POWERS OF THE SECULAR MODERN

Cultural Memory
 in
 the
 Present

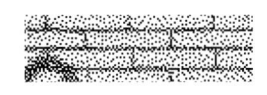

Mieke Bal and Hent de Vries, Editors

POWERS OF THE SECULAR MODERN

Talal Asad and His Interlocutors

*Edited by David Scott and
Charles Hirschkind*

STANFORD UNIVERSITY PRESS
STANFORD, CALIFORNIA
2006

Stanford University Press
Stanford, California

© 2006 by the Board of Trustees of the
Leland Stanford Junior University.
All rights reserved.

No part of this book may be reproduced or transmitted in any form
or by any means, electronic or mechanical, including photocopying
and recording, or in any information storage or retrieval system
without the prior written permission of Stanford University Press.

Printed in the United States of America
on acid-free, archival-quality paper

Library of Congress Cataloging-in-Publication Data

Powers of the secular modern : Talal Asad and his interlocutors
   / edited by David Scott and Charles Hirschkind.
      p.   cm. — (Cultural memory in the present)
   Includes bibliographical references and index.
   ISBN 0-8047-5265-6 (cloth : alk. paper)
   ISBN 0-8047-5266-4 (pbk. : alk. paper)
      1. Ethnology—Philosophy. 2. Ethnology—Eastern Hemisphere—
Philosophy. 3. Postcolonialism—Eastern Hemisphere. 4. Secularization—
Eastern Hemisphere. 5. Asad, Talal—Criticism and interpretation.
I. Scott, David, 1958– II. Hirschkind, Charles. III. Series.

GN345.P66 2006
306'.01—dc22

2005013565

Original Printing 2006

Last figure below indicates year of this printing:
15   14   13   12   11   10   09   08   07   06

For Tanya

Contents

1. Introduction: The Anthropological Skepticism of Talal Asad
   David Scott and Charles Hirschkind — 1

2. Secularization Revisited: A Reply to Talal Asad
   José Casanova — 12

3. What Is an "Authorizing Discourse"?
   Steven C. Caton — 31

4. Fasting for Bin Laden: The Politics of Secularization in Contemporary India
   Partha Chatterjee — 57

5. Europe: A Minor Tradition
   William E. Connolly — 75

6. Secularism and the Argument from Nature
   Veena Das — 93

7. On General and Divine Economy: Talal Asad's Genealogy of the Secular and Emmanuel Levinas's Critique of Capitalism, Colonialism, and Money
   Hent de Vries — 113

8. The Tragic Sensibility of Talal Asad
   David Scott — 134

9. Redemption, Secularization, and Politics
   George Shulman — 154

10 Subjects and Agents in the History of Imperialism
  and Resistance
    Jon E. Wilson   180
11 Responses
    Talal Asad   206

Appendix: The Trouble of Thinking:
An Interview with Talal Asad
   David Scott   *243*
Notes   *305*
Talal Asad: A Bibliography
   Compiled by Zainab Saleh   *333*
Contributors   *339*
Index   *341*

Introduction: The Anthropological Skepticism of Talal Asad

David Scott and Charles Hirschkind

For more than three decades, Talal Asad has been engaged in a distinctive critical exploration of the conceptual assumptions that govern the West's knowledges—especially its disciplinary and disciplining knowledges—of the non-Western world. The investigations that comprise this by no means concluded intellectual project have of course been varied in the objects and topics taken up for inquiry, but they have all been characterized, we suggest, by a profoundly questioning attitude, an attitude of *skepticism*. Asad's skepticism—articulated largely (though not exclusively) in relation to anthropological claims—has been directed toward systematically throwing doubt on Enlightenment reason's pretensions to the truth about the reasons of non-European traditions. This is not to make out Asad to be a mere subverter of the desire for positive knowledge. Rather his impulse is guided, we think, by the Wittgensteinian dictum that whether a proposition turns out to be true or false depends on what is made to *count* as its determinants or criteria; it will depend on the language-game in which it is employed.[1] And language-games, for Asad, are historical and political and therefore *ideological* matters potentially warranting deconstructive as well as reconstructive investigation.

I

Adumbrations of this intellectual stance of skepticism can already be discerned in the manner in which Asad entered the anthropological upheaval of the late 1960s and early 1970s. As is well known, these were years in which the British social anthropological establishment (in which Asad was trained and in which he spent the first two decades of his academic life, largely at the University of Hull) was coming under attack for its alleged role in the administrative functioning and ideological legitimization of the British colonial enterprise. Indeed, in some Left quarters anthropology was being criticized as the very "handmaiden" of colonial subjection and its practitioners reviled for their racism (remember that Bronislaw Malinowski's diaries were published in 1967 and set off a mini-scandal in the discipline of which he was a revered founder).[2] While sympathetic to the anticolonial rejection of anthropology's hubristic will-to-omniscient-knowledge, however, Asad very early articulated a doubt about the *register* and *direction* of this criticism. He doubted not only whether anthropology was as important to colonial rule as its detractors often alleged, but also whether the reactive and defensive moralizing posture of assertion and counterassertion was at all constructive. In interrogating the colonial question in anthropology, he urged, what is important is the *conceptual* structure of the discipline and the relation of this structure to the conditions of power in which the discipline realized itself as authoritative knowledge.

Take, for example, his first book, *The Kababish Arabs*, published in 1970 and no doubt little read today.[3] It is, in many ways, a very recognizable monograph in the British anthropological tradition. Its formal concern is an analytical description of the organization of power, authority, and consent among the Kababish of northern Sudan. Undoubtedly the colonial question haunts the book's concerns; however, Asad takes aim not at the supposed motivations of colonial anthropologists but at the *ideological* character of their dominant theoretical paradigm, namely functionalism.

In the colonial environment in which early social anthropologists encountered their primitive polities, and in the atmosphere of philosophical positivism surrounding the early development of social anthropology, it seemed appropriate and possible to take primitive political structures for granted and view them with detachment as aspects of identifiable "natural systems." Viewed functionally in relation to a total natural system, political activity emerged primarily as a mode of maintaining the coherence or identity of a given society. If classic functionalism had not existed, it would have been necessary for anthropologists to invent it, for it enabled them to analyze primitive political systems without having to consider alternative political possibilities. The character of political domination remained unproblematic because it was part of the natural order of things.[4]

The passage is a characteristic one. The issue (and he makes it more explicit in a footnote)[5] that requires our attention is not the attitude of anthropologists toward their native informants (however reprehensible that may be) but the *ideological* conditions that give point and force to the *theoretical* apparatuses employed to describe and objectify them and their worlds.

Of course, the delineation of the problem of anthropology's relationship with colonialism was even more sharply articulated in Asad's edited volume, *Anthropology and the Colonial Encounter*, published in 1973.[6] In many ways a landmark intervention, Asad sought in his framing introduction to redirect attention away from the anthropology-as-tool story toward the analysis of the ideological character of anthropological knowledge. Locating anthropology's crisis in the altered worldly conditions of decolonization following the Second World War, Asad urged that anthropologists remind themselves "that anthropology does not only apprehend the world in which it is located, but that the world also determines how it will apprehend it."[7] He noted the "curious refusal" of anthropologists to think seriously and critically about the unequal relation between the West and the Third World in which anthropology produces knowledge, and argued programmatically: "We must begin from the fact that the basic reality which made the pre-war social anthropology a feasible and effective enterprise was the power relationship between dominating (European) and dominated (non-European) cultures. We then need to ask ourselves how this relationship has affected the practical pre-conditions of social anthropology; the uses to which its knowledge was put; the theoretical treatment of particular topics; the mode of perceiving and objectifying alien societies; and the anthropologist's claim of political neutrality."[8]

This set of concerns was not necessarily shared by all the contributors to the volume, needless to say, but it was exemplified in the critical practice of Asad's own essay, "Two European Images of Non-European Rule."[9] A model instance of historicizing conceptual interrogation, it anticipated by many years the later "postcolonial" theorization of the relation between power and disciplinary knowledge. Asad's doubt here concerned the unexamined contrast between the images of non-European political order constructed respectively by the functionalist anthropology of African societies and the orientalist study of Islamic societies. On the one hand, the functionalist anthropology of African societies stressed the *integrated* character of the political order and the *consensual* basis of political authority; on the other hand, orientalism emphasized *force* and *repression* on the part of Islamic leaders and *submission* and *indifference* on the part of the ruled. Asad's interest, however, was not merely these differences themselves, but their connection to the *historical formation* of their respective disciplines, one emerging after the advent of colonialism in the societies studied (African anthropology), and the other rooted in an older European experience (orientalism). In short, Asad was beginning to develop a skeptical mode of anthropological inquiry attuned to the ideological character of objectification and, therefore, the historical and political conditions of formation of the apparatuses of scholarly investigation. The rest of the 1970s were to see him engage this question variously in a number of remarkable essays.[10]

The 1980s, however, were a period of transitions for Asad—transitions in geographic and institutional location, and transitions in intellectual direction. In 1988 he relocated to the United States from Britain to take up a position in the Department of Anthropology at the Graduate Faculty of the New School for Social Research in New York. Although he would never be seamlessly integrated into either its professional or scholarly ethos, Asad would nevertheless now be more systematically part of the landscape of argument that constituted U.S. anthropology. In the 1980s that landscape was animated (*decentered*, in the jargon of the moment) by debates about power and representation that had entered the humanities and social sciences by way of the linguistic and poststructuralist turns. Edward Said's *Orientalism*, published in 1978, vividly brought together the themes of power/knowledge and the questioning of the West and helped to create the intellectual space for the revival (as well as *recharacterization*) of the *colonial* question. Within U.S. anthropology, the volume that most embodied the new theoretical self-consciousness was, of course, *Writing Culture*, edited by the cultural historian James Clifford and the anthropologist George Marcus, and published in 1986.[11] The essays that comprised this volume were diverse, but the project, so far at least as the editors were concerned, aimed at questioning the seeming naiveté of anthropological representation, in particular bringing recent developments in literary analysis to bear on the conventions of ethnographic *writing*.

Asad, interestingly, was a contributor to this volume, though he stood at something of an angle to some of its central concerns with ethnography and textuality. It may be true that what ethnographers do is write, as Clifford and Marcus asserted, but is it the case that *ethnography* ought *necessarily* to be thought of as what anthropologists do? Asad has never assumed this relation between anthropology and ethnography—indeed, recently he has suggested that anthropology is best thought of as the comparative study of concepts across space and time.[12] Which is perhaps why, in his contribution to *Writing Culture*, he focused his attention on an explicitly *theoretical*—as opposed to an ethnographic—text, namely Ernest Gellner's famous essay, "Concepts and Society." "The Concept of Cultural Translation" is an essay that works through a number of moves that together expose the assumptions underlying Gellner's argument about translation and interpretation. In particular, Asad was interested in thinking about the tendency to understand "translation" as a practice involving "reading the implicit" into the enunciations of native informants; the translator/interpreter seems always able to discern or reveal meanings hidden from the native speakers themselves. Part of the problem with arguments such as Gellner's, Asad maintained, is that they systematically missed or obscured the *inequality* in the relations of power between the languages of Third World societies and the languages of Western societies. "My point," Asad argued, "is only that the process of cultural translation is enmeshed in conditions of power—professional, national, international. And among these conditions is the authority of ethnographers to uncover the implicit meanings of subordinate societies. Given that this is so, the interesting question for enquiry is not whether, and if so to what extent, anthropologists should be relativists or rationalists, critical or charitable, toward other cultures, but how power enters into the process of 'cultural translation,' seen both as a discursive and as a non-discursive practice."[13]

II

Since the 1980s, Asad has turned his attention more and more systematically to the study of religion—not merely to the study of *a* religion (Islam, Christianity), but to the question of what it means for a discipline like anthropology to be engaged in the study of "religion" at all. The body of work to emerge from this inquiry will explore the various ways in which the historical shifts giving shape to the complexly interrelated categories of the secular and the religious have been decisive in the emergence of modern Europe and the modes of knowledge and power it deploys. Asad's entrance into this question takes place via an extended discussion of the notion of religion as found in the work of the noted anthropologist Clifford Geertz.[14] In a critique that constantly tacks between the historical and the conceptual, Asad carefully demonstrates how the universal definition of religion propounded by Geertz rests on a conceptual architecture deeply indebted to developments within early modern Christianity, and thus is of limited value in the analysis of other traditions. Importantly, the problem he identifies in Geertz's model is not simply its privileging of one religion (Christianity) at the expense of others, something that might be overcome by a careful elimination of its specifically Christian and eurocentric assumptions. Rather, the very idea of religion as a universal category of human experience owes directly to developments within seventeenth- and eighteenth-century theology, and specifically to the emergence of the concept of Natural Religion—namely, the idea that religion is a feature of all societies, evident in the universality of systems of belief, practices of worship, and codes of ethics. As Asad notes,

> What appears to anthropologists today to be self-evident, namely that religion today is essentially a matter of symbolic meanings linked to ideas of general order (expressed through either or both rite and doctrine), that it has generic functions/features, and that it must not be confused with any of its particular historical or cultural forms, is in fact a view that has a specific Christian history. From being a concrete set of practical rules attached to specific processes of power and knowledge, religion has come to be abstracted and universalized. In this movement we have not merely an increase in religious toleration, certainly not merely a new scientific discovery, but the mutation of a concept and a range of social practices which is itself part of a wider change in the modern landscape of power and knowledge.[15]

Here again we see Asad's concern with the ideological location of anthropological knowledge, with the genealogy of the discipline's moral preferences. The various traditions that anthropologists call religions cannot be understood as cultural elaborations of a universal form of experience, a sui generis category of human knowledge, but must be analyzed in their particularity, as the products of specific practices of discipline, authority, and power. In his attempt to delineate the contours of such an inquiry, Asad will find it increasingly necessary to engage religion's other, the secular, insomuch as it is this concept, and the practices and deployments of power that it has brought into play, that continues to anchor the modern interpretation of religion as a unique (and uniquely distorted) form of human understanding.

While Asad's engagement with Geertz's work centered on the latter's attempt to establish a universal definition of religion, his critique of Geertz's use of the notions of symbol and meaning had implications that extended well beyond any single author or area of inquiry. Against what at the time was a growing tendency within anthropology to understand culture as fundamentally textual—a "system of symbols," as Geertz put it, whose meaning it was the anthropologist's task to decipher—Asad insists that the meaning of symbols must be understood in relation to both the practical contexts within which those symbols function and the forms of social discipline by which certain readings are authorized and accomplished. When anthropologists or historians approach cultural phenomena as texts to be read, they are in a sense adopting the stance of modern theology, one that takes religion to be fundamentally about the affirmation of propositions expressed in symbolic form. "Can we know," Asad asks in this essay, "what [religious symbols] mean without regard to the social disciplines by which their correct reading is secured?"[16] It is precisely this disciplinary dimension that Asad foregrounds in two subsequent articles addressing the use of language and symbol within monastic programs geared to the formation of the virtues.[17] His concern in these pieces with the materiality of discourse, with attending to the practical contexts in which words are used, and particularly to the conditions of power, authority, and discipline by which practices (linguistic and otherwise) are learned and reproduced, anticipated poststructuralist emphases on the exteriority of language, on what Gumbrecht has referred to as "the totality of phenomena contributing to the constitution of meaning without being meaning themselves."[18]

In his concern with the overvaluing of consciousness within theories of human action, including Marxian theories based on a distinction between (material) force and (subjective) consent (or between "structure" and "agency"), Asad has increasingly directed his attention to aspects of human embodiment, exploring some of the various ways that pain, emotion, embodied aptitude, and the senses connect with and structure traditional practices. As in his other work, he has eschewed programmatic understandings of the body in favor of a genealogical approach attentive to the way the corporeal is thematized and deployed within cultural practices. The somatic concepts he deploys in his approach to different historical problems—for instance, disciplined sensibility, pain, suffering, embodied aptitude, gesture—do not assume any one kind of body but, on the contrary, take the plurality of historical bodies as a necessary presupposition of genealogical analysis. In framing such questions of human embodiment, Asad will privilege an analytical style that resists the conventional schematic opposing discourse to that which lies outside it. Though given explicit elaboration at only a few junctures in his work, Alasdair MacIntyre's notion of tradition will provide Asad with a key conceptual device for thinking beyond the division of body and culture, so as to open up an inquiry into historically specific responses to the task of embodied existence.[19] In his essay, "The Idea of an Anthropology of Islam," published in 1986, Asad had suggested that anthropologists approach Islam through the concept of a "discursive tradition": those discourses and practices of argumentation, conceptually articulated with an exemplary past and dependent on an interpretive engagement with a set of foundational texts, by which practitioners of a tradition distinguish correct actions from incorrect ones.[20] In his later writings, he increasingly comes to view this formulation as failing to adequately appreciate the embodied aspects of traditional action. His rethinking of this point bears the imprint of two authors in particular: Marcel Mauss, specifically his provocative essay on body techniques, with its conception of the body as a "technical instrument"—what Asad will gloss as a "developable means for achieving a range of human objectives"[21]—and Michel Foucault, whose genealogies of the diverse ways the "docile body" has been constructed by power had an obvious influence on Asad's approach to medieval Christian discipline.[22]

Asad continues to explore the theme of embodiment in his most recent book, *Formations of the Secular*, but compliments it with greater emphasis on those aspects of corporeality that constitute what might be called a generative friction within traditions—aspects such as pain, aging, and childbirth.[23] As in his earlier inquiries, it is the genealogy of modern power that orients the questions he poses in regard to both secularism and the corporal. Pain provides a strategic point of entry, due both to the way it resists containment within the binaries of mind/body (or culture/nature) and to the role a certain normative understanding of pain plays within modern conceptions of the human being. In chapters addressing such varied topics as human rights, sadomasochism, and torture, he explores secular-liberal sensibilities to pain as embedded within Western popular, legal, and administrative discourses, as well as the deployments of power such sensibilities serve to authorize. Asad shows that the commitment to prevent unnecessary pain and suffering that has served to define a modernist moral outlook does not give rise to a project aiming at their elimination, but rather to one geared to their regulation in accord with certain ideas of utility and proportionality. Thus the use of violence against domestic populations and foreign adversaries remains a key element of modern political technique but, exercised in accord with a utilitarian rationality, such practices frequently pass below the threshold of moral thematization and response. As elsewhere in his work, the argument here seeks to uncover the forms of violence authorized by the modern project of humanizing the world, of forcibly (and often violently) transforming both Western and non-Western societies on the basis of what are taken to be universal standards of acceptable and unacceptable suffering.

In attempting to open up a space for assessing the assumptions underlying such standards, Asad intersperses his analysis with examples of the way pain has been conceived of and lived in different cultural and historical sites. The sense of tradition that begins to emerge here (particularly in the chapter "Thinking about Agency and Pain") suggests a collection of temporally structured techniques by which human beings adjust to such existential bodily conditions, understood simultaneously as sources of friction on human designs and enabling instruments for distinct human goals. Pain and other dimensions of corporeality acquire their significance not only through the distinct cultural meanings assigned to them but also, and more importantly, by the economies of action they make possible: "What a subject experiences as painful, and how, are not simply mediated culturally and physically, *they are themselves modes of living a relationship*. The ability to live such relationships over time transforms pain from a passive experience into an active one, and thus defines one of the ways of living sanely in the world."[24] Bodies—disciplined, suffered, scrutinized, and differentially invested with significance—constitute a structuring condition for action and moral agency. This approach diverges both from phenomenology, where cultural practices are analyzed in relation to a set of innate bodily orientations, and from an understanding of the body as a surface upon which culture inscribes different meanings. For Asad, language and the body are distinct, co-constituent elements of human life, whose complex imbrications cannot be reduced a priori to any structure of determinations but must be examined in their diversity and cultural specificity.

Finally, Asad's contribution to the theorization and analysis of contemporary Islam has been profound. Both in the above-mentioned article, "The Idea of an Anthropology of Islam," and elsewhere in his writings, he has articulated a challenge to anthropologists and other scholars of Islam that remains an ineluctable point of reference for scholarship in the field. His interventions in this arena have been primarily through an engagement with a variety of anthropological and historical writings on Islam, an engagement in which he has sought to genealogically unpack many of the key concepts used in the description of Muslim societies. Here, as elsewhere in his work, Asad remains attentive not only to the work performed by such concepts within a text's analytical apparatus but also, and more importantly, to their historical embeddedness within modern forms of power, their authorizing function within projects of destruction and remaking. In an essay addressing the impact of secularizing reform in modern Egypt, for example, he explores how modern legal, moral, and political vocabularies created new spaces of (secular) action but were also inflected by sensibilities and embodied aptitudes rooted in traditions of Islam.[25] Key to this exploration is an argument that the secular be approached not simply in terms of the doctrinal separation of religious and political authority, but as a concept that has brought together sensibilities, knowledges, and behaviors in new and distinct ways.

In a set of more overtly political writings, Asad has applied his style of critical analysis to an examination of contemporary European discourse on the status of Muslim minorities in Europe. Key to this work has been an investigation of the way the categories of secular liberal society—from the idea of toleration to the discourses of assimilation and integration—constitute a barrier to the possibility of Muslims (and particularly those Muslims who view their religion as important to their politics) being accepted into and accommodated by the nations of Europe.

The essays comprising this volume take up diverse aspects of this remarkable body of work. While the specific themes and arguments addressed by the individual contributors range widely, the collection of essays cohere in a shared orientation of both critical engagement and productive extension. It is important to note that this is not a Festschrift, nor a celebratory farewell, but a series of engagements with a thinker whose work is in full spate but which deserves to be far better known and understood.

Secularization Revisited: A Reply to Talal Asad

José Casanova

In his insightful and incisive criticism of my reformulation of the theory of secularization, Talal Asad claims that my position is not "an entirely coherent one. For if the legitimate role for deprivatized religion is carried out effectively," the other two components of the thesis—the differentiation of the secular spheres and the declining significance of religious beliefs, practices, and institutions—are also undermined. As a consequence, according to Asad, "It seems that nothing retrievable remains of the secularization thesis."[1]

Let me restate my thesis in order first to clarify what I deem to be a misreading of my position, and then to address what I consider to be Asad's valid criticism.[2] The main purpose of my reformulation of the thesis of secularization was to disaggregate what usually passes for a single theory of secularization into three separate propositions, which in my view need to be treated differently: 1) secularization as a differentiation of the secular spheres from religious institutions and norms, 2) secularization as a decline of religious beliefs and practices, and 3) secularization as a marginalization of religion to a privatized sphere. I insisted that the core component of the theory of secularization was the conceptualization of societal modernization as a process of functional differentiation and emancipation of the secular spheres—primarily the modern state, the capitalist market economy, and modern science—from the religious sphere, and the concomitant differentiation and specialization of religion within its own newly found religious sphere. I argued that this was still the defensible core of the theory of secularization. I will examine later whether and to what extent this core is still defensible after Asad's compelling critique.

The other two subtheses, which are thought to explain what happens to religion in the modern world as a result of secular differentiation, I insisted are not defensible as general propositions either empirically or normatively, in the sense that they are not inherently concomitant with modernity. The assumption that religion tends to decline with progressive modernization, a notion that, as I pointed out, "has proven patently false as a general empirical proposition," was traced genealogically back to the Enlightenment critique of religion.[3] Asad has therefore misrepresented my position when he states that I hold this as a "viable" element of the thesis of secularization. As to the third component of the theory, the thesis of privatization, I argued that "the related proposition that modern differentiation *necessarily* entails the marginalization and privatization of religion, [and] its logical counterpart that public religions *necessarily* endanger the differentiated structures of modernity" are equally indefensible.

While recognizing the validity, or at least the suggestive promise, of my argument, Asad takes me to task for going only halfway by drawing an analytical distinction between those *kinds* of public religion that are compatible with modern differentiated structures, with liberal democratic norms, and with individual liberties, and those that are not. It is true that since my argument was directed primarily at liberal secular theories of the public sphere, I was particularly interested in examining those modern forms of public religion that are not intrinsically incompatible with differentiated modern structures and that are "desirable" from a modern normative perspective in that they could actually contribute to strengthening the public sphere of modern civil societies. But nowhere did I argue that forms of political religion which seek to undermine civil society or individual liberties are "indeed a rebellion against modernity and the universal values of Enlightenment."[4] They are simply religions that follow or are constituted by different norms. Moreover, it is a misrepresentation of my position to state that "only religions that have accepted the assumptions of liberal discourse are being commended." In my argument, the litmus test for a modern public religion was not the commitment to liberal "tolerance on the basis of a distinctive relation between law and morality," but the recognition of freedom of conscience as an inviolable individual right. Such recognition does not need to be—and historically for many religious people it has not usually been—based on liberal or secular values.

Nor was the conception of a modern public sphere that I proposed reduced to a discursive communicative space restricted to rational debate. A more careful reading will show that on this point I clearly sought to distance myself from Habermas. I envision the modern public sphere as "a discursive or agonic space in principle open to all citizens and all issues," including issues of power and the power to set the terms of the debate.[5] Moreover, there is not a single public sphere; there are many competing and interrelated publics and a multiplicity of public spaces. I fully concur with Asad when he states that "when religion becomes an integral part of modern politics, it is not indifferent to debates about how the economy should be run, or which scientific projects should be funded, or what the broader aims of a national education system should be."[6] In principle I also have no objection to the creation of modern "hybrids" that may result from the entry of religion into these debates. My conception of modern differentiation or of the boundaries between the differentiated spheres is neither as rigid nor as fixed as Asad seems to imply. As I pointed out, not disapprovingly, "Religions throughout the world are entering the public sphere and the arena of political contestation . . . to participate in the very struggles to define and set the modern boundaries between the private and public spheres, between system and life-world, between legality and morality, between individual and society, between family, civil society, and state, between nations, states, civilizations and the world system."[7] The purpose of such interventions in the undifferentiated public sphere is not simply to "enrich public debate," but to challenge the very claims of the secular spheres to differentiated autonomy exempt from extrinsic normative constraints.

I also do not recognize as my own Asad's examination of "*the kind* of religion that enlightened intellectuals like Casanova see as compatible with modernity."[8] For, as I pointed out, "The very resurgence or reassertion of religious traditions may be viewed as a sign of the failure of the Enlightenment to redeem its own promises. Religious traditions are now confronting the differentiated secular spheres, challenging them to face their own obscurantist, ideological, and inauthentic claims. In many of these confrontations, it is religion which, as often as not, appears to be on the side of human enlightenment."⁹ Furthermore, the purpose of such a confrontation is not simply to "evoke the moral sensibilities" of the nation by appealing to its conscience. I take the moral heterogeneity of modern societies for granted, and for that very reason I distinguished my position from neo-Durkheimian or communitarian theories of "civil religion."

But if my own true position, rather than the one misrepresented by Asad, does not seem so distant from Asad's position, it is still legitimate to ask whether anything retrievable remains of the secularization thesis. Why go through the trouble of reformulating the theory, rather than discarding it altogether as a myth? My reasons then and now, I submit, would seem to be the same ones that have led Asad to reconstruct a genealogy of the secular. I agree with Asad that to examine critically the formations of the secular and construct an anthropology of secularism remains one of the most relevant tasks for the social sciences today. To drop the concept or the theory of secularization would leave us analytically impoverished and without adequate conceptual tools in trying to trace the "genealogy" and "archeology" of Western modernity and to reveal the modern "order of things." Our approaches, however, are somewhat different. Asad follows a Foucauldian genealogical approach with illuminating results. I follow a more traditional comparative historical sociological analysis.

My purpose in attempting to offer a reformulation of the theory of secularization was to mediate in what I considered to be a fruitless and futile debate between European and American sociologists of religion concerning the validity of the theory of secularization. The fact that the contentious debate has continued unabated only indicates how unsuccessful my attempted mediation has proven to be and how ingrained are the positions.¹⁰ Most European sociologists continue to hold unreflexively and uncritically to the traditional theory of secularization. For them the drastic secularization of European societies appears to be an empirically irrefutable fait accompli. Most American sociologists of religion, by contrast, have reduced the meaning of the concept of secularization to such an extent that they are convinced they have proven that secularization is a *myth* once they are able to show that, at least in the United States, none of the so-called "indicators" of secularization—such as church attendance, belief in God, frequency of prayer, and so on evince any long-term declining trend.

In the European context, secularization is a concept overloaded with multiple historically sedimented meanings that simply points to the ubiquitous and undeniable long-term historical shrinkage of the size, power, and functions of ecclesiastical institutions vis-à-vis other secular institutions. As the dictionary of any Western European language will show, to secularize means "to make worldly," to convert or transfer persons, things, meanings, and so on from religious or ecclesiastical to secular or civil use. But Europeans tend to use the term in a double sense, switching unconsciously back and forth between this traditional meaning of *secularization* and a second meaning that points to the progressive decline of religious beliefs and practices among individuals. This narrower meaning of secularization is secondary, posterior, and mainly derivative from the primary meaning. Europeans, however, see the two meanings of the term as intrinsically related because they view the two realities—the decline in the societal significance of religious institutions and the decline of religious beliefs and practices—as structurally related. Supposedly, one leads necessarily to the other.

American sociologists of religion tend to view things differently and practically restrict the use of the term *secularization* to its narrower meaning of decline of religious beliefs and practices among individuals. It is not so much that they question the secularization of society, but simply that they take it for granted as an unremarkable fact. The United States, they assume, has always been, at least constitutionally since independence, a secular society, as secular if not more so than any European society. Yet they see no evidence that this unquestionable fact has led to a progressive decline in the religious beliefs and practices of the American people. If anything, the historical evidence points in the opposite direction: progressive growth in religious beliefs and practices and progressive *churching* of the American population since independence.[11] Consequently, many American sociologists of religion tend to discard the theory of secularization as a European myth.[12]

Even after discounting the tendency of Americans to inflate their rates of church attendance and to exaggerate the depth and seriousness of their religious beliefs, the fact remains that Americans are generally more religious than most Europeans, with the possible exception of the Irish and the Poles.[13] Moreover, the very tendency of the Americans to exaggerate their religiousness, in contrast to the opposite tendency of Europeans to discount and undercount their own persistent religiosity—tendencies that are evident among ordinary people as well as among scholars—are themselves part of the very different and consequential definitions of the situation in both places. Americans think that they are supposed to be religious, while Europeans think that they are supposed to be irreligious.

The progressive, though highly uneven, secularization of Europe is an undeniable social fact. An increasing majority of the European population has ceased participating in traditional religious practices, at least on a regular basis, even though they may still maintain relatively high levels of private individual religious beliefs.[14] But the standard explanations of the phenomenon in terms of general processes of modernization are not persuasive, since similar processes of modernization elsewhere (in the United States or in the cultural areas of other world religions) are not accompanied by the same secularizing results. We need to entertain seriously the proposition that secularization became a self-fulfilling prophecy in Europe once large sectors of the population of Western European societies, including the Christian churches, accepted the basic premises of the theory of secularization: that secularization is a teleological process of modern social change; that the more modern a society the more secular it becomes; that "secularity" is "a *sign of the times.*" If such a proposition is correct, then the secularization of Western European societies can be explained better in terms of the triumph of the knowledge regime of secularism than in terms of structural processes of socio-economic development, such as urbanization, education, rationalization, and so on.

In such a context, the study of modern secularism, as an ideology, as a generalized worldview, and as a social movement, and of its role as a crucial carrier of processes of secularization and as a catalyst for counter-secularization responses should be high on the agenda of a self-reflexive comparative historical sociology of secularization. Otherwise, teleological theories of secularization become themselves conscious or unconscious vehicles for the transmission of secularist ideologies and worldviews. What makes the European situation so unique and exceptional when compared with the rest of the world is precisely the triumph of secularism as a teleological theory of religious development. The ideological critique of religion developed by the Enlightenment and carried out by a series of social movements throughout Europe from the eighteenth to the twentieth century has informed European theories of secularization in such a way that those theories came to function not only as descriptive theories of social processes but also and more significantly as critical-genealogical theories of religion and as normative-teleological theories of religious development that presupposed religious decline as the telos of history.

It is time to abandon the eurocentric view that modern Western European developments, including the secularization of European Christianity, are general universal processes. The more one adopts a global perspective, the more it becomes obvious that the drastic secularization of Western European societies is a rather exceptional phenomenon, with few parallels elsewhere, other than in European settler societies such as New Zealand, Quebec, or Uruguay. Such an exceptional phenomenon demands, therefore, a more particular historical explanation. The collapse of the plausibility structures of European Christianity is so extraordinary that we need a better explanation than simply referring to general processes of modernization. Holding onto the traditional theory of secularization, by contrast, reassures modern secular Europeans, including sociologists of religion, that this collapse was natural, teleological, and quasi-providential. Such a view of secularization tends to make the phenomenon of secularization into something practically inevitable and irreversible. It turns into a self-fulfilling prophecy.

It is in reaction to the European failure to confront seriously the evidence of American religious vitality that a new American paradigm has emerged, offering an alternative explanation of the American religious dynamics that challenges the basic premises of the European theory of secularization.[15] In and of itself, the explanation of religious vitality in terms of the beneficial effects of the dual clause of the First Amendment to the U.S. Constitution, "no establishment" and "free exercise" of religion, is not novel. Tocqueville, and Marx following him, had already maintained this basic insight.[16] The combination they observed of high secularization in the broad primary sense of social differentiation (i.e., "perfect disestablishment") and low secularization in the narrower secondary sense of religious decline ("land of religiosity par excellence") already put into question the alleged structural relationship between the two dimensions of secularization in the orthodox model. Tocqueville (p. 309), moreover, had already used the American evidence to question two basic premises of modern theories of secularization, which, as he pointed out, had their origins in the Enlightenment critique of religion under the ancien régime: that the advancement of rationalism (i.e., education and scientific knowledge) and individualism (i.e., liberal democracy and individual freedoms) would necessarily lead to the decline of religion.

What is refreshingly new in the American paradigm is the move to turn the European model of secularization on its head and to use the American evidence to postulate an equally general structural relationship between disestablishment or state deregulation, open free competitive and pluralistic religious markets, and high levels of individual religiosity.[17] With this reversal, what was until now the American exception attains normative status, while the previous European rule is now demoted to a deviation from the American norm. But it is this very move to turn a persuasive account of the exceptionally pluralistic and competitive American religious market into a universal general theory of religious economies that is problematic. The perils are precisely the same that led the European theory astray by turning a plausible account of the European historical process of secularization into a general theory of modern development.

Nevertheless, I believe that the theory of secularization is still useful, not only as a way of reconstructing analytically the transformations of modern European societies, but also as an analytical framework for a comparative research agenda that aims to examine the historical transformation of all world religions under conditions of modern structural differentiation, as long as the outcome of this transformation is not predetermined by the theory, and as long as we do not label as religious fundamentalism any countersecularization, or any religious transformation that does not follow the prescribed model.

The story of secularization is primarily a story of the tensions, conflicts, and patterns of differentiation between religious and worldly regimes. The European concept of secularization refers to a particular historical process of the transformation of Western Christendom and might not be directly applicable to other world religions with very different modes of structuration of the sacred and profane realms. It could hardly be applicable, for instance, to such "religions" as Confucianism or Taoism, insofar as they are not characterized by high tension with "the world" and have no ecclesiastical organization. In a sense those religions that have always been "worldly" and "lay" do not need to undergo a process of secularization. To secularize—that is, "to make worldly" or "to transfer from ecclesiastical to civil use"—is a process that does not make much sense in such a civilizational context. But to ask how religions like Confucianism or Taoism, or any other religion for that matter, respond to the imposition of the new global worldly regime of Western modernity becomes a very relevant question.

In the rest of this paper I would like to address what I consider to be the most valid aspect of Asad's critique. In my view, the fundamental question is whether the core of the theory of secularization—namely, the differentiation of the secular spheres from each other *and* from religious institutions and norms—is still defensible. I believe that secularization, as an empirical proposition and as an adequate way of conceptualizing analytically the historical transformation of Western European societies, is defensible.[18] But even if this is a valid claim, it raises two further questions that need to be scrutinized more critically than I was prepared to do. Firstly, to what extent is it possible to dissociate this analytical reconstruction of the historical process of differentiation of Western European societies from general theories of modernity that present secular differentiation as a normative project for all "modern" societies? As I pointed out then, "The theory of secularization is so intrinsically interwoven with all the theories of the modern world and with the self-understanding of modernity that one cannot simply discard the theory of secularization without putting into question the entire web, including much of the understanding of the social sciences."[19] Self-definitions of modernity are tautological insofar as secular differentiation is precisely what defines a society as modern. But can the analytical definition be dissociated from the normative project of turning the temporal age of modernity into a homogeneous global space until all contemporary societies *in* modernity but not *of* modernity become liberal modern secular societies?

Asad's parallel genealogies of religion and of the secular offer a way of deconstructing the secular self-understanding of modernity that is constitutive of the social sciences. Therein lies in my view his main critical contribution. But his analysis raises a further question, namely which of the possible alternative genealogies of the secular is one going to privilege? I do not have a ready answer to this question, but in my view Asad's genealogy of the secular is too indebted to the triumphalist self-genealogies of secularism he has so aptly exposed. I fully agree with Asad that "the secular" "should not be thought of as the space in which *real* human life gradually emancipates itself from the controlling power of 'religion' and thus achieves the latter's relocation."[20] This is so precisely because in the historical process of secularization, the religious and the secular are inextricably bound together and mutually condition each other. Asad's statement that "the genealogy of secularism has to be traced through the concept of the secular—in part to the Renaissance doctrine of humanism, in part to the Enlightenment concept of nature, and in part to Hegel's philosophy of history,"[21] fails to recognize the extent to which the formation of the secular is linked with the internal transformation of European Christianity, particularly through the Protestant Reformation. Should one define this transformation as a process of internal secularization of Christianity?

This has been, of course, an ardently contested issue, and Asad is, in my view, correct in distancing himself from the two contentious poles in the debate, from Karl Löwith, who, following Nietzsche, traced the genealogy of the secular idea of progress through the internal secularization of Christian postmillennial eschatology, as well as from Hans Blumenberg, who offered a "secularist" defense of the legitimacy of the Modern Age in order to cleanse secular modernity from any dubious religious pedigree.[22] Each of these antithetical genealogies, moreover, can have opposite readings. Parallel to Löwith's critical reading of secular teleologies, there is a celebratory Protestant reading of modernity, going from Hegel's *Early Theological Writings* through the Weber-Troeltsch axis to Talcott Parsons's interpretation of modern societies as the institutionalization of Christian principles.[23] Such a reading is operative, moreover, not only at the level of intellectual history but at the more popular level in the seemingly perennial postmillennial visions of America as "a City on a Hill," "beacon of freedom," and redeemer nation. While inverting Blumenberg's triumphalist evaluation, it seems to me that Asad's critical genealogy is nonetheless too close to Blumenberg's insofar as Asad seems to assign to the secular the power to constitute not only its own near-absolute modern hegemony but also the very category of the religious and its circumscribed space within the secular regime.

Following a more traditional comparative historical analysis, David Martin has shown convincingly that it is necessary to take into account two very different historical patterns of secularization. In the Latin-Catholic cultural area, and to some extent throughout continental Europe, there was a collision between religion and the differentiated secular spheres, that is, between Catholic Christianity and modern science, modern capitalism, and the modern state. As a result of this protracted clash, the Enlightenment critique of religion found ample resonance there; the secularist genealogy of modernity was constructed as a triumphant emancipation of reason, freedom, and worldly pursuits from the constraints of religion, and practically every "progressive" European social movement from the time of the French Revolution to the present was informed by secularism.

In the Anglo-Protestant cultural area, by contrast, particularly in the United States, there was collusion between religion and the secular differentiated spheres. Irrespective of how one evaluates the elective affinities between ascetic Protestantism and the spirit of capitalism analyzed by Weber, there is little historical evidence of tension between American Protestantism and capitalism. There is also no manifest tension between science and religion in America prior to the Darwinian crisis at the end of the nineteenth century, and the secularization of the American university dates only from this period. The American Enlightenment had hardly any antireligious component. Even the separation of church and state that was constitutionally codified in the dual clause of the First Amendment had as much the purpose of protecting "the free exercise" of religion from state interference as that of protecting the federal state from any religious entanglement. James Madison's *Remonstrance*, the text that provided the rationale for the Virginia Statute on Religious Liberty, upon which the First Amendment was based, is a theological discourse on religious liberty as an inviolable individual right in need of protection from any political or religious establishment rather than a liberal secular discourse on overlapping consensus or the need to protect the liberal state and the public sphere from religious "infection." It is rare, at least until very recently, to find any progressive social movement in America appealing to secularist values. The appeals to the Gospel and to Christian values are certainly much more common throughout the history of American social movements as well as in the discourse of American presidents. Indeed, as jarring as such a discourse might sound to the enlightened ears of modern secular individuals, particularly European ones, no candidate for electoral office in America can afford to don a secularist or even an agnostic face in public.

The purpose of this comparison is not to reiterate the well-known fact that American society is more religious and therefore less secular than

European societies. While the first may be true, the second proposition does not follow. On the contrary, the United States has always been the paradigmatic form of a modern secular, differentiated society. Yet the triumph of the secular came aided by religion rather than at its expense. The point I am trying to make is that Christianity, particularly Protestant Christianity is intrinsically implicated in the development of secular modernity. One could say that the existence of a theological discourse of the "saeculum" within medieval Christianity was the very condition of possibility and the point of departure of the process of secularization. This process, however, has two trajectories. The more familiar trajectory is envisioned in secularist narratives as the emancipation and expansion of the secular spheres at the expense of a much-diminished and confined religious sphere. Here the boundaries are well-kept, but they are relocated drastically, pushing religion into the margins. The other trajectory is one in which the monastery walls—that is, the symbolic boundaries between the secular and religious spheres—are shattered, allowing for a mutual penetration of religion by the secular and of the secular by religion. The boundaries themselves become so diffuse that it is not clear where religion begins and the secular ends.

Of course, one could also offer a secularist interpretation of this trajectory by arguing that what we are dealing with here is no longer "authentic" religion, but rather an accommodation of religion to secular demands in order to survive. Supposedly, religion becomes so secularized that it does not count as "religion" anymore.[24] But, as Asad has noted concerning this secularist understanding, "The interesting thing about this view is that although religion is regarded as alien to the secular, the latter is also seen to have generated religion. . . . Thus the insistence on a sharp separation between the religious and the secular goes with the paradoxical claim that the latter continually produces the former."[25] The notion of an "authentic" religion is no less problematic, as Asad's persistent critique of essentialist constructions of Islam and of the Islamic tradition has shown so persuasively. Is modern Christianity less authentic and therefore less Christian than medieval or ancient Christianity? Is Eastern less authentic than Western Christianity, or Catholic less authentic than Protestant Christianity? It should be obvious that social science should not be in the business of authenticating authoritatively what true religion or true tradition might be, even when it cannot eschew making analytical distinctions.

The problem is that in the modern secular world the boundaries between the religious and the secular are so fluid that one ought to be very cautious when drawing such analytical distinctions. Let me illustrate this point through an analysis of the implication of religion in the crafting of what Asad views as "secular" human rights. Obviously I cannot attempt here a systematic reconstruction of the complex and multiple trajectories from medieval theological and canonical debates over natural law and natural rights, through early modern debates in secular legal and political theory, to modern declarations of universal human rights. Undoubtedly, the rise of bourgeois capitalism and the absolutist administrative state, the European colonial expansion, and the subjugation of conquered peoples and the slave trade were all crucial catalysts in these reformulations. But certainly the dissolution of medieval Christendom, the proliferation of competing churches unable to enforce their claims to territorial monopoly over the means of salvation, and the proliferation of dissenting sects challenging the claims of established state churches were equally relevant catalysts in "separating the individual right to (religious) belief from the authority of the state" and, one should add, from the authority of the church. To attribute this separation, as Asad seems to do, to the doctrine of secularism and to argue that "it is on this basis that the secularist principle of the right to freedom of belief and expression was crafted" is an overtly secularist reading of this process that overlooks the historical role of religious dissenters in claiming and securing their own rights.

Christian sects, particularly Baptists who on religious-theological grounds gave up the model of church, played a crucial role in the first historical codification of human rights in the Bills of Rights of the colonies and postcolonial states. Certainly the coalition of the secularist Jefferson, the religiously antiestablishmentarian Madison, and the mobilized Baptists was crucial in overcoming the resistance and securing the passage of the Virginia Statue on Religious Liberty. Today Christians continue to play an active role in the globalization of the discourse of human rights. The contemporary role of Catholics in this process is particularly striking and instructive. After all, the Catholic church had vehemently opposed the principle of human rights since the principle emerged at the time of the American and French revolutions. Pope Pius VI viewed the Declaration of the Rights of Man by the French National Assembly as a direct attack on the Catholic church. His 1791 papal Brief *Caritas* condemned the Declaration, stating that the formulation of the rights to freedom of religion and freedom of the press, as well as the Declaration on the Equality of All Men, was contrary to the divine principles of the church.[26] Pope Gregory XVI reiterated the condemnation in his encyclicals *Mirari vos* (1832) and *Singulari nos* (1834). Pius IX included the principle of human rights and most modern freedoms in the *Syllabus* (1864) of errors, pronouncing them anathema and irreconcilable with the Catholic faith. The principle of religious freedom was particularly odious, since it implied making equal the true religion and the false ones, as well as legitimizing separation of church and state.

But as part of the process of *aggiornamento* of the 1960s, the Catholic church has embraced the secular discourse of human rights, giving it a theological justification. John XXIII's encyclical *Pacem in Terris* (1963) was the first to adopt the modern discourse, which has remained thereafter part of every papal encyclical and of most episcopal pastoral letters.[27] Papal pronouncements have consistently presented the protection of the human rights of every person as the moral foundation of a just social and political global order.[28] Moreover, while earlier encyclicals were usually addressed to the Catholic faithful, beginning with *Pacem in Terris* the popes have tended to address their pronouncements to the entire world and to all people.

The Second Vatican Council's Declaration on Religious Freedom, *Dignitatis Humanae*, recognized the inalienable right of every individual to freedom of conscience, based on the sacred dignity of the human person. As the American theologian John Courtney Murray, one of the main drafters of the declaration, explained, theologically this entailed the transference of the principle of *libertas ecclesiae,* which the church had guarded so zealously through the ages, to the individual human person, from *libertas ecclesiae* to *libertas personae*.[29] Besides the unanimous support of the American bishops, the most eloquent arguments in support of the vehemently contested declaration came from Cardinal Karol Wojtyła from Cracow, who had learned from the experience of trying to defend the freedom of the church under communism that the best line of defense, both theoretically and practically, was the defense of the inalienable right of the human person to freedom of conscience.

From now on, the most effective way for the papacy to protect the freedom of the church worldwide would no longer be to enter into concordats with individual states, trying to extract from both friendly and unfriendly regimes the most favorable conditions possible for Catholic subjects, but rather to proclaim *urbi et orbi* the sacred right of each and every person to freedom of religion and to remind every government, not through discreet diplomatic channels but publicly, of their duty to protect this sacred human right. In particular, John Paul II became an untiring world traveler proclaiming everywhere the sacred dignity of the human person, claiming to be the self-appointed spokesman of humanity and *defensor hominis*. The pope learned to play, perhaps more effectively than any competitor, the role of first citizen of a catholic (i.e., global and universal) human society. One could almost say that the pope is becoming the high priest of a new global civil religion of humanity.[30]

There can be no doubt about the geopolitical impact of this doctrinal transformation upon the democratization of Catholic societies throughout the world.[31] But how are we going to interpret this theological reformulation of the Catholic tradition? Are we going to view it as the final capitulation to the inevitable triumph of secular modernity after centuries of apparently futile resistance? Certainly the very concept of *aggiornamento*, with its semantic connotation of "bringing up to date" and "catching up" with the spirit of the age, would seem to warrant such a reading. The Pastoral Constitution on the Church in the Modern World, *Gaudium et Spes*—undoubtedly the most important and consequential document of the Second Vatican Council—explicitly recognizes the legitimacy of the modern *saeculum*, of the modern age and the modern world. From now on, action on behalf of peace and justice and participation in the transformation of the world will be a constitutive dimension of the church's divine mission. In the last decades, Catholic churches, Catholic movements, and Catholic elites everywhere have turned inner-worldly with a vengeance. How is one to evaluate this process of internal secularization of the Catholic tradition?

About the authoritative nature of the theological reformulation there can be no doubt. The Church Fathers, gathered in ecumenical council, claimed to be inspired by the Holy Spirit.[32] But even if one were, from a secular perspective, to discount this theological claim as nothing but a subterfuge to mask and legitimate the radical reform, it would not follow that it constituted an illegitimate break with Catholic tradition. As Asad has rightly pointed out, "The selectivity with which people approach their tradition doesn't necessarily undermine their claim to its integrity. Nor does the attempt to adapt the older concerns of a tradition's followers to their new predicament in itself dissolve the coherence of that tradition."[33] But could it not be viewed perhaps as an instance of unwitting accommodation to the cunning of secular liberal reason? The bishops would certainly protest such a reading, and it would seem farfetched to accuse John Paul II of secular or liberal reasoning. Certainly his explicit critiques of secularism and liberalism are as coherent as those provided by Asad.

Although the Second Vatican Council recognized the autonomy of the secular spheres, the Catholic church does not accept the claims of these spheres to be detached from public morality. It resists the relegation of religion and morality to the private sphere, insisting on the links between private and public morality. It criticizes the radical individualism that accompanies privatization and stresses the collective and communal—the ecclesial—character of the proclamation of faith and of religious practices, while simultaneously upholding the absolute rights of the individual conscience. It simultaneously affirms dogma (i.e., authoritative obligatory doctrines of faith) and freedom of conscience. It also maintains the principle of communal ethical life that demands that all parts of society work toward the common good and be subordinated to higher moral principles.

Despite some continuity, there is a clear break with traditional Catholic organicism. The common good is no longer tied to a static, ontological view of natural law, itself tied to a conception of a natural social order. The church's claim that it is the depository of the common good is no longer tied to its alleged expertise in a divinely prescribed natural law but rather to a newly claimed "expertise in humanity." It is the transcendent, divinized humanity revealed in Jesus Christ that serves to ground the sacred dignity of the human person, as well as the absolute values of human life and freedom. Ironically, the church escapes the nominalist critique of the traditional ontological conception of natural law by embracing the historicism implicit in the biblical message. It is this historicism that permits maintaining both the religious particularity and the anthropological universality of the Christian message. With some lingering neo-Thomist strains, this is the core of Karol Wojtyła's theology, equally visible in his prepapal writings and in his papal pronouncements.[34]

The fact that the pope links these allegedly universal norms and values—the sacred dignity of the human person as well as the inalienable rights to human autonomy and self-determination—to a particular religious tradition is certainly bound to affect the reception of these universalistic claims by non-Christians. But conversely, in places where this particular religious tradition is still alive, it will serve to sanctify and legitimate modern liberal secular norms and values as Christian ones. The legitimation of liberal democracy is a case in point.

The traditional position of the Catholic church regarding modern political regimes had been neutrality toward all forms of government. While expressing its preference and the Catholic affinity for hierarchic and corporatist over republican and liberal democratic forms of government, the church also stressed its willingness to tolerate and coexist with the latter. Above all, the church always reminded the faithful to obey the rightful authorities. So long as the policies of these governments did not infringe systematically upon the corporate rights of the church to religious freedom, *libertas ecclesiae*, and to the exercise of its functions as *mater et magistra*, the church would not question their legitimacy. Only most rarely in those instances would the church resort to its traditional doctrine of lawful rebellion.[35]

The assumption of the modern doctrine of human rights has entailed not only the acceptance of democracy as a legitimate form of government but the recognition that modern democracy is a type of polity based on the universalist principles of individual freedom and individual rights. One can surely find continuity between the contemporary Catholic defense of human and civil rights against the modern authoritarian state and traditional Catholic critiques of tyranny and despotic rule. Against the arbitrary rule of tyrants as well as against the absolutist claims of the secular state, the church has always argued that the legitimacy of the state ought to be subordinated to the common good. But there is a fundamental difference between the traditional opposition to immoral rule because it violates natural law and the natural social order, and opposition to modern authoritarian rule because it violates the dignity of the human person and the inalienable rights to freedom, autonomy, and self-determination.

The purpose of this seeming digression into Catholic political theology has been to question what I consider to be the most problematic aspect of Asad's genealogy of the secular. Asad has presented a stark picture of the secular, liberal democracy, and the human rights regime, all blurred into an undifferentiated totality of Western modernity. If such a perspective is plausible, it would mean that the Catholic *aggiornamento* has contributed to the triumph of the secular regime across Catholic societies throughout the world. But Catholicism is not the only world religion undergoing similar *aggiornamentos*. Indeed, all world religions are challenged to respond to the global expansion of modernity by reformulating their traditions in an attempt to fashion their own versions of modernity. As I've pointed out elsewhere, it may be appropriate to interpret contemporary Islamic revival movements as types of *aggiornamento*.[36]

There are, of course, obvious differences between the contemporary Catholic and Islamic reforms. While the Catholic church has a clerical and hierarchic centralized administrative structure, the Islamic *umma*, at least within the Sunni tradition, has a more laic, egalitarian, and decentralized structure. Moreover, in comparison with the canonical and dogmatic modes of official infallible definition and interpretation of divine doctrines, Islam has more open, competitive, and pluralistic authoritative schools of law and interpretation, with a more fluid and decentralized organization of the *ulama*. Consequently, the Catholic *aggiornamento* had the character of an official, relatively uniform, and swift reform from above that encountered little contestation from below and could easily be enforced across the Catholic world, generating as a result a remarkable global homogenization of Catholic culture, at least among the elites. Lacking centralized institutions and administrative structures to define and enforce official doctrines, the ongoing Muslim responses to modern global realities and predicaments are and will likely remain plural, with multiple, diverse, and often contradictory outcomes. Actually, if there is anything on which most observers and analysts of contemporary Islam agree, it is that the Islamic tradition in the very recent past has undergone an unprecedented process of pluralization and fragmentation of religious authority, comparable to that initiated by the Protestant Reformation and operative ever since within Protestant Christianity.

Rather than furthering secularization, however, the general "modernization" or detraditionalization of Muslim societies has actually led to greater and wider access to religious education, which is moreover no longer under the control of the traditional *ulama*. As a result, not only Muslim intellectuals but ordinary Muslims across the world are engaged in contentious debates over their tradition and over the relationship of Islam to democracy, human rights, civil society, the public sphere, and the nation-state.[37] In order to be attuned and appreciate the multiple modernities that are likely to be fashioned by the diverse Muslim practices informed by these debates, we need better and more critical analytical tools than those provided by the traditional theory of secularization and corresponding theories of religious fundamentalism. Asad's *Formations of the Secular* offers a much more helpful analytical approach.

3

What Is an "Authorizing Discourse"?

Steven C. Caton

> July 2002. Sana'a, Republic of Yemen. The monsoon season but no rain. People are worried that the crops will fail, as they have in the previous five summers. Even the president has gone on TV to ask the country to pray for rain. One can hear them in the mosques all over the city and far into the night.
>
> —S. CATON, DIARY ENTRY

As in other parts of the Middle East, the Republic of Yemen has suffered a long-term drought, though it has been more severe perhaps in Yemen than elsewhere in the region. Drought is not the only problem where water shortage is concerned, however. Due to overuse of bore-hole drilling, spurred on by overly ambitious agricultural development plans of the 1980s and 1990s, the water table has been dropping precipitously and in some parts of the country is below the level at which farming is still profitable or even in some cases possible, leading to the wholesale abandonment of once self-sufficient villages. According to some predictions, Sana'a, the capital, will run out of potable water by the year 2008 unless something drastic is done. Just what that something might be, however, is anyone's guess. Though it would help to restrict the depth to which wells may be drilled for water extraction, finding new or additional sources of water is unlikely. Nor can Yemen afford the relatively expensive process of water desalinization, and transporting water over great distances—much less the fantastical idea of floating icebergs from the Antarctic—is nothing more than science fiction for one of the poorest countries on earth. As it seems that nothing less than a miracle will save them, is it any wonder that the people of Yemen have turned to prayers for rain? As I listened to the murmurs in the mosques that July, I asked myself the question Talal Asad might have posed of such a religious practice: what discourse "authorized" the ritual, constructing such categories of belief and practice? In what theological or other "official" discourse (including traditional sources) were these prayers commented upon or enjoined?

The publication of Talal Asad's *Genealogies of Religion* in 1993 was a landmark event in anthropology. Among other things, it reframed the analysis of religion in terms of a Foucauldian theory of discourse. Simply and perhaps too baldly put, it argued that religion (as well as ritual) is a historically constructed category, which in anthropology, moreover, owes a great deal to Christian theological discourse and religious practice—though Asad charged that anthropologists from Frazer to Geertz had forgotten this genealogy when they put forward allegedly universalist or essentialist definitions of their subject. In the manner of a Foucauldian analysis, Asad proceeded to "excavate" the category of "religion" through an examination of a vast discursive field constituted by historical texts mainly in the Christian but also in the Islamic theological traditions, along with some forays into journalism and literature (notably, *The Satanic Verses* and the firestorm it generated in the 1980s, known as the Salman Rushdie Affair). As a result of this intervention, written texts, or perhaps more precisely textual practices, have come into prominence as legitimate and important objects of analysis in ways that arguably had not been seen before in anthropology. Theoretical conceptions have shifted along with this new datum. If religion was once understood primarily as a cognitive or metaphysical system (as a worldview, or a way of "making sense" of the world or of nature)—or, to put it differently, if religion like any other hermeneutic system was once viewed as a system for encoding or decoding meaning—it is now approached as a discursive practice, tied closely to social action and especially to bodily discipline. I cannot think of another theoretical text as important as *The Genealogies of Religion* in shifting anthropology's conversation on religion onto this new terrain. In my teaching of this book, I have found the essay "The Construction of Religion as an Anthropological Category" to be the one which students read with the greatest interest, the one that seems to have the most impact on their understanding of religion as a discursively constituted category. In order to bring his own point of view into bold relief, in that essay Asad takes a deeply critical look at Clifford Geertz's famous interpretive or hermeneutic approach to religion, itself developed in an equally famous and widely influential essay entitled "Religion as a Cultural System."[1] In his reading of that essay, Asad argues that Geertz puts forward a "universal" or "trans-historical" definition of religion as a cultural system, a definition that purports to tell us the ontological essence of religion for now and always. Asad then scrutinizes the various constituent parts of the definition in an effort to demonstrate that it cannot, in fact, work in the way that Geertz claims it does. But he takes aim at the definition largely in order to show that Geertz's entire theoretical approach, sometimes called interpretive, sometimes hermeneutic anthropology, is confused, if not downright wrong. Certainly among the most important ideas to have come out of Asad's critique of Geertz in the essay "The Construction of Religion as a Cultural System" is the notion of an authorizing discourse, which I see as the linchpin of his entire argument on how a religious category is constructed in a particular society and indeed how power operates discursively through it. My essay asks two questions: What does Asad mean by this phrase in this essay and other writings on religion? And are his explicit statements on authorizing discourses sufficient to explain how religion works in practice?

Before we get to that point, however, it is necessary to examine more closely Asad's critical discussion of Geertz's ideas on religion. Since I disagree with the way Asad has characterized Geertz's project, I have, by necessity, had to say more about what I think Geertz was up to in the 1960s and 1970s than I ever intended to before beginning this essay. My aim is not to defend Geertz, or at least not the hermeneutic anthropology that he might stand for, even though we do have something in common, namely a desire to know how signs are used in social contexts and concomitantly how cultural meaning is constituted through them—an aim that I suspect all of us, Asad included, are interested in to one degree or another. However, I tend to approach this problem through linguistic pragmatics, and it remains to be seen how closely that approach might be affiliated with

Asad's notions of embodiment and discursive practice (let alone Geertz's hermeneutic anthropology). I try to explain why I think a particular idea that comes out of linguistic pragmatics—namely, the metapragmatic function of discourse—underlies not only what Geertz was talking about but, even more crucially, what Asad calls an authorizing discourse.

As already mentioned, Asad criticizes Geertz for his allegedly universalist or transhistorical definition of religion, a definition that assumes that religion "has an autonomous essence—not to be confused with the essence of science, or of politics, or of common sense—[and that insistence] invites us to define religion [like any essence] as a transhistorical and transcultural phenomenon." Asad goes on to state, "My argument is that there cannot be a universal definition of religion, not only because its constituent elements and relationships are historically specific, but because that definition is itself the historical product of discursive processes."[2]

One might ask whether, in fact, Geertz claims to provide an analytical definition of religion derived from certain theoretical propositions or whether his claims are indeed essentialist and universalistic in the sense that he is saying something ontological about religion as a transhistorical object. In my opinion, Asad cannot fault him for the former, for certainly Asad's definition of an authorizing discourse is no less theoretical or paradigmatic in that sense. There are reasons to believe, however, that Geertz is not making universalist claims, and in "Religion as a Cultural System" he explicitly says he is not. It is worth quoting the crucial passage in full:

> The notion that religion tunes human actions to an envisaged cosmic order and projects images of cosmic order onto the plane of human experience is hardly novel. But it is hardly envisaged either, so that we have very little idea of how, in empirical terms, this particular miracle is accomplished. We just know that it is done, annually, weekly, daily, for some people almost hourly; and we have an enormous ethnographic literature to demonstrate it. But the *theoretical framework* which would enable us to provide an analytic account of it, an account of the sort that we can provide for lineage segmentation, political succession, labor exchange, or the socialization of the child, does not exist.
>
> Let us, therefore, *reduce our paradigm to a definition*, for, although it is notorious that definitions establish nothing, in themselves they do, if they are carefully enough constructed, provide a useful orientation, or reorientation, of thought, such that an extended unpacking of them can be an effective way of *developing and controlling a novel line of inquiry*.[3]

In this passage, it is clear that Geertz does indeed intend to build a definition, but as a shorthand for what he takes to be a "theoretical framework" through which he hopes to reorient anthropological thought on religion. I cannot see that this is any different in intention, at least, from what Asad intends by the theoretical idea of an authorizing discourse. What he proposes to accomplish is to redirect our thinking about religion along, say, Foucauldian lines as bodily discipline. Asad goes on to claim that the distinguishing features of what Geertz takes to be religion as a cultural system are in fact deeply embedded in Christian theology and, he suspects, derived from it—unconsciously, one assumes. He concludes that Geertz's categories have a genealogy to which Geertz is either blind or not sufficiently attentive. It is an important criticism that may very well be true. That is a hazard all theoretical definitions face, of course, but if it were true, it would only call into question the validity of the framework, not whether Geertz actually intends to "essentialize" or "universalize" it.

But in my reading of Asad's essay, this point is not as interesting or as subtle as what he goes on to do next, which is to interrogate Geertz's notion of religion (and of culture and symbols) in such a way as to characterize it as "cognitive" and divorced at the outset of its theoretical formulation from the problem of social practice. Asad's characterization of Geertz goes something like this. Following Weber and Parsons, Geertz conceptualizes religion as an "autonomous sphere" (what this might mean is considered below), and as such he disengages it ontologically from the sphere of action in the world and society, and, more seriously still, from the problem of power (to which I also return below). Asad's point is not that Geertz is unconcerned with action (or power for that matter) but that he conceptualizes the symbolic realm of culture as being separable at the *outset* of the analysis from action in society—and that he then attempts to reconnect or re-engage culture and social action in an ad hoc or ex post facto fashion. This analytical fallacy, it is claimed, leads to others in Geertz's scheme, the most serious of which is a separation of thought from (social) action, resulting in what might be called cognitivism, which might be defined as the claim that thoughts are in the mind to begin with and only need to be expressed through symbols or signs in order to be communicated and acted upon. Asad rightly critiques cognitivism in psychology, drawing upon the work of the Soviet psychologist Lev Vygotsky, who argued that thinking is a process that takes place through signs as they are used in social context, and as such is embedded from the start in (unequal) social relations. In other words, to understand thought in the Vygotskyan view is to analyze it as emergent and constituted in social action through the mediation of signs. My argument is not with Asad's leaning toward a Vygotskyan theory of mind (quite to the contrary, for it is at the heart of the pragmatic tradition, which I have espoused elsewhere)[4] but rather in his surmise that Geertz is so very far from it.

Asad charges Geertz's definition with certain inconsistencies that, as far as I can see, lead him to view Geertz as a "cognitivist." Let us look first at what Asad has to say about Geertz's theory of symbols. Geertz states that practically anything can serve as a symbol, which in turn serves as a vehicle for some conception or meaning, a definition that Asad finds simple, clear, and seemingly straightforward. He finds more controversial or problematic the fact that Geertz supplements the definition with statements that are "not entirely consistent with it, for it turns out that the symbol is not an object that serves as a vehicle for a conception, it is itself the conception." He cites Geertz's discussion of the number 6 as an example of such inconsistency: "The number 6, written, imagined, laid out as a row of stones, or even punched into the program tapes of a computer, is a symbol."[5] Asad observes that "what constitutes all these diverse representations as versions of the same symbol ('the number 6') is of course a conception."[6] It is not altogether clear to me, however, that Asad's reading of Geertz's sentence is a necessary or correct one. For example, what would have been punched into the program tapes of a computer is a set of instructions that, if followed mechanically, would result in the representation of the symbol "6" on a printout or a computer screen, but those instructions and the number 6 as symbol are hardly "versions" of each other (nor is there reason to suppose that Geertz presumes them to be). Nor are the computer instructions a "conception of the number 6" in any straightforward way that Asad seems to have in mind by the "conception" behind a symbol. Asad gives Geertz's sentence a reductive reading; that is, reducing the symbol to its conception or what Saussure would have called its signified, and thereby leaving Geertz open to the charge of cognitivism. However, Geertz's sentence could also read, and to my mind this is the more plausible reading, as saying that the *symbol* 6 can be re-presented or retranslated by other quite different symbols (six stones laid in a row, the Latin numeral VI, six notes struck by a clock, and so forth) or be arrived at through any number of computational or mechanical ways, but those facts do not alter its ontological status qua symbol—which is a reading that does not commit us to an understanding of a symbol as a conception.

Asad goes on to assert that Geertz is inconsistent in an even more important sense when he says that a symbol "has an intrinsic connection with empirical events from which it is merely 'theoretically' separable" but then insists upon "the importance of keeping symbols and empirical objects quite separate."[7] For Asad, the "inconsistency" is symptomatic of a larger problem in Geertz's theoretical formulation, namely the idea that symbols are "autonomous" with regard to social action, which I take to mean both that they are not caused or determined by action in society and that they have an internal logic that cannot be reduced to a pattern to be found in social action. As it happens, Asad is touching upon one of Geertz's more famous examples, which comes up again in a later portion of that section of "Religion as a Cultural System"—namely the difference between a model "of" some aspect of the real world (say, the floor plan of a house) and that which it stands "for" or models (the house to be built). The model of / model for idea is presumably an instance of Geertz distinguishing ontologically between the symbol and the real world (and one can hardly see how it could be otherwise); however, if the floor plan has been made by an architect with a client in mind, it does indeed have "an intrinsic connection with empirical events" (namely the imminent building of a house). Surely, both propositions can be true in the very same sign phenomenon as Geertz would have it: that the plan is not the same ontologically as the house, but the plan nevertheless has an intrinsic connection to the house. In a footnote, Asad constructively cites Charles S. Peirce as being more rigorous on the question of sign-representation than Geertz—which may be true—but he fails to take up Peirce's tripartite mode of icon, index, and symbol, which would help us to understand how signs may be intrinsically or existentially connected to what they stand for and yet may still be ontologically distinct. Thus, regarding the example of the floor plan, Peirce might have said that it is, of course, an icon in that it is presumed to bear a resemblance to what it stands for, and insofar as it is supposed to stand for an *actual* building (whether already existent or to be constructed in the future), it is also an index that stands for something in temporal or spatial contiguity to itself (hence the sign "is in intrinsic connection with empirical events or objects").

Having argued that Geertz is inconsistent in these ways, Asad then concludes: "These divergencies are symptoms of the fact that cognitive questions are mixed up in this account with communicative ones, and this makes it difficult to inquire into the ways in which discourse and understanding are connected in social practice."[8] It is not clear what "mixing up" means in this passage. One reading of the criticism might be that Geertz allegedly separates thinking or understanding (or cognition) from the problem of communication or the intersubjective and interactive social process in which meanings are conveyed through symbols (and symbols in turn are interpreted for their meanings). In any case, Asad goes on to state:

We might say, as a number of writers have done, that a symbol is not an object or event that serves to carry a meaning but a set of relationships between objects or events uniquely brought together as complexes or as concepts, *having at once an intellectual, instrumental, and emotional significance.* If we define symbol along these lines, a number of questions can be raised about the conditions that explain how much complexes and concepts can be formed, and in particular how their formation is related to varieties of practice.[9]

Note the multiple significances that a symbol can have, according to Asad, a point that I will take up later when I look more closely at Geertz's notion of symbolic action. What I take exception to here is the characterization of Geertz as a cognitivist tout court, a move that is not a little ironic when one recalls what passed for cognitivist anthropology in the 1970s, a movement Geertz vehemently distanced himself from in interpretive essays published in 1973: the structuralism of Levi-Strauss—most obviously—but also the componential analysis of kinship terminologies (variously called ethnoscience or cognitive anthropology), spearheaded by Ward Goodenough, Floyd Lounsbury, and others in the 1960s. And it was such formalistic and cognitivist approaches to the study of culture that Geertz opposed—as he stated in his essay "Thick Description"[10]—for fear that his own might be mistaken for them.

As for Asad's point about Geertz's separation of the cultural system from social practice, it is also helpful to recall that he distinguished his own position from that of another famous symbolic anthropologist of the 1960s and 1970s, David Schneider, who in Geertz's estimation had treated cultural systems as too hermetically self-contained, too divorced from social action. Geertz does not explicitly mention Schneider in "Thick Description," but in the following passage the allusion to and critique of what might be called a Schneiderian approach is unmistakable:

> Now, this proposition, that it is not in our interest to bleach human behavior of the very properties that interest us before we begin to examine it, has sometimes been escalated into a larger claim: namely, that as it is only those properties that interest us, we need not attend, save cursorily, to behavior at all. Culture is more effectively treated, the argument goes, purely as a symbolic system (the catch phrase is, "in its own terms"), by isolating its elements, specifying the internal relationships among those elements, and then characterizing the whole system in some general way—according to the core symbols around which it is organized, the underlying structures of which it is a surface expression, or the ideological principles upon which it is based. Though a distinct improvement over "learned behavior" and "mental phenomena" notions of what culture is, and the source of some of the most powerful theoretical ideas in contemporary anthropology, this hermetical approach to things seems to me to run the danger (and increasingly to have been overtaken by it) of locking cultural analysis away from its proper object, the informal logic of actual life. There is little profit in extricating a concept from the defects of psychologism only to plunge it immediately into those of schematicism.
>
> Behavior must be attended to, and with some exactness, because it is through the flow of behavior—or more precisely, social action—that cultural forms find articulation. They find it as well, of course, in various sorts of artifacts, and various sorts of consciousness; *but these draw their meaning from the role they play (Wittgenstein would say their "use") in an ongoing pattern of life, not from any intrinsic relationship they bear to one another.*[11]

Schneider countered such accusations by sharply criticizing Weberian anthropologists such as Geertz, among others, for not making culture more autonomous. As Schneider confessed in his class lectures in the 1970s at the University of Chicago, he feared that symbols and their meanings would become "lost" or "obscure" to the symbolic anthropologist if they were not abstracted from social institutional settings and from social action.[12] It is certainly true, as Asad points out, that Geertz was a student of Parsons, as was Schneider, but Geertz also distanced himself from his mentor's more extreme positions. More importantly for our purposes, the passage reveals that Geertz conceptualizes action in terms that are closer to the pragmatist tradition, both philosophical and otherwise, than Asad seems willing to grant. Thus the reference to Wittgenstein and his *Philosophical Investigations* is incomprehensible were Geertz a dyed-in-the-wool cognitivist or semanticist. Rather than saying in the above passage that ideas are simply hatched a priori in the brain and then "executed" in communicative action (a position that is closer to the Saussurean langue/parole distinction), Geertz is arguing, with Wittgenstein, that action plays a far more important constitutive role in the formation of ideas than the cognitivists or semanticists would allow.

Of course, these statements of Geertz's may still not alter the fundamental problem with his theory as Asad sees it, which is to conceptualize culture qua system of symbols and their meanings as being separate at the outset from the domain of social action as well as social structure, such that it is only in a specific empirical or ethnographic analysis that the two are conjoined. I don't disagree with Asad when he criticizes the way in which Geertz formulated the relationship of cultural meaning to social practice, for there are several key passages (which Asad cites) that do indeed suggest a break or separation between two distinct orders that is perhaps sharper than Geertz—at least in hindsight—might have intended. My own interpretation of these passages is that Geertz wanted to avoid a reduction of culture to the realms of society and politics that he found in more materialist or Marxist anthropologists of his generation, such as Marvin Harris. But does that mean that Geertz, as a consequence, analytically separated the problem of symbolic meaning from action at the outset or that he had failed to incorporate an "action" view within his notion of culture, which did in fact entail social relations?

I believe the answer to this question lies in what Geertz meant by "symbolic action," a phrase he borrowed from the literary critic Kenneth Burke.[13] Though this phrase might be interpreted as action in which symbolic meaning is merely instantiated (as in the idea of meaning being "enacted"), this is not, in fact, what Burke had in mind, nor what I believe Geertz, following Burke, construed it to mean. For Burke, a poem, for example, was never simply an "expression" of an emotion or an idea (as if it were simply a vehicle or container for something already in the mind and heart of the poet that then gets connected to words on a page) but a *communicative act*—a framework that turns the poem into a social act comprising an addressor, an addressee, their social relationship, the channel or medium of their communication, and the effects the poem may have on a wider social context.[14] It is my contention that Geertz attempted to analyze a cultural system as symbolic action in an analogous fashion. Indeed, when one returns to the definition of religion that Geertz gave, it is striking how strongly he conceived of it in terms of action: "a system of symbols which acts." It is not simply that one has culture on one side as a self-contained system and action on the other (as when culture becomes connected to practices within social institutions) but that culture is always already a symbolic act, though for Geertz never reducible to the wider ground of social institutions and material realities that influence it (and vice versa). In this view, the "model of" aspect of religion is intrinsic to cultural systems insofar as they try to say something about the world (whether presupposed or imagined) and corresponds to what Burke called the "mapping function" in speaking of the literary text.[15] Indeed, it is what Asad above referred to as one of the "significances" of a practice, namely its referential one. But that is only one of the functions or purposes (goals) of communication that a text may have, in addition to culture understood as a symbolic act. What Burke called the "exhortative" or "hortatory" purpose of address has its parallel in what Geertz delineated as religion's propensity to "establish powerful, pervasive and long-lasting moods and motivations in men [sic]." And, of course, one could go on to delineate more such purposes or goals.

Having hopefully clarified what Geertz intended by the phrase "symbolic action," it might be helpful at this point to take up one of the most important criticisms of his approach—his apparent lack of concern for the "problem of power." Of course, this criticism has been made before by such materialist and Marxist-inspired anthropologists as Eric Wolf and William Roseberry, and while Asad has from time to time been a Marxist theoretician, his criticism of Geertz is more subtle than to say that his definition does not address power.[16] There is, after all, no a priori reason that a definition of culture must take power into account, and the reason that Geertz's definition is found wanting may be a consequence of shifting interests and priorities in anthropology. But Asad is asserting something more subtle and potentially more damaging: that Geertz's definition of religion as a cultural system cannot work on its own terms without taking power into account at the very outset of its formulation.

To respond adequately to this criticism would require more space than is available in this essay. I would claim that Geertz does have such a notion of power, though we might call it rhetorical, in the sense that it is closely tied to the persuasiveness of symbols in communicative action. In this vein, one might interpret the statements on power and symbolic action in his study of the Balinese theater state as a "spectacle" of power.[17] But I would not want to suggest that this is the only way to conceptualize the connection between symbolic action and power effects within a communicative model of action; rather I would claim that the notion of metapragmatics also has a critical contribution to make. The crucial question for me is whether Asad's point is a different one, when he states that "the authoritative status of representations/discourses is dependent on the appropriate production of other representations/discourses; the two are intrinsically and not just temporally connected."[18] This is what Asad has termed an "authorizing discourse," and it is here that one arrives at the central point or the main criticism of Geertz: what gets constructed as "religion" in any given society is a priori a matter of other discourses that *authorize* that construction. "The argument that a particular disposition is religious partly because it occupies a conceptual place within a cosmic framework appears plausible, but only because it presupposes a question that must be made explicit: how do authorizing processes represent practices, utterances, or dispositions so that they can be discursively related to general (cosmic) ideas of order? In short, the question pertains to the authorizing process by which 'religion' is created."[19] I would ask: and to what extent is a metapragmatic notion of discourse essential here?

It is time now to examine more closely Asad's important and influential idea of an "authorizing discourse." In "The Idea of an Anthropology of Islam," he writes:

If one wants to write an anthropology of Islam one should begin, as Muslims do, from the concept of a discursive tradition that includes and relates itself to the founding texts of the Qur'an and the Hadith. Islam is neither a distinctive social structure nor a heterogeneous collection of beliefs, artifacts, customs, and morals. It is a tradition. . . .

What is a tradition? A tradition consists essentially of discourses that seek to instruct practitioners regarding the correct form and purpose of a given practice that, precisely because it is established, has a history.[20]

A tradition, then, is constituted minimally by a set of discourses that "instruct" the individual in what he or she ought to do in order to be a "proper" Muslim. Asad reiterates this point several times in this paper. "For the anthropologist of Islam, the proper theoretical beginning is therefore an instituted practice [set in a particular context, and having a particular history] into which Muslims are inducted *as* Muslims. . . . A practice is Islamic because it is authorized by the discursive traditions of Islam, and is taught by Muslims—whether by an *'alim*, a *khatib*, a Sufi *shaykh*, or an untutored parent."[21] One might note, however, that there are several discursive practices at work in the above statements, which are arguably also analytically distinct. There is the primarily written liturgical discourse consisting of the Qur'an, the hadith, the fiqh, and other "official" sources, which theoretically constitute the categories of belief and practice that are said to be Islamic. But these discourses, though they are clearly meant to be instructional, are not necessarily the same as "an instituted practice [set in a particular context, and having a particular history] into which Muslims are inducted *as* Muslims," and Asad makes this plain when he says, "It may be worth recalling here that etymologically 'doctrine' means teaching, and that orthodox doctrine therefore denotes the correct process of teaching, as well as the correct statement of what is to be learned."[22] Thus it is useful to distinguish between what we might call a theory of Islam, gleaned from liturgical and other kinds of discourses, and the ways in which a Muslim is instructed through the use of these texts in specific and concrete settings in order to act as a "proper" Muslim. In other words, Asad's definition of discursive tradition allows for what might be called a "gap" between the instructional texts as given in the Qur'an, the hadith, and so forth and concrete Islamic practices, for it is not necessarily the case that the latter are merely imitative or mere instantiations of what has been thought to come before.

Clearly, not everything Muslims say and do belongs to an Islamic discursive tradition. Nor is an Islamic tradition in this sense necessarily imitative of what was done in the past. For even where traditional practices appear to the anthropologist to be imitative of what has gone before, it will be the practitioners' conceptions of what is an *apt performance*, and of how the past is related to present practices, that will be crucial for tradition, not the apparent repetition of an old form.[23]

I take this passage to mean that not everything a Muslim says or does qua Muslim need be a repetition of the past—it is only necessary that *practitio-*

ners thinks it is so and that what they say or do is therefore proper according to their own lights. But if this is so, then who or what authorizes them to think so? Indeed, the passage seems to imply that it is not only that a tradition authorizes Islamic practice; by presupposing a past that "is related to present practice," practitioners "authorize" the tradition and thereby also their own practices, even or perhaps especially when one cannot find a textual source in that tradition for that purpose. The two discourses—the liturgical tradition and the practice that presupposes a tradition—are placed in dialectical relationship to each other.

This state of affairs raises a fundamental analytical question, or so it seems to me. It is easy enough to see how a pre-existent text authorizes a present Islamic practice; it is harder to see how practices "authorize" themselves, not to mention tradition, in the absence of the former. I am not sure that there is a clear answer to this in the *Genealogies of Religion*. In that text, an authorizing discourse *appears* to be distinct from the religious discourse or practice it authorizes; in other words, the discourse that authorizes always stands outside of what it represents and legitimates. That this assumption is warranted is clear, I think, from the following. After having claimed that Geertz wrongly separates a symbolic system from action, Asad criticizes him for not adequately distinguishing them—for example, a traditional religious practice like a prayer, must be distinct from the theological discourse that dictates that a prayer "should" be conducted and how:

> One consequence of assuming a symbolic system separate from practices is that important distinctions are sometimes obscured, or even explicitly denied. "That the symbols or symbols systems which induce and define dispositions we set off as religious and those which place those dispositions in a cosmic framework are the same symbols ought to occasion no surprise" (Geertz, 98). But it does surprise! Let us grant that religious dispositions are crucially dependent on certain religious symbols, that such symbols operate in a way integral to religious motivation and religious mood. Even so, the symbolic process by which the concepts of religious motivation and mood are placed within "a cosmic framework" is surely quite a different operation, and therefore the signs involved are quite different. Put another way, theological discourse is not identical with either moral attitudes or liturgical discourses—of which, among other things, theology speaks. . . . *Discourse involved in practice is not the same as that involved in speaking about practice.*[24]

According to this passage, in other words, an authorizing discourse is distinct from *other* discourses (as well as nondiscursive practices, one presumes) which it comments upon or in some way gives authority to; by that logic, a discourse may not refer to or authorize itself. There is a certain irony in insisting on this point, for in deciding to keep distinct discourse and practice, Asad seems to create for his schema the same problem he finds fault with in Geertz, and in the end, one has to figure out how a discursively constructed category and its deployment in social action are somehow connected.

My argument is that the problem lies with Asad's notion of an authorizing discourse as prior or anterior to the practice itself. Linguistic pragmatics may help us understand this point. The notion of an authorizing discourse needs reformulation so as to be attuned to the ways in which (1) any discourse can operate metadiscursively, not only in the sense that Asad intends it by commenting on another practice, but also in its capacity to comment on *itself* (a capacity that all signs have because of their multifunctional communicative nature);[25] and (2) its authorizing power is dependent upon both kinds of metapragmatic processes—to a discourse that is "other" than itself and to its own powers of metareferentiality—but especially the latter.

Let me now return to the ethnographic example for a fuller discussion of some of these points about the metapragmatic nature of an authorizing discourse. In the summer of 2002 I became aware of a fervent preoccupation in Yemen with "rain prayers," the result of a drought that had afflicted the country for several years. I asked the Asadean question: who authorized these prayers and how did they construct the categories of belief and practice? In what theological or other official discourse were these prayers commented upon or enjoined?

I asked my friend Kamal, a devout and highly educated young man, about the rain prayers. Apparently, I had conflated in my mind two very different genres of discourse, which he proceeded to distinguish for me. He explained the difference between a call or supplication (*du'a*) for rain and the prayer (*Salaah*) for rain itself, though one could hear both in the mosque at night. The latter is done collectively and has the same words, gestures, and movements as any other prayer, the only difference being in the appearance of the worshippers (to which I will return in a moment).

The *du'a*, on the other hand, can be intoned either individually by the imam after the prayer has been completed or collectively. I heard an example of one such *du'a* from the Grand Mosque in Sana'a, which Kamal taped for me, two slightly different textual versions of which are given below.

1. O Lord, we ask Your forgiveness, for You truly are forgiving. Make the sky send water down to us! Lord, irrigate us with Your succor. Shed our fear! Don't turn us into hopeless and hapless beings! Don't destroy our livelihood with years of drought! Lord, give us succor, benevolent rains . . . with no wrath in it, Lord, provide us with the succor of the days in our hearts, the succor of mercy in our stomachs, the succor of forgiveness and blessing in our bodies. Lord, irrigate us with mercy, don't irrigate us with suffering (this latter sentence repeated three times). Lord, truly we plead for help and now not later: irrigate the land and be merciful to mankind, You who possess the world and the hereafter. To You is (the way of) the hereafter. Lord, irrigate us with succor, with Your blessing, O most Merciful One, most Helpful One (repeated three times). Our Lord, the trees have withered, the rivers gone dry, the animals gone hungry. We've had misfortune, want, and poverty. We complain to you, Lord, and none other, for there is no life for us except for the rain that falls from the sky. Lord, help us now not later, O most Merciful One.

2. Lord, don't keep the rain imprisoned because of our sins. Don't blame us for what we've done, nor what the fools among us have done and the ignorant. Lord, let the crops grow, give fodder to the animals, and waft to us from the blessings of the sky that which we require. Lord, our crops have been destroyed, our animals have gone hungry. Relieve us from that which we are in the midst of, O most Merciful One. Lord, discoverer of misfortune, overhearer of every secret conversation, remove this calamity from us with Your mercy, O Lord, O He who gives life to decaying bones, revive Your land of Yemen with rains, most Merciful One.

After the imam has finished this *individual* invocation, Kamal went on to explain, he or some other person in the first row of the congregation "spontaneously" begins the *collective* invocation. The text is more or less the same all over Yemen, though the words may vary slightly, an observation of Kamal's that was confirmed by several friends from different regions of the country. Thus the text in the Grand Mosque in Sana'a is the same as that in Sa'dah to the north or villages in Khawlan aT-Tiyal. Here's the text as it is chanted by the entire congregation in the Grand Mosque:

> O Merciful One, take pity on us.
> And be compassionate toward us.
> And turn toward us
> And send us rain, O Lord.
> There is no God but God.
> O most compassionate of all the compassionate
> There is no sanctuary except in You.
> "There is no God but God."
> Our instrument—"There is no God but God."
> Our sanctuary—"There is no God but God."
> O Merciful One, O Compassionate One
> Grant us rain!

The words are not spoken but chanted: Kamal was quite insistent upon this point. In his estimation, the chant as opposed to a delivery in "plain voice" facilitated the collective performance of the call for rain—the *du'a jama'i* (collective invocation)—which in turn underscored the unity of purpose behind the plea for forgiveness. In other words, it was not just an individual but the entire community that was now asking for God's help, and that fact, it was believed, made the call even more urgent and effective. In turn, the more intense the drought, the greater the number of invocations (as well as rain prayer) are heard during the week. It was no wonder, then, that it seemed all night long of every night of the month of July I heard these invocations coming from the mosques of Sana'a, the voice of the imam filled with ever more pathos and the worshipful congregation with ever more fervor as the weeks went by—but without the hoped-for rain clouds massing on the horizon.

As for other parts of Yemen, especially in the smaller villages and more remote areas of the country, it is common, according to Kamal, to perform an invocation *collectively* after the prayer for rain in the mosque and to do it on returning from the mosque, perhaps in the *sayilah* (flood plain) or some other public gathering place. When I asked some friends who live outside the capital, they confirmed much of what Kamal said, but gave slightly different texts:

> O Merciful One, O Benefactor,
> Bless us with rains,
> "There is no God but God."

> In the name of Taha and [the well of] Zamzam and its water
> And Mekka, which are protected,
> Irrigate us with rain, O Lord
> Exonerate Yemen.
> "There is no God but God."
> The despairing ones are shriveled up
> (This is) the calamity of the poor.

Regardless of the particular text or its provenance, one presupposition they all share is that the supplicants are guilty of sin and it is for this reason that God has punished Yemen with drought. This is more obvious perhaps in the second text, but Kamal confirmed this interpretation for me, qualifying it by explaining that one area of Yemen always got rain even when the rest of the country was dry: the city of Ibb, located in the center of the country. Popular belief has it that when the Prophet Muhammad learned that Ibb always paid the *zakkat* tax (each Muslim's obligation of providing money for the poor), he asked the Lord to bless it. Ever since, or so it is believed, Ibb has never lacked water, which is why it is known as "the green district." Kamal, who hails from Ibb, mentioned that when people discover his origin, they acknowledge the almost sacred status of the city by saluting him with the phrase "God's blessings are upon you." On the other hand, the opposite of Ibb in the popular imagination is the iniquitous village of al-Muqaddishah, located in the tribal region belonging to the 'Ans. Rather than paying the *zakkat*, this village was apparently too concerned with making war on its neighbors, so that the Prophet invoked the curses of God upon it, and the Muqaddishah have been plagued ever since by drought and other calamities. It is worth pointing out that these are allegorical narratives and as such are meant to produce certain political effects. Thus it is not surprising that the central portion of the country, which historically has been the backbone of central authority in Yemen since at least the days of the Rasulids, imagines itself as "blessed" in comparison to those regions in the east that attempt to resist its authority and are considered "damned"; nor is it surprising that this self-serving rhetoric is countered or simply ignored by others.

But the days are long gone (if they ever existed) when only the village of al-Muqaddishah was blamed for calamities, for now the entire country is experiencing a severe drought and not even Ibb has been completely spared. It follows, therefore, that everyone is somehow implicated in the metaphysical problem of evil thought to be at the root of this calamity, and therefore all Yemenis must beg God's forgiveness for their sins.

And it is here that we come to the rain prayer and the way in which the sinner makes his appearance in the Grand Mosque in Sana'a like a character in an ancient morality play. Kamal said that the scene inspired him with awe. Worshippers came with their clothing reversed or turned inside out. Jackets were worn backwards, thobs inside out, headdresses with the patterned or printed side hidden underneath, watches with their faces down, and so forth. "You have to understand," Kamal explained. "All these people are usually so careful about their attire but now appear to humiliate themselves. And it isn't only their clothing that has been altered. Their eyes are downcast, even their postures are different. They slouch with their shoulders stooped and their heads inclined downwards, and sometimes they even shuffle across the floor like old men. It's an incredible sight, the wealthiest and most powerful men of the city looking like the lowliest and most downtrodden." After a pause, he went on, in even more reverential tones, "The point, of course, is for the great to humble themselves before God." Again, this presupposes that one is seeking forgiveness for something; when pressed to be more specific, Kamal said that it had to do more with one's state of moral being rather than specific misdeeds one had committed: the sin of pride, for example, even arrogance, and lack of compassion toward the poor. "The belief is that one has to change one's entire attitude to ensure that the correct social behavior will follow and, accordingly, that God will bless the penitent with rain." The worse the drought became, the more sinful, it was presumed, mankind had been, thus requiring even more penitential practices on the part of the people.

I asked Kamal whether the invocations were thought to be ancient, and he replied that it was not known exactly how old they were, though there were stories about such penitence being performed in the reign of Queen Arwa and even before her time by the pre-Islamic Prophet Suleyman, as related in this story.

> It is related that when the Prophet Sulaiman, peace be upon him, went outside to pray for rain on behalf of the people, an ant thrown onto its back in the middle of the *wadi* intoned, "Lord, I'm a creature of your Creation, don't spare us Your rain (irrigation) and Your Compassion." And the Prophet Suleyman, peace

be upon him, said to his people, "Go back (to your homes), for you have already been irrigated by the call of someone else."

Kamal could not say where this story came from. He thought it was part of an ancient folkloric tradition, but when pressed to describe it further or to cite a body of texts or sayings, he drew a blank. Although practitioners do not know if there was a tradition of stories (as in the sense of a discursive field), of which the story of Solomon is a part, such a tradition is *presupposed* by the way the story is told. The metapragmatic frame "It is related that . . . " sets up the presupposition that this story has been told again and again as part of what might be called collective memory. To put it more provocatively, it is as though the story authorizes the tradition *as* an authorizing discourse, a rather more complicated process than the notion developed in Asad's essay, that the tradition authorizes the story. I was surprised to learn from Kamal that there are no theological texts or texts of religious learning that prescribe the invocations or describe how they are to be performed. I asked him to check on this to make sure and he consulted with QaDhi Isma'el al-Ikwa, perhaps the most eminent authority on Yemeni history, theology, and jurisprudence, who told him, "This [the rain invocation] is considered something that the people do unofficially and as if spontaneously and therefore beyond the need for regulation or prescription." To be sure, other authorities should be consulted to verify this conclusion. Nevertheless, a categorical distinction was produced between what it was thought necessary to regulate and supervise in religious life and what apparently could be left to its own unfolding and development, but beyond that there were no specific prescriptions of behavior.

There are at least two ways to conceptualize a metapragmatic discourse. One is quite close, I think, to what Asad has in mind when he talks about an authorizing discourse. We know that metapragmatic discourses do indeed comment on discourses or modes of speaking in the way Asad has in mind; thus an old-fashioned etiquette manual might instruct the reader to say "May I?" rather than "Can I?" in order to do or obtain something, where the metapragmatic or instructional discourse is quite separate from the particular instance of discourse in which the polite form "May I?" occurs, but nonetheless is meant to apply to it. But there is another way in which to conceptualize a metapragmatic discourse that is distinct from the former, for we also know that a discourse may refer to *itself* in the very *same* instance of its occurrence or utterance. This is largely because of the multifunctional nature of linguistic communication, in which what has variously been called the metalingual or metacommunicative function is but one of many.[26]

One of the most interesting ways to clarify this kind of discourse is to delve into the writings of Bakhtin and Voloshinov, which, in fact, Asad cites at various points in his essay to suggest not only how one might theorize the connection of sign to practice, of consciousness to action in the world, but also the authorizing discourse that is so important to his own thinking about religion. In what ways do these writers touch upon, if only implicitly, the problem of metapragmatic discourse in their theoretical formulations of language, thought, and ideology?

Let us start with *Marxism and the Philosophy of Language,* whose precise authorship is controversial even to this day, some maintaining that it was written by Voloshinov, a Communist Party functionary and student of Bakhtin, others that it was the work of Bakhtin, who published it under Voloshinov's name because he was not in favor with the party, and still others that it was a collaboration between the two though presented as a mono-vocal text. This book proposes that there are two kinds of ideologies: an official one, which emanates from various state apparatuses and other institutions of power and operates rather like Asad's authorizing discourse, as well as an everyday or unofficial ideology (what the text refers to as a "behavioral" ideology), which emerges through social interaction and in what they call dialogue. They make the important point that the study of ideology had been confined largely to official ideology and that its operations in everyday behavior, especially linguistic behavior, had been neglected. But this neglect or oversight is unfortunate, for one can only understand how the official ideology sustains itself and leads to some sort of regulated social practice through the behavioral (dialogical) one. Indeed, according to their thinking, it is the everyday or behavioral ideology that "authorizes" the official one—and vice versa, for the two are in dialectical relation to each other. However, because it is a dialectical relation, the behavioral ideology may also implicitly "comment on" or "frame" the official ideology in ways that subtly undermine or subvert rather than merely authorize it.

Let us, then, take a closer look at "behavioral" ideology and how Bakhtin/Voloshinov envisioned its operation. In particular, we want to see if it might be (implicitly) metapragmatic and in an important sense arrogate to itself the power to authorize itself without depending upon or waiting for an official ideology. The author(s) of *Marxism and the Philosophy of Language* is/are particularly interested in what they call "dialogue" and the grammatical or linguistic ways in which it is instantiated. By "dialogue" they understand not the formal theatrical or dramatic structure of two characters taking turns in speaking (A speaks and then B, A speaks again and then B) but a dialogue *internal* to a given turn of speaking: a person, while speaking, is at once replying to a previous "said" of discourse (either her own or someone else's) *and* anticipating a reply or answer to her own, and insofar as the stretch of speech may be said to contain these multiple voices of self/selves and other(s), it is "poly-vocal." Geertz's model of/model for operation is apposite here: on the one hand, the discourse provides a model "of" something (both what was said by another but also perhaps what the reporter of that speech thinks or feels about it) as well as a model "for" (that is, a model of how the dialogue is meant to proceed, at least from the point of view of the speaker, a kind of prefiguring of discourse). For Bakhtin/Voloshinov, this dialogue could occur within a sentence or large stretch of "monological" speech, or even in a single word.

> Dialogue is studied merely as a compositional form in the structuring of speech, but the internal dialogism of the word (which occurs in a monologic utterance as well as in a rejoinder), the dialogism that penetrates its entire structure, all its semantic and expressive layers, is almost entirely ignored. But it is precisely this internal dialogism of the word, which does not assume any external compositional forms of dialogue, that cannot be isolated as an independent act, separate from the word's ability to form a concept of its object—it is precisely this internal dialogism that has such enormous power to shape style.[27]

Note that at the end of this passage, Bakhtin connects dialogicality with a certain power, and—since Asad is mindful of the ways in which discursive practices are intrinsically connected to power—one might want to dwell further on this point. Dialogue, understood in Bakhtin's sense, has at least as much to do with understanding how power operates discursively as does Asad's authorizing discourse, which operates outside an actual instance of utterance that it authorizes. We need both notions, however, not just one of them, to understand power as a discursive practice.

If dialogue is the most important theoretical concept here, how is it instantiated in grammatical forms of everyday speech? And in turn we must ask how the latter can be seen to be metapragmatic? To begin with, it is salutary to realize how pervasive and consequential reported speech is in everyday life in Bakhtin's view.

In real life people talk most of all about what others talk about—they transmit, recall, weigh and pass judgment on other people's words, opinions, assertions, information; people are upset by others' words, or agree with them, contest them, refer to them and so forth. Were we to eavesdrop on snatches of raw dialogue in the street, in a crowd, in a foyer and so forth, we would hear how often the words "he says," "people say," "he said . . . " are repeated, and in the conversational hurly-burly of people in a crowd, everything often fuses into one big "he says . . . you say . . . I say. . . . " Reflect how enormous is the weight of "everyone says" and "it is said" in public opinion, public rumor, gossip, slander and so forth. One must also consider the psychological importance in our lives of what others say about us, and the importance, for us, of understanding and interpreting these words of others [living hermeneutics].[28]

Note that "he says . . . you say . . . I say" are all examples of reported speech, of which there are several forms, the most important perhaps being direct versus indirect. An example of the direct form would be, "He said, 'I want to go to Union Square tonight,'" in which, presumably, the exact words of the person denoted by the pronoun *I* are reported. The indirect form would be, "He said he wanted to go to Union Square tonight," in which the speech of the person denoted in the narrated event is paraphrased rather than quoted in full. In Bakhtin's perspective, reported speech is a dialogical entity in the sense that it contains at least two voices—the speaker and the person whose speech is being reported. In the above examples, the voice of the speaker may sound "neutral," but it is not passive reporting—for even neutrality is a position one must take, and in taking that position, one constitutes oneself to the audience as a "reliable" or "unbiased" or "objective" reporter and that which is re-presented as actual or authentic. But Bakhtin was even more interested in the ways in which the speaker of reported speech may, in the same event of reporting, inflect or color the said of discourse, either through a certain tone of voice or through a verbal descriptive phrase that refers to the manner in which something was uttered (for example, "He said sarcastically, 'I want to go to Union Square tonight'"), which indicates that the speech being reported ought not to be taken at face value. It is, to return to the Geertz of "Thick Description," the verbal equivalent of Cohen's winks. Reported speech is thus metapragmatic in the most minimal sense in that it re-presents what has been said but always also in such a way as to make an (implicit or explicit) commentary on it. But that is not all, for not only does it comment on the said of a previous discourse, but it also comments on its own present moment of speaking as being either in agreement or disagreement with the previous discourse, and even prefigures the discourse to come as hopefully "univocal" with the speaker's own. Thus, in this view, an actual instance of reported speech is a miniature power struggle between the various voices in a dialogue, each hoping to have its representation of discourse (or metapragmatic framing) prevail.

However, to limit the dialogical forms of speaking to direct and indirect speech would be too narrow a view of what Bakhtin and Voloshinov had in mind. "Syntactic means for formulating the transmitted speech of another are far from exhausted by the grammatical paradigms of direct and indirect discourse: the means for its incorporation, for its formulation, and for indicating different degrees of shading are highly varied. This must be kept in mind if we are to make good our claim that of all words uttered in everyday life, no less than half belong to someone else."[29] Hence Bakhtin's interest in parody, for example, where someone else's discourse is re-presented but in a malicious or subversive way—and of course one might add irony, satire, and so forth. Someone else's discourse is mimicked but always in such a way that one is at least implicitly commenting on or somehow referring to it and at the same time implying that one's discourse is in opposition to or in alignment with it. That is to say, one is engaged in a complex metapragmatic operation.

> Let us return now to the ethnographic example and the question of an authorizing discourse and its relation to religious prayer. The Qur'an clearly would be an authorizing discourse of the sort Asad has in mind, but how does one understand its operation in authorizing the performance of the invocation? To my knowledge, the Qur'an does not anywhere state the specific invocation to God for rain, much less state what its form or content might look like in any specific instance of its utterance (though, of course, it has much to say about the obligation to pray to God as well as about the words and movements to be performed in prayer). The Qur'an is in other respects a rich source of metapragmatic instruction, which I have discussed elsewhere.[30] For example, it instructs the devout person on

how to greet another, stipulating the exact phrase to be used and the exact phrase to say in return (salaam 'alay-kum / w-alay-kum as-salaam), but as for knowing how an invocation to God for rain is to be performed, one could not derive this from the Qur'an itself.

It is interesting to consider how various liturgical literatures in Islam, mostly Sufi-based, have in fact spoken at length about invocation as well as prayer for rain or *istisqa*. Sufi treatises (such as al-Badjuri), acknowledging the importance of uttering the correct words in the appropriate circumstances in order to secure the most efficacious results, are highly prescriptive of ritual practice.[31] For example, in the case of the rain prayer in the mosque, the number of *rak'as* and the ritual of the "turning of the cloak" (described above) are both prescribed. Yet this liturgical tradition was not referenced by Sana'a's greatest religious scholar when talking about the authority for the religious practices Kamal had described to me. Given the predominance of the Zaidis, a sect of Shia Islam that has little truck with Sufi Islam, this fact is not surprising. However, that the *qaDhi* left these practices outside official liturgical discourse of any kind is perhaps more surprising, and occasions the question of where they derive their authorization.

What, then, does the invocation for rain look like as a pragmatic genre of speaking? The ethnographic texts provided earlier in this essay contain, more or less, the following three elements: an address to God ("O Merciful One") that uses one of His Names as given in the Qur'an; a set of speech acts that are in the imperative (perhaps "implorative" mood might be a better designation), such as "turn toward us . . . send us rain, O Lord"; and the phrase "There is no God but God," which concludes each stanza, an expression that, of course, is one of the central (if not *the* central) tenets of Islam and is taken directly from the Qur'an in the form of what Voloshinov/Bakhtin would have called reported speech. Thus the invocation cites Qur'anic discourse in order, metapragmatically, to authorize its own performance or instance of speaking, and it does so in order to call forth a response from God that is material in the form of rain but also spiritual as a sign of forgiveness. It is a dialogical act, or attempts to be one, between man and God. Precisely because there is no explicit metapragmatic discourse in the Qur'an, the hadith, the sunna, the fiqh, or elsewhere in Zaidi doctrine that says what the rain prayer should be, it must constitute itself as an event in the world—it must authorize itself—and does so metapragmatically. To be sure, like reported speech, without something like the text of the Qur'an to depend on it would not be entirely persuasive, but it nonetheless constitutes or creates itself in its own utterance.

To the nonlinguist, this may all seem a bit nitpicking. The larger theoretical point is that I agree with Asad that if one wants to understand religious practice, one has to understand it as a construction—but the question is, How it may be constructed and performed? Is it constructed in an authorizing discourse that exists apart from or outside it, even though it may be ontologically dependent upon this authorizing discourse? This may be one way of conceiving of the problem of construction, but it is not the only one, or even the most important one, if understanding actual or concrete social action is at stake. One must also be attentive to the ways in which a discourse can constitute itself metapragmatically, citing as it must an anterior discourse but constituting something other than this discourse. And it is this *creative* or *emergent* process that one must grasp if one is to understand, in turn, how power is constituted in action.

By the way, the rains came at the end of last summer, for the first time in five years, flooding the streets of Sana'a. The ordeal was over, and the rain prayers and invocations consequently came to an end. No one was in doubt, however, as to their efficaciousness.

4

Fasting for Bin Laden: The Politics of Secularization in Contemporary India

Partha Chatterjee

I

In an essay published a few years ago, I attempted, in the context of a sometimes quite bitter debate over the rights of minority religious communities in India, to identify two contradictions of the politics of secularism in that country.[1] I pointed out, first, that although a significant section of Indian political leaders shared the desire to separate religion and politics, the Indian nation-state, for various historical reasons, had no option but to involve itself in the regulation, funding, and in some cases, even the administration of various religious institutions. Second, even though sections of Indian citizens were legally demarcated as belonging to minority religious communities following their own personal laws and possessing the right to establish and administer their own educational institutions, there was no procedure to determine who would represent these minority communities in their dealings with the state. I suggested that these contradictions had produced an impasse. On the one hand, the tendencies toward religious reform within the minority communities were blocked by fears that reform would mean capitulation to majoritarian homogenization and loss of identity. On the other hand, the secular state was seen as hopelessly compromised by its legal protection of the differential and allegedly backward practices of the minority communities. Since all projects of changing social practices by law are fundamentally coercive, I said that the only fair and legitimate method that would be acceptable to the minorities in India for reform of their personal laws was democratic consent—not legislation by a majority of the general population of the country but democratic consent *within* each legally constituted minority community. I had suggested, tongue in cheek, that I could hear my critics accusing me of calling for the convening of Muslim and Christian parliaments in India. As it happened, not only was my argument immediately labeled antisecularist, but it was also condemned for allegedly advocating the dismantling of the nation-state.[2]

The publication of Talal Asad's *Formations of the Secular* gave me the opportunity to revisit that debate and underline what I think still remains at stake in the relations between modernity, religion, and the nation-state.[3] Asad's incisive examination of the discursive as well as the practical aspects of this question, putting into doubt many comfortable philosophical and sociological certainties, makes possible a more rigorous theoretical treatment of the subject.

Let me begin with Asad's consideration of the so-called secularization thesis. Derived from Max Weber, the secularization thesis became a standard component of twentieth-century sociological theory. It claimed that modernity entailed (1) an increasing structural differentiation resulting in the separation of religion from politics, economy, science, art, and so on; (2) the privatization of religion; and (3) the declining social significance of religious belief and institutions.[4] The history of the modern West, it was argued, had demonstrated the truth of this thesis. With the expansion of modernity into other regions of the globe, the thesis would be confirmed. Most modernization theories of the 1950s and 1960s, whether Weberian or Marxian, subscribed to this thesis and expected a process of secularization to take place in the newly independent and industrializing countries of Asia and Africa.

Instead, there was an explosion of politicized religion in the last decades of the twentieth century in both modernizing and modern countries. It became clear that the secularization thesis was not being borne out. One response was to turn it into a normative rather than a sociological claim: secularization had to happen if modernity was to be achieved; if some countries were not becoming secular, it was because they were insufficiently modern or because their modernizing project had gone astray. The other response was to save the sociological thesis by claiming that not all three elements of secularization were necessary for modernity. Thus, it was possible for religion to exist in the public political space without necessarily threatening the essential components of modernity. Asad shows with consummate analytical skill that this claim is incoherent. If religion becomes an integral part of modern politics, then the domains of the economy and education and art cannot be insulated from religious arguments and positions. Neither could it be said that religion has lost its social significance simply because there is a decline, let us say, in religious observance or ceremony. If secularization is an essential component of modernity, then religion cannot be an integral part of modern politics.[5]

So what is to be done about the fact that the secularization thesis is failing in the contemporary political world? Asad shows us the implications of the liberal responses to this challenge for the *practices* of modern politics. The new claim that religious movements and parties may well have a legitimate place in modern politics *if* they agree to confine themselves to rational debate and persuasion and not resort to intolerant and violent methods is, he shows, only a plea for a *particular kind* of religion. Because, first, it is the experience of religion in the so-called private sphere of domestic, educational, and cultural life that will determine the kind of political subject who will or will not be ready to listen to religious arguments in the public sphere. Hence, the demand that religious groups in the political domain confine themselves to certain kinds of rational debate and tolerant behavior could easily entail a further demand that particular kinds of religious teachings and practices be prohibited or promoted in the "private" domains of education and culture. Second, in making themselves heard in the public spaces of politics, can religious arguments simply fit into existing "nonreligious" discursive structures without disrupting the established practices of political debate? If they do disrupt those practices, by challenging the moral beliefs and cultural sensibilities of nonbelievers, can they still be said to be operating in a rational and tolerant way? Third, if the proponents of religious politics find that they cannot break through the existing structures of consensus and persuade others to negotiate regarding their moral beliefs, what do they do? Asad perceptively points out that they do what all secular politicians do in mass democracies: they try to manipulate the conditions in which citizens act by using instruments of propaganda and mobilization aimed at the desires and anxieties of people. In other words, far from staying within the bounds of rational debate and moral persuasion, the presence of religion in the political domain necessarily comes up against the structures of coercive power that seek to lay down and police the sanctioned forms of political practice in modern democracies.[6]

It is because Talal Asad persistently examines secularism as a new set of *practices* producing a new political subject that he is able to cut through the make-believe discursive screens of analytical philosophy and multicultural ethics to reach the stark facts of power that underlie and surround the entire process of secularization. In all countries and in every historical period, secularization has been a coercive process in which the legal powers of the state, the disciplinary powers of family and school, and the persuasive powers of government and media have been used to produce the secular citizen who agrees to keep religion in the private domain. Sometimes this has been done by putting external and forcible constraints on the public political presence of religion, as in the Jacobin tradition of *laïcisme*, or in the Soviet Union and contemporary China, or in Kemalist Turkey. More compatible with liberal political values, however, and in many ways the more successful process has been the secularization resulting from an internal reform of religion itself. Thus, secularization in England and France gained decisively in the late nineteenth century from Tractarianism and Ultramontanism, respectively—both religious movements seeking to extricate the church from its dependence on the state. Asad closes his book with an insightful study of religious reform in Egypt as a process of secularization deeply entangled with the legal institutions of the state.[7]

I will draw two threads of argument from Asad's discussion of secularization and weave them into my treatment of secularism and minority rights in India. First, I point to the role of coercive power—indeed, the centrality of the legal institutions of the state—in directing and shaping the process of secularization in modern societies and to the still unresolved question of the legitimacy and limits of such coercion in modern mass democracies. Asad's historical treatment of the subject in *Genealogies of Religion* and in *Formations of the Secular* reminds us that the discursive and institutional tasks of separating religion from politics and producing a new set of secular subjects and secular practices in the political domain were accomplished in the countries of Western Europe and North America *before* the era of mass democracies based on universal franchise.[8] The "problem" of secularism has thus emerged in those countries as a *new* question concerning, first, the role as citizens of new immigrants who follow religions (such as Islam) that were not a party to the original compact that privatized religion, and second, the assertion of religious beliefs in law-making and governance by politically mobilized Christian groups. It is for this reason that the problem of secularism is often posed as one of the "intrusion" of religion into politics or of the conditions under which religious arguments may be "allowed" in the arena of political debate. In the countries of Asia and Africa, however, the question of secularism is largely coeval with the very emergence of modern nation-states in the twentieth century. The idea of the secular state exists there principally as one model of the modern state derived from the Western historical experience. It often represents a normative project rather than a set of actually existing practices. The crucial political question then becomes: what are the ethical and strategic considerations in carrying out a project of secularization that carries the imprint of popular legitimacy and democratic consent?

The second argument I draw from Asad is about the role of majorities and minorities. As far as contemporary Western democracies are concerned, the new Muslim immigrants in European countries seek the protection of the laws of the secular state to maintain their freedoms and identities as religious minorities, while Christian political groups try to mobilize electoral power to make laws that reflect what they assert are the moral beliefs of the majority. In either case, the demands raise complex questions of the neutrality of the state in matters of religion and equal treatment of all citizens. Thus, if Muslims in France insist that their daughters be allowed to wear the headscarf in schools, the question is asked if this is not a discriminatory privilege being granted to some citizens on grounds of their religion. This, of course, only begs the further question of how the supposedly neutral and religiously unmarked school uniform was agreed upon in the first place and whether this is not in fact a practice, now conventionalized as secular, that emerged out of the secularization of a specifically Christian culture. On the other hand, when politically mobilized Christian groups in the United States demand prayers in public schools or a ban on abortions, or when they resist the legal recognition of same-sex marriage, they seek to use the sanctioned forms of democratic campaigning to wield the moral opinions, grounded in religious beliefs, of a majority of the electorate in order to influence the laws of the state or the policies of the government. In either case, the question of secularism gets entangled with the historically constituted structures of power and the authorized forms of coercion in Western democracies.

In the case of the countries of Asia and Africa, secularization is necessarily a normative project formulated and directed by an elite minority. The historical challenge before this elite is to steer the project by using the coercive legal powers of the state as well as the processes of reform of religious doctrine and practice—all within a global context where power must be legitimized by a large measure of popular consent. This is a task that is unprecedented in Western history. As Asad points out, it calls for the discovery of new paths toward secularization.

I present below a recent controversy from the Indian state of West Bengal, ruled since 1977 by a communist-led government that has won five successive electoral terms through popular elections. It raises several of the questions mentioned above regarding legitimate and democratic forms of secularization.

II

On January 19, 2002, speaking at a public meeting in Siliguri, Buddhadeb Bhattacharya, chief minister of West Bengal, said that there were many madrasahs (Muslim religious schools), not affiliated to the West Bengal Madrasah Board, where antinational terrorists, including operatives of the Pakistan intelligence agency, were active. These unauthorized madrasahs would have to be shut down. This remark, however, might not have had the effect it did if a major incident had not happened in Calcutta three days later.

On January 22, 2002, in the early hours of the morning, two motorbikes drove up in front of the American Center in Calcutta. The policemen on security duty there were changing shifts at the time. Suddenly, the riders on the back of the motorbikes pulled out automatic rifles and began to shoot. The policemen were apparently so taken aback by this unexpected attack that they were unable to respond. After forty seconds, during which the two riflemen fired more than sixty rounds of bullets, the motorbikes sped away, leaving five policemen dead and several others injured. The incident immediately made international headlines, and the first presumption was that it was another attack by Islamic terrorists against the United States. It later transpired that the attack had been launched by a criminal gang based in Dubai, which was seeking revenge for the death of one of its associates in an encounter with the police. But the criminal network overlapped with that of suspected Islamic militants operating in different parts of India. One of the first suspects arrested in connection with the killings was a mathematics teacher of a madrasah in North 24-Parganas, from a place about thirty miles north of Calcutta. He was said to be a member of SIMI, the banned Islamic students' organization. Another madrasah teacher, said to be a Bangladeshi national with connections to the Pakistani intelligence services, was arrested in Murshidabad district.

On January 24, speaking to the press in Calcutta, Buddhadeb Bhattacharya clarified his earlier remarks: "Certain madrasahs, not all madrasahs—I repeat, certain madrasahs—are involved in anti-national propaganda. We have definite information on this. This cannot be allowed." Four days later, at a public meeting at Domkal in Murshidabad, he said that all madrasahs would have to seek affiliation with the Madrasah Board. "We will not allow unaffiliated madrasahs to run here," he said. He instructed the district administration to carry out a survey of all madrasahs in Murshidabad and report on the number of students, teachers, boarders, and sources of funding.[9]

The chief minister's comments, reported in the press, immediately sparked off a controversy. It was alleged that by suggesting police surveillance of madrasahs, the chief minister had maligned the entire Muslim community of West Bengal. If there were specific allegations against particular institutions, the offenders should be punished, but why should an entire system of minority educational institutions be tarred with the same brush? At a demonstration of madrasah students in Calcutta, an apology was demanded from the chief minister. The students said that madrasah teachers were being harassed and that a witch-hunt atmosphere had been created because of "misinformation and poor understanding" of the system of madrasah education. It was reported that the Urdu press was comparing Bhattacharya not only with Hindu right-wing leaders like L. K. Advani and Bal Thackeray but also with "Musharraf, the military dictator of Pakistan."[10] The protests came not only from those who claimed to speak on behalf of Muslim organizations or from the opposition political parties, but also from partners of the ruling Left Front. Several Front leaders said that the chief minister's remarks sounded alarmingly like those of Bharatiya Janata Party (BJP) leaders in Delhi and that this would send wrong signals to the minority community in the state. In fact, an emergency meeting of the Left Front was called on February 6 to clarify the government's position.[11]

On January 31, the state Minority Commission organized a meeting of Muslim intellectuals and academics at which Mohammed Salim, the Communist Party of India (Marxist) minister for minority affairs, explained that the chief minister had not made a blanket allegation against all madrasahs and that there was not going to be any witch hunt. In fact, he praised the initiative taken by community leaders to set up madrasahs. "These institutions are a national asset. It is laudable that some individuals or organizations have reached remote rural areas to spread some sort of education even before the government could open a school there." But he defended the chief minister by saying that the government must take steps against "anti-national and communal forces along the Indo-Bangla border as the area has become a second front for anti-Indian forces. Terrorism is not religion-specific. There will be a crackdown irrespective of whether it is a madrasah, mosque, temple or club."[12]

Nevertheless, there continued to be reports that Muslims were agitated about what they regarded as an unprovoked accusation of complicity with terrorism directed against an entire community. They alleged that several teachers in madrasahs had been picked up by the police after the American Center killings and later released because nothing was found against them.[13] The police, it was alleged, were proceeding on the basis of preconceived and unsubstantiated stereotypes. There were even reports from several places in the border districts of North 24–Parganas and Nadia that Communist Party members belonging to the minority community were alarmed that the chief minister's remarks sounded so much like those of the BJP home minister Advani. "Such statements from the chief minister will only encourage the terrorists as they will get a fertile ground among the irate Muslims to spread their organization," said Waris Sheikh, who had been a member of the Communist Party for forty years.[14] On February 4, a surprisingly large rally organized in Calcutta by the Jamiat-e-Ulema-e-Hind, an association of Muslim religious scholars, once again demanded a public apology from Buddhadeb Bhattacharya, this time calling him an agent of the United States and Israel.[15]

The matter had clearly gone too far. It was announced that the chief minister had called a meeting of Muslim organizations and intellectuals on February 7, in which he would explain his position.[16] He also claimed that his remarks in Siliguri had been misquoted by the press and even by the CPI(M) party newspaper *Ganashakti*. At a meeting of the Left Front on February 6, Buddhadeb Bhattacharya was apparently roundly criticized by partners of the Front and even by the former chief minister Jyoti Basu.[17]

By this time, a strategy to handle the fallout appears to have been worked out. The crucial move was to separate the issue of terrorism from that of madrasah education. It was explained that neither the chief minister nor the government had ever suggested that all madrasahs were involved in terrorist propaganda or recruitment. Only when there was specific evidence of such involvement would the government move against particular organizations or individuals, and that according to the law. The issue of madrasah education was a completely separate matter, and the press had misrepresented the chief minister's remarks on this subject by tying it to the question of terrorism. As far as madrasah education was concerned, the Left Front government in West Bengal had done more than any other government in India. Biman Bose, the chairman of the Left Front, explained that in the nearly two hundred years since 1780, when the Alia Madrasah was founded in Calcutta by Warren Hastings, to 1977, when the Left Front came to power, a total of 238 madrasahs had been set up in West Bengal with government approval. In the twenty-five years since 1977, this number had more than doubled. In 1977, the government expenditure on madrasah education was 500,000 rupees; in 2001, it was 1,150 million rupees, an increase of more than two thousand times. The entire financial responsibility, including salaries of teachers and supporting staff, of madrasahs affiliated to the state Madrasah Board was borne by the government. Students graduating from affiliated madrasahs in West Bengal were entitled to admission to all universities and all professional courses. This was unprecedented in independent India.[18]

On February 7, the chief minister met a gathering of Muslim leaders and intellectuals, including writers, journalists, teachers, doctors, and imams of mosques. He admitted that his words as reported by the media might have caused confusion and anxiety; he was prepared to share the blame for this and expressed his regret. He reiterated that antinational elements were active in the state, but clarified that such activities were not confined to madrasahs. Just as there were fundamentalist Hindu organizations, so there were outfits like the Lashkar-e-Taiba that were involved in antinational and terrorist acts. He had never suggested that all madrasahs were under a cloud of suspicion. There was no legal obligation for madrasahs to seek the approval of the government, and there was no law by which the government could close down private schools, no matter who ran them. "The constitution guarantees minorities the right to run their educational institutions," he said. "Christian missionaries and Hindu organizations are also running their own schools." But the question of modernization of the madrasah curriculum was an urgent issue. The government had appointed a committee headed by Professor A. R. Kidwai, former governor, to look into the matter. "We will try and persuade the unrecognized madrasahs to revise their curricula so that modern subjects could be introduced along with religious studies. We will urge them to join the educational mainstream." He urged Muslim community leaders to think seriously of ways to educate Muslim children so that they might have better skills for entry into professional employment and not become isolated from the rest of the nation. At the end of the meeting, the imams of two leading mosques said that a lot of tension had been created in the past few days as a result of the chief minister's remarks. Some of that communication gap had now been bridged.[19]

The media in general interpreted the chief minister's clarifications as backtracking forced on him by the adverse reaction both inside and outside the party and in the Left Front. Several commentators alleged that a courageous initiative to tackle the problem of Islamic fundamentalism from within the parameters of secular politics in India had been stymied because of the relentless pressure of the minority vote bank. Two interesting organizational changes were also reported. First, it was suggested that in view of the misunderstanding and controversy, the affairs of madrasah administration would be taken away from Kanti Biswas, the school education minister, and given to Mohammed Salim, the minority affairs minister. It was said that Biswas had taken a hard line on madrasah reform and was pushing for the conversion of government-supported senior madrasahs, which provided religious education, to high madrasahs, which followed a strictly secular curriculum. "Why should the government pay the salaries of teachers who provide religious education in madrasahs when it did not do so in other religious schools?" Biswas had apparently asked.[20] The other significant change was within the CPI(M) party daily *Ganashakti*. The chief minister had alleged that his remarks had been misrepresented, even in the report published by the party newspaper. Dipen Ghosh, senior trade unionist and former member of parliament, was asked to relinquish his position as editor of the daily, and on February 25, Narayan Dutta, a relatively inconspicuous member of the state committee, was appointed in his place.

III

Reconstructing the controversy, both the possibilities and the constraints of a secular state policy on religious minorities in India become apparent. The Left Front in West Bengal, and the CPI(M) in particular, have always proclaimed, with justified pride, that in spite of having a large Muslim minority and a long history of communal conflict up to the 1960s, for the last twenty-five years the state has seen undisturbed communal peace. With the exception of a brief outburst, controlled quickly by prompt administrative and political action, in 1992 following the Babari Masjid demolition and attacks on Hindu temples in Bangladesh, there has been no communal violence in West Bengal under Left Front rule. According to most observers of elections in West Bengal, the Left has consistently won the greater part of the Muslim vote. The parties of the Left, and once again the CPI(M) in particular, have recruited leaders from the minority community in several districts. It is likely that many of these young leaders were attracted to the parties of the Left because of their image as secular, modern, progressive organizations.

Although the issue of modernization of madrasahs suddenly appeared in the public limelight because of its association with the question of terrorism, there is reason to believe that the CPI(M) leadership had long been engaged with the issue. Alongside the extension of government financial support to madrasahs affiliated to the Madrasah Board, the Front initiated in the 1980s a process of change by which the high and junior high madrasahs—some four hundred in number—came to follow the same curriculum as regular secondary schools except for a single compulsory course in Arabic. In fact, the point was made during the recent controversy that high madrasahs in the state had significant numbers of non-Muslim students as well as teachers. They also had more female than male students, reflecting the fact that many Muslim families felt more comfortable sending their daughters to madrasahs than to regular secondary schools. Teachers were recruited through the same School Service Commission that chose teachers for all other secondary schools. The hundred-odd senior madrasahs, affiliated with the Madrasah Board and financially supported by the government, followed a revised curriculum in which about two-thirds of the courses consisted of English, Bengali, physical and life sciences, mathematics, history, and geography, and about one-third were on Islamic religion and law. It was alleged that senior madrasahs had become an anomaly because they did not prepare their students adequately for either the religious or the secular professions. There were fewer and fewer students, those wanting a religious education preferring to go to one of the many private madrasahs outside the Madrasah Board system.[21] There was a renewed initiative now to further modernize the madrasah curriculum. A committee had been set up, with Professor A. R. Kidwai as chairman, to look into the matter. Kidwai himself, in an interview given during the recent controversy, suggested that traditional Yunani medicine and modern Arabic might be introduced into the madrasahs to make their curricula more suitable for new employment opportunities.[22]

Nonetheless, it remains a fact that the involvement of nonaffiliated madrasahs with the activities and propaganda of militant Islamic groups began to worry the party leadership even before the American Center killings, and not merely because there were police intelligence reports suggesting such involvement. The Muslim leaders of the party themselves became aware of the impact that fundamentalist propaganda was producing in Muslim neighborhoods. A striking example was provided by Anisur Rahaman, a CPI(M) minister, in an op-ed article in *Ganashakti*.[23] Entitled "Fasting for Laden," the article describes the leader's visit to a Muslim village, where he is told that people are observing a fast. Surprised because the month of Ramadan is a long time away, he asks the villagers what the fast is for. The villagers explain that they are praying for the safety of Osama bin Laden, who was a target of attack by the imperialist Americans. The meeting the minister is to address begins late in the evening after everyone has broken the fast. The rest of the article is a summary of a speech by Rahman Chacha, a village elder, who makes several arguments, having to do with political ethics as well as tactics, on why Muslims in India have no reason to support Bin Laden. The fact that these arguments are presented in the voice of a nonpolitical "wise man" of the community and not in that of the Communist minister is interesting, but the most striking thing about the article is its recognition of the impact that a few "hot-headed and thoughtless young men" were having on many ordinary Muslims.

The most contentious issue, of course, was that of the private madrasahs, which everyone agreed were growing rapidly in number. No one really had a good estimate of how many *khariji* madrasahs there were not affiliated to the Madrasah Board. Many said there were ten times as many private madrasahs as there were state-supported ones. It was widely argued that private madrasahs were popular because they offered food and often board and lodging to their students. In the words of Mohammad Salim, the CPI(M) minister, "Children whose families cannot afford a square meal would prefer these madrasahs which provide them food, shelter and some sort of education."[24] The point was made repeatedly that madrasahs were never the first choice considered by Muslim parents, at least for their sons. They always preferred the regular secondary school if they could afford it. The religious professions did not hold much attraction for most young Muslims, who went into them only because the alternative was low-paid unskilled manual work. Even those who spoke so loudly about the right of minorities to run their own schools did not send their children to madrasahs. Private madrasahs were coming up because there was a social need that the state had been unable to fill; the community was stepping in where the government had failed. How did the private madrasahs raise funds? Community leaders insisted that charity was a religious duty for Muslims, and many took that obligation seriously. Most private madrasahs ran on money and food collected from families in the neighborhood. There were also a few large Islamic foundations, even some that received funds from international foundations based in Saudi Arabia and the Gulf states, and these sometimes made grants to private madrasahs. A few private madrasahs in West Bengal possessed large buildings and provided free boarding to three or four hundred students each; such resources could not have been raised locally. However, the administrators of these madrasahs resented the suggestion that this was tainted money. All grants, they insisted, were legal and were cleared by the relevant ministries in Delhi.[25] What about the content of the courses taught at these private madrasahs? There were some sensational stories in the mainstream press that quoted from primers that allegedly glorified *jihadi* warriors and demanded that the civil code be replaced by the sharia.[26] But once again it was clear that most Muslim representatives, irrespective of political loyalties, had a low opinion of the quality of education offered by the private madrasahs. Their complaint was that the state-supported schools were few and not necessarily better run, and alternative secular private education was too expensive.

The West Bengal debate highlights an important fact that seems crucial in judging the conditions for a democratic politics of secularism. The issue cannot be successfully posed as one of a secularizing state versus a minority community seeking to preserve its cultural identity. Although that understanding of secularism was powerful, it did not win the day. There were several interventions suggesting that the question of social reform was emerging *from within* the Muslim community. This understanding too was by no means decisive, but it was there. Not only that, it was strongly influencing the question of who represents the minority community.

The issues were delineated in an article by Mainul Hasan, a CPI(M) member of parliament from Murshidabad.[27] After going through the history of madrasah education and the recent changes in curricula, Mainul Hasan disputes the argument that private madrasahs were growing because there were not enough secondary schools. Speaking as an insider, he argues that a major reason for the madrasahs was the need to provide jobs for young Muslim men. Most madrasahs were set up as a result of local community initiative, often with the support of political parties. It was possible to raise funds from within the community through charitable donations (*zaqat*, *fitra*, etc.). Most madrasahs ran on shoestring budgets, but they provided employment to educated Muslims, who could teach in private madrasahs, become *maulvis* in mosques, and lecture year-round at religious congregations. These were necessary, if not very lucrative, functions, and Muslims with a smattering of education had few other opportunities open to them.

The rest of the article is a strong plea for further modernization of madrasahs. No Muslim would claim that modern education was unnecessary. On the other hand, everyone agreed that private madrasahs did not provide modern education. Why then should not the government come forward to start modern madrasahs that were not "factories for producing mullahs"? The Muslim community should not only support this policy but also actively contribute, even financially, to setting up madrasahs that offer modern education.

Finally, on the question of subversive propaganda and terrorism, Mainul Hasan takes the clear position that administering the law and providing security for the country are the government's responsibility. It is childish, he says, to claim that the community and not the police would act against organizations that are involved in subversive activities. Rather, the duty of the community is to provide the necessary context within which the government could enact correct policies and implement them properly. Suppose, he says, the imam of a mosque is liked and respected by the community; he has been leading the prayers for many years. It then turns out that he is actually from Bangladesh and does not have the right papers to live and work in this country. No one can dispute the fact that his status is illegal, but it may be that the correct policy would be to persuade the authorities to help him get the right papers. This the community must try to do, but it cannot insist that the state not act when there is a violation of the law.

IV

Who represents the religious minorities? The question was raised directly in the debate over madrasahs. After the chief minister's meeting with Muslim intellectuals and madrasah teachers, complaints were heard in party circles over the ceremonial recitation from the Qur'an at the meeting.[28] Why should a meeting with representatives of the Muslim community inevitably mean a meeting with imams and *maulanas*? The answer clearly is that there are few organized forums in the public sphere outside the religious institutions that could claim to be representative of a community that is marked as a *religious* minority. Why is that the case in West Bengal, where a fifth of the population is Muslim and where there is a growing Muslim middle class? Because, as several Muslim professionals explained, community organizations tend to be dominated by men from the religious occupations who are suspicious and resentful of those Muslims who have successfully made it into the urban secular professions. The overwhelming majority of Muslims in West Bengal are rural and poor; urban middle-class Muslims are not able, and perhaps do not wish, to represent them. As one Muslim bureaucrat remarked, "The uneducated or semi-educated lot is intolerant, fanatical and dangerous."[29] It is not uncommon for professional Muslims with liberal opinions to be targeted for vilification by communal organizations. As a result, such persons usually choose to stay away from community organizations altogether, leaving them to the unchallenged sway of men flaunting their religious credentials. As one correspondent writing to a leading Bengali daily put it, almost 20 percent of all students in regular secondary schools in West Bengal are Muslims. Yet it is the private madrasah question, involving only a few thousand students, that agitates the political circle. "How much longer will political leaders succumb to the imams and put a lid on reforms within Muslim society?" she asked. Muslim politicians in state and national politics have invariably been educated in mainstream institutions and are often in the secular professions. Yet every time there is a debate over reform in Muslim society, it is the imams who are listened to as representatives of the community. "The principal obstacle," she claimed, "in the fight against Muslim fundamentalism and religious bigotry is the silence of the growing educated and enlightened section of Muslim society."[30]

The question then arises: what are the appropriate institutions through which the debate over change within minority communities can be conducted in a secular polity? Ever since independence, while the modernizing state in India has often sought to change traditional social institutions and practices by legal and administrative intervention, an accompanying demand has always been that the minority religious communities must have the right to protect their religious and cultural identities, because otherwise they would be at the mercy of a majoritarian politics of homogenization. The Indian state, in general, has largely stayed away from pushing an interventionist agenda of modernization with respect to the institutions and practices of minority communities. This in turn has produced a vicious campaign in recent years from the Hindu right wing accusing the Indian state and the parties of the Center and the Left of "pseudo-secularism and appeasement of minorities." Even in the case of West

Bengal, as we saw, the suggestion that private madrasahs might come under government regulation provoked enough of an outcry from those who claimed to represent the Muslim community to force the government to make what many saw as an about-face. The alternative, to work for reform from within the community institutions, is seen by most potential reformers as infeasible. Once again, even in the case of West Bengal, we have seen that factors of class, occupation, and ideological orientation prevent liberal middle-class Muslims from engaging in community institutions.

There is, however, a third possibility, which, it seems to me, is apparent even in the recent West Bengal debate. It is not a dominant tendency, but it has become a distinct presence. This reformist intervention does not take place exclusively within the legal-administrative apparatus of the state. Nor does it take place in the nonpolitical zone of civil society. Rather, it works in that overlap between the extensive governmental functions of development and welfare and the workings of community institutions that I have elsewhere called *political society*.[31] This is often a zone of paralegal practices opposed to the civic norms of proper citizenship. Yet there are attempts here to devise new, and often contextual and transitory, norms of fairness and justice in making available the welfare and developmental functions of government to large sections of poor and underprivileged people. There are claims of representation here that have to be established in that overlapping zone between governmental functions and community institutions. I see in the West Bengal case an attempt to pursue a campaign of reform through the agency of *political* representatives rather than through either state intervention or civil social action. Those political representatives of the left parties in West Bengal who are Muslims usually have large popular support among their Muslim constituents because of their promise, if not their ability, to deliver benefits such as jobs, health, education, water, roads, and electricity. But as political representatives of the minority community, they do not necessarily relinquish their right to speak on the internal affairs of the community, if only because the community institutions are also tied into the network of governmental functions. As Mainul Hasan pointed out, even the private madrasahs had to be set up with the active involvement of local political leaders. This is the zone where a different mode of reformist intervention can take place that straddles government and community, outside and inside. It can potentially democratize the question of who represents the religious minorities in the public political domain.

Once again, let me reiterate that what I have brought up in this paper is only the hint of a different modality of secular politics for which I find theoretical justification in Talal Asad's wide-ranging treatment of the question. I am stressing its significance as a potential, but I must not exaggerate its actuality. As a student of Hindu-Muslim relations in Bengal in the twentieth century, I have lived far too closely with the massive evidence of communal violence there to have rosy ideas about any sort of innate secularism of the Bengali people, whether Hindu or Muslim. Indeed, I often worry about the complacency of many left and liberal persons who think that the communal question has been somehow resolved in West Bengal and Bangladesh. However, I do think that there is a deeply democratic implication of the massive political mobilization that has taken place in rural West Bengal in the last three decades. It is well known that democracy is no guarantee of secularism, since electoral majorities can often be mobilized against minority communities: we saw this only too well recently in the western Indian state of Gujarat. On the other hand, it is also true that protected minority rights give a premium to traditionalists, and sometimes even political extremists, within the minority communities unless the question of who represents them is allowed to be negotiated within a more effective democratic process. With Talal Asad's help, I see something of this process going on in West Bengal's political society.

5

Europe: A Minor Tradition

William E. Connolly

Secularism and Belief

Talal Asad complicates terms of comparison that many anthropologists, theologians, philosophers, and political theorists receive as the unexamined background of thinking, judgment, and action as such. By doing so, he creates clearings, opening new possibilities of communication, connection, and creative invention where opposition or studied indifference prevailed. The Asad slogan might be, Where simple or fixed opposition appears, let numerous connections across subtle differences emerge. Nonetheless, out of these nuanced interrogations a few organizing themes become discernible. They inform his interventions into the established unconscious of European culture. Here are a few that command attention, particularly the attention of political theorists seeking to rethink secularism and pluralism within and across states in an age that demands rethinking:

1. Secularism is not merely the division between public and private realms that allows religious diversity to flourish in the latter. It can itself be a carrier of harsh exclusions. And it secretes a new definition of "religion" that conceals some of its most problematic practices from itself.

2. In creating its characteristic division between secular public space and religious private space, European secularism sought to shuffle ritual and discipline into the private realm. In doing so, however, it loses touch with the ways in which embodied practices of conduct help to constitute culture, including European culture.

3. The constitution of modern Europe, as a continent and a secular civilization, makes it incumbent to treat Muslims in its midst on the one hand as abstract citizens and on the other as a distinctive minority either to be tolerated (the liberal orientation) or restricted (the nationalist orientation), depending on the politics of the day.

4. European, modern, secular constitutions of Islam, in cumulative effect, converge upon a series of simple contrasts between themselves and Islamic practices. These terms of contrast falsify the deep grammar of European secularism and contribute to the culture wars some bearers of these very definitions seek to ameliorate.

It is risky and, well, coarse to state these Asadian themes so brashly. For even if they have been identified reasonably well, it is the *way* Asad articulates each with the particular issue under examination and in relation to the other three that does the work.

Let me, then, allow Asad to articulate his orientation more closely in his own words. We begin with his critique of Wilfred Cantwell Smith, a Canadian scholar of comparative religions writing in the 1960s who sought to distill the essence of "religion" from several cultures, drawing upon that distillation to compare Islam, Christianity, and Judaism. Smith, Asad says, thinks of a religious tradition "as a cognitive framework, not as a practical mode of living, not as techniques for teaching body and mind to cultivate specific virtues and abilities that have been authorized, passed on, and reformulated down the generations."[1] As Smith distills a putative universal called "religion" out of the materialities of culture, he also obscures the operation of these materialities in the religious life of Europe, misses the historic-territorial link between "universal" religion and European secular culture, and tends to define the palpable operation of ritual in Islam as a sign of its underdeveloped character. All this flows from the way his secular reading of religion bypasses an important component of culture itself—its embodiment in practices that help to constitute the dispositions and sensibilities through which meaning is lived and intellectual creeds are set. "My concern," says Asad, "is to argue that various questions about the connection between formal practices and religiosity cannot be addressed if we confine our perspectives to Smith's—to what is in effect a pietistic conception of religion as faith that is essentially individual and otherworldly."[2] Smith's very distillation of religion situates it within a secular image of the world.

The upshot of these concerns becomes more visible in Asad's recent book, *Formations of the Secular*. Here Asad traces how the dominant European idea of religion expresses the cultural unconscious discernible in Smith's work. He contrasts this understanding to religious experience in the European Middle Ages; then when "the devotee heard God speak there was a sensuous connection between the inside and outside, a fusion between signifier and signified. The proper reading of scripture . . . depended on disciplining the senses (especially hearing, speech, and sight)."[3] This inner connection between education of the senses and devotional practice gets lost or diminished in later European representations: "Where faith [within Europe] had once been a virtue, it now acquired an epistemological sense. Faith became a way of knowing supernatural objects, parallel to the knowledge of nature (the *real* world) that reason and observation provided."[4]

Of course, if Asad is right, the practices in which we participate continue to be organized into circuits between institutional arrangements and lived layers of human embodiment, but many secularists, theologians, and anthropologists interpret such practices within a cognitive framework that ignores them, diminishes their importance, or reduces them to modes of cultural manipulation that could in principle be surpassed. Many cultural theorists talk endlessly about the body—how it is represented and symbolized through ritual, and even how it exceeds the best cultural representations of it. But many still construe ritual to be only a mechanism through which beliefs are portrayed and symbolized rather than a medium through which embodied habits, dispositions, sensibilities, and capacities of performance are consolidated. Atheists also participate in this reduction whenever they act as if the key question is whether you "believe" in a transcendent God, thus accepting the assumption that cognitive belief or disbelief is both a separable factor and the critical element. "The idea that there is a single clear 'logic of atheism' is itself the product of a modern binary—belief or unbelief in a supernatural being."[5]

The drive to secularism in late nineteenth- and early twentieth-century Egypt recapitulates some of these tendencies. In traditional Islam, *iman*, typically translated into English as "faith," "is not a singular epistemological means that guarantees God's existence for the believer. It is better translated as the virtue of faithfulness toward God, an unquestioning habit of obedience . . . , a disposition that has to be cultivated like any other."[6] But some Islamic jurists, pursuing secularism in Egypt, sought to open a clean division between belief and *habitus*, thinking that to do so would enable the state to set limits to religious *conduct* while appreciating a reasonable diversity of religious *belief.*

Contemporary European secularists—both the majority of secularists who are believers and the minority of whom are nonbelievers—seize this issue, contending that the problem of "Islamic faith" inside and outside Europe is engendered by the failure of its adherents to accept the division between freedom of private faith-belief and participation as abstract citizens in governance of the state. Both nationalists on the Right and secular liberals contend that "the de-essentialization of Islam is paradigmatic for all thinking about the assimilation of non-European peoples to European civilization."[7] Asad specifically does not claim that Muslims inside Europe have made no contribution to the difficulties they face. He suggests, rather, that negotiation of a new pluralism within Europe will *also* involve a reassessment on the part of believers and nonbelievers in secular, enlightened Europe of the tendency to treat belief as separable from disciplinary practices and the living flesh.

Indeed, the best definition of Europe itself—as presented by those constituencies assuming themselves to be qualified to define its core authoritatively—is the idea that to be European is to express religious beliefs in the private realm and to participate as abstract citizens in the public realm. This innocent and tolerant-sounding definition promotes Christian secularism into the center of Europe and reduces Islamic peoples into a minority unlike other minorities; they are distinctive because they alone are unwilling or unable to abide by the modern agenda. The definition, one might add, carries important implications for the current debates in Europe about immigration policy. You might even say that the inner connection between Christianity and Europe today is not that all Christians still demand common belief in Christianity as a condition of citizenship—though too many still do; rather it resides in the demand, growing out of the Christian Enlightenment, to disconnect the expression of religious belief from participation in embodied practices, so that it becomes possible to imagine a world in which everyone is a citizen because religious belief is relegated to the private realm and the interior of the self.

As Asad makes the point, "The definition of religious toleration that helps to define a state as secular begins with the premise that because religious belief cannot be coerced, religion should be regarded by the political authorities with indifference as long as it remains in the private domain."[8]

And, one might add, religion can safely be relegated to the private realm only because, according to secular believers and nonbelievers, there is an independent way of reaching authoritative public agreements without recourse to religious beliefs, so understood. The problem here is that several secular doctrines converge on setting such an agenda for public life but diverge significantly on what that authoritative practice is or could be. Some place faith in reason, others in deliberative consensus, others in implicit contractual agreements, and others yet in a "myth" of equality citizens have decided to accept *as if* it were ontologically grounded. This failure to agree on the authoritative public mode of resolution expresses, below the threshold of secular awareness, the persistent connection between belief and practice.

Asad does not link his genealogy of secularism to the need to construct a new theocentric regime. Rather, he points cautiously toward a new pluralism inside and outside Europe, in which "multiple ways of life" collaborate and negotiate because each defines itself to be a minority among other minorities.[9] This would also make Christianity a minority among minorities—even if a majority of citizens were Christian. It would do so because Christianity itself would drop the implicit insistence that its legacy provides the authoritative center around which other traditions are compelled to rotate. It would also install within each minority a heightened appreciation of the elemental connection between a set of practices and the consolidation of specific capacities of being. It would, in another vocabulary, correct the tradition of "intellectualism"—the name William James and Henri Bergson give to doctrines that depreciate lived connections between modes of embodied being and expressions of belief—that shapes the thinking of many protestant, secular intellectuals.

A Minor Tradition

I have profited from Asad's exploration of the constitutive role of practice, and I seek to learn more yet from his presentations of the diversity of practices that make up Islam today. My concern here is to explore, albeit briefly, a persistent, minor tradition in Europe that flows against the grain that Asad identifies while making contact with some of his themes. It might be called the minor Enlightenment of Europe. It is a mode of Enlightenment because its supporters love freedom and seek ways of being that are more inclusive in character. It is minor because it contests central themes emerging from the dominant Enlightenment in Europe, at least as that latter tradition is constituted retrospectively by most Euro-American intellectuals. It is if and as such strains are uncovered and pursued that the plurality of connections across religious practices that Asad admires will emerge as a promising possibility within Europe.

Asad identifies Kant as a key figure who prepared the intellectual ground for central tendencies in modern, secular European orientations to religion, morality, and secular public life. He grounds, for instance, the modern concept of conscience and the autonomous agent in Kantian philosophy. Much of what Asad says seems right to me, although—and I imagine Asad may agree—the contemporary focus on Kant as *the* key figure of the Enlightenment speaks as much to the assumptions and demands of contemporary academic politics as it does to the plurality of perspectives in play during the seventeenth and eighteenth centuries.

Kant, for instance, thought that of all ecclesiastical creeds in the world, Christianity comes the closest to the essence of "universal religion" as such. It does so because it gives priority to the human will and acknowledges the very essence of morality as law. He therefore places Christianity at the top of his list of ecclesiastical faiths, even though he elevates "universal religion" above every ecclesiastical practice. And, in line with Asad's reading, he reduces rational faith in universal religion to a series of "postulates" that follow, albeit with universal and subjective necessity, from the unity of reason as he defines it.

There are also strains in Kant, however, that point hesitantly toward Asad's themes. First, Kant construes the moral agent to be a being that must limit its drives to act on its own inclinations, and he thought that this process of moral acculturation was best promoted through a process of self-humiliation. The very "respect" (*Achtung*) the subject cultivates for the moral law is grounded in a process by which its "self-conceit" is "humiliated." "The moral law, which alone is truly, i.e., in every respect, objective, completely excludes the influence of self-love from the highest practical principle and forever checks self-conceit. . . . If anything checks our self-conceit in our own judgment, it humiliates. Therefore, the moral law inevitably humbles everyone when he compares the sensuous propensities of his nature with the law."[10]

It is through the painful experience of "healthy humiliation" that you come to recognize more clearly that morality takes the form of law and that you accept the imperative to restrict the agency of inclination in favor of agency as *obedience* to the moral law. The centrality of the theme of obedience in the Kantian conception of agency may make contact with the cultivation of surrender in Islam. More pertinent yet, for Kant it is through practices of "gymnastics" that rough human "inclinations" are educated until they become soft enough to accept the dictates of the moral law inscribed in human will. As Kant puts it, "Ethical gymnastics, therefore, consists only in combating natural impulses sufficiently to be able to master them when a situation comes up in which they threaten morality; hence it makes one valiant and cheerful in the consciousness of one's restored freedom."[11] It is this combination of gymnastics and self-humiliation that enables the ("nonsensuous") feeling of respect for morality as law to emerge. Finally, as Ian Hunter has shown, Kant concludes that the culture in which the right sort of gymnastics is available will be one in which Christian revelation prepares the way.[12] The Kantian ranking of Christianity as first among ecclesiastical religions, then, does not overturn similar tendencies in the history of Judaism and Islam. It simply applies them to a different object.

These themes in Kant may already suggest that a minority voice lurks within the majority expression of the Enlightenment in Europe; it may even point to the fact that the equation between the Enlightenment and the Kantian tradition is more a product of contemporary retrospection than of the actual distribution of perspectives during the period in question.

Let me turn now, then, to a minor European tradition, a tradition that makes deeper contact with themes Asad articulates even while dissenting on one or two points. The loosely bounded assemblage I have in mind finds harassed expression at several junctures. Early forerunners are Epicurus and Lucretius, before the hegemony of Christendom constituted the "continent" (which is not actually a continent) as Europe. Spinoza reactivates and redefines critical strains in the seventeenth century. His work challenges several perspectives, including ecclesiastical practices in the two dominant religious traditions, the dominant voices of Enlightenment and secularism elaborated later, and even the scientific atheism that became another minor voice in the Enlightenment. More recent Euro-American thinkers, such as Nietzsche, Kafka, Henri Bergson, William James, Stuart Hampshire, Michel Foucault, Gilles Deleuze, the Nobel prize–winning chemist Ilya Prigogine, and the American neuroscientist Antonio Damasio, continue this tradition, drawing part of their sustenance from Spinoza and modifying aspects of the minor tradition as they proceed. Asad is touched by this tradition through his engagement with the genealogical perspective of Michel Foucault. My point now, however, is to articulate it as a tradition, a minor tradition within Europe that has been subjugated by those who insist that Christianity, or the Judeo-Christian tradition, or Judeo-Christian *secularism* constitute the essence of Europe.

To discern the logic of double exclusion through which this tradition was launched inside Europe, consider the *herem* pronounced against Baruch Spinoza by Jewish Elders in Amsterdam when the young man refused to commit himself publicly to the orthodoxy they promulgated:

The gentlemen . . . have endeavored by various ways and promises to draw him back from his evil ways; and not being able to remedy him, but on the contrary, receiving every day more news about the horrible heresies he practiced . . . , and the awful deeds he performed . . . , they resolved that the said . . . be put to the ban and banished . . . , as indeed they proclaim the following *herem* on him:

"By the decree of the Angels and the word of the Saints we ban, cut off, curse and anathematize . . . , with all the curses written in the Torah; cursed be he by day and cursed by night. Cursed in his lying down and cursed in his waking up, cursed in his going forth and cursed in his coming in; and may the Lord not want his pardon, and may the Lord's wrath and zeal burn upon him.

We warn that none may contact him orally or in writing, nor do him any favor, nor stay under the same roof with him, nor read any paper he made or wrote."[13]

This excommunication was delivered by the Ruling Council in Amsterdam on July 27, 1656 to the twenty-four-year-old Spinoza. Baruch's parents had been Marrano Christians, Jews in Portugal and Spain who were first compelled to convert to Christianity and then subjected to the Inquisition because of doubts about the authenticity of the conversion. These forced conversions were loosely coordinated with the conquest of

Islam in Spain, a combination that closed through violence several centuries in which three religions of the Book had coexisted, albeit uneasily, on the peninsula.[14] Those conquests in turn helped to consolidate Europe as a continent-civilization grounded first in Christendom and then in the secular complex growing out of it. Many Marranos fled to Holland, as did Baruch's parents, joining a synagogue in Amsterdam. But the young Baruch—as he was called before changing his name after the ban—found himself unable to endorse either Jewish or Christian orthodoxy. The toll taken on the stubborn young man by the logic of double exclusion somehow released a new adventure of thought that offended all the ecclesiastical faiths of his day and continues to puzzle Euro-American secularists today. Benedict, as he named himself after the *herem*, was treated as a non-Jew by Jews and a Jewish philosopher by many Christians philosophers, even as numerous intellectuals of his day and later fed surreptitiously upon the ideas he promulgated.

The logic of double exclusion to which Spinoza was subjected sounds like a good recipe to foster either a philosophy of transcendence—to rise above the turmoil around him—or of adamant atheism, to expel "completely" the ecclesiastical traditions that excluded him. But Benedict cooked up a new dish. His metaphysical monism refuses the dualism of God/nature and mind/body; and it is not reducible to finalism either. His work depicts a *monism* in which "God or Nature" is *immanent* in the movement of things rather than forming a commanding, juridical order above them. It issues as well in a philosophy of *parallelism* in which mind and body express different aspects of the same substance. An important upshot of parallelism is that every change in a mode of mind or thinking is paralleled by a change in bodily state or capacity and, as a corollary, every change in the state of the body is accompanied by a parallel change in mind or thinking. The philosophy of monism, immanence, and parallelism in turn encourages Spinoza to fold affect into ideas and ideas into affect, so that it becomes impossible to separate them in life: "By emotion [*affectus*] I understand the affections of the body by which the body's power of activity is increased or diminished, assisted or checked, together with the ideas of these affections."[15] And lest a reader misconstrue him to be a philosopher of atomism, Spinoza emphasizes how negative and positive "compositions" between human beings engender larger complexes, which take the form of "bodies."

Spinoza builds upon this nonreductionist break with dualism to articulate an ethic of cultivation, in which cultivation of the body contributes to the cultivation of the mind and vice versa, and in which a positive ethos of cultural composition is needed to inaugurate the vision of democratic pluralism he embraces even before later, less pluralistic ideals of democracy became popular in Europe. Benedict becomes, that is, a philosopher of ethics not as *obedience* to the command of a personal God *or* a categorical imperative, but as cultivation by tactical means of *hilaritus*, a love of life that infuses the body/brain/culture network in which we move and live. *Hilaritus,* you might say, is a positive predisposition to being alive, even amidst the suffering life inevitably brings with it. It can be kindled to some degree by tactical means but is not entirely under the direct, willful control of people. When it flows into the higher intellectual registers and is joined to "adequate concepts" of the world, it issues in a generous sensibility that is crucial to the ethical life of the individual and, potentially, to the ethos of an entire regime. It is this embodied-spiritual understanding of *hilaritus* and the ethic of cultivation to which it is attached that makes it inappropriate to think of Spinoza as a secularist. Spinoza is not well read as a precursor to European secularism because he resists in advance the thin intellectualism that grips secularism—that is, the idea that thinking can be separated from its affective dimension and that exercises of the self and collective rituals merely represent or symbolize beliefs. But his thought does not fit well within either of the two European theological traditions either. He thus activates a minor tradition, a nonsecular, nonecclesiastical Enlightenment.

To bring out some of the dimensions in the minor tradition he activated, I will review a few ideas by Euro-American contemporaries indebted to him.[16] Take Stuart Hampshire, the English analytic philosopher writing in the late twentieth century. After writing a fine study of Spinoza in the 1960s,[17] Hampshire himself embraced an immanent, layered materialism in which confused and vague affects inhabiting the lower registers of the lived body can be crafted into a refined ethic of thought-imbued dispositions by a combination of corporeal techniques and reflexive thought. For Hampshire claims that just as techniques of the body help to compose patterns of thought, a change in thinking touches in some way the embodied habits of the thinker. Thus new knowledge about the body/brain network

can be translated into techniques that recipients of the knowledge can use to work upon themselves. The reflexive thinker, Hampshire says, aware of the neuro-chemical instrument of thinking, knows that if "the condition of the instrument is grossly changed, as by drugs, the power of thought is grossly changed also." Hampshire thus emphasizes the importance of "shifting attention back and forth from the consideration of persons as active observers of the physical world to the consideration of them as also observed objects, with their bodies in a dual role, as both purposely used instruments of exploration and observed objects."[18] He might be positively disposed, for instance, to the new neuro-therapy, where patient reads instruments that record their brain states and then act upon themselves to modify those states in specific directions; however, the instruments needed to pursue such therapies were not yet available when Hampshire wrote the essay in question.

Hampshire not only resurrects the reflexive relation between thought and the cultivation of ethical dispositions that is so critical to Spinoza, he also dissolves the aura of demonstration with which Spinoza surrounded his metaphysic of immanence.[19] He thus hitches the Spinoza tradition to the modern task of cultivating appreciation between alternative philosophies/faiths of the extent to which each remains legitimately contestable in the eyes of the bearers of other traditions. In this, too, he breaks with the version of contemporary thought that points back to the Kantian combination of modesty in metaphysics and dogmatism about the unity of reason. The following is a sample of how Hampshire joins appreciation of the power of Spinoza's thought to acknowledgment of the contestability of its deepest premises. The tradition of morality to which he refers critically is the Augustinian-Kantian tradition:

It is at least possible that Spinoza is right in his opinion that traditional ethics is the pursuit of an illusion, and that gradually, in the course of years, he may be shown to be right. . . . The confirmation, if it comes, will not be like the confirmation of an empirical hypothesis. . . . Rather the confirmation would be that some notions closely resembling Spinoza's key notions become widely accepted as peculiarly appropriate in studying and in evaluating human behavior. New psychological knowledge might fit better into this framework than into any other. . . . Certainly anyone who altogether rejects Spinoza's naturalistic standpoint, and anyone who has some religious and transcendental ground for his moral beliefs, would remain unpersuaded, and given his premises, justifiably so. But those of us who have no such transcendental grounds may at least pause and consider the possibility that our habitual moralizing about the ends of action is altogether mistaken. Certainly we should not deceive ourselves by dismissing Spinoza as the kind of determinist who allows no possibility of deliberate self-improvement, as if this were the dividing line between him and the traditional moralists. It is not.[20]

Consider, as well, how Antonio Damasio, a leading neuroscientist of our day, draws upon Spinoza to inform his research findings. Modern cognitive science and neuroscience alike, Damasio says, for too long ignored the embodied, affective dimension of thinking and judgment. For there is no thinking without affect and no affect without its entanglement in thought at some level. This conviction was consolidated early for Damasio—against his training and earlier hypotheses, when he encountered patients in whom "when the ongoing brain mapping of the body was suspended so was the mind. In a way, removing the mental presence of the body was like pulling the rug from under the mind. A radical interruption in the flow of body representations that support our feelings and our sense of continuity might entail, in and of itself, a radical interruption of our thoughts of objects and situations."[21]

Damasio commits himself to a version of parallelism, then, and, moreover, to Spinoza's idea that ethics cannot advance far unless a background attachment to life is folded deeply into thought-imbued emotional life. The human body/brain network is the critical system of experimental inquiry for him, a network in which various subsystems in the brain respond to signs from the body and in turn relay messages back to it. In recent correspondence with me, he concurs that the larger object of inquiry in neuroscience must become the body/brain/culture network.[22] That is, neuroscience and anthropology need to be brought into closer coordination. To me, that means anthropology can profit from experimental studies of how the body/brain network works, and neuroscience can learn from anthropology how social disciplines and techniques of the self fold cultural modalities into multiple layers of the body/brain complex.[23]

Michel Foucault, writing in a different genre than either Hampshire or Damasio, nonetheless joins Spinoza and them in playing up the importance to ethics of technique and exercises. And Gilles Deleuze, who has written two books on Spinoza, pursues the issue further, extending technique to the field of politics. He attends to the ubiquity of "micropolitics" in the consolidation of an ethos of politics. I have dealt with these issues elsewhere, so I turn now to additional contributions Deleuze makes to the Spinoza tradition.

Deleuze translates Spinoza's monism of substance as stable immanence into the theme of a mobile or "pure" immanence, an immanence that participates in a world of becoming. In a world of eternal becoming, the whole is never given; it is always in the process of emergence, as differential forces set on different tiers of time collide, merge, divert, and melt into one another. If you think about modes of becoming set on different tiers of time, such as the rapid movement of a thought across the body/brain network, the emergence of an adult from childhood, the consolidation or dissolution of a state, the evolution of the three Indo-European monotheisms, the open course of biological evolution, and the evolution of the universe, the upshot of Deleuze's radicalization of Spinoza's philosophy of immanence into a philosophy of time becomes apparent. It is when surprising intersections eventuate between diverse temporalities of becoming that something new and unpredictable sometimes surges into being. Stephen Gould's contention that the course of biological evolution underwent a radical turn when a meteor shower changed the world's climate constitutes an excellent example of what Deleuze has in mind. Here is an articulation by Deleuze and Guattari of the idea of immanence as mobility:

So how are we to define this matter-movement, this matter-energy, this matter-flow, this matter in variation that enters assemblages and leaves them? It is a destratified, deterritorialized matter. It seems to us that Husserl has brought thought a decisive step forward when he discovered the region of *vague and material essences* (in other words, essences that are vagabond, anexact and yet rigorous), distinguishing them from fixed, metric and formal essences. . . . They constitute fuzzy aggregates. They relate to a *corporeality* (materiality) that is not to be confused either with an intelligible formal essentiality or a sensible, formed thinghood.[24]

It is apparent, perhaps, how modest an intellectual shift is needed to transmute the Spinozist immanence of substance into the temporal mobility of immanence, in which the element of becoming is accentuated and the relative openness of the whole is underlined, but the implications are large. Perhaps such an ontology of becoming gains greater credibility during a time when the pace of the fastest cultural processes has accelerated in military life, media communications, tourist travel, disease transmission, and population migrations and the gap has enlarged between the slowest modes of being and the fastest modes of becoming. It takes much longer to alter the mores of a populace, for instance, than to defeat it militarily with a high-tech military arsenal. These shifts in the modern experience of temporality tempt multiple constituencies to fundamentalize traditions in which they have been immersed, in order to stem a tide of change that feels overwhelming and disorienting.

But Deleuze, in a Spinozistic spirit, tempers the desire (or wish) to slow time down, even while resisting the logic of military conquest. His fear is that today any such attempt to slow down the world could only be realized through fascist means. His most basic ambition, then, is to find ways to fold "belief in this world" more deeply into the fiber of cultural life. "This world" refers in part to a time in which becoming has accelerated, disrupting some operative assumptions of both secular intellectualism and ecclesiastical faith. It is how he comprehends the layering of "belief" or "faith" that interests me. It is interesting because it speaks to Asad's thesis about the role of technique in composing individuals and constituencies and because it propels Spinoza's idea of cultivating *hilaritus* into the late-modern whirlwind.

In *Cinema II* Deleuze reviews efforts by a small group of film directors to "restore" belief in this world. Film is timely because it is one of the media—alongside churches, schools, labor processes, television, and regimes of military discipline—that combine image, music, sound, words, and rhythms to compose or modify aspects of the body/brain/culture network. Film is noteworthy among these practices, however, because—unlike the other media much of the time—some directors experiment through film with ways to deepen faith in this world. That is, they experiment with ways to foment affirmation of a contemporary world marked by both acceleration on the fastest tiers and an enlarged gap between the fastest and slowest zones of time. It is above all these changes in the experience of time that insinuate alienation into the embodied experience of contemporary life. The task is to combat the suffering that subtends radical dislocation while finding ways to mute the sense of existential suffering that accompanies the quickening of pace itself. It is not an easy agenda to enact.

The Deleuzian idea is not that film alone could accomplish the needed task, but that this is a task that needs to be pursued within media and religious institutions today, and is not being pursued sufficiently in the prevailing religious and secular practices. The wager, again, is that a drive to slow time down in the contemporary age would engender worse suffering than attempts to affirm the new world while combating the dislocations it engenders. Here are a few formulations through which Deleuze poses the issue and a possible direction of response to it:

*The modern fact is that we no longer believe in this world. It is clear from the outset that cinema had a special relation with belief. There is a Catholic quality to cinema. . . .

*Restoring belief in this world—this is the power of modern cinema. Whether we are Christians or atheists, in our universal schizophrenia, we need reasons to believe in this world.

*What is certain is that believing is no longer believing in another world, or in a transformed world. It is only, it is simply, believing in the body. It is giving discourses to the body, and, for this purpose, reaching the body before discourses, before words before things are named. . . .

*Give words back to the body, to the flesh.

*We need an ethic or a faith, which makes fools laugh; it is not a need to believe in something else, but a need to believe in this world, of which fools are a part.[25]

The fools, I think, are those who grasp that time is always "out of joint," that the way in which past and future gnaw into the present, as they constitute its complex mode of duration, introduces a split or ineliminable element of dissonance into the very flow of time.

Deleuze is aware that we live in a world in which the electronic media play a critical role in fashioning both the affective ideas we carry into politics and the underlying sense of being in which they are set. He was not fully aware, when *Cinema II* was written in the mid-1980s, of the extent to which rightwing moguls would take over the image-reports-political debates on the electronic media in the United States, but he sensed the drift. Film, in some of its manifestations, appreciates the power of modern media while contesting the dominant tones of the electronic media. But to what effect? As I read him, Deleuze is taken with films that seek to infuse into the flesh presumptive affirmation of the contemporary world of speed and temporal multiplicity.

The stakes are high, even when institutional control of the media is so highly skewed. For it is when and as such affirmative presumptiveness becomes layered into life that we can hope for energetic political movements to foster a richer, more multidimensional pluralism within and across regimes. A pluralism of religious practices is sought—including Islamic, Buddhist, Christian, Hindu, Jewish, and Spinozistic practices—in which many exude faith in this or that vision of transcendence and a few embrace a world of pure immanence. In such a pluralism, some constituencies on either side of this divide—and other divides as well—occasionally hear a whisper that confounds them, but they do not respond to this disturbance by dogmatizing their own faith. The Spinozist-Deleuzian wager is that effective movements of pluralization, and particularly of generous responses to such movements, are grounded in part on affirmative, generous energies—on *hilaritus* and not on suffering alone. If and as the scope of religious diversity is extended, a multidimensional pluralism of gender practices, ethnic habits, and linguistic affiliations might also be installed more effectively.

I will turn to the relation between alternative faiths in a moment. But within this minor tradition the aspiration to spawn a new pluralism of multiple minorities is linked to the quest to imbue belief in this world: the two are joined together like Siamese twins. Even if one sets aside the uneven distribution of institutional power over the media, it may require more than Deleuze admits to foster such dispositions. People and constituencies may need opportunities to withdraw periodically from the whirlwind to prepare to re-enter it affirmatively. Such a dissonant combination might help to foment the culture of "rhizomatic" pluralism that Deleuze and I admire, a pluralism in which multiple minorities connect at disparate points, participating in forging a generous ethos of engagement through their negotiations. Even to articulate the points in this way, however, is to see that Deleuze stands in a relation to politics in our day not all that far from Spinoza's stance in regard to the European Christianity and Judaism of his day.

An Ethos of Minorities

Late modern Spinozists—as I call those who seek to adjust Spinoza to the contemporary condition—bring a distinctive set of orientations and dispositions to the contemporary world. You can call us carriers of the minor Enlightenment, an Enlightenment that reworks the images of nature, morality, culture, causality, embodiment, and time pursued under the mantles of Locke, Kant, Habermas, Rawls, Benhabib, Nussbaum, Gutmann, and that gang, while nonetheless remaining recognizable as a mode of Enlightenment. Carriers of this minor tradition do not seek to define Spinozism as the frame in which all other orientations must be set. This all-too-familiar ambition would define others to be minorities revolving around the center we occupy. It would define us as arboreal pluralists, when we aspire in fact to a world in which the rhizomatic dimension of multiple connections is pronounced and the arboreal dimension is toned down. We seek, then, to become a recognized minority in a world of interconnected minorities. The task is to modify the terms of engagement within Europe writ large by projecting the minor tradition of enlightenment more vibrantly onto the field of politics, and to build upon that entry to inspire a new spiritualization of political engagement inside and outside Europe.

One thing seems clear, however. If and as you come to terms with the layered and embodied character of culture amidst the acceleration of pace in the fastest zones of life, every tradition faces obstacles in deepening belief in this world. During such a time, some factions within *each* tradition—including the one outlined here—are tempted to dogmatize its own faith-practice-assemblage to fix and secure itself. The question is how to combat this tendency. It is, perhaps, as each party invents reflective techniques to *fold back into its own faith a moment of modesty and appreciation of its deep contestability in the bodies and brains of others that the formation of a new pluralism becomes more promising.* The first imperative is not to insist that other traditions advance down this path before you start, for such a stance intensifies the negative dialectic already under way; rather it is to start down the path yourself, hoping that bearers of other traditions will be inspired by the example you embody.

The themes that the minor Spinoza tradition presses upon secular intellectualism—that is, upon a vision that plays up the autonomy of the intellect and plays down the layering of affect-imbued ideas into the flesh—provoke a more enlightened sense of what it would take to *be* a pluralist today, a more profound appreciation of why the new pluralism is *needed*, and a deepened sense of the challenges to its *attainment*. These themes would exert similar pressure upon the dominant ecclesiastical traditions of Europe.

I approach Talal Asad as an agonistic partner in exploring the dangers and possibilities of deep, multidimensional pluralism in the late modern age. He is an *agonistic* partner, if I read him correctly, in that his faith is invested in something beyond, as well as in, pure immanence. He is an agonistic *partner* in that he appreciates the layered, embodied character of culture, the importance of technique to ethico-religious life, the significance of cultivating affirmation of this world, and the role that these components might play together in fomenting a new ethos of pluralism.

6

Secularism and the Argument from Nature

Veena Das

Talal Asad's authoritative work on secularism as an object of anthropological inquiry takes us to the practices of the self, and especially to the way the subject comes to be attached to the nation-state and its law.[1] As Asad states it, secularism is not simply an intellectual argument offered in response to a question about enduring social peace and toleration—it is also a way of distributing and rearranging forms of suffering so that it becomes legitimate to acknowledge some forms of suffering and to practice indifference (or worse) toward others. To the usual claim that secularism was instrumental as the ideology of modern liberal states in bringing about peace in the context of warring religions in European history, Asad offers the counterargument that the issue is not one of *ending* violence but one of *shifting* the violence of religious wars into the violence of national and colonial wars.

It follows from the above argument that there are specific ways in which the secular state assigns responsibility for cruelty so that as Asad says, "the suffering that the individual sustains as a citizen—*as the national of a particular state*—is distinguished from the suffering he undergoes as *a human being*" (p. 129, emphasis in original). This duality of the person is reflected in two distinct ideas—that of the unattached human in an imagined state of nature and that of the citizen/subject, attached to the state through both regulation and the creation of sentiments like patriotism. The duality of the person, Asad argues, arranges law, violence, and the notion of rights under modern secular regimes. This is a complex weave, within which I will steer a more limited course of trying to delineate one strand: how birth and reproduction are implicated in the creation of citizen/subjects and how themes of suffering and death are reinserted by this route in the realm of the secular. Underlying this entire issue, as Asad detects, is the place of nature in thinking about the creation of the political. The problem, as I see it, is that once the idea of God as the author of nature and time is displaced and the political body is seen as subject to death and decay, secular means have to be crafted to ensure that the sovereign receives life beyond the lifetime of individual members. Thus, the state has to reimagine its relation to the family in more complex ways than simply assigning the family to the realm of the private.

Let me enter the discussion with an observation that Asad makes about active and passive rights. He argues that the question of what is human in human rights is based on the idea of a previous state of nature in which a person is entitled to natural rights independently of social and political institutions. Thus the notion of the human located in nature (but not in any social institutions), he argues, meshes more comfortably with theories that use a concept of active rights rather than passive rights. This is because active rights are those in which the individual is pitted *against* others, whereas passive rights are embedded in obligations to others and hence assume a state of social relatedness. While I agree with Asad that the state of nature is the point of mythic origin of the state (in Hobbes, for instance), it seems to me that the imagination of bodies in nature invites us to consider various sites in which notions of rights are engaged.

One frequently cited sentence in Hobbes is the mushroom analogy, in which we are asked to consider men as having sprung out of the earth and suddenly "like mushrooms, come to full maturity, without all kind of engagement to each other."[2] Many feminist scholars have noted the exclusion of the woman, especially the mother, from this originary imagination of social order. Thus, Carol Pateman notes that the invitation to think of men as springing up like mushrooms is designed to obscure the fact that contractual individualism is grounded in the husband's subjugation of the wife.³ Similarly, Seyla Benhabib cites this analogy as evidence that the denial of being born of a woman frees the male ego from the natural bonds of dependence on the mother.⁴ While this line of argumentation is powerful in showing how the profoundly masculine Leviathan is based on the explicit exclusion of women, I think there is some scope for thinking this issue beyond questions of exclusion.

One point of entry into these questions is to track the way the so-called natural life enters into the mechanisms and calculations of power—in short, the domain of biopolitics. In his recent writings, Giorgio Agamben offers us the concept of bare life as a constitutive principle of modernity to suggest the coinciding of biological life with the life of the citizen.⁵ In Agamben's words, "European democracy placed at the center of its battle against absolutism not *bios*, the qualified life of the citizen but *zoē*, the bare, anonymous life that is as such taken into the sovereign ban." He locates the first rendering of bare life as the new political subject in the 1679 writ of habeas corpus, for here he finds the idea that the body has to be produced literally before the law. "It is not the free man with his statues and the prerogatives, nor even simply *homo*, but rather *corpus*—that is the new subject of politics" (p. 125). This bears some affinity to the idea of the individual sprung from the earth, although its location is shifted from the origin of social contract to that of anonymous life as the subject of the law. It may provide some support to Asad's contention that the notion of human rights under the regime of modernity privileges active rights because the person is placed in nature rather than in already constituted social relationships. I propose a different trajectory and argue that even when the law is demanding a body to be produced before it, this body is already constituted as a socio-legal subject rather than a natural body. This will have some bearing on the various impasses that confront the liberal imagination in thinking of the social order as constituted through the gathering together of autonomous male subjects. More importantly, I claim that if the individual located in nature is a sexed individual, then the state of nature turns out to be a state of social relatedness, providing the grounds for imagining political community. But I am running ahead of my argument.

Law, Paternity, and the Facts of Nature

How, then, is nature constituted in the legal imagination? The colonial archive is particularly instructive in this regard, since taken-for-granted notions of nature and culture had to be explicitly articulated in the context of subjects whose integration into the law was mediated by the notion of custom, as well as for citizens who were domiciled away from metropolitan centers. In this section, I draw from judgments rendered in the Supreme Court in Bombay in the mid-nineteenth century regarding questions such as the "natural" rights of the father over his child after he had converted to Christianity, or the validity of marriages when the stipulated legal provisions could not be fulfilled. Since the British view of their role in India was not that of aggressive proselytizers, such cases raise important issues regarding what is natural and universal and what belongs to the domain of custom and religion. Beyond raising obvious questions about how colonialism had to adjust to local conditions, these cases are important, in my view, for addressing the place of nature in secular modernity through birth and reproduction. I hope to show that there are subtle connections between the regulation of birth and the figuration of death in the formulation of sovereignty and citizenship—a theme I take up in the last section of this chapter.

I start with a particular problem that colonial law faced in India: did conversion to Christianity alter the rights of the father to custody of his child? The first case I present—the Queen versus Shapurji Vezonzi and Bezanzi Edalji—came before justices C. J. Roper and J. Perry on February 28, 1843.[6] It concerned a Parsi man named Hormazji Pestonji who had converted to Christianity, and consequently denied access to his wife and female child by his father-in-law. The petition by the father-in-law submitted that the Parsi Panchayat had already rendered judgment on the matter, dissolving Hormazji Pestonji's marriage, and his wife had now married another Parsi man. Further, the petition stated that the child over whom he sought custody was already betrothed—and that her grandfather had settled three thousand rupees upon her. The petitioner submitted that these were sufficient grounds (the dissolution of the marriage and the betrothal of the child) for denying Hormazji Pestonji any claims over his wife and child. I will not go into all the questions raised by the case, but will concentrate on the observations of the court regarding the natural rights of the father over his child. The case summary provided by the judges goes as follows:

> It appeared from the affidavit on which the ruling of habeas corpus was sought on behalf of Hormazji Pestonji, the father of the child, that he was converted to Christianity in 1839. Before this conversion, he used to live with his father-in-law, the defendant. After his conversion, however, he took up his abode at the house of the mission of the Church of Scotland, leaving his wife and child at her old residence; and he swore that he abstained from going to his father-in-law's house, through fear of ill treatment on account of his change of religion. He submitted that he had frequently applied to Shapurji that his wife and child should be given up to him, but the defendant refused, on the ground that his conversion to Christianity constituted dissolution of the marriage; and on January this year the defendant and his family married off Hormazji's wife to another Parsi man. It was also sworn that the defendant was about to betroth Hormazji's daughter according to the custom of the Parsis, that he had refused to give her up to him, and that they believed that the child would be removed out of the jurisdiction if the writ of habeas corpus did not issue.

The question before the court, then, was whether Hormazji Pestonji's actions amounted to desertion of his wife and child, and whether the custom of the Parsi community, as the court put it, was ascendant over the natural rights of the father to have custody of his child. The petition from the child's grandfather and the woman's new husband claimed that the man Hormazji had deserted his wife and child and, further, that he had consented to the child's betrothal, so that effectively he had agreed to forgo custody. The observations of the court on this matter are worth producing in detail.

Justice Perry stated that none of the affidavits submitted to the court supported the claim that the father consented to the child's betrothal:

If Hormazji is sincere in his embracing of Christianity, it is impossible that he could ever consent to his child being educated in a faith that he believes to be false. . . . The cases in which a father has been held to have waived his right to custody of his children, all shew [sic] either gross immorality on the part of the father or a distinct assent on his part to a separate custody in which case the arrangements having been made on the strength of such assent, court would not allow the father capriciously to interfere; . . . but here the whole conduct of the father shews that he has always been desirous to have his wife and child restored to him. Rex v Green . . . is a clear decision that the proper custody of an infant child is with the father. . . . There is a statement in this return that bears improbability on the face of it. The child was betrothed, it is said, a month after the baptism of the father. She must then have been betrothed at the age of one year. Is it in accordance with the custom of the Parsis to betroth so early? I believe it is not; let me be corrected if I am mistaken. Say, it was betrothed; it was plainly done to annoy the father. Done by whom? By the grandfather; but the grandfather had not the slightest right to do so. If he betrothed the child, the father not consenting, then the betrothment was decidedly an illegal act. The man had embraced Christianity and therefore he is to be deprived of his natural right as a father? I can only say that if the Parsis set up such a claim as that, they will find they are grossly mistaken.

There were similar cases in which the issue of conversion and custody of children came before the court (e.g., the Queen v. Rev. Robert Nesbitt [1843]). The application of the writ of habeas corpus was always described as producing a body that was under illegal detention, but in determining what constituted illegal detention it was the socially constituted person that was at stake rather than a biological body. Thus, for instance, the failure to produce the child in court had to be juridically interpreted: was it illegal for the grandfather to refuse to give custody of the child to its father? Did it violate the natural rights of the father? But in interpreting the conditions under which such *natural rights* could be asserted, the court had to give due consideration to Parsi custom. It had to further determine whether conversion to Christianity constituted an act of desertion. Thus, the centrality accorded to the "natural rights" of the father arose not from the mere fact of the birth but from the acknowledgment of the father as one who transforms birth from a natural event to a social one.

I suggest that the body of the child to which the writ of habeas corpus was applied in the court of law was not a simple body unattached to any form of the social, as Agamben's argument would have us believe, but the body of a socially and legally constituted person already located in a system of relationships.[7] It is the symbolic weight of the father that makes the court read the biological function of fathering in this particular way, for no corresponding discussion occurs on the natural rights of the mother over the child. It is paternity that is seen to transform sexuality from private pleasure to an obligation of the citizen in reproducing the political community. Thus the right of the father regarding the child, which seems to stem from the natural fact of birth and thus to cut across race and religion, in effect carried already constituted ideas of paternity that linked family and state.

In the latter part of the chapter, I provide the intellectual and moral context that makes the father such a pivotal figure in the imagining of the political community. I want to consider one more case—Maclean v. Cristall—that came before Justices Perry and Yardley in September 1849 in the same court to show how issues of reproduction and citizenship were linked. The essential question here was whether the common law of England regarding marriage, as it applied to British citizens living in India, imported with it the provisions that made the presence of a minister in holy orders essential, as it was in England.

On the 6th of November 1834, a ceremony of marriage was performed between the plaintiff and Miss Mary Lewis Pelly, a resident of Surat. Both parties to the marriage were members of the Church of England. One Mr. William Fyre, a missionary who was then residing at Surat, performed the ceremony. The court noted that Mr. Fyre had not been episcopally ordained; he belonged to the Congregationist sect and had signed the register in which the marriage was entered as "Minister of the Gospel and Missionary." The court further noted that no person of holy orders was present at the time of the marriage and that although there were several civil functionaries who lived in Surat, a person of the holy order was not easy to find. In their summary of the case, the justices put the question before the court as follows: "The question for the opinion of the Court, is, whether the preceding facts constitute a valid marriage, as stated in the plaint."

The council for the plaintiff brought a passage from an earlier judgment (Reading v. Smith) before the court. "What is the law of marriage in all foreign establishments, settled in counties professing a religion essentially different? . . . An English resident at St. Petersburg does not look to the ritual of the Greek Church, but to the rubric of the Church of England, when he contracts a marriage with an English woman. Nobody can suppose that while the Mogul empire existed, an Englishman was bound to consult the Koran for the celebration of his marriage." Another council suggested that only parts of English law were suitable to the conditions in India, so that it was open for the court to consider whether this portion of the common law was indeed appropriate to the circumstances of the country.

The judges themselves were quite clear that the "common law of

England is the law of this country [i.e., India] so far as respects Europeans." This would imply that the marriage would have to be declared void. But, as Justice Perry noted, "The effect of such a conclusion would be to pronounce a vast number of marriages that have taken place in India during the last 250 years invalid, to extend the stain of illegitimacy to many a pedigree hitherto deemed spotless, and, above all, to carry error and dismay into numerous innocent and unsuspecting households." Accordingly, Justice Perry concluded that "the fund of good sense which is contained in the most valuable collection of jurisprudence in the world—I mean the English Law Reports—furnishes forth ample authority for denying a rule so inconvenient to mankind as has been alleged at our Bar to exist."

The historical and anthropological literature on colonialism recognizes that the entire process of applying legal rules to new circumstances arising from the expansion of empire led to adaptations of the law to local circumstances. The very question of where authority of law is to be located became debatable. Thus, for instance, Justice Perry talked about the *unstable* foundations of law in such a case as the present one. Reflecting on the conflicting opinions on this question in the judicial archive, Justice Perry referred to the great masters in law, the classical Roman jurists who, when they found that propositions and dicta laid down in early times led to a conclusion opposed to the best interests of the Commonwealth, "vigorously appealed to the foundation of all human law." He saw these foundations to lie in common sense and the principle of *utilitas causa* and *jus sigulare ad consequential non productur*. Thus, if the consequences were against the welfare of mankind, the law was to be rejected.

We now have the building blocks necessary for me to make my argument on how the appeal to common sense regarding the "natural rights" of the father and the welfare of mankind reveals how reproduction linked the citizen to the state even in the absence of biblical arguments regarding the will of God. After all, certainty about paternity is not necessary to reproduce the population conceived as a numerical entity, but the reproduction of the social body seems to call for reiterating the role of the father. To anticipate my later argument, I claim that regulating birth and reproduction is the other side of the concern with the sovereign's rights over life and death, and that life for the political body requires not only that "correct" children be born but that, as *citizens*, they should be ready to die for continuity of the political body.[8] Thus, while the father's rights over the life of his son was reconfigured so that even the natural right of the father seems to stem now from some notion of consent and capacity to provide care for the child, the sovereign now demands that citizens be ready to give life to the sovereign *voluntarily*. However, such citizens are seen as springing not from the earth but rather from the normatively configured order of the family, as we saw in the judgments of the Supreme Court.

Revisiting an Old Debate

Asad's account of the genealogy of the secular traces it in part to the Renaissance doctrine of humanism, in part to the Enlightenment concept of nature, and in part to Hegel's philosophy of history. Before the Reformation, he points out, the term *secularization* denoted a legal transition from monastic life to the life of canons. Later, after the Reformation, it signified the freeing of property from Church hands and its transfer into the hands of private owners and thus into the market for circulation. "Finally," Asad concludes, "in the discourse of modernity, 'the secular' presents itself as the ground from which theological discourse was generated (as a form of false consciousness) and from which it gradually emancipated itself in its march to freedom."[9] This is clearly one description of the secular, and Asad is cautious in pointing out the inversions and paradoxes entailed in claims that secularism itself generated a new form of religiosity.

One of the problems I face in Asad's rendering of the genealogy of secularism is that the Begriffsgeschichte School (on which Asad relies in part), is committed to the history of words but has a somewhat restricted notion of context. This creates a picture of the secular as a unitary system or a notionally complete totality of legal rules. However, Asad's own work has repeatedly emphasized the importance of colonized spaces in producing the forms of knowledge in Europe, broadening the idea of context far beyond the work of the Begriffsgeschichte historians. As we saw in the cases I presented, the justices had access only to partial forms of legal knowledge, and they were unsure of the extent to which their legal rules were applicable to the countries in which they were obliged to apply them.

This scene of colonialism obliged administrators and judges to refer to a world populated with other religions and customs; their notions of natural rights were pitted against other people's ideas of what constituted nature. Thus a form of secular reasoning had to be applied to cases in which the private domains of marriage and reproduction overlapped the public domain of making loyal subjects and citizens for the nation. As we saw in the Maclean v. Cristall case, this was not a matter of religious rites becoming redundant as marriage became a secular affair; instead, we witness the concerns of state in producing legitimate members of the political body when this body was dispersed over sites far from home. The judges seem to have rearranged the relative importance of legal rules concerning legitimate marriage and used an argument based on the welfare of mankind for suspending the application of the rules in these particular cases. This is, then, not a simple story of the secular emerging out of the religious and leaving it behind, nor is it one in which religious life is consigned to the sphere of the private; what is at stake is precisely that marriage cannot be relegated to a private arrangement. Instead, these cases support Asad's point that secular concerns of the state are ascendant over other concerns as far as the production of legitimate subjects or citizens is concerned. Thus, the founding moment of the social order that conceives of a state of nature as consisting of autonomous individuals meets its limit in the sexed individual whose reproductive functions situate the individual as being born within a family rather than being produced from the earth.

The line of argument proposed here does not see family simply as an institution from which civil society arises and separates itself but proposes that sovereignty continues to draw life from the family. It troubles some aspects of Asad's argument. For instance, with regard to legal reform in Egypt, Asad says that he sees citizen rights as integral to the process of governance and to the normalization of conduct in a modern secular state. "In this scheme of things, the individual acquires his or her rights mediated by various domains of social life—including the public domain of politics and the private domain of the family as articulated by law. The state embodies, sanctions and administers the law in the interests of its self-governing citizens" (p. 227). I have argued instead that "the law" is not the unitary sovereign presence suggested by an exclusive reading of the history of concepts as discursive entities. Thus, though the justices of the Supreme Court of Bombay did not once utter the word *secular*, it seems to me that this experience rightly belongs to the history of secularism both in Europe and in India. So one returns to the question of why reproduction is the point at which the private and the public are joined rather than separated.

An important debate that has bearing on this question relates to the nature of patriarchal authority in seventeenth- and eighteenth-century England, when the framework for a liberal polity based on consent was in the process of formation. Was patriarchal authority derived from God, so that the father was the head of the family according to the divine law of nature? Or was secular or civil power to be seen as instituted by men? Another way of putting this question is to ask whether the power of the king was an extension of the power of the father, or whether one could argue that power was given to the multitude by the king, who ruled by their consent. Whichever events we emphasize in determining what constituted the historical context—the execution of King Charles in January 1649, the problems of succession, Reformation, or the discovery of Aristotle via Arabic texts—there is little doubt that theological considerations informed questions of political philosophy.[10]

My interest in revisiting the debate over the relation between family and the state is for the limited purpose of thinking the relation between reproduction, death, and sovereignty. Was the place of the father under what has been called the new framework for liberal thought a complete break from earlier patriarchal doctrine, a transformation, or a transfiguration? I suggest that if we look at reproduction and death in relation to continuities of the political body, then the symbolic weight of the father is transfigured (in the way in which, say, a walk may be transfigured into a dance or speaking may be transfigured into singing), but he does not disappear from the political scene nor does his authority become redundant in the efforts to reimagine the place of family within political community.

In Sir Robert Filmer's *Patriarcha*, fatherly or patriarchal authority was derived from God and the authority of the father over his children was similar to the authority of the king over his subjects—in fact, the latter was a direct extension of the former.[11] Filmer states that the father was head of the family according to the divine law of nature: his wife, children, and servants owed obedience by the will of God. As he states: "Fatherly power over the family was natural and God was the author of nature" (p. 31). Thus fatherly power was not authored by law—rather the social order was itself founded on the fact that this power embodied the law. The father of the family governs by no other law than his own will, not by the laws or will of his sons or servants. Filmer's insistence on grounding kingly power on the natural and originary authority of fatherly power escaped the impasse that Hobbes faced in somehow deriving the social from the fully formed autonomous individual arising from nature and contracting to constitute the political.

In an acute analysis of the relation between fatherly authority and the possibility of a woman citizen, Mary Laura Severance argues that in Hobbes we have a predication of fatherly authority based on consent rather than something natural or originary.[12] But, as she notes, the consent of the family to be ruled by the father effectively neutralizes his power to kill. For Filmer, the family is insulated from the father's power to kill because laws of nature ensure that the father does not use this power but instead does his best to preserve the family.[13] Analogically, the king also would not use his power to kill under normal circumstances. Since the father (and by extension the monarch) *embodies* rather than *represents law*, it is up to him to decide what constitutes the state of exception, and there can be no legal remedy against this. "There is no nation that allows children any action or remedy for being unjustly governed and yet for all this every father is bound by the law of nature to do the best for the preservation of his family. By the same move is the king tied by the same laws of nature to keep his general ground that the safety of his kingdom be his general law" (p. 42).

By grounding the power of the father in the consent of the family, Hobbes is able to draw a distinction between fatherly and sovereign authority as two distinct but artificial spheres. However, this is done within the framework of the seventeenth-century doctrine that women are unfit for civil business and must be represented (or concluded) by their husbands. The sexual contract and the social contract are, then, two separate realms, but the relation between these two is much more vexed than Asad grants. Certainly, as Severance notes, the idea of the state of nature as one in which every man is in a state of war with every other man, should be modified to read: in which every father as the head of the family is in a state of war against every other father. In her words, "The members of each individual family 'consent' not to the sovereign's but to the father's absolute rule; they are not parties to the 'contract' that brings the commonwealth into existence" (p. 6). Unlike the consent to be ruled by the father, which protects the family against him, such that political society stops at the doorstep of the family, the consent to the social contract protects individuals from each other by vesting power in the sovereign.

Paternity, Secular Time, and the Life of the Sovereign

One might expect that once biblical notions of time were displaced in the nineteenth century by secular notions of time derived from evolutionary theory, the symbolic weight of the father in determining the nature of political community would be lifted. If we turn to the studies of kinship instituted by legal scholars, such as Johann Bachofen, John Mclennan, and Lewis H. Morgan,[14] we find that though family now acquires a history, this history is staged around the curious question of the conditions under which it became possible to ascertain paternity. Thus, for instance, Bachofen characterized primitive promiscuity as problematic because it made it impossible to determine paternity with certainty. Mclennan similarly thought that the problem with polyandry was that while the mother was known under this system of marriage, it was impossible to determine who the father was. Morgan and later Engels asserted that the beginning of civilization can be traced to the decisive victory of the monogamous family, "the express purpose being to produce children of undisputed paternity."[15] Though Engels saw in the rise of monogamy the establishment of the power of men and the "world historic defeat" of women, there are passages in both authors that suggest that the desire to pass on property to sons was a *natural* desire. Bachofen famously talked about the "spurious" children brought about by the women of the Cecrops, who were not bound to any one man.

Although Filmer's claim that the father had an absolute right over the life and death of his son was refuted by Locke on the ground that the facts of begetting would give joint dominion over the child to both parents, he too thought that women were by nature weak and hence needed to be represented by their husbands. Moreover, Locke claimed that the father's authority over the child, which is necessary in childhood, has a natural limit when the child becomes older. It is interesting that in introducing a temporal element into the relationship, Locke shifts the emphasis to the anatomical child, whereas for Filmer the status of the son was relational (i.e., even adult sons were children of their fathers). Severance points out that the performative nature of the father's authority is overlooked in discussions of Locke, especially by those who believe he did not go far enough in refuting the patriarchal grounds of political authority.

Does the father then act in the Lockean view only as the symbolic placeholder for the political order? For Severance, the Father functions not as an individual but as a symbolic principle: "He is a necessary presupposition in Locke's attempt to maintain a distinction not between the natural and the political but the political and the social." Yet, as the legal scholarship at the moment of the institution of kinship studies attests, because certainty of paternity is a necessary condition for the establishment of the political in the context of the state, we cannot get rid of the "natural" so easily. The symbolic weight of patriarchy, it seems, can only be borne by biological fathers, and the evolution of the monogamous family is the best guarantee within evolutionary time for political authority to be securely grounded in fatherly authority. So how is the sexed individual to be placed in the imagination of the secular? If individuals are sexed, then they are also mortal—both are facts that the mushroom analogy manages to obscure.

On the Sexed and Mortal Individual, or Rousseau's Woman

Many Rousseau scholars have held the view that the Book 5, "Sophie, or, The Woman," is a minor text marked among other things by a break in genre from earlier sections of the book.[16] Ronald Grimsley argues that not only are Rousseau's ideas on men and women conservative and reactionary but also that in this section he is unable to detach himself from his personal fantasies.[17] Others have abstracted the observations on the masculine and the political from this section but hold that the figure of Sophie does not offer any philosophical challenge. I want to address a limited point here: what promise does the figure of the woman hold for introducing the themes of love and citizenship, and how are these themes conjoined?[18]

At the conclusion of Book 4, the tutor announced that Emile is not made to live alone, rather he is a member of society and must fulfill his duties as such. Thus the appearance of a woman, first crafted in imagination and then given a name and thus made concrete, is to teach Emile the meaning of sociality. Sophie, as the tutor says, is the name of a good omen.

If Emile is a man of nature not spoiled by artifice, then Sophie is not so much the symmetrical opposite as the obligatory passage through which the man must move along the road of marriage, paternity, and citizenship. While the scene of seduction is necessary for the pupil to be inserted into the social, his capability of becoming a citizen is proved by learning how to renounce the very lure of the woman that was his passage into sociality. In an intriguing episode, when Emile and Sophie are betrothed, the tutor tells Emile that he must leave Sophie. The argument presented to Emile is that he must wait until Sophie is older and able to bear healthy children. But an earlier episode, in which the tutor tells Emile that Sophie is dead in order to test his reaction, shows that there is a close relation between learning how to inhabit society through an engagement with sex and becoming a good citizen by overcoming the fear of separation and death. It is worth pausing to reflect on this.

In educating Emile such that his natural inclinations are not shrouded by the artifice of society, the tutor had taken care to see that he overcome the fear of death, which Rousseau sees as a sign of this artifice. "Death is the cure for the evils you bring upon yourself," he exhorts. "Nature would not have you suffer perpetually" (p. 146). So, when Sophie's death is announced, Emile has already learned not to fear death in general. But what of death in particular, or the death of the known other? In fearing that Sophie might be dead, Emile learns that the fear of death can be expanded to include those one loves. "You know how to suffer and die; you know how to bear the heavy yoke of necessary ills of today; but you have not yet learnt to give a law to the desires of your heart; and the difficulties of life that arise rather from our affections than from our needs" (p. 146).

It is then from Emile's journey into citizenship that we understand the multiple chains of signification in which the figure of Sophie is inserted. She is the chimera who is inserted into the text—the figure of seduction, the future mother of a family, and one through whom Emile learns that to be a good citizen is to overcome his fear of her death by giving a law to the desires of his heart. Hence, she is a seductress in the present, the maternal in the future, and the teacher of duty and a code of conduct. Without her he can overcome physical ills, but with her and then despite her he will become a virtuous citizen. "When you become the head of a family, you are going to become a member of the state, and do you know what it is to be a member of the state? Do you know what government, laws, and fatherland are? *Do you know what the price is of your being permitted to live and for whom you ought to die?*" (p. 448; emphasis added).

There are two thoughts: first, that in order to be a citizen of the state you must be the head of a household, and second, that you must know for whom you ought to die. It is important not to confuse the virtue of readiness to die with some simple picture of the heroic. In earlier sections, while learning about the arts, Emile had expressed derision over the idea of the heroic, and in considering the careers that do not obstruct the naturalness of Emile, the tutor says with irony, "You may hire yourself out at very high wages to go to kill men who never did you any harm" (p. 420). What does the readiness to die signify?

A woman's duty as a citizen is confounded with her duty to her husband. A woman's comportment must be such that not only her husband but also his neighbors and friends believe in her fidelity. When she gives her husband children who are not his own, we are told, she is false both to him and to them, and her crime is "*not infidelity but treason*" (p. 325). Thus, woman as seductress holds danger for the man, because she may use her powers of seduction to make the man too attached to life and thus unable to decipher who and what is worth dying for. In her role as mother, she may prevent him from being a proper head of the household by giving him counterfeit children. That this is treason and not infidelity shows how the mother, who was completely excluded as a figure of thought in Filmer and Hobbes, is incorporated into the duties of citizenship. For Rousseau, the individual on whose consent political community is built is, no doubt, a sexed individual, but the woman has the special role of not only introducing the man to forms of sociality but also teaching him to renounce his attachment to her in order to give life to the political community.

The fear of death in Rousseau is aligned with the fear of extinction. "My personal identity," the tutor tells Emile, "depends upon my memory. In order to be the same self, I must remember that I have existed" (p. 246). But then existence is not only a matter of bodily continuity, for "the life of the soul only begins with the death of the body." Thus, for Rousseau, self-preservation demands that the person be initiated into citizenship by overcoming his fear of bodily death; what, then, is the life of the soul that he talks about? In Book 5, where the figure of Sophie appears, we also find that the child is taught that the beginning of the human race is the father and mother who did not have a father and mother, and the end of the human race will come when there are children who do not have children. There are no references to creation and apocalypse, hence the complex relation between the obligation to reproduce, the idea of individual mortality, and the fear of extinction. I submit that the relation between the state, as a passive entity whose active face is sovereignty, allows a slippage between the idea of human race as biologically defined and the idea of life invested in the sovereign, for as a passive entity the state could be replenished by any means to augment its population, such as immigration or birth of illegitimate children, but in order to receive "life," it must command the allegiance of properly born citizens who are willing to both reproduce for it and die for it. This is evident when Rousseau expounds on the idea of good government and says that an increase in population provides a kind of moral compass by which we can judge the goodness of a government. Thus, good governance is indexed in the fact that citizens want to reproduce and population is augmented not by "artificial" means, such as colonization, but by natural means of reproduction.[19]

Within this scheme, women's allegiance to the state is proved by bearing legitimate children (recall the remark about the crime of bringing illegitimate children in the world being not about infidelity but about treason), whereas men become good citizens by being prepared to die in order to give life to the sovereign. To be sure, there is a shift in the conception of paternity, for if the father's authority provides the foundation for the authority of the sovereign, this is not because the father has a right over the life and death of his son but because the natural right of the father stems from his natural tenderness toward his son.[20] There is a natural joining of the will of the father and the son that provides the model for the joining of the will of sovereign and citizen in Rousseau, but as I have indicated, the symbolic weight of paternity continues. For the individual to be located in the state as citizen (and not merely a subject who obeys laws), he must first pass through the detour of sexuality and seduction. This is a more complex picture than the simple opposition of active and passive rights would suggest and gives at least a clue as to why paternity remains at the center of debates about citizenship and sovereignty. I prefer to think of this as a transfiguration rather than a transformation in the figure of the paternal and the sovereign.

By Way of Conclusion

To conclude, I would like to try to construct an imaginary matrix in which the figure of the father provides a kind of keyhole through which we can see the complex relations between ideas of god and nature, family and political community, and what constitutes sovereignty. Instead of starting with Justice Perry as I did in the body of the paper, I will work back to his arguments.[21]

For Filmer, God is the author of nature and Adam as his direct creation is the figure of the father who combines different kinds of power. Thus for Filmer, political power is fatherly power and earthly fathers, the direct descendants of Adam, have absolute power over the life and death of their sons. Inasmuch as fathers embody law rather than simply representing it and kingly power is simply an extension of fatherly power, it is laws of nature that instill in both fathers and kings the desire to preserve their children and their subjects, respectively. This is the only protection that sons and subjects have in the face of the sovereign's right to kill. Hobbes, on the other hand, would place God and family completely offstage in his imagination of political community. In his rendering, there are two kinds of contracts: the family consents to be ruled by the father, and this is their protection against the father's power to kill. The men who arise like mushrooms from the earth are, nevertheless, heads of households. In the war of men against men (read fathers) in the state of nature, the ability to enter into a social contract produces the sovereign, who gives men protection against each other. The sexed individual is recognized but placed just at the threshold of political community.

In disputing Filmer's patriarchal absolutism, Locke famously argued that God is the maker of mankind, and thus even if his power is to be read as fatherly power, it excludes all pretense that earthly fathers are the makers of their children. In the earthly register, begetting would give men and women joint dominion over their children, but since it is God who is the maker, the dominion over children does not give either parent rights over life and death. One could argue that the father is merely the placeholder, a name in Locke, as argued by Severance,[22] but the slippage between the father as the biological begetter and the father as the symbolic placeholder for the Law does not vanish.

Once the individual is recognized as social because he is sexed, he is also recognized as mortal. In Rousseau, we saw that man is said to receive life from the sovereign. Political community as a population is dependent on reproduction, but the citizen's investment of affect in the political community is attested by his desire to reproduce and to give the political community legitimate, "natural" children. A corollary is that immigration is not an authentic way to augment population—and further that a woman's infidelity is an offense not only against the family but also against the sovereignty of the state. After biblical time is replaced by secular time, the entire course of the history of the family is arranged around the certainty of paternity, on which institutions of private property and the state are made to rest.

Within this particular field of forces, we can see now that colonial encounters would pose significant questions about the relation between family and state. Since the political community becomes dispersed and pluralized under colonialism, the person has to be seen as situated in a socially and legally constituted community, with possibilities of changing his or her religion. Conversion, then, opens up the space for imagining bodies as legally and socially constituted even at the moment when bare life is being asserted, as in cases where writs of habeas corpus are brought before courts. Family cannot be left offstage in imaginings of the political, but fathers now cannot be seen as either embodying or representing law. The rights of husbands or fathers over children or wives have to be ascertained in the face of the astounding possibility that religion cuts through and divides family rather than uniting it. What nature is under these circumstances has to be built block-by-block on dispersed sites.

I cannot resist quoting from a detailed exposition of the matter in another case adjudicated by Justice Perry in 1852, in which a Hindu man who converted to Christianity applied for a habeas corpus to bring up "the body of his wife," who had left him after his conversion. In the words of the learned Justice: "In all these cases of conflicting personal rights, wherein social interests and different religious persuasions so strongly combine to call the most potent feelings of our nature into operation, and thus to cloud the judgment . . . there is one simple clue for ascertaining what the dictates of justice require, which I always employ myself, and which may possibly be found useful to others. I always ask myself, what the sound decision would appear to me to be if my own case had to be presented to a Hindu or Mussalman Judge."[23]

Asad's major theoretical concern—showing how subjects are constituted within the realm of the secular—rightly addresses the place of nature in imagining the human. However, instead of proposing a simple opposition between the sacred and the secular, the private and the public, the sexual contract and the social contract, it invites us to see the problematic relation between the state and the family. Since the sovereign, within the regime of the secular, is seen to give life to the political community and to receive life from it, the father becomes the key figure in establishing the grounds for the social in the political. Asad's book has opened up for me the entire issue of the duality of the individual with regard to the constant struggle to reimagine nature in the context of Western theories of liberalism. In working through his essays, I came to understand why certain types of family—e.g., the African American family—were considered problematic within American culture, because of their supposed lack of strong paternal figures, as stated in the famous Moynihan report.[24] I also began to understand the problematic character of white paternity with regard to interracial sexual unions. I am aware that I have not been able to tie all the threads of my argument together, but I now see that the story of the secular is much more enmeshed within the theological imagination than I had thought. I look forward to taking this conversation further.

7

On General and Divine Economy:
Talal Asad's Genealogy of the Secular
and Emmanuel Levinas's Critique of
Capitalism, Colonialism, and Money

Hent de Vries

In recent years, we have seen increasing attention to the importance, the incredible opportunities, and the considerable downsides of globalization, global capital, and new technological media, and at the same time an unexpected, increasingly unpredictable return of religions—indeed, a turn to the religious—as a political factor of worldwide, indeed global, significance. The result seems to be an ever more globalized and, I will suggest, "global" concern with "religion"—one that is dislocated, mediated, mediatized, virtualized, yet also deprivatized or politicized, and whose implications and consequences extend well beyond the assumptions concerning differentiation, disenchantment, and rationalization held by most theories of modernization, which until recently remained unquestioned. Such "global religion" seems at least in part inaccessible to established empiricist scholarly approaches, which seek to explain this renewed—and oftentimes quite novel—presence of "religion" in terms of a turn to given imagined communal commitments or values and hence tend to privilege "local"—that is to say, national, ethnic, or otherwise identitarian—contexts of origin, including diverse forms of authority, legitimacy, and so on. By and large, these approaches, which have typified both contemporary religious studies and even the more classical modern approaches to confessional theology (including those of the progressivist-emancipatory variety, as in the liberation and so-called genitive theologies), leave in place an all too naïve and often downright essentialist—or, which comes down to the same, historicist, sociologistic, psychologistic, and, more recently, culturalist—definition and understanding of their referent, "religion." The recent collection entitled *Global Religions* (in the plural) and edited by Mark Juergensmeyer, seems an exception to the rule. It seeks to "think globally about religion," queries "religion in a global age" and "in global perspective," investigates "the global future of religion," the "global resurgence of religion," "the global religious scene," and, against this background, discusses also the implications of an opposed tendency, namely that of "antiglobal religion." But this book does not theorize the structural features of "globality" and "the religious" that interest me here and instead presents itself as a guide to understanding "the state of *worldwide* religion in the twenty-first century," while emphasizing the diversity—indeed, plurality—of religions even (or especially?) today. It seem to shun the temptations of generalization and abstraction by organizing its chapters into sections devoted to three major monotheisms (Christianity, Judaism, and Islam), Hinduism, and Buddhism, adding two chapters, "African Religion" and "Local Religious Societies."

Yet, the return of "religions" and "the religious" on a "global" scale could, perhaps, be philosophically approached quite otherwise—along with the apparent simultaneous *emptying out* of the concept, if not the practice, of "religion" (its increasing formalization and apparent universalization, but also its reification and even commodification). Such a change of perspective can, I believe, provide insight into the more protracted yet highly volatile process of what emerges as an ongoing and ever increasing profanization, by contrast to previous notions of an undisturbed and fairly linear narrative of secularization. Even more than the concept of secularization, this category of an observed no less than professed profanization—like all idolatry, blasphemy, fetishization, superstition, and kitsch, including the critique that accompanies them—remains irrevocably tied to the very tradition it tends (or intentionally seeks) to subvert or substitute for once and for all, according to a logic and dynamic whose workings and effects we have hardly begun to understand. Here contemporary philosophy, in "solidarity with metaphysics at the very moment of its downfall," as Adorno diagnosed the task of thinking today, still has important contributions to make, even though it cannot make them alone. In order for such philosophical thinking to—quite literally—*work out* its concepts, that is to say, give them the material or, if you like, materialist (I am not saying: naturalist) grounding, as well as sufficient leeway to fit nonidentical contexts, it must engage with and learn from the very same disciplines (history and anthropology, political science and economy, studies of new media and recent biology) whose conceptual schemes it begins by pointing out.

In what follows, I will turn to some of the most telling analyses of these questions available in contemporary philosophy and anthropology in order to illustrate where such philosophical inquiry might lead us. The result is not so much a formal (a priori and transcendental) analysis or reconstruction of religion, let alone its essence, "as such," nor an apologetic (and by definition dogmatic) justification of any of its historical truth claims but, I would suggest with an ironic appreciation of one of Theodor W. Adorno's central intuitions, a *minimal* theology at most. But what could this mean? And how does such theological *minimalism* pair with the supposed *globalism* and, indeed, *globality* of its object or reference, that is to say, of "religion," the religiosity of religions and, perhaps, not of religions alone? In what sense might "the secular," "secularization," and "secularism"—religion's antipode and mirror image, as Talal Asad reminds us—be said to obey the same logic?

The task of answering these questions is enormous, not least because whenever we speak of what Derrida, in "Faith and Knowledge," calls this "single word, the clearest and most obscure: religion," we "act as if we had some common sense of what 'religion' means through languages that we believe . . . we know how to speak." Indeed, Derrida goes on to say:

We believe in the *minimal* trustworthiness of this word. Like Heidegger, concerning what he calls the *Faktum* of the vocabulary of being (at the beginning of *Sein und Zeit*), we believe (or believe it is obligatory to believe) that we pre-understand the meaning of this word, if only to be able to question and in order to interrogate ourselves on this subject. Well, nothing is less pre-assured than such a *Faktum* . . . and the entire question of religion comes down, *perhaps*, to this lack of assurance.[1]

In the opening chapters of *Genealogies of Religion* as well in his critical review of Cantwell Smith's *The Meaning and the End of Religion*, Talal Asad has convincingly demonstrated that such (partly linguistic or terminological and etymological, partly ontological and existential) uncertainty extends to the scholarly definition of "religion"—and hence to the very epistemology of the field of religious studies and anthropology—as well. Moreover, the same would hold true for its counterpart, its shadow concept, of the secular in its distinction of and intrinsic relation with the process of secularization and the societal project of secularism, which form the central themes of *Formations of the Secular*. This constellation would imply two central assumptions: first, that modernity "is neither a totally coherent object nor a clearly bounded one, and that many of its elements originate in relations with the histories of peoples outside Europe";[2] second, that the same project of modernity is "not primarily a matter of cognizing the real but of living-in-the-world," and since, Asad immediately adds, "this is true of every epoch, what is distinctive about modernity *as a historical epoch* includes modernity as a political-economic project."[3] Indeed, the latter reveals itself as intrinsically "related to the secular as an ontology and an epistemology."[4] These philosophical—or, in Wittgenstein's sense, "grammatical"—questions would be central to anthropology, that is to say, "the discipline that has sought to understand the strangeness of the non-European world," and that seeks to capture the meaning and effect of "religion" not least by way of a genealogy of the formations of its "other," namely the "modern" and the "secular."[5]

It would be naïve, Asad suggests, to assume that "today," after the Cold War, "no single struggle spans the globe," and to believe that the last "universal historical teleology" could be attributed "solely to a defeated Communism." We should not disregard, Asad continues, "U.S. attempts to promote a single social model over the globe": "If this project has not been entirely successful on a global scale—if its result is more often further instability than homogeneity—it is certainly not because those in a position to make far-reaching decisions about the affairs of the world reject the doctrine of a single destiny—a transcendent truth?—for all countries."[6] The global aspirations of a certain politico-juridico-economic model, therefore, should not be underestimated, nor should we overlook that its intellectual-cultural conditions require a genealogical study in their own right. Hence a major premise of Asad's work: the assumption "that 'the secular' is conceptually prior to the political doctrine of 'secularism,' that over time a variety of concepts, practices, and sensibilities have come together to form 'the secular.'"⁷ With regard to the secular, secularism, and secularization, a critical anthropological genealogy—hardly a "substitute" for "social" or "real history" but "a way of working back from our present to the contingencies that have come together to give us our certainties"—would aim at "questioning its self-evident character while asserting at the same time that it nevertheless is something real."⁸ The task of anthropology thus conceived would depart from the fixation on the "research technique (participant observation) carried out in a circumscribed field," that is to say, the method of so-called fieldwork geared toward local particularities and their "thick description" (a term introduced by Gilbert Ryle and adopted by Clifford Geertz), and move (back) in the direction of Marcel Mauss's original program of a "systematic inquiry into cultural concepts."⁹ Indeed, Asad notes, such "conceptual analysis" is, in fact, "as old as philosophy": "What is distinctive about modern anthropology is the comparison of embedded concepts (representations) between societies differently located in time and space. The important thing in this comparison is not their origin (Western or non-Western), but the forms of life that articulate them, the powers they release or enable."¹⁰ Both "the secular" and the religious, Asad concludes, constitute such "embedded" notions, whose implications and varying features have lost nothing of their relevance in the present day and age.

With the term "global religion," I seek to designate the way in which, in modernity, within political liberalism and its cosmopolitan or, if one prefers, expansionist empire no less than in its economic infrastructure, religion's proper names, rituals, and institutions continue, on a globally increasing scale, to mark the present, though they do so as voided—or empty—signifiers, as mechanical gestures or petrified structures whose historical origin and meaning, contemporary function, and future role have become *virtually* unclear, irrelevant, or obsolete. The religious legacy, it would seem, has not quite ceded its place to secular terms, mundane practices, autonomous individual agency, laic-republican political formations (as was long expected). "Religion" thus retains a seemingly diminished yet abiding presence, intelligibility, even an explanatory force, not least in the socio-juridical, multicultural, transnational, and postcolonial realm—

in short, wherever the problematic of the theological-political periodically gains new prominence.

If, on this view, the religious and theological legacies can no longer master their current valence yet have not quite faded into oblivion, what use might we still have for terms such as "religion" in describing contemporary geopolitical, globalized, and globalizing trends? Why risk an even more excessive expression, "global religion," in an attempt to capture religion's continued or renewed manifestation and significance—displaced yet recited and recycled, evanescent yet ever more insistent, at once promising and pernicious? Redescription of historical "revealed" or "positive" religion—marked by the utmost respect and disrespect at once—can still, I believe, be of strategic use in bringing out some of the problems and aims that "secularism" variously sought to theorize and realize, without falling prey to its reductionist naturalism, in epistemology and method no less than in politics.

I thus offer the term "global religion" as a heuristic and, admittedly, provisional understanding in order to account for and respond to the simultaneous pluralization and, as it were, virtualization of public spheres and lifeworlds said to be taking place today, within the circulation and concentration of capital, the "informationalism" of the "network society" (as Manuel Castells would have it). This term, understood here in an emphatic as well as slightly ironic sense, seeks to capture the qualities of a dislocation and deterritorialization that increasingly characterize a terrain that has lost all fixed boundaries (such as, say, Europe or the West) and that we—for both historical and analytical, conceptual, and, perhaps, sentimental reasons—can begin to explore under the heading of "religion."

In saying this, I am not referring to some self-evident historical phenomenon, an abstract assertion about the world, but picking up on a recognizable and compelling problematic in twentieth-century European thought, one that makes itself heard, for example, in Jürgen Habermas's arguments concerning modernity. Habermas, basing himself in large part on the theory of rationalization detailed by Max Weber, keeps circling around the fact that there was something precious in modernity's "universalizing" tendencies, however violent their effects.

According to Habermas's formal pragmatic, modernity has been characterized by a "linguistification of the sacred" that comes down to what he calls a "liquefaction [*Verflüssigung*] of the basic religious consensus." Habermas holds the rationalization of worldviews to be marked by an irreversible development "in which the more purely the structures of universal religions [*Universalreligionen*] emerge, merely the kernel [*Kernbestand*] of a universalistic morality remains." That is to say, a certain globalization—an expansion, generalization, and universalization—of the religious goes hand in hand with a formalization of its historical, positive, and ontic content. He posits that in this historical process a procedure of reconstruction and quasi-transcendental reduction empties or thins out the original referents of religion, revealing its "kernel" to be morality. The result, as in Kant, is a purely moral religion, but one whose features are now naturalized, reformulated in formal—that is, no longer substantialist but interactive, indeed pragmatic—terms.

Interestingly, such transposition and translation of the religious into the secular, the profane, the exoteric, and the public constitutes at once a *purification* and *intensification* of its supposedly ultimate concern and the *trivialization* or *profanation* of religion itself: a global or globalized religion, but a merely global—that is, a minimally theological—sense of what "religion" once meant. Yet there are no historical or conceptual means for deciding whether this "secularization" does not, in the very process of minimizing religion, realize it in a more fundamental and promising way—that is to say, whether heterodoxy is not, after all, the "kernel" and final consequence of orthodoxy. Conversely, there are no historical or conceptual means for deciding whether this process—by merely repeating the same in a seemingly senseless, nonformal tautology—does not produce something radically new as well: the heterology of some undeterminable, as Derrida would say, undecidable (now religious, then nonreligious) other.

The Disorientation and De-Europeanization of the West

> Only the play of the world permits us *to think the essence* of God. In a sense that our language—and Levinas's also—accommodates poorly, the play of the world precedes God.
> —DERRIDA, *Writing and Difference*

Some of the more surprising aspects of Emmanuel Levinas's concepts of ethics, sociality, and the political can further illuminate the global trends that are all too often—and all too globally—described using such terms as "Enlightenment," "disenchantment," "secularization," "rationalization," "differentiation," "privatization," "democratization," "liberalization," and perhaps even "globalization"—that is, as tendencies whose basic premises are unambiguously and undialectically conceived and whose linear, teleological, and salutary, not to say redemptive, outcomes are taken to be all but certain.

In Levinas, as in Husserl and Heidegger—who, after Bergson, were his main sources of philosophical inspiration—we find, as Derrida has noted, a "recourse [*recours*]" to tradition—but one "which has nothing of traditionalism."[11] Even though in these authors the "entirety of philosophy is conceived on the basis of its Greek source," this does not imply an "occidentalism" or "historicism," which is to say, "relativism."[12] The reason for this has everything to do with the transcendental—if not necessarily metaphysical and ontological, phenomenological or genealogical—argument upon which such inquiry relies. In Derrida's view, the conceptual strategies of Husserl, Heidegger, Bergson, and Levinas make their mark at once from within and from beyond the tradition and the intellectual or even political history of the West and its expansion—and do so in complex, paradoxical, and aporetic ways: "The truth of philosophy does not depend upon its relation to the actuality of the Greek or European event. On the contrary, we must gain access to the Greek or European *eidos* through an irruption or a call [*appel*] whose provenance is variously determined by Husserl and Heidegger"[13]—and, we could add, still differently by Bergson and Levinas. Nonetheless, for all four thinkers, this "irruption" of the philosophical—its "Aufbruch" or "Einbruch," as Husserl calls it in *The Crisis of European Sciences and Transcendental Phenomenology*—remains the primary feature of a certain "Europe" and its "spiritual figure."[14] It would be impossible to philosophize outside the "element"[15] of the fundamental categories of Greco-European thought, even—and especially—in the most radical attempts to dislodge their hegemony.

Yet, in this very fidelity, the "archaeology" of reason such thinkers pursue "prescribes, each time, a subordination or transgression, in any event a *reduction of metaphysics*. Even though, for each, this gesture has an entirely different meaning, or at least does so apparently."[16] As we will see, in Levinas the "category of the *ethical* is not only dissociated from metaphysics but subordinated to [*ordonnée à*] something other than itself, a previous and more radical instance [*instance*]."¹⁷ Levinas's thought, even more radically than that of his teachers, summons us "to a dislocation of the Greek logos, to a dislocation of our identity, and perhaps of identity in general; it summons us to depart from the Greek site [*lieu*] and perhaps from any site in general, and to move toward what is no longer a source or a site (too welcoming to the gods), but rather an *exhalation* [*une* respiration], toward a prophetic speech already emitted not only nearer to the source than Plato or the pre-Socratics, but inside the Greek origin, close to the other of the Greek."¹⁸

Confronted by an interviewer with the question of the multiplicity of cultures, and hence the decentering and dis-orientation (literally, in his own idiom, the un-Easting, *dés-orientation*) of the West—or of Occidental rationality, as Max Weber or Habermas would prefer to say—Levinas responded, therefore, ambiguously: To be sure, he acknowledges, there are many cultures, most of which can rightfully claim to play a significant role in the "general economy of being" and whose "national literatures" contribute to the ontological pluralism and ontic "separation" without which no responsible ordering of the political beyond mythic participation in the primitive collective—and also beyond totalizing ideologies in their affinity with totalitarianism—would ever be possible. But, he insists, "It is Europe which, alongside its numerous atrocities, invented the idea of 'de-Europeanization.'" This, he concludes, ultimately "represents a victory of European generosity."¹⁹ "The European [*L'Européen*]," as the "convergence" of the tradition of Greek philosophical thought and the Bible—"Old or New Testament—but it is in the Old Testament that everything, in my opinion, is born"—would thus remain "central, in spite of all that has happened to us during this century, in spite of 'the savage mind [*pensée sauvage*].'"²⁰

Indeed, Levinas continues, Claude Lévi-Strauss's classic *La Pensée sauvage*, dedicated to the memory of Maurice Merleau-Ponty, is only able to make its point (and impact) by way of a performative contradiction of sorts:

The "Savage Mind" is a thinking that a European knew to discover, it was not the savage thinkers who discovered our thinking. There is a kind of envelopment [*une espèce d'enveloppement*] of all thinking by the European subject. Europe has many things to be reproached for, its history has been one of blood and war, but it is also the place where this blood and war have been regretted and constitute a bad conscience, a bad conscience of Europe which is also the return [*retour*] of Europe, not toward Greece, but toward the Bible . . . : man is Europe and the Bible, and all the rest can be translated from there.[21]

A little later, the incomprehension of—and impatience with—the structuralist anthropological view is repeated once more:

No, structuralism, I still do not understand today. Of course the most eminent mind of the century is Lévi-Strauss, but I do not at all see where the target of his vision is. It certainly responds, from a moral perspective, to what one calls decolonization and the end of a dominating Europe, but my reaction is primary—it is, I know, worse than primitive: can one compare the scientific intellect of Einstein with the "savage mind," whatever the complications, the complexities, that the "savage mind" may gather or accomplish?

How can a world of scientific thinking and of communication through scientific thinking be compared to it? No doubt I have not read as I should.[22]

But then, could one not arrive at a feeling of similar generosity and "comparative compassion" starting from, say, the practices and texts of Buddhism just as easily as from Western monotheism? Levinas is careful not to make exclusionary claims when he immediately adds: "For me, of course, the Bible is the model of excellence; but I say this knowing nothing of Buddhism." Like so many other of his contemporaries—like most of us today—it would thus seem that he owns his philosophical position as *his own*, from a position that is unique to him, not pretending otherwise, and in this he remains worthy of emulation.

However, for Levinas, "de-Europeanization" also has a completely different face: a contrary movement or perverse side, in a reverse transcendence that, again, finds an unexpected ally in Occidental rationalism and its technology. Indeed, the best, the better, and the worst—more precisely, the *possibility* of the best, the better, and the worst (that is, both "religion" and the deprivation of all meaning and sense, of every norm and law)—correspond in secret, troubling, and incalculable ways. This conviction constitutes the radicality and the radical modernity of Levinas's *propos*, as well as the modernism of its rhetorical strategy, its aesthetic preoccupation, its "down-to-earth morality" (indeed, economy), and so on.

Just as the relation to the other—essential, for Levinas, in the definition of religion, creation, revelation, messianism, and eschatology—protects us from the obscure realm of diffuse nondifferentiation as well as from the imperialist luminosity of organicist or mechanistic forms of historical determinism, as they culminated in the fascist and Stalinist nation-states, so an opening toward the other and toward others, to whom one cannot close one's eyes, can correct movements that are supposedly antagonistic to such determinism: libertarian atomism, anarchism, procedural liberalism, and identitarian politics. Too much relation and not enough relation are both undercut by the "relation without relation" that makes up the ethical "optics" that, in Levinas's view, defines the "religion of adults" at its deepest. It circumvents equally communal fusion, formalist theories of natural rights, and foundational fictions concerning the miraculous emergence of the social contract out of an original war of all against all.

In yet another passage, transcribed from the notes on his final lecture course, which were published as *God, Death, and Time*, Levinas speaks of

> an affinity [*convenance*] between the secularization of the idolatry that becomes ontology (i.e., the intelligibility of the cosmos, representation and presence measuring and equaling each other) and the good practical sense of men gnawed by hunger, inhabiting their houses, residing and building. Every practical relationship with the world is representation, and the world represented is economic. There is a universality of economic life that opens it to the life of being. Greece is the site of this intersection [and despite the diversity of cultures, Messer Gaster ("Sir Belly" in Rabelais's *Pantagruel*), companion to Prometheus, is the world's first master of arts]. Nothing is therefore more comprehensible than European civilization with its technologies, its science, and its atheism. In this sense, European values are absolutely exportable.[23]

But is Levinas merely repeating here the Western mid-twentieth-century commonplace that European technology helps combat hunger—an assertion that is greatly problematic both pro and con?

Two further remarks on the phrase "European values are absolutely exportable" seem in order: first, the fact that European values are "absolutely exportable" does not mean that they have value per se—only that they can be transposed in an absolute mode, can be translated in an absolute fashion. What remains, what absolves and absolutes itself, is only their *form*, their inalienable gesturing, their transcending, away from myth and idolatry, the primitivism of all participation in the totalities of groups and peoples, party and state.

Second, if Europe's—or Greece's—exemplary role in (and definition of) the general economy of being is tied to its engagement and elective affinity with science, technology, atheism, and capital, then this alliance is far from unproblematic either: "No one is mad enough to fail to recognize technology's contradictions,"[24] Levinas goes on to say. True, this acknowledgment falls short of proclaiming the "dialectic," let alone the "critique" of instrumental reason that neo-Hegelians or neo-Marxists such as Adorno and Horkheimer empirically diagnose and rhetorically exaggerate, or that the later Heidegger turned into a drama of almost (or more than) ontological proportions. In Levinas's words:

The balance of gains and losses that we habitually draw rests upon no rigorous principle of accounting. The condemnation of technology has become a comfortable rhetoric. Yet technology as secularization is destructive of pagan gods. Through it, certain gods are now dead: those gods of astrology's conjunction of the planets, the gods of destiny [*fatum*], local gods, gods of place and countryside, all the gods inhabiting consciousness and reproducing, in anguish and terror, the gods of the skies. Technology teaches us that these gods are of the world, and therefore are things, and being things they are nothing much [*pas grand chose*]. In this sense, secularizing technology figures in the progress of the human spirit. But it is not its end.[25]

Not the end, it has, again, no value in and of itself—but, in its solidarity with the iconoclasm of critical thought, it helps. Its function is limited, an insufficient but necessary condition of moral progress, if ever there was one. More carefully, since no precise "rigorous principle of accounting" can help us here, its affinity with the "religion of adults" is not causally determining but merely elective, happy coincidence.

In thus speaking of "secularizing technology," Levinas adopts a position almost diametrically opposed to that of Marx. Instead of analyzing—and deploring—the reification of human relationships having theological, godlike qualities, Levinas envisions a process of *reverse reification* in which gods, fetishes, magic, and the sacred are immobilized and turned into things, no longer able to relate to human beings or to enchant their ways. By contrast, the self that singularizes itself in being made responsible to the point of substitution for the other—to the point of suffering, testimony, and martyrdom, as Levinas says—is described as subjectivity "prior to reification," and Levinas adds: "The things we have at our disposal are in their rest as substances indifferent to themselves. The subjectivity prior to this indifference is the passivity of persecution."[26]

There is a sense, however, in which this process of reification can go into reverse, that is to say, can run amok and end up in a different form of "de-Europeanization"—one that deformalizes but this time also dehumanizes, in a contrary movement in which transcendence is perverted in a Faustian dynamic. Dialectically put, when left to themselves, Occidental rationalism, as well as Western science and technology, will almost inevitably produce their opposites and thereby contribute to their own disintegration, disqualification, and ultimate demise. The perfectibility of Western axiology (of its epistemology and the general categories of experience, perception, and action) implies rather than excludes a reversal, whose ultimate possibilities Levinas sees exemplified by the atrocities committed during the twentieth century and all other expressions "of that very same antisemitism" (his words). Referring to the testimony of Vasili Grossman's great Russian novel *Life and Fate*,[27] he speaks of the retrospective projection of the principle of "organization" and its inevitable culmination in "*de-humanization*"—from the Holy Roman Empire to Orthodox czarist Russia and Stalin, from modern Europe to Hitler—back into its earliest origins. Grossman projects the seeds of this development into the event of Christ's *speaking*: where he "*preaches*, there is already this first organization."[28] From here on, Levinas paraphrases: "There is nothing to be done!"[29]

In Levinas's view, Grossman,

outside his value as a great writer, is witness to the end of a certain Europe, the definitive end of the hope of instituting charity in the guise of a regime, the end of the socialist hope. The end of socialism, in the horror of Stalinism, is the greatest spiritual crisis in modern Europe. Marxism represented a generosity, whatever the way in which one understands the materialist doctrine which is its basis. There is in Marxism the recognition of the other [*autrui*]; there is certainly the idea that the other must himself struggle for this recognition, that the other must become egoist. But the noble hope consists in *healing everything* [tout réparer] in installing, beyond the chances of the individual charity, a regime without evil [*sans mal*]. And the regime of charity becomes Stalinism and Hitlerian horror. That's what Grossman shows, who was there, who participated in the enthusiasm of the beginnings. An absolutely overwhelming testimony and a complete despair.[30]

But then, even when carried to its extreme, this process touches as well upon something "indestructible" (as Blanchot would say)—or, in Levinas's words, on "something positive . . . modestly consoling, or marvellous."³¹ Even where the worst violence seems the sole possible consequence of the principle of "organization" as such, Grossman's novel, in its history of the "decomposition of Europe" in the camps, succeeds in presenting a "fable" of acts of "small goodness [*la petite bonté*]"³² that are not completely vanquished. Levinas speaks of a "*justice behind justice*" that, not least in a "liberal State," one "*must* [il faut]" take into account: "goodness [*la bonté*] without regime, the miracle of goodness, the only thing that remains,"³³ appearing in "certain isolated acts," "exterior to all system,"³⁴ alone. This, then, would be the "terrible lucidity" in Grossman's *Life and Fate*: "There isn't any solution to the human drama by a change of regime, no system of salvation [*salut*]. The only thing that remains is individual goodness, from man to man [*d'homme à homme*]. . . . Ethics without ethical system."³⁵ Or, as Levinas formulates it in another interview: "The essential thing in this book is simply what the character Ikonnikov says—'There is neither God nor the Good, but there is goodness'—which is also my thesis. That is all that is left to mankind." There are acts of goodness that are absolutely gratuitous, unforeseen. "There are acts of stupid, senseless goodness. . . . The human pierces the crust of being. Only an idiot can believe in this goodness."³⁶ And the protagonist of Dostoyevsky's *The Idiot* exemplifies nothing else. Levinas continues: "Grossman writes that all organization is already ideology. When Christ begins to preach, there is already the Church, and with the Church the whole organization of the good. The opposition of Ikonnikov to Christianity is not directed against this or that part of the teaching of Christ, but against the history of Christianity and of the Church with all the horrors it allows."³⁷

Grossman, Levinas summarizes,

thinks that the little act of goodness [*la petite bonté*] from one person to his neighbor is lost and deformed as soon it seeks organization and universality and system, as soon as it opts for doctrine, a treatise of politics and theology, a party, a state, and even a church. Yet it remains the sole refuge of the good in being. Unbeaten, it undergoes the violence of evil, which, as little goodness, it can neither vanquish nor drive out. The little goodness going only from man to man, not crossing distances to get to the places where events and forces unfold! A remarkable utopia of the good or the secret of its beyond.³⁸

Capital Revisited

> Essence ... works as an invincible persistence in essence, filling up every interval of nothingness which would interrupt its exercise. *Esse* is *interesse*; essence interest. This being interested does not appear only to the mind surprised by the relativity of its negation, and to the man resigned to the meaninglessness of his death; it is not reducible to just this refutation of negativity. It is confirmed positively to be the *conatus* of beings. And what else can positivity mean but this *conatus*? Being's interest takes dramatic form in egoisms struggling with one another, each against all, in the multiplicity of allergic egoisms which are with one another and are thus together. War is the deed or the drama of the essence's interest. ... Does not essence revert into its other by peace, in which reason, which suspend the immediate clash of beings, reigns? Beings become patient, and renounce the allergic intolerance of their persistence in being; do they not then dramatize the *otherwise than being*? But this rational peace, a patience and length of time, is calculation, mediation, and politics. The struggle of each against all becomes exchange and commerce. ... Commerce is better than war.
>
> —LEVINAS, *Otherwise than Being*

The example of money (as opposed to economy, a term Levinas uses in a somewhat idiosyncratic, etymological, and almost Bataillean way) can help clarify this point. On several occasions, most directly in an invited (and thus far untranslated) lecture given to the collected Belgian national banks (the *Groupement Belge des Banques d'Epargne*) in 1986 and entitled "Socialité et argent [Sociality and Money]," Levinas sets out two seemingly contradictory viewpoints. Speaking of the "institution" of money in its "empirical" nature and "planet-wide extension," which it has derived from the "sciences and technologies of the European genius,"[39] Levinas asserts, this time following a basic thesis of Marx's *Capital*, that money is "the universal equivalent" mediating natural and acquired needs, objects, goods, services, and, last but not least, persons. He adds the insight that this equivalence—like technology—rids the world of false equivocities in which selves are drawn into diffuse totalities (in Levinas's words, "mythical" and "primitive" ones), into realms of otherness not yet severed by acts of divine creation and ontological (that is to say, Greek) separation.

By contrast, he also puts forward the view that equivalences—hence a fortiori the universal equivalent of global capital, money—equalize the unequal, undo the differentiation of what is different, and, in short, repress and violate the other, who (or that?) has neither use value nor exchange value but in his (or its?) uniqueness regards me uniquely. Hence, for Levinas, a first important axiom, an "axiology of saintliness" or "gratuity"—and, ultimately, of offering and sacrifice—is that the other is not for sale, not exchangeable in any currency, irreducible to and unrecognizable by any measure of comparison. The relative and limited separation and hence transcendence that economy—precisely as a "community of genre"—invests in the general economy of being is, in the end, to be distinguished from (and is dependent upon) the relationship between two unique instances (the self and the other, the other and the other), which is an "extraordinary ontological event of dis-interestedness"[40] irreducible to any economy: an anomaly of "expenditure" in the general economy of being whose dominant principle, the *conatus essendi*, the perseverance of all beings in their being (to cite Spinoza), it divests of its ontological value. Hence also the limitation of the universal principle and form of equivalence, the minimal margin—the internal and external others figured by the widow, the orphan, the stranger, the poor, the "proletarian"—from whose perspective capital and capitalism, like history in its finiteness and totality, can be criticized, indeed *judged*, at every instant long before having run its course.

Yet in this insertion of the "value of saintliness" and "gratuity" into the circulation of goods, services, things, and people, the value of equivalence—that is to say, of money—reasserts its place and function: "All the values of interest regain their signification at a higher level, that of dis-interestedness, in giving [*le donner*]. Conversion [*retournement*] of interest into dis-interestedness in the realm [or in view] of transcendence."[41] Conversely, there is a sense in which justice—the comparison between unique others—requires of the "spontaneity" and "totality of dis-interestedness" (a surprising formulation) what Levinas calls "a first violence" and "first injustice"[42]—in other words, a "necessity in justice to come back to economy."[43] This (ontological? logical? axiological? theological?) "necessity" to respond to two different and even contradictory requirements—"the ambiguity of persons *at once* submitted to an axiology exterior to that of need *and* integrated in the economy as market value"[44]—would impose an intrinsic "limit" upon all "charity," the "necessity of a sharing and splitting [*partage*]" of justice that would be "justified" and "the very structure of spirituality itself."[45] Paradoxically, justice—doing justice to more than one other—carries itself out "against the integral inequality of the devotion [*devouement*]"[46] that characterizes the relationship between the self and one other, without whose corrective asymmetry all symmetry would become total, totalizing, and totalitarian. By the same token, the "totality of dis-interestedness," in its "integrality" and hence integrity could not stand on its own and requires a "return to knowledge, research, inquiry, organization, a return also of institutions that will come to judge and thereby the return to a political life," to the "good" or "best" politics (*la bonne politique*).[47] Last but not least, this referral back to a certain economy—in the restricted sense—requires a return of "money, to be administered for the other," as well as the "homogeneity of everything that has a value and thus to a justice that remains a just calculation [*un juste calcul*]," in short: the "State."[48] This, Levinas says, occurs whenever there is a third person and, "beginning with the third, who is not third but a billion [*qui n'est pas tiers mais qui est milliard*]—the whole of humanity."[49]

Yet even the most just state ought to "recognize what is already lost in the relation to the compassion [*miséricorde*] and spontaneity of charity in [the process of] calculation."[50] For the state to recognize the discrepancy of this primary and inevitable—empirical and transcendental—violence is to acknowledge that "the universal rule of justice it discovers [is] not definitive," that there are always other possibilities that "approach more" the "first spontaneity" of the face-to-face.[51] The "liberal State" would be the state that "admits the reprisal [*la reprise*], the possibility of changing existing laws, of finding in human inspiration and in the future of the human [*de l'humain*] a better justice."[52] Implied in this, Levinas says, would be the insight that the "idea of charity" cannot be fully "exhausted [or satisfied, *satisfaite*]" by "justice."[53] Insisting on this irreducible discrepancy, Levinas continues, would mark the distinction between "public justice" and the "temptation to construct *a-regime-of-justice* [un-régime-de-justice]" that would be "definitive."[54] This was the temptation of Stalinism, as well as all other regimes that are premised on "*not allowing* [laisser] *justice in its permanent renewal* [dans son permanent renouvellement]."[55] The difference between the Greek polis, the totalitarian "regime," and the liberal state would thus be a certain relaxation of the "rigor," "deduction," and "administration" of justice, precisely because justice, in political liberalism, is "not complete."[56] The biblical examples of kings criticized by prophets who, being "*just*," put into question the "just political act" and, in that respect, are echoed in the presence of "love in Marxism [il y a de l'amour dans le marxisme],"[57] testify to this.

A poignant example of this "love" and, indeed, its metaphysical, that is to say, anti-ontological and antinaturalist, implications Levinas views in the protests of the "youth" who marched in the streets of Paris and elsewhere in late 1960s and early 1970s:

> It is interesting to note the dominance, among the most imperative "sentiments" of May 1968, of the refusal of a humanity defined by its satisfaction, by its receipts and expenditures, and not by its vulnerability more passive than all passivity; its debt to the other. What was contested, beyond capitalism and exploitation, was their conditions: the individual taken as accumulation in being, by honors, titles, professional competence—ontological tumefaction weighing so heavily on others as to crush them, instituting a hierarchical society that maintains itself beyond the necessities of consumption and that no religious breath could make more egalitarian. Behind the capital in *having* weighed a capital in *being*.[58]

But then, the very same contested state—and the same movement of the money of interest to this money's dis-interested use for the other, *and back*—could help to mediate and mitigate problems and relationships, not of possession or dispossession but of "irreparable," even unspeakable "crime."[59] In the means that money and the state provide, we could find a "possibility of overcoming violence" by way of another "pay-back [*rachat*]" than that of "death itself."[60] With this "bloodless redemption," Levinas goes on to suggest, money could "substitute for the infernal or vicious circle of vengeance and universal pardon, which always constitutes an inequality with regard to the third" and an "encouragement to crime and, consequently, a possibility to be feared by the third."[61] For all the justice that one might attribute to the biblical prophet Amos, in his condemnation of treating the other as merchandise (see Amos 2:6, as well as its echo in the *Communist Manifesto*)[62] there lies an even greater justice—and, perhaps, Levinas writes, an element of "charity"—in seeking in pecuniary retribution for the in fact (and in principle) "incomparable crime" another way out of the dilemma between the "impunity of pardon" and the "cruelty of revenge."[63]

Here we would confront the "necessity to compare, to compare the incomparable, to introduce calculation and, in consequence, all the rest"; here, moreover, "the whole of Greece is present [*toute la Grèce est là*]. Aristotle already speaks of all this."⁶⁴ But neither Aristotle's *Nichomachean Ethics* (cf. Book IV, chapter 1) nor the whole of Greece provides any understanding of the "modality" under which this *comparative compassion* (miséricorde) can—indeed, must and ought to—become truly "universal."⁶⁵ Here, Levinas suggests, following a classical and modern—in fact, almost Hegelian topos—the contribution of the great monotheisms of the West remains essential.

Toward a Critique of Political Idolatry

I have been drawing on an author (Levinas) and on commentators (Derrida, in particular) in the fields that I know best, but I trust that despite this inevitable limitation my remarks will speak to the central problem and questions that concern Talal Asad's multifaceted and profound genealogies of the formation of "religion" and "the secular."

Levinas's thought distinguishes itself from any form of rationalization of religious salvation or even any hermeneutics of faith. Indeed, "to be Jewish," in Levinas's view, is "not a particularity; it is a modality," to which he provocatively adds: "Everyone is a little bit Jewish, and if there are men on Mars, one will find Jews among them. Moreover, Jews are people who doubt themselves, who in a certain sense, belong to a religion of unbelievers"; more specifically, Levinas refers to the passage in which "God says to Joshua, 'I will not abandon you' [and, in the subsequent phrase]: 'nor will I let you escape,'"⁶⁶ thus evoking the possibility of a dwelling in contradiction that is not merely a paralyzing double bind—easy though it would be to read God's words to Joshua thus. Dwelling in contradiction—this and nothing else is the "modality" of the spiritual life, the religion of adults, beyond myth and participation, "primitive" fusion and overrationalized totality, in its differentiation, privatization, and the like. Nothing more—and nothing less—than an inflection of the intersubjective, public, and political realm, "religion" (in its very concept and, increasingly, its practice) would not so much designate a set of beliefs and prohibitions, imageries and hopes, but the destructuring movement, always and everywhere to be found, away from identity (whether semantic, propositional, political, or national).

What use, then, could we have for such a formal—a global—definition of religion in terms of its "modality"? How should we evaluate this *generalization* and *universalization* of "religion," of its concept and practice, into meaning nothing more or less than the structuring and dislocation—the "curvature"—of what Levinas, following Durkheim, calls "social space"? Doesn't this stretching and emptying out of the concept entail a *trivialization* of its historical meaning and its axiological weight? Yet such a substitution of "religion" for almost every relationship between humans—and, ultimately, between them and anything else, repeating the term, if not all of its connotations, if not for the infinite's sake then at least ad infinitum and ad absurdum—also, paradoxically, *intensifies* "religion" as well. For good and for ill. Only the turn—and repeated return—to religion would prepare the possibility of its eventual demise. For good and for ill.

Levinas is, I have been suggesting, a case in point. His de-essentializing and detranscendentalizing concepts and arguments, couched in a rhetorical language punctuated by figures of speech that can sometimes be maddening, go hand in hand with an attempt to concretize and hence, as he says, deformalize the various themes of "religion" (such as creation, revelation, messianism, and eschatology). Yet in the process the central referent—religion itself—remains *unconquered, unoccupied.* The result is what, to borrow a term from Raymond Aron,[67] I would like to call a critique of the idolatry of (political) history, indeed, of political economy, which does not allow its rationale and objective to be fixed in any determinate way, which resists context and identity, and which enhances our hospitality with respect to otherness and strangeness, both within and without.

Talal Asad seems to envision a similar task for anthropological critique as it emancipates itself from an all too unmediated—"pseudo-scientific"—conception of fieldwork and local knowledge and moves in the direction of an "epistemology" or even "ontology" of "religion" in its relation to the broader historical category of "the secular" and its differentiated yet overlapping practices and forms of life. His emphasis on a more "complex space" and "complex time" (adopting and expanding on a terminology introduced by John Milbank), that is to say, of "embodied practices rooted in multiple traditions" and "simultaneous temporalities" implying "more than a simple process of secular time," seem to come close to what Levinas—not accidentally taking his first intellectual leads from Durkheim and Lévy-Bruehl—ultimately chooses to articulate with the help of the phenomenological idiom that he helped introduce into the French philosophical debate. Do the notions of "complex space" and time, on the one hand, and the "curvature of social space" convey a similar insight in the structuring and destructuring of culture and economy, of justice and the law? Does Levinas's singular evocation of exteriority and transcendence, of intersubjectivity and disinterestedness let themselves be mapped on Asad's use of Wittgenstein's categories of "grammar," "practices," and "forms of life"? Perhaps not. But the "systematic inquiry into cultural concepts" introduced in modern anthropology by Mauss and the conceptual—Levinas will say, intentional—analysis proper to philosophy from its earliest beginnings to twentieth-century phenomenological, existential, and hermeneutic phenomenology nonetheless yield a similar result: a *complementary* interrogation of the historical and structural relationship and, indeed, co-implication of the religious of the secular, of seemingly singular identities and the sociality imposed or enabled by the universal equivalent. Money and whatever comes to take its place would form only the most significant example of this more general economy—the "play of the world"—whose enabling and disabling function reveals the divine for what it is, must and can be.

8

The Tragic Sensibility of Talal Asad

David Scott

The ethics of passionate necessity encompasses tragedy.

Talal Asad, whose poignantly paradoxical remark this is, is a *tragic* theorist.[1] I do not mean by this, of course, that he is a theorist of tragedy per se, that is, a theorist of tragic drama (although we will shortly see in him a discerning reader of Sophocles' *Oedipus*) or of the *idea* of tragedy. I mean rather that he is a thinker with a tragic *sensibility*. Asad is a thinker responsive to the tragic in human life, to the antagonism between our determined will and the varied contingencies that often thwart and sometimes reverse it, our propensity to the sorts of moral conflict that lead toward disappointment, suffering, and even catastrophe. A rueful gray colors his mind's activity. Asad's thinking about history and human action, and about human action as our mode of being *in* history, is alert to the frailties and opacities that make us less than the self-sufficient reasoners we suppose ourselves to be, and that expose us to aspects of ourselves and our worlds over which we have little or no rational control. In this sense he practices a discerning and respectful—yet at the same time unsentimental—attunement to the scripts already written for us by the accumulated histories in which we find ourselves: the palpable volume and the unrelievable weight that are the signatures of our unrequited historical burden. In short, I believe Asad's is an intellectual ethos appreciative of the "passionate necessity" to which our human life is subject and by which it is often propelled, and through which we make up, as best we can, the dramatic projects of our lives.

I want to consider some aspects of Asad's tragic sensibility and its implications for his thought—and for ours. His tragic sense, I think, is the leaven that binds together several dimensions of his work over the past decade or so, on historical change and modernity, on agency and moral action, on the body and its dispositions, on genealogy and tradition—in many ways the larger ideas that form the intellectual context and conceptual horizon of his specific arguments about religion and the secular. His tragic sensibility, further, is a sensibility for our time. For ours, I judge, is a damaged time in which the once familiar temporalities of past-present-future that provided the historical reason for our ideas about change (change-as-succession, for example, or change-as-*revolutionary*-succession) no longer line up quite so conveniently, so progressively, so administratively, as they once did; the present no longer appears as the tidy dialectical negation of an unwanted, oppressive past awaiting its own overcoming in a bright and busy Hegelian future. Inerasable residues from the past stick to the hinges of the temporality we have come to rely on to secure our way, and consequently time is not quite as yielding as we have grown to expect it to be. Perhaps, then, a tragic sensibility is a timely one. And if so, it may be wise—if unfashionable—to attend more patiently, more searchingly, more modestly, to the intractable, the contingent, the ordinary, the remainder, and even the malignant, to which our lives are persistently, and sometimes inescapably, exposed.

Part of my overall preoccupation here, I should say, is to try to gain some measure of Asad's work as a mode of moral and social inquiry into our present. I sometimes feel, in this regard, that Asad has been often misread, or certainly *too quickly* read, into the neat classifications that drive the currents of contemporary oppositional scholarship. His identification, of course, is with the Left—a good deal of his work (from the 1970s through the early 1980s) has constituted a sympathetic internal dialogue with Marxism, especially around the problem of ideology. Needless to say, he has never been comfortable with Marxism's Laws-of-History mentality, nor with the high-minded and secularist rationalisms that have often informed its views of the ordinary and religion, but he has remained faithful to what he takes to be Marx's lasting insight, namely, that domination need not depend upon either coercion or consent. It is insufficiently recognized or appreciated, I think, that Asad's interest in religion does not grow out of an a priori view of the privilege of the religious, but rather out of a larger concern with understanding the way authority *binds* practice toward certain ends—virtues—without recourse to brute force or reflexive reason.

Similarly, his identification has been postcolonial and poststructuralist, to name two more recent trends of social critique to which he has contributed. But his criticisms of the European Enlightenment, and the modern West it has helped to give rise to, have not always conformed to the standard formulations, or indeed the standard aspirations. They have, for example, rarely if ever been informed by anti-essentialism's counter-rationalism, that is to say, its *theoreticist* desire to overcome or destroy its theoretical nemesis, foundationalism. Asad obviously shares the "postie" critique of essential meanings (he has written instructively against this in anthropological theory);[2] but the inclination of his thought is antirationalist, studiously so, which is why he is drawn to the work of thinkers (philosophers of science, often) such as Thomas Kuhn, Ian Hacking, and Stephen Toulmin, and in general to more pragmatist styles of reasoning, such as the cases-and-circumstances approach of casuistry, which eschew arguing from invariant principles, however up-to-date.[3]

For these reasons too, I think, Asad often draws back from the explicit stance of the critic, at least insofar as "criticism" often suggests too much, or too sharply, a radical cutting away of everything that already exists, of *any* ground on which to stand. This, anyway, is not the *temper* of Asad's thinking. For him, as we will see, it is important—it is in fact necessary—to begin where one contingently is and with what one contingently has, with the intellectual and practical knowledges that contingently make one who one is and that enable one to see what one sees. On this view, critical inquiry has always to be *situated* inquiry, undertaken in an attitude of affirmation as well as disaffirmation. Indeed, in Asad, in some of his moods at least, there is a doubt about rational criticism *tout court*, that is to say, a doubt about the intersubjective receptiveness to cognitive persuasion that rational criticism must depend upon in order to be binding. It is not surprising, therefore, that the concept of *habitus* has attractions for him.

Moreover, the critic often appears as someone who *already* knows at least the directions in which her or his dissatisfactions *ought* to lead. This again is not Asad's mode of inquiry. His inquiries always have about them a deliberatively *exploratory* and *provisional* character. His style of investigation is that of the very tentative cartographer wandering into unmapped or incompletely mapped territories, "sketching landscapes" (to use Wittgenstein's apt metaphor) over the course of "long and involved journeyings" whose end he cannot see in advance. His work, therefore, constitutes more an inventory of outlines (or, again, to invoke Wittgenstein, an "album" of thought-pieces), than a series of monographs compiling comprehensive accounts of the way the world is *there*—or *then*.[4]

I have a modest and somewhat circumscribed objective in this essay, and to achieve it I proceed in the following way: First, I consider the question of whether and to what extent genealogy and tradition are compatible modes of moral and social inquiry. As any careful reader of his work will quickly recognize, Asad has affiliations with both, so to speak, with Michel Foucault on the one hand and Alasdair MacIntyre on the other; but he has not, so far as I can tell, given specific attention to how their seemingly antagonistic relation might be properly conceived. Pulling as they seem to do in radically different directions—one in the direction of subversion of the status quo, and the other in the direction of a respect for given modes of life—how might the tension between them be productively held together, if not entirely resolved? Second, I will have a look—an admittedly admiring look—at one very suggestive way of thinking about tragedy (Greek tragedy principally) as a mode of moral understanding that seeks to answer precisely this question. The genius of tragedy, so it might be suggested, is that it stitches together a sort of paradoxical bridge between the *discontinuities* of genealogy on the one hand, and the *continuities* of tradition on the other. And finally, third, I come back to Asad's own work and consider a brief but very suggestive discussion by him of Sophocles' *Oedipus* in the context of an inquiry into agency, pain, and responsibility. All of Asad, in a manner of speaking, is at work in a condensed form in this piece of writing, but what is most instructive to me, or what anyway I want to underline for my purposes here, is the way he finds himself working through the connections between *habitus* and tragedy to give voice to the worldly paradoxes of action and suffering he seeks to explicate.

My aim in all this, it may already be evident, is less to subject Asad's work to a mode of *fault*-finding or *lack*-finding criticism (I owe too much to his example to adopt the tendentious attitude this stance entails) than to draw out what I think is already implicitly at work in his sensibility as a moral and social thinker. But I also aim, speaking as someone who has learned to read—and above all to read *in*—his idiom of inquiry, to press him to think more self-consciously, perhaps even more systematically, than he has so far done, about some of the tensions internal to his work, in particular the tension between genealogy and tradition; and to urge him to follow out more closely than he has seemed willing to do up to now the implications for a history of the present of explicitly drafting tragedy into his thinking about agency, suffering, and history. My suspicion is that the tragic ethos of passionate necessity to which he seeks to attune our faculties is very much an ethos for our disconsolate time, and in consequence merits our respectful regard as much as our studied attention.

I

Asad, avowedly, is a genealogist. It would be easy to show the affinities between his work and Michel Foucault's. His histories are less *social* histories, tracking the movement forward from past to present of some idea or institution or practice (though he by no means disparages this kind of scholarly enterprise and indeed often relies on the scholars who engage in it),[5] and more "effective" histories in the sense now associated with Foucault's reading of Nietzsche. In his famous homage to Jean Hyppolite, it will be remembered, Foucault repudiated the search for "origins" characteristic of traditional social history, and with it the idea of interpretation understood as "the slow exposure of the meaning hidden in an origin."[6] Against this "image of a primordial truth fully adequate to itself," he commended a practice of genealogy thought of as a subversive exercise in *counter-memory*; a perspectival form of historical analysis concerned with tracing out discontinuous lines of "descent" (identifying "the accidents, the minute deviations—or conversely the complete reversals—the errors, the false appraisals, and the faulty calculations that gave birth to those things that continue to exist and have value for us"), as well as "emergence" (that is, the particular play of forces and powers that produce effects of knowledge).⁷ For genealogy, as Foucault put it, summing up, it "is no longer a question of judging the past in the name of a truth that only we can possess in the present, but of risking the destruction of the subject who seeks knowledge in the endless deployment of the will to knowledge."⁸

This is a conceptual, antihumanist, and antiprogressivist approach that Asad has brought to his doubts about the West's autobiographical knowledges—including, of course, specifically anthropological ones. Take, for example, his engagement with the problem of religion, an engagement that absorbed his scholarly preoccupations in the 1980s and led eventually to the publication of his seminal book, *Genealogies of Religion*.⁹ Notably, Asad's guiding historical questions about religion have tended *not* to be of the following sort: What is the history of this or that religious practice or institution? How are these religious rituals to be interpreted? What function does religion play in other social fields? These questions assume that we already know what "religion" is, in effect that "religion" is a transparent category of Universal History. Rather, Asad has been inclined to begin with a different complex of questions: What are the conceptual and ideological assumptions through which the modern West (and anthropology in particular) thinks about "religion"? What is the history of power through which this way of thinking has been established? And what are the ways—conceptual, institutional, ideological—in which the modern West's understanding of religion has materially altered the modes of life of the people it conquered and dominates? These are questions pitched at the problem of the *formation* of objects of anthropological inquiry. How anthropology (and the modern West of which anthropology is an integral part) makes its disciplinary object ("religion," say) has consequences for how it names, describes, and analyzes the discourses and practices it encounters in the non-European world. And therefore, to adequately understand the history of Europe's Others, it is important to critically consider the concepts and categories through which Europe's epistemological practices have sought to assimilate—and sometimes change—them.

This is, of course, why in thinking about the problem of religion Asad begins as he does with a genealogical inquiry into one very prominent contemporary anthropological attempt to produce a universal definition, that of Clifford Geertz.¹⁰ The idea that religion is essentially a symbolic system that requires interpretation ("the slow exposure," in Foucault's inimitable phrase, "of the meaning hidden in an origin") is one that has become conventional across the humanities and social sciences in the North Atlantic academy. Asad works to interrupt and unsettle this idea by showing some of the ideological and conceptual sources in the West's history (its Christian history especially) that make it up.[11] In this sense his intervention aims at demonstrating the contingent character of the present; historicizing anthropological categories in the way he does is a way of producing a contrast-effect that helps to defamiliarize (*shock*, as he might say these days) our ready assumptions about the present order of things.[12]

Asad, then, is a genealogist, and a genealogist of accomplishment and illumination. It is hardly possible to think the problem of religion (or indeed of the West or colonialism) without finding oneself confronted with Asad's questions regarding the conceptual-ideological underpinnings of our inquiry. But there is too, in Asad's work, something at odds with Foucault and genealogy, something that does not sit—or anyway, not *comfortably*—with the ethos, style, and drive of the genealogical mode of inquiry, a doubt or discomfort that draws him in the direction of Alasdair MacIntyre and the concept of a tradition. If Asad is incited by a Nietzschean skepticism regarding power's knowledges (especially *modern* power's universalist knowledges) and is ever urged in consequence to interrogate their conditions and effects, he is also prompted by a counter-preoccupation with the ways in which historical forms of life, binding experience to authority, are built up over periods of time into regularities of practice, mentality, and disposition, and into specific conceptions of the virtues, and distinctive complexes of values. This is partly why, for example, *Genealogies of Religion* (despite the dispersion its title suggests) does not take the form of a thoroughgoing deconstruction of a wide cross-section of contemporary anthropological understandings of religion, but moves on quickly to describe (or better, redescribe) aspects of two contrasting religious traditions: medieval Christianity and Islam. In Asad's work, in short, there is something of a tension—and, I think, to a degree an unexplored and *therefore* unresolved tension—between genealogy and tradition. And this bears consideration: in what sense or senses are these modes of inquiry compatible with each other? Are they, in fact, mutually antagonistic stances toward moral and social inquiry? Is there a way—a register, perhaps, a discipline, an idiom—in which they can be brought into an explicit and fertile (even if not seamlessly harmonious) dialogue?

Of course, MacIntyre himself has directly addressed the question of the relation between genealogy and tradition, and in some detail.[13] It will be helpful, therefore, to consider some of the ways in which he negotiated them and the way he understands himself to have finally settled the matter, and settled it *against* genealogy and in favor of tradition. In setting out his idea of a tradition and his case for the distinctive virtues of tradition as a mode of moral inquiry, MacIntyre draws a contrast between tradition and two other modes, namely, encyclopedia, which finds its paradigmatic embodiment in the late nineteenth-century project of the ninth edition of the *Encyclopaedia Britannica*, but which is also in many ways still the governing ethos of the twentieth-century academy; and genealogy, the exemplifications of which are to be found in the works and stances of Nietzsche, and subsequently Foucault. Not surprisingly, MacIntyre has little real sympathy for the objectivist pretensions of encyclopedia—a mode of inquiry whose "guiding presupposition" is "that substantive rationality is unitary, that there is a single, if perhaps complex, conception of what the standards and the achievements of rationality are, one which every educated person can without too much difficulty be brought to agree in acknowledging."[14] True, he does try, as he puts it, to learn its idiom "from within as a new first language" (and this in view of its continued role in the academy), but it is clear that it does not command his intellectual respect.

Genealogy, by contrast, is another matter, and MacIntyre provides a sympathetic (if selective) picture of this mode of inquiry. In his exploration of Nietzsche, MacIntyre focuses his attention on the stance of *subversion* implicit or (as often) explicit in genealogical investigations. The practice of genealogy very often appears as an attitude of writing *against*, as a fundamental act of *undoing*, as an absolute *break* with the established or conventional modes of understanding or idioms of inquiry—those of encyclopedia most emphatically. Nietzsche urged a radical *perspectivalism* that repudiated the whole conceptual and psychological foundation sustaining the view of language and reality upon which encyclopedia's moral and epistemological truth-claims rested. Truth, in Nietzsche's memorable formulation, is a mere linguistic regime, a worldly matter of metaphor and power. These illusions of truth, of course, are not inconsequential; to the contrary, they are held in place by an "unacknowledged motivation," a drive Nietzsche would call the Will-to-Power. And this purposeful blindness obscures the plurality of perspectives *from* which—and the plurality of idioms *in* which—the world can be described and understood.

While sympathetic to the deconstruction of encyclopedia's pretensions to a unified truth, however, MacIntyre has doubts about Nietzsche's radical perspectivalism. He wonders whether it doesn't, after all, undermine itself; whether it doesn't itself *in the end* cash out into a *non*perspectival theory of truth. Nietzsche's "denials of truth to Judaism, to Christianity, to Kant's philosophy, and to utilitarianism," MacIntyre argues, "do seem to have the force of unconditional and universal nonperspectival denials. And insofar as Nietzsche's affirmations are the counterpart of such denials, they too may seem to have the same kind of force. So the assertion that there are a multiplicity of perspectives as a counterpart to the denial that there is one world, 'the world,' beyond and sustaining all perspectives, may itself perhaps seem to have an ontological, nonperspectival import and status."[15] Part of the instability MacIntyre discerns in Nietzsche inheres in the unresolved relation between two distinctive voices or selves—the voice or self who offers a critical or subverting or ironical commentary from a seeming metaposition, and a voice or self who speaks out of or from *a* perspective.

One of the ways in which Nietzsche sought to negotiate (or *suppress*) this dilemma, MacIntyre argues, is by speaking through aphorisms—in *Human, All Too Human* (1878), for example, or the later *Beyond Good and Evil* (1886). The aphorism is a mode of subversive, anti-academic insight in which the serial adoption of various temporary masks allows the genealogical self enough provisionality and enough mobility to *evade* the sticky metaphysics of presence.[16] But Nietzsche is, of course, also the author of *The Genealogy of Morals* (published in 1887), a text that, however radical in argument, nevertheless bears the traces of a conventional academic exercise. Nietzsche, MacIntyre suggests, is caught in a paradoxical bind: "If his views were not in fact almost universally rejected, they could not be vindicated"; in other words, "on his account assent by those inhabiting the culture of his age could only be accorded to theories infected by distortion and illusion."[17] *The Genealogy of Morals* may be many things, MacIntyre argues, but it is hard to read it "otherwise than as one more magisterial treatise, better and more stylishly written than the books of Kant . . . but deploying arguments and appealing to sources in the same way, plainly constrained by the same standards of factual accuracy and no more obviously polemical against rival views. . . . If so, then genealogy in the course of defending itself has both relapsed and collapsed into encyclopaedia."[18]

MacIntyre may be overstating the case here, but it is clear enough that his doubts about the Nietzschean project of perspectivalist subversion are grave ones; he believes the project is fatally flawed on its *own terms* even though he is willing to concede that, at least where the *aphoristic* Nietzsche is concerned, there remain some areas of ambiguity. Nietzsche's illusiveness, the mobility of his several masks, enabled in part by his repudiation of the academy, is enough to provoke a strong *suspicion* of some metaphysics of presence, if not enough to sustain the indictment unambiguously. But this is not exactly the case with Nietzsche's best-known disciple, Michel Foucault, who after all sought to translate Nietzsche's insights into a full-blown research program housed precisely in the academy. "Nietzsche's progress was from professor to genealogist, Foucault's was from being neither to being both simultaneously."[19]

On MacIntyre's view, Foucault spoke in a less ambiguously academic voice than Nietzsche ever did; or anyway, he *increasingly* did so after what was (often accusingly) called his "structuralist" phase, from the mid-1970s onward. The temporalities that defined his later historical schemas of discipline, sexuality, and government were, if not exactly conventional, still not completely alien to the academic modes of understanding that genealogy purported to subvert. And therefore the question poses itself with more force than it did with Nietzsche: "How far can the genealogist, first in characterizing and explaining his project, to him or herself as much as to others, and later in evaluating his or her success or failure in the genealogist's own terms, avoid falling back into a nongenealogical, academic mode, difficult to discriminate from that encyclopedist's or professorial academic mode in the repudiation of which the genealogical project had its genesis and its rationale?"[20] It is a hard question, admittedly. And for MacIntyre this dilemma becomes all the more vivid in the plain, expository, and simplifying style of "that wearisome multitude of interviews" in which Foucault offered "explanations of his explanations," and in which "the academic deference evident in the questions is never rejected . . . in his answers."[21] In short, in seeking to destroy once and for all the pretensions of encyclopedia, genealogy undermined itself by suppressing the ways in which its subversive voice, like any other voice of moral inquiry, depends on standards and affiliations, continuities and groundings that make it necessarily part of something ongoing, however agonistic, argumentative, or dissonant—part of what MacIntyre calls a tradition.

For MacIntyre, the concept of a tradition offers an alternative mode of moral inquiry, one that does much of the critical work against encyclopedia that genealogy does, but also does *more*, and does it perhaps with a different overall *point*. Tradition shares, as MacIntyre says, genealogy's *diagnosis* of encyclopedia (namely that it rests on a mistaken conception of Truth), but not the grounds for it. Genealogy's grounds, remember, are (so the genealogist would say) *anti*-grounds—that is to say, they constitute the repudiation of the continuity and identity and accountability that grounds require to do the moral and epistemological work of securing claims. Genealogy contests encyclopedia's assumption of nonperspectival grounds, not to offer in its place a reconstitution of the very idea of perspectives so as to revise our understanding of grounds, but to dismiss grounds altogether as necessarily a universalizing Will-to-Power. If adherents of tradition agree with the genealogist's suspicions of encyclopaedia's claims about transcendental grounds, their overall aim is not to dismiss grounds per se, but to reformulate our understanding of them as being *internal* to traditions and as requiring investigation *on those terms*.

Against genealogy, then, tradition argues that the claim to absolute groundlessness is unsustainable. MacIntyre, remember, is not convinced that genealogy can completely do without some notion of a stable self, however surreptitious that notion may be. He sees, more in Foucault than in Nietzsche perhaps, a use of language (especially the *pronominal* use of language that pervades the interview as a genre of speaking) that inevitably presupposes some amount of metaphysical presence. Even the idea that genealogy is an emancipation from deception and self-deception, he argues, requires the identity and continuity of the self that is deceived. And this is precisely what tradition seeks more systematically to explore and complicate. Tradition brings with it a more self-conscious and a more robust conception of moral and epistemological *location* within embodied and historical contexts. In MacIntyre's well-known formulation, our life has the form of an enacted dramatic narrative, and therefore, from the point of view of tradition, "every claim has to be understood in its context as the work of someone who has made him or herself accountable by his or her utterance in some community whose history has produced a highly determinate shared set of capacities for understanding, evaluating, and responding to that utterance."²² In contrast to the seemingly infinite multiplicity of interpretive perspectives the genealogist offers, in which truth as such is ridiculed as the mere pretense of power, tradition urges the conception of a more determinately situated understanding of what *counts* as truth, and how what counts as truth is advanced, criticized, developed, debated, and perhaps even transformed from within. In this sense, tradition has far greater regard than genealogy does for the extent to which our selves are already-scripted, and consequently for the often ineradicable continuities of identity they bear.

For MacIntyre, then, tradition *defeats* genealogy. I wonder how Asad would answer this argument of MacIntyre's against Foucault's. I wonder what he takes the implications to be for his own appeals to genealogy. Can one agree with *both* MacIntyre and Nietzsche/Foucault? There is room, I think, to suggest that MacIntyre's account of Foucault is self-servingly one-sided, or anyway that Foucault's genealogy (perhaps more so than Nietzsche's) was not only subversive but also reconstructive as well, roughing out the unforeseen conditions and connections of "emergence" of hitherto unrecognized traditions. After all, this is one way of describing the volumes of his late work on the *History of Sexuality*. But still, does this satisfy MacIntyre's chief complaint, namely, that even were this a suggestive way of describing Foucault's work, it continues to be the case that the genealogical self remains an unsustainably traditionless one—a mode of critical subjectivity that does not make itself *accountable* to any community? How might Asad answer? Is his persistent location of his own work inside an explicitly *anthropological* tradition one kind of implicit reply? Or again, are there other idioms in which the tensions between genealogy and tradition might be (more explicitly) addressed? Does Asad's sense of the tragic, for example, suggest one direction in which this idea might be pursued?

II

In recent years, tragedy has emerged as a focus of inquiry in some quarters of moral, literary, and political theory. Much the more interesting instances of this work have been concerned to explore the ways in which tragedy—largely Greek tragedy—might offer resources for reorienting inquiry away from some of the constructivist shibboleths about agency and history that have become so orthodox a feature of contemporary social theory. Part of what is richly attractive about Greek tragedy—in particular, the extant tragedies of Sophocles (and of these, most especially the *Oedipus* and the *Antigone*)—for contemporary critical theory is that it suggests a sensibility subtle enough in the relevant ways to lever us out of the dead ends into which we have been led by the resolute one-sidedness of structure/agency debates that consumed so much of the 1970s and 1980s. The tragic sensibility pulls *both* against the idea of a self-sufficient subject as well as the idea of an overdetermined one; it *both* affirms the enlightened rationality of the subject's potentially transforming relation to history and doubts the assumption that the self-mastering self can ever entirely transcend the past's reach into—and hold on—the present. In short, the tragic sensibility, or at any rate the Sophoclean one, is a *paradoxical* sensibility, more both/and than either/or in its handling of social and moral quandaries.[23] There is already a good deal here, I think, in tragedy's self-understanding that Asad's ethos of engagement—his ethics of passionate necessity—would be at home in.

One political theorist whose work has sought to explore the resources of tragedy for rethinking aspects of contemporary moral and political criticism is J. Peter Euben.[24] An acute and subtle thinker, Euben is particularly helpful to consider in relation to Asad and the tension between tradition and genealogy, because one focus of his exploration of tragedy has centered precisely on its resemblance to Foucault's genealogy. Euben's starting point is to take issue with the ways in which tragedy has been positioned in relation to philosophy, in effect as *antithetical* to it. This idea, he urges, depends equally on an impoverished conception of philosophy (that is, a foundationalist, ahistorical, and antitraditional view of philosophy) and a mistaken reading of Greek tragedy (which sees it as more emotive than cognitive and more conservative than critical). Both views are unsustainable, Euben argues. In the first place, with the linguistic, pragmatic, and hermeneutic turns in Anglo-American and continental philosophy, the view of philosophy as having no connection to poetics is less convincing than it once was. In the second place, he argues, Greek tragedy was an important public institutional dimension of the democratic life of fifth-century Athens, and as such participated in the cultivation of the cognitive virtues of citizenship, fostering insight and enhancing judgment. Moreover, Euben argues that contrary to the conventional view, tragedy was neither conservative nor critical, but *both* together. Tragedy, he suggests, provided a performative occasion where the city's traditions could be, simultaneously, reflected upon, questioned, and sustained. In this view, the important point about tragedy is precisely that as a discursive and institutional form it embodied in a compelling way a distinctive capacity for ambiguity and paradox, a capacity to look in several competing directions at once—in the direction of a self-appraisive reflexivity and in the direction of an appreciation of the constitutive ground of tradition.

In developing this argument, Euben draws attention to the similarities between the work of tragedy and the work of genealogy. Tragedy and genealogy have a family resemblance, he suggests. Needless to say, Euben is well aware of Foucault's dismissive attitude toward the place of ancient Greek theater in the story of modernity. "We are much less Greek than we believe," he wrote in *Discipline and Punish*. "We are neither in the amphitheater, nor on the stage, but in the panoptic machine, invested by its effects of power."[25] Foucault's suspicion of the Greeks is of course part of his suspicion of humanism and the Enlightenment narratives about knowledge and freedom that trace their history from it. But beyond this, Euben discerns a more profound connection. Foucault's genealogical insight is Sophoclean. Like Sophocles' tragedies—the *Oedipus* and the *Antigone* perhaps most especially—Foucault's genealogical inquiries are meant to disrupt the progressivist assumptions embedded in civilizational narratives that run from "darkness and chaos to light and freedom, from disease, madness, and transgression to health, sanity, and salvation, or from monstrosity to normalcy."[26] This is because genealogy, like tragedy, plays with the given and the contingent; or, perhaps more accurately, plays with the way the latter appears as the former.

Like Foucault's genealogy, "tragedy does not present otherness as a disease to be cured but leaves the other as other. The great Sophoclean heroes and heroines remain liminal figures, saviors and polluters, touching gods and beasts at once. They do not instigate a third term in which warring principles are fully subsumed and silenced."[27] And Euben goes on: "To the degree tragedy confronted its audience with the fictive aspects of its otherwise lived past and warned of the mind's propensity for theoretical closure, it was itself a genealogical activity. But it was also a warning about genealogy's insufficiencies. The tragedians tend to portray discourses that fix, define, center, and ground us as simultaneously closing us off from other possible modes of speaking and acting and giving us place and identity."²⁸

This is why Euben sees in tragedy a way of articulating his doubts about those readings of genealogy (on the whole the most prominent ones, and to some extent MacIntyre's) that see it merely as debunking, as merely subversive, overturning, unconnected to where it is subverting *from*. As Euben has said eloquently in regard to such readings of Nietzsche, he is not sure whether "critics are attentive enough to the practical implications of what it means for 'us' to believe that we are the creators of our own purposes, values, and natures, and whether they are as appreciative of the mythopoetic Nietzsche as the deconstructive Nietzsche."²⁹ In short, part of what makes tragedy so instructive a form to think with in our time is precisely the way in which it keeps alive a paradoxical tension between genealogy and tradition. Tragedy avows the mastering desire of enlightened, problem-solving reason, but it also cautions against too one-sided an investment or confidence in it; it urges us to be cognizant of the fact that enlightened reason is often insufficient to secure us against the contingencies of nature—including our own passional natures and the mythopoetic scripts through which they are experienced and lived—and cautions us, moreover, that the drive for such security often impoverishes us in significant ways. In the view of tragedy, for readers like Euben, to act in the world *is* to expose ourselves to uncertainties over which we can have no *final* mastery.

III

That tragedy might constitute a form in which the rival practices of tradition and genealogy as modes of inquiry sustain a paradoxical relationship has not escaped Asad's implicit notice. Or anyway, there is at least one suggestive instance in which he *turns* to Greek tragedy in order to illustrate an argument that draws insights from both genealogy and tradition. I am thinking here of his essay, "Thinking about Agency and Pain," and especially of its closing section, in which he discusses the problem of "responsibility."³⁰ The essay appears in *Formations of the Secular*, the book that follows by a little over a decade the magisterial *Genealogies of Religion*. There is a sense—a rough-and-ready sense to be sure—in which these books stand to each other as genealogy does to tradition. Each, needless to say, practices *both* modes of social/moral inquiry; but, again in a rough-and-ready sense, one might be thought of as depending *more* on the critical concern to reconstructively explore different kinds of understandings, while the other is more deeply indebted to a deconstructive agenda.[31]

In the section on responsibility in "Thinking about Agency and Pain," Asad is interested, he says, in "whether intention, responsibility, and punishment are together necessary to the notion of agency with which we have become familiar in secular ethics."[32] And in this exploration he takes issue with a prominent reading of Sophocles' *Oedipus Tyrannus* in which Oedipus's actions are conceived in terms of "responsibility." The outline of that drama is familiar enough, and Asad provides only a thumbnail sketch, sufficient to bring into focus the specific issue he is going to attend to. As he briefly relates it, the tragedy of *Oedipus* depicts a profound paradox: "A story of suffering and disempowerment that is neither voluntary nor involuntary."[33] Oedipus is doubtlessly an agent inasmuch as he acts consciously and with foresight when he is set upon at the crossroads. But he does not know the terrible deed he has in fact committed, since he knows neither the true identity of the man in the chariot (Laius) nor his own (the son of Laius); and to this extent, he is not the *author* of the deed of killing his father. If Oedipus is the very embodiment of the rational actor, the problem-solving *subject of* enlightened mastery, he is also, and in a most perverse way, *subject to* circumstance and contingency that are beyond his conscious mastery. In the famous scene when he finally discovers who he is and the enormity of what he has done, he swiftly takes action: he inflicts wounds upon "the body that performed them," as Asad puts it, "the self that can neither be recognized nor repudiated."[34] Oedipus's actions are characterized by a disturbing paradox of agency.

One view of the action Oedipus takes of renouncing his kingship and exiling himself from Thebes—that is, his conscious disempowerment of himself—when he discovers the nature of his deed is that it constitutes an acknowledgment of "responsibility" for killing his father, and by this acknowledgment an affirmation of himself as a *moral* agent.[35] Asad disagrees with this view; he disagrees that the notion of "responsibility" is an appropriate one here. "If we take that notion [of responsibility] as containing the element of imputability and liability to punishment it seems to me that

Oedipus is not responsible to any authority. He does not have to answer to any court (human or divine) for his actions."[36] For Asad, *answerability* is a necessary component of the concept of responsibility. Turning to the later play, *Oedipus at Colonus*, that depicts the broken, exiled, and disempowered Oedipus about to enter into a new kind of empowerment, Asad shows that Oedipus explicitly *denies* that his transgressions were, strictly speaking, his own acts. In his memorable plea, he says: "I was attacked—I struck in self-defense./Why even if I had known what I was doing,/how could that make me guilty?"[37] As Asad suggests, it is important to see exactly what it is that Oedipus affirms and what he denies. He affirms that he caused the death of a man at a crossroads, but he denies that he murdered his father. Oedipus "recognizes himself as the owner of a responsible act (as an agent),"[38] namely the agency of a conscious act of violence, but not the one of which he is accused, that of patricide.

When Oedipus discovers what he has done, he knows he must act. This is indisputable. But in Asad's view, this is not because Oedipus either admits or claims responsibility, but because he cannot *live* with the knowledge of who he is and what he has done. Oedipus is making no appeal to a higher authority; he is in the grip of a driven, *passional* predicament in which living in a particular way has become intolerable, impossible: unbearable. It is, says Asad, *this* predicament that demands immediate resolution, and one need not have recourse to a concept of responsibility or answerability to understand its ethical significance. An altogether different kind of concept than these is needed here. In Asad's view, the nature of Oedipus's moral conduct upon discovering what he has done might more usefully be understood in terms of Marcel Mauss's idea of *habitus*, that is, "an embodied capacity that is more than physical ability in that it also includes cultivated sensibilities and passions, an orchestration of the senses."[39] The idea of *habitus*, in other words, is attuned to a dimension of ethical being and ethical conduct in which we are propelled, not by self-reflexive rejection or acceptance of the authority of a transcendent moral code (the Kantian idea) but by the active propensities, predispositions, and aptitudes of embodied sensibilities. On this view, Oedipus inflicted pain upon himself not because he judged himself responsible and therefore to be punished, "but as a passionate performance of an embodied ethical sensibility. Oedipus suffers not because he is guilty but because he is virtuous."[40] Oedipus does not do what he might, but what he *must*: he "puts out his own eyes not because his conscience or his god considers that he deserves to be punished for failing to be responsible—or because he thinks he does—but because (as he says) he cannot bear the thought of having to look his father and his mother in the eyes when he joins them beyond the grave, or see his children, 'begotten as they were begotten.' He acts as he does necessarily, out of the passion that is his *habitus*."[41]

For Asad, then, Oedipus's agency and his *habitus* are not counterposed to each other, as though his agency were to be understood as the overcoming of constraint. To the contrary, his habitus traces the outline of the plot in which his agency is constituted and unfolds, and in which he is able to choose among the range of possibilities that are recognized as options. With the idea of *habitus*, in other words, Asad is reaching after a concept in which action is not simply the result or realization of the conscious, reflexive intention of a unified subject. Secular ethics (and in many ways, as MacIntyre suggests, modern secular ethics *is* Kantian ethics) demands a conception of action and responsibility in which a rational agent is understood as antecedent to any particular shaping experience and therefore prior to its ends. The deontological self, morally and foundationally, is a free chooser between ends.[42] It is this fundamental capacity to exercise reason unencumbered by the ineluctable incursions of contingency and unmolested by irreversible passions that marks the agent as fully autonomous.

Asad rejects this flight from heteronomy. This is why, as he says, tragedy, like pain, "may be actively lived as a necessary form of life, one that no amount of social reform and individual therapy can eliminate forever. The tragedy of Oedipus does not illustrate 'how institutions may paralyze action,' as Feyerabend and others have put it. It shows how the past—whether secular or religious—constitutes agency. An 'impossible choice' is a choice between terrible alternatives that have been pre-scripted for one—but it is still possible to choose, and to act on that choice."[43] The concept of *habitus* therefore invites us to honor the tragic inasmuch it urges us to be responsive to the intractable ways in which the past lives on in the present and is not merely escapable by an act of conscious decision or reflexive reason.

IV

A good deal of contemporary moral, social, political, and cultural criticism is *anti*-tragic in the sense that it is driven by an appeal to an agent who, with conscious intention, and by resisting or overcoming the constraints of *habitus*, makes history. There is a familiar and not irrelevant critical humanism attached to this confidence (or confident hope) in the conscious agency of the human subject resisting dominant power, tilting heroically against the grain of the given. In the best formulations—or anyway the ones that solicit our most sympathetic consideration and sometimes even our solidarity—this humanism is articulated in the outline of a subaltern subject who, in however small and barely visible ways, contributes to remaking her or his own world from below. The conception of this history-making agent is sustained by the familiar constructivist picture of a thin or deontological self whose relation to the past is a purely instrumental or utilitarian or contingent one. In the mythos of the West, the story-form of this drama of being human is Romance. But this story-form derives its point in large measure from the assumption of an imagined horizon of emancipation toward which the subaltern subject strives. The past is there to be overcome on the way to a preconstituted future. It seems to me, however, that ours is a time in which such an imagined horizon is harder and harder to sustain; the hoped-for futures that inspired and gave shape to the expectation of emancipation are now themselves in ruin; in Reinhart Koselleck's grim but still felicitous phrase, they are futures past.[44]

This is why a tragic sensibility is a timely one. It is not by any means that a sense of the tragic is bereft of moral and political hope or unmoved by the sufferings that spur the desire for emancipation. But the tragic sense doubts the romantic humanist story that carries that hope forward on a progressive teleological rhythm: Dark at length giving way to Light, Evil to Good. The tragic sensibility is more cognizant of the historical disruption in the temporalities that gave the longing for emancipation its philosophical as well as its political drive, that generated the end at the beginning. In tragedy, past, present, and future are not sequential successive moments in an epic or dialectical trajectory. They do not align themselves neatly, as though history were heading somewhere—from Despair to Triumph, from Bondage to Freedom—as though the past could be banished by an act of heroic agency. The past may not go away so easily. A tragic sensibility is more attuned to (is more respectful of) the myriad ways in which we carry our pasts within ourselves as the not-always-legible scripts of our *habitus*. In contrast to the constructivist (indeed too, as we have seen, the genealogical) emphasis on the self as little more than a series of invented—and therefore chooseable, replaceable—masks behind which lies an echoless metaphysical vacancy, the tragic sensibility is poignantly aware of the ineradicable metaphysical traces that connect us to what we leave behind—to the leavings that stick to the soles of our various departures.

It is in this foreboding sense of the often chanciness of life, I believe, the restless doubt about the possibility or desirability of self-mastery, that the force of Asad's mode of reasoning is felt, drawing us away from the glad hubris that the world (including our own worldly selves) is there for the molding or the escaping and toward a more somber appreciation of the debt we owe to the past (including the past in ourselves) and the extent to which we are shaped by its contingent, passional, and sometimes catastrophic necessities.

Redemption, Secularization, and Politics

George Shulman

Talal Asad's recent work seeks to create an "anthropology of the secular" in two related ways. Partly, it tracks the changing grammar of concepts central to modernity—such as secular, sacred, religion, and myth—while situating these concepts in a social and political geography of state power, disciplinary practices, and academic discourses. Through this genealogy, Asad questions the ideology of "secularism" and the grand narrative of "secularization" that have been central to anthropology, liberal nationalism, and Western domination of a world called premodern. Partly, he troubles the binary distinctions—modern and premodern, sacred and profane, myth and disenchantment—that underpin the self-understanding of modernizing elites and academics. He does so by showing how secularism as an ideology requires and constructs its other, tying any "modern" identity to the differences on which it depends. Partly, he depicts liberal modernity as a political project implicated in the violence, myths, and creedal passions it has disavowed. By exposing how liberal ideals entail disciplinary power and exclusionary violence as they are embedded in the necessarily messy realm of practice, he shows their inevitably ambiguous meaning. His refusal to simplify is a crucial antidote to the contending moralisms that have been violently intensified since 9/11. This chapter analyzes the idea of redemption in Asad's richly textured argument about the secular.

Asad's account begins with the Romantics, who tried to reconcile the conflict between believers (who saw prophets as spokesmen for God) and skeptics (who saw prophets as charlatans) by arguing that prophets were "inspired" poets. For Coleridge, says Asad, "prophets were not men who sought to predict the future, but creative poets who expressed a vision of their community's past—the past both as a renewal of the present and as a promise for the future."[1] Coleridge follows German biblical criticism, but also Blake, whose prophets exemplify "poetic genius," which repeatedly invents the gods and epics by which people live. Shelley depicts poets as "legislators" because they found not the law but the vision that frames how people practice life, the optic that shapes how they endow the past with meaning, action with purpose, and life with a horizon of expectation. (So Whitman declares: what I assume, you shall assume.)[2]

By showing how the practice or office of prophecy, historically linked to divinity, is reconfigured in relation to inspiration and poetry, Asad retells a story of secularization. In it, "poetry" signifies all the arts, separating themselves from theism but opposing a modernity deformed by disembodied Cartesian subjectivity, narrowly instrumental reason, and predatory individualism. From Blake to Whitman, "poetry" retains the ecstatic or libidinal dimension of prophetic (then protestant) "enthusiasm," joined to a democratizing project opposed to middle-class domination and moralized state power. "Poetry" thus shows the changing meaning of "myth." For "if Biblical prophets and apostles . . . were now to be seen as performing, in mythic mode, a poetic function," says Asad about those who secularized prophecy, "modern geniuses could reach into themselves and express spiritual truths by employing the same method."[3] What was called God's word is thus renamed myth, the fruit of human poesis.

For Blake or Coleridge, though, poesis reveals what is, and so remains linked to revelation, whereas Elliot links poetry and myth so as to theorize a *fiction* that gives order and form to the world. While romantics use myth and poetic vision to contact and reveal spiritual reality, for modernists like Elliot, myths provide "fictional ground for secular values that are sensed to be ultimately without foundation," as Asad puts it, and such fictions must be used to "impose aesthetic unity on a disjoined and ephemeral reality."⁴ Within a secular frame, "myth" is thus recast from the voice of tradition to the basis of modernity, just as Wallace Stevens imagines a "supreme fiction" created by "words free from mysticism," a groundless ground that refuses any reference to an independent spiritual reality. What is at stake in this aesthetic project? According to Simon Critchley, modern disenchantment drives romanticism and then modernism to address "what counts as a meaning for life, a meaningful life, after one has rejected the founding certainties of religion. The naivete of romanticism is the conviction that the crisis of the modern world can best be addressed in the form of art." As poetry means poesis, so art suggests a more general human possibility of creative transfiguration, both of human character and of everyday life. Stevens puts the stakes more simply: "After one has abandoned a belief in god, poetry . . . takes its place as life's redemption." Does what Stevens calls "the pressure of reality" shift the meaning and not only agency of redemption?⁵

Asad does not address this question in his story about prophecy and poetry, but he does in his parallel story about myth and liberal nationalism. He focuses on the claim of political theorist Margaret Canovan that, in his words, "a secular liberal state depends crucially for its public virtues (equality, tolerance, liberty) on political myth—that is, on origin narratives that provide a foundation for its political values and a coherent framework for its public and private morality."⁶ Liberalism initially claimed that rights were wired into the nature of things, but it can best counter conservative or radical critics, she argues, by recognizing that it rests not on nature but on assumptions—about nature, human nature, and the nature of society—that are contestable and contested fictions. A liberal language of rights should be seen not as an "account of the world," but as "a project to be realized." As Asad quotes her:

The essence of the myth of liberalism . . . is to assert human rights precisely because they are NOT built into the structure of the universe [but] go against the grain of human and social nature. Liberalism is not a matter of clearing away a few accidental obstacles and allowing humanity to unfold its natural essence. It is more like *making a garden in a jungle that is continually encroaching*. . . . [The] element of truth in this gloomy picture . . . makes the project of realizing liberal principles all the more urgent. *The world is a dark place which needs redemption by the light of a myth.*⁷

As Asad notes, striking images of garden and jungle not only invite but enact a mythic approach that, in the name of overcoming violence, justifies it. "For to make an enlightened space," he says, "the liberal must continually attack the darkness of the outside world that threatens to overwhelm that space." A myth of *redemption* thus underwrites the political and legal disciplines that "forcefully protect sacred things (individual conscience, property, liberty, experience) against whatever violates them." Asad thus uses Canovan to reveal how the mythic basis and redemptive meaning of liberalism generates both imperial violence and disciplinary social practices.[8]

Indeed, as social movements and not only elite actors invoke the liberty and the health of "the people," they justify projects of redemption involving the state, through the "soft tyranny" Tocqueville calls democratic despotism and by literal coercion of those deemed intractable. "Redemption" of the people, to secure its plenitude and liberty from threat, has been a democratic—not only a liberal—aspiration continually replenishing and authorizing state power. If redeeming the people inevitably means depicting threats and enacting exclusion, then wider participation is as likely to authorize as disrupt this logic. The reality of danger, and the imperatives of "human" potential, make redemption an unending necessity and an endless process. Says Asad:

The thought that the world needs to be redeemed is more than merely an idea. Since the eighteenth century, it has animated a variety of intellectual and social projects within Christendom and beyond, in European global empires. In practice they have varied from country to country, unified only by the aspiration toward liberal modernity.[9]

Liberal modernity thus reworks Christian ideas of redemption, but Asad insists that liberal projects are not "simple restatements of sacred myths," not "apparently secular but in reality religious." The "missionary history" of Christianity did make "the modern concept" of redemption possible, but each "articulates different subjectivities, mobilizes different kinds of social activity, and invokes different modalities of time."[10]

I have retold Asad's account of prophecy and poetry, myth and liberalism to foreground how ideas of redemption are central to the secular, both in the "office" of poetry (or idea of culture) after the death of God, and in the political projects of liberal modernity. Like Asad, I want to explore the *political* bearing of the redemptive language drawn from prophecy for modern cultural and political projects. The issue is not only analytic, for in the wake of 9/11 the redemptive meaning of American liberal nationalism, informed by a prophetic "civil religion," is again justifying violence abroad and repressive unity in the "homeland." But Asad's story, I think, flattens out both the complex meaning of redemptive language and its ambiguous political significance.

On the one hand, he suggests that redemptive language, as such, justifies exclusion and violence in the name of "redeeming" its unsaved others, even as it abstracts "higher" causes from worldly practices of power. In this regard I ask: Has he recognized something inherent in the concept that engenders domination? Has he (also) reduced a grammar—which makes a concept available for multiple uses—to a single meaning? The grammar of the concept surely entails dangers, but are these contingent, subject to political mediation? Is the task, therefore, to disillusion actors who no longer imagine their suffering, freedom, and future by way of redemptive frameworks? Or is the task rather to emphasize the meanings of redemption as, say, repair or healing rather than deliverance or transcendence, to make redemption a practice tied to the local and quotidian, not the epochal and heroic? In other words, do we refuse or rework the concept?

On the other hand, his account locates danger not so much in redemption as a concept as in its deployment (especially but not only by states) to authorize power. In this regard I ask: Can democratic resistance to domination be fostered, and state power chastened, by repudiating—or using—redemptive language? Could redemptive language be a political resource, and at the same time, might democratic practices mitigate its dangers? By these questions, I mean to suggest, contra Asad, that the grammar of the concept and the practices it has entailed offer political resources and not only dangers.

Asad's account precludes asking such questions and pursuing such possibilities: given the nation-state, in his view, redemptive language only abets power, and democratic ideals only justify disciplining sentient bodies in the name of redeeming them. He does not respond to the redemptive rhetoric of state power in liberal modernity by a counterfaith in democratic practices, let alone by investing redemptive meaning in them. Rather than rework the concept on behalf of democratic politics or imagine how democratic practices could chasten the redemptive logics he exposes in the liberal state, he speaks in the critical voice of disenchantment about the fateful bond between redemptive language and disciplinary power in *any* political form. He thus seems driven into the sterile trap of seeking redemption from redemption. My intention is not to redeem redemption or democracy from Asad's critique, for he surely identifies real dangers in each. My goal, rather, is to complicate his view of redemptive language by offering an account that shows why it seems unavoidable and how it may be politically fruitful, even essential, and not only dangerous. I would sustain this tension as I relate redemptive language to democratic ideals and practices of power.

Any argument about the meaning of redemption and how it has been practiced must begin with the damage it has wrought. First is overt violence: Hebrew redemption from Egypt requires dispossession of Canaanites, and violence—against pagans and racialized others—bridges the redemptive practice of Christianity and liberalism. Second, for Weber's heirs, Protestant religiosity generates worldly asceticism, which infuses redemptive meaning into the instrumental reason and acquisitive practices that destroy nature and drain life from our common world. Third, for heirs of Nietzsche, redemptive rhetorics in Christianity and Marx devalue the conditions of plurality and incompletion that make politics necessary and valuable. Promises of redemption, even when secularized, seem to warrant self-righteous action hostile to the divided nature and plural condition of human beings. This antipolitical animus seems crucial to the histories of both liberalism and Marxism, but also to identity politics in its national, racial, and gendered forms. Any dream of "more perfect union," of a community that redeems its members, seems to entail dogmatism about identity while mobilizing resentment of difference; by such dreams, people(s) would fix what went wrong in their histories, but a quest for redemption binds them to injury and rancor about it, imprisoning them in the past.

Rhetorics of redemption take various forms but always seem to produce the saved by marking and stigmatizing the damned, to evoke a true world (of fulfillment and freedom) by devaluing the actual world. People seek redemption from real oppression and grievous injustices, to be sure, but sometimes they do so in ways that turn them, resentfully, against ineradicable or valuable aspects of life and against a past they can neither change nor escape. This seems as true of redemption in Christian rhetoric as in the romance of "the American Dream." The true or redeemed world—projected in time as a Promised Land or authentic community, or out of time as eternal life—seems to promise a resolution of the conflicts, a closure of the uncertainties, a settling of the ambiguities in which politics and freedom actually live. The promise of a (future) life beyond power or suffering, the very desire to "redeem" life, seems to devalue the actualities of the present. People lodge hope for meaning in their future or children, their work, art, or possessions, their community or political action, but redemptive desire enacts an imprisoning investment. Any history of redemption impels us to ask: Who must people become, and what must they do to themselves and others, and to their world, to gain redemption as they understand it?

The great writers about redemption—Hebrew prophets, Marx, Nietzsche, and American figures like William Faulkner, James Baldwin, and Toni Morrison—are acute critics of the motives and worldly consequences of the ways their audiences understand and practice redemption. They show how the desire for redemption drives us into brutally violent but also self-denying and bewilderingly self-defeating forms of action, how pervasive ways of understanding and practicing redemption subvert rather than foster freedom. Yet, even as figures from Jeremiah to Nietzsche and Baldwin denounce how we mean and practice what we *call* redemption, they also name what is necessary and valuable in ideas of redemption.

Unlike Jeremiah and Martin Luther King Jr., of course, Nietzsche and Baldwin question rather than expound the idea of deliverance from captivity, trouble rather than avow the idea of a redemptive promise in politics, dramatize what is problematic and not just needful in efforts to redeem the past, and mark the limits and not only the power of language to redeem suffering. They stage redemption as a problem, but they make it a problem impossible to escape, as they struggle to redeem the history whose crimes and failures they narrate unblinkingly. No less than Jeremiah and King, therefore, they ask not *whether* we seek redemption but *how*.

Given the costs and dangers in the idea, why rework it and recast how we practice it? Are there better and worse—more or less political—ways to conceive and practice redemption? Indeed, could redemptive language enable more political ways of imagining democracy and more democratic ways of practicing politics? These questions reframe what it might mean to "secularize" redemption but still leave us asking: in what ways can *any* quest for redemption go awry?[11]

I pursue these questions by exploring the Hebrew prophets and then their greatest critic, Nietzsche. Surely those prophets originated the political and national, also the personal and what we now call religious, meanings of redemption so powerful today, especially in America, while the problematic in this rhetoric is engaged best by Nietzsche. For he shows how redemption comes to mean the purifying of what Philip Roth calls "the human stain," even as his own effort to "redeem" a problematic past, to enable a different future, speaks to those defending democratic projects now.[12]

Redemption in Hebrew Prophecy

Begin with the *Oxford English Dictionary*.[13] "Redeem" and "redemption" derive from the Latin *redimere*, to buy back. To buy back a hostage, specifically: to redeem is to ransom, rescue, or deliver; redemption thus connotes liberation from bondage or captivity. Second, to redeem means to regain, recover, or repossess: a redeemed captive recovers a prior condition of freedom or an innate capacity for action. Third, to redeem also means to make up for, make amends for or make right a fault or defect: we redeem a tainted reputation, shameful deed, or wounding experience by finding something of value in it; we thus would redeem our history (or suffering) by making it meaningful. In this third sense, we also redeem a promise or potential by making good on it, by making it good. We seek redemption *from* worldly bondage, sin, or suffering but also seek the redemption *of* history or suffering. Redemption from and of create a semantic field in which redeeming involves both making-free and making-meaning. (Arendt deems politics redemptive and Nietzsche calls *amor fati* "my redemption" because they grasp this double meaning.)

In part, therefore, Hebrew prophets link redemption to freedom as exemplified by exodus. "I redeemed thee from slavery, for I brought thee up out of the land of Egypt," says Micah's god. "In all their affliction [God] was afflicted . . . and in his love he redeemed them," says Isaiah about the exodus. To redeem is to *free* (deliver or liberate) *from* worldly conditions of captivity. Weber thus claims: "[Yahweh] was and always remained a god of salvation and promise. What mattered chiefly, however, was that salvation as well as promise concerned actual political, not intimate personal affairs.

The god offered salvation from Egyptian bondage, not from a senseless world out of joint. He promised not transcendent values but dominion over Canaan . . . and a good life."[14]

But movement from Egypt to a "promised land" occurs through a "wilderness" in which Hebrews learn to make covenants, and the practice of promising constitutes them as ethical subjects and as a political community. If promising is a practice that links freedom and redemption, it also entails joint liability, the idea that each bears responsibility for the fate of the rest. Redemption thus appears to be worldly, collective, political: if each is responsible for and no one is exempt from the fate of the whole, there is no individual salvation, and if people are delivered from captivity, not history, then redemption is a practice (of covenanting) and not a fantasy of plenitude.

Still, questions abound: Do images of a "redeemed" future entail the wish that people, once and for all, could fully escape the legacy of their past? Does the idea of deliverance, and so of a before-and-after, devalue the actuality of freedom, the limited, in-between space in which politics lives? Does an image of "the" promised land entail internal and external enemies and authorize violence against them? Still, do struggles against domination and its internalized grip depend on faith in a redeemed future, though there are better and worse forms of this aspiration?

The canonical prophets do not raise these questions. After three hundred years of monarchy, they are impelled to reconceive redemption, to reimagine its temporal meaning as well as its internal and worldly dimensions. They invoke redemption from Egypt but tell a story about the *corruption* of a people whose monarchical regime betrays the founding promises that redeemed them from Egyptian bondage. Prophets cast core elements of their society, long deemed legitimate, as violations of first principles: social inequality, priestly and kingly power, ritualized worship of Yahweh and the worship of other gods. The prophets' god implores his people to repent or "turn" away from idols like kings, priests, and other gods toward covenanting as an ongoing practice and toward substantive promises to "love justice." This god promises punishment if they do not amend their ways, (re)turn to their origins, rightly understood.

Whereas Nietzsche and Baldwin invoke a nightmarish history we cannot change or escape but must "redeem" by artful narration and painful working-through, the prophets—like Machiavelli later—invoke "first principles," lament their desecration, and call people to (re)turn to them, and so to themselves. Deliverance from captivity to idols and kings here requires redemptive acts of repossession. But what is the goodness that prophets recover? To what do they re/turn us, which would free—redeem—us? Does their "jeremiad" necessarily entail idealization of the legacy from which they would derive us?

In one reading, prophets seek to return literally to a lost way of life—to the egalitarian prestate confederation of tribes before kingship introduced state centralization, social inequality, and idolatry. This story erases the founding violence of the Hebrews, and their ongoing mixing with surrounding cultures, to project a pure origin people have betrayed—but can recover. This dream of return, nostalgic and resentful in its wishing backward, prophets call redemption: to recover a lost way of life is to be delivered from corruption or captivity now. But this reading is too literal-minded, though not about American populism and the Right's "cultural war."

In a second (Machiavellian) reading, prophets (re)turn to first principles, demanding what Buber calls "decision" about the terms on which people live. Just as Jeremiah denounces a regime that speaks in God's name but worships other gods (and God) falsely, so Frederick Douglass and Henry Thoreau say that Americans claim to worship equality but conceive and practice it falsely, while worshiping gods antithetical to it. Like Jeremiah, each casts himself as a truly faithful heir of first principles their people profess yet desecrate, but they do not so much conserve intact a fixed principle as freshly interpret it, to make it anew. This creative reinterpretation of the past and principles prophets call redemption, for it delivers people from self-betrayal and failure by returning them to what is best in their themselves and their history.

In a third reading, however, prophets re/turn people not to principles, but to a founding "event." For if founding signals generativity, a return to origins means recovering not a law or even a specific commitment, but freedom as the capacity to begin, initiate, and create. By claiming that prophets re/turn Hebrews to a "primal religiosity" to defeat formalized or ritualized worship, Buber depicts a dialectic between the demotic energy Arendt calls "a lost revolutionary treasure" and the forms it generates, which ossify and must be made anew. If idolatry is the name prophets give to reified forms, a return to origins is called redemption because it means (re)claiming generative power.

In these readings, people can be "delivered" from relations of domination, inequality, and subjection to idolatry by (re)turning to an original goodness that prophets link to natality, practices of covenanting, and a commitment to justice passionately lived out. Redemption then seems not an abstract *promise* of "deliverance" in the future but a practice of freedom in the present, by way of acknowledgments and acts that, Machiavelli says, (re)turn people "to themselves," that is, to their principles, their capacity for action, and themselves as a political community. Atonement and covenant renewal "redeem" people by reanimating capacities for promising and acting, but their deliverance from reification depends on "redeeming" the past by altering how the Hebrews judge what is problematic and valuable in it. Redemption *from* captivity depends on redemption *of* the past: by reimagining the past and its meaning to disclose an alternate legacy from which people could derive themselves, prophets recast pervasive practices long deemed legitimate and reconstitute community.[15]

But this reading of redemption through politics and narrative is not credible unless it addresses how this-worldly practice comes to mean deliverance from a "stain" that taints all worldly and historical endeavor. In part, redemption takes on a richly charged meaning when Hosea first depicts Hebrews as God's adulterous spouse who must be "redeemed" from the idolatry holding her captive to kings, priests, and other gods, the impulses driving her to adultery with these "lovers," and the stain of her crime. To be "freed" from these captivities (and so from self-betrayal) is to be restored to *worthiness*. So Isaiah's god laments, "How the faithful city has become a harlot," and implores: "Wash you, make yourself clean, put away evil doings from before my eyes, cease to do evil, learn to do well, seek judgment, relieve the oppressed, loose the bands of wickedness, undo heavy burdens, let the oppressed go free that you break every yoke." As Heschel argues, the core sin for the prophets is *pride*, a false sense of sovereignty, a refusal to acknowledge finitude.[16]

Freedom from worldly captivity (to empires and idols) depends on justice in social relations, and freedom and justice depend on overcoming pride, which denies human incompletion and interdependence. Desire and imagination themselves seem captive to or distorted by a "pride" whose worldly emblem is social inequality and domination. Overcoming the proud in the world and the pride in the heart are two sides of a redemptive project seeking to establish righteousness (or justice) in self and world. So Hosea's god promises his spouse: "I will betroth thee to me forever, in righteousness, in judgment, in loving kindness, and in mercies. . . . And I will say unto them which were not my people, thou art my people, and they shall say, thou art our god." A "redeemed" people refound Canaan: they "shall abide without a king, without a prince, without sacrifice, and without an image."[17]

Prophets testify that worldly redemption has an internal dimension. They ask: what must people overcome, not only amongst themselves but within themselves? But the inner and worldly dimensions of this project generate the same question: when deliverance is figured as cleansing or purification, does this mean ongoing struggle with pride as an inescapable aspect of human life or the erasure once and for all of a willfulness and partiality seen as a "stain"? Does the "honest indignation" at injustice that Blake affirms in the prophets become, through the trope of a female body contaminated by wayward desire, what Roth calls an "ecstasy of sanctimony" about corruption? The language of pride and the apparently all-or-nothing logic of a before-and-after "cleansing" suggest two ways in which redemptive language entails, even authorizes, inner and worldly violence. The problem inheres in the idiom of deliverance looking forward, but also in the idiom of return, even as a (re)turn to a generative event, *if* it means a once-and-for-all overcoming of, say, the reification and docility, or domination and predatory individualism, in a corrupt present.[18]

Redemption is also linked to violence through the narrative of a spouse who is corrupted but can be redeemed. We can credit covenant renewal as a redemptive political practice, but it presumes repentance and signals a desire for pardon. Prophets authorize it through a story in which Hebrews' conduct elicits God's judgment and their response elicits divine punishment or forgiveness (or punishment and then forgiveness). By this story, prophets create what Weber calls an "ethically rational" universe in which good fortune is a sign of right conduct and worldly difficulty signals God's just punishment. Until prophets advanced this story, Hebrews assumed that God was unconditionally supportive, so that their besieged position between empires indicated God's lack of power. In response, Amos invented a theodicy: "Of all the families in the world only you have I known," his god says; "therefore, I will punish your transgressions." God destroyed the northern kingdom, later prophets argued, because its people refused to mend their ways, but the southern kingdom can forestall this fate by atonement, which will elicit God's forgiveness.

Here is the pedagogy: if people interpret worldly difficulty as God's punishment, they take on God's judgment as their own, assume responsibility for their situation, and become agents seeking to redeem themselves, by making amends for their failures, and by making good their promise(s) as a people. Prophets endorse the divine wrath they announce because they identify with their god's anger at Hebrew injustice. If people could be moved to take this judgment as their own, they would see their conduct and history critically, and real grief would transform conduct. But when this "turn" is refused, prophets endorse a punishment they depict as educative and transforming. Isaiah's god promises to "wash away the filth of the daughter of Zion and purge the blood of Jerusalem . . . by the spirit of judgment and burning." Indeed, "Zion shall be redeemed with righteousness. . . . For the day of the lord shall be upon everyone that is proud and lofty and upon everyone that is lifted up, who will be brought low." Invasion and exile are God's punishment, but as *this* suffering compels genuine atonement, God forgives their trespass and "redeems" them from exile. How shall we interpret this prophetic story of crime, punishment, and redemption?

One reading follows Nietzsche: this theodicy projects a moral logic into life by attributing to it a stain that warrants punishment and requires redemption. Prophets thus constitute agency in subjection: as a superego rhetoric, redemption means taking up a chosen subjection to God's authority, which establishes an ethical and a collective subject as people take responsibility for their acts, "cleanse" the willful desire that stains them, and seek the pardon that redeems them from their guilt and its consequences. Agency and redemption require taking up the position of wayward people as unclean spouse that is created by this prophetic story. "Owning" their sin is the condition of seeking to be redeemed; by embracing deserved suffering, subjects prove their worthiness and gain pardon. Their quest for redemption binds them to abjection in the name of ending it; abjection and redemption are the two faces of agency as prophets conceive its ethical and collective form, and violence is its necessary consequence.[19]

In an alternative reading, though, their god's righteous wrath is the voice not of the law as a command, but of justice outraged by evil and human indifference to it. If this god is "the face of the other," as Levinas says, it "summons" people to acknowledge their connection. Then the premise of theodicy is not abjection but interdependence, and their story of sinful sovereignty and redemptive reconciliation calls people not to renounce desire but to acknowledge the reality (and suffering) of the other, and their own capacity to act differently. Prophetic theodicy does not compel purification but solicits such acknowledgments, which usually are a condition of forgiving one another, as well as a condition of community, which survives only if practices of atonement and forgiveness repair inevitable trespass and injustice. Prophets thus introduce practices of judgment and forgiveness into (political) life. For forgiveness is essential if people are to remain free and together, as Arendt must have learned from the prophets: it is redemptive because, if people do not release each other from trespass and rancor about it, they remain imprisoned by the past and the injuries it bequeaths.[20]

We might endorse Arendt's "secularizing" effort to extract practices of promising and forgiving from the enchantment of theodicy—Nietzsche says "true world" or "moral world-order"—that first authorized them. When judging, promising, and forgiving are practiced not by way of God's authority but by differently positioned actors, violence is deprived of transcendental sanction, and actors are put at (moral) risk by actions whose consequences they cannot know or control. Once the fate of community has no guarantee beyond political conduct itself, promising and forgiving bear a redemption that is separated from deliverance and violence and linked instead to limitation and repair.

But the prophets' theodicy also discloses the insufficiency of Arendt's "secular" account of the redemptive meaning of promising and forgiving. Partly, she does not credit the *politics* of seeking and gaining forgiveness: prophets must "wrestle" with people who do not readily acknowledge the consequences of their conduct. Partly, she does not credit that people often recognize their situation only when it is too late, when no act can redeem them from or repair the relentlessly unfolding consequences of earlier choices. (Isn't this the point of Baldwin's title, "The Fire Next Time"?) Prophets must say: you cannot forestall the consequences of past choices; no acts, now, can redeem you. You are going down. *False* prophets give reassurance about redemption, which is not absolute but conditional.

To gain acceptance of *this* disaster then becomes the purpose of prophetic wrestling, but in the process redemption is again reconceived, fatefully. Redemption still means deliverance, but from exile not domination and by God's grace alone. Hear Jeremiah:

> I shall establish a new covenant with the people of Israel and Judah. It will not be like the covenant I made with their fore-fathers when I took them by the hand to lead them out of Egypt, a covenant they broke though I was patient with them. . . . For I shall set my law within them, writing it on their hearts. I shall be their God and they shall be my people. No longer need they teach one another . . . to know the Lord; all of them . . . will know me.

By a "new covenant," Jeremiah dreams of a community delivered from kings and priests but also, apparently, from pride and resentment, as members internalize the same law, which "circumcizes the heart." Instead of wrestling with pride as an ongoing element in human being, he closes the gap between human desire and God's law, and renders politics (and teachers) unnecessary. This dream bespeaks a profound wish to vanquish not only injustice but pride itself, not only unjust social divisions but plurality itself, not only hierarchy but the pathos of distance that separates singular selves, not only social exclusion but all alienation. By a dream of internalization, Jeremiah would *guarantee* righteousness, making redemption certain and final, not contingent and ongoing.

Does this vision only intensify the redemption that pre-exilic prophets sought by practices of atonement and covenant renewal? Their images of a betrothal or a marriage renewed, of people restored to harmony with each other and God, surely bespeak a dream of communitarian fullness. *This* dream of redemption, not the practices it authorizes, may be the antipolitical core of Hebrew prophecy. Still, does some such imagination of profound solidarity, of community as a *space together*, enable democratic wrestling about covenants, liability, and forgiveness? Do we witness a contradiction or paradox between an image of a redeemed community and practices of freedom?[21]

Exile also foregrounds the fact that we seek redemption *from* a condition, but also redemption *of* it. Jeremiah and post-exile prophets evince an intense need to "redeem"—heal, justify, make meaningful—a history they depict as dominated by suffering and ruptured by exile. Lincoln invokes this sense of redeem when he calls on "we the living" to make good the "unfinished" work consecrated by the dead at Gettysburg. We must redeem their suffering and sacrifice, as well as the proposition for which they died, by our own dedication and sacrifice on its behalf; otherwise, the violence of slavery and civil war, and so the promise of America, remain unredeemed. When King calls people to "redeem" the American promise, he means make good on it, which would justify it at last. In this sense of redemption, people "make right" (which entails making amends for) what has been flawed or corrupted; they "make whole" what has been rent or injured. They redeem a dismal experience by finding value in it or redeem (seek what is redemptive in) painful experiences of oppression or suffering. Nietzsche and Arendt thus say that the past, or crimes and suffering, or lives and people *must* be "redeemed," that is, endowed with meaning, even as they question whether our meaning-making can bear that burden without creating a "true world" that escapes the actual one.

Hebrew prophets do not identify this sense of redemption, but they enact it. By their story of origins, guilt, punishment, and deliverance, they "redeem" Hebrew suffering; they make it meaningful—intelligible, purposeful—by making an ethically rational universe. Prophets do not only "promise" redemption in the future but enact redemption, now, by *bestowing* meaning on life. People are "redeemed" not by freeing themselves from suffering but by making it meaningful. This desire to redeem the past—to justify suffering, bring good out of horror, make amends for failure, project value into injury—seems inescapable but is fraught with danger and easily goes awry.

As the example of Lincoln (or 9/11) attests, people feel driven to redeem violence and death in ways that authorize more violence and death, and often our meaning-making is a way to avoid their full horror, to close over our haunting by the *problem* of their meaning. Acknowledgment of loss and calls to remember never seem enough, and not only in politics. To ensure that suffering is not "in vain," we would make it purposeful, but we project that meaning into the very order of things, as if to close the gap between words and the world and deliver ourselves from the problem of suffering's meaning. We also endorse violence, literal and figurative, against carnal bodies and imperfect actuality to secure the meaning we project, the story we tell.

Redemption—*from* domination and *of* suffering—is tightly tied to the practices of freedom that prophets endorse, like commitment-making and forgiving, collective liability, political judgment, and action in concert. But does redemption go awry because the idiom of deliverance necessarily entails a purifying logic, while the idiom of redeeming suffering necessarily invests in language an impossible burden? Danger lies not (only) in the grammar of the concept but (also) in the way Pauline Christianity reconfigures Hebrew ideas of redemption and the ways liberalism and Marxism rework or "secularize" this redemptive religiosity.

Secularizing Redemption

According to Paul, we are "redeemed from" bondage to "sin," and so from subjection to "the law," by our faith in Jesus *as Christ*, as God's chosen son resurrected. If slavery is a social condition Orlando Patterson calls "social death," then Paul conceives the "death of death," using a trope of rebirth to transpose emancipation from slavery into entirely internal and individual—thus universal—terms that indeed represent a wish to escape history and embodiment, not only violence and oppression. But as Milton later says: "Christ has redeemed us from the entire Mosaic law, [which] is abolished by the gospel. . . . The result is Christian liberty, God's law written in the hearts of believers [whose works] never run contrary to the love of God and of our neighbor, which is the sum of the law." As faith fosters capacities for love, so love is redemptive for Milton and Blake, and as love is enacted in historical time and antinomian tones, so English Protestantism explicitly recovers the collective and historical, the worldly and national dimensions of Hebrew redemption. As Puritan leaders cast their colony as a "city on a hill," so liberal nationalists cast the United States as a "chosen" and indeed "redeemer nation," called by God to deliver other nations from despotism by the example—and coercive expansion—of "liberty."[22]

The redemptive promise of that liberty is conceived as a capacity for personal and political self-determination that brings deliverance from "old world" despotism and tradition—a redemption from slavery that is the redemption of history. To annul the power of history is to create a "new world" of freedom and plenitude, a "new nation" that redeems every member. Tom Paine thus invokes the exodus story to declare that "we have it in our power to begin the world over again." The "we" of nationhood is redemptive because it replaces despotism with democracy, which is redemptive because it enables the individual to live out, or incarnate, such dreams of rebirth, from sin to liberty and from ascription to self-definition. Millions enact a redemptive narrative of starting over and self-making, by way of the willful practices of self-denial Weber calls worldly asceticism or through recurrent rebellions against the iron cages it creates. Ideas of redemption suffuse American culture in every regard and subject position, framing the meaning of white supremacy and xenophobia, of immigrant hopes and upward mobility, and of political struggles against exclusion or domination.

Redemption thus binds Christian religiosity and stories of self-making into a distinctive culture that takes national form as the story of a people who, like the Hebrews, have been corrupted but can redeem their sacred origin and special promise. Elites repeatedly justify imperial expansion, racial violence, and social control as efforts to redeem America from captivity or corruption attributed to subversive threats, while social movements repeatedly redeem an American promise by freeing people from the captivities that prevent its realization. Since a redemptive view of freedom remains central to the mythology of democratic self-determination constituting "America" as an imagined community, legitimacy in political struggles still depends on invoking, rather than refusing or even questioning, "America" as a site of special possibility.[23]

In this condensed story about "secularizing" redemption, Marx is noteworthy in two ways. On the one hand, he follows liberalism by relocating other-worldly Christian redemption in worldly human action, but he shifts the agent of redemption from nation to class: "A class must be formed which . . . can only redeem itself by a total redemption of humanity."[24] By freeing itself from captivity, the proletariat recovers the generative power and capacity for action that marks humanity, and also "makes good"—completes, heals, and justifies—all of human history and its suffering. Redemption *from* alienation is the redemption *of* a history defined by injustice and suffering. Making theodicy into historical telos and human beings into their own redeemers, Marx reworks the redemptive dream whose religious form he unmasks: "The world has long been dreaming of something it can acquire if only it becomes conscious of it."[25]

On the other hand, the example of Marxist practice—its self-righteousness and violence in the name of truth, its hostility to difference in the name of true identity, and its devaluation of politics in the name of justice—suggests that bringing redemptive dreams "down to earth" does not suffice to address the dangers in redemptive rhetorics. How then do we explain pressures toward unity and closure in even this-worldly views of redemption?[26]

There is the other Marxism, Groucho's, a voice of irreverent play, endlessly fertile and disruptive, which opposes every form of order and authority, every piety and virtue. This iconoclastic yet inventive negativity sees meaning-making itself as coercive, an imposition of order and propriety, while any specific form of meaning appears as a vain fiction—an idol—warranting ridicule. If every effort to redeem life is an arrogant vanity, devaluing life to bestow meaning on it, and if people inevitably are imprisoned by the forms of meaning they make for themselves and impose on others, then the only way to escape self-defeat is to use shameless irreverence to disrupt the art that elicits human participation in schemes of redemption.

On the one hand, we enact a willful secularity to expose illusion in all motivational frameworks to undermine conviction, as if for the sake of life itself against the violence entailed by meaning-making. On the other hand, carnal pleasure appears as what Phillip Roth calls "the redeeming corruption, that de-idealizes the species and keeps us everlastingly mindful of the matter we are." As Groucho's heir celebrates sexuality through *words*, and finds sexual pleasure in fecund and not only disillusioning play with words, his practice subverts his point, but still he recasts redemption (as de-idealization) rather than refusing it. Consider, then, how the trope of redemption from redemption was initially used by Nietzsche: because his critique of the ascetic ideal diagnoses those (like Marx) who claim to secularize redemption, while his Zarathustra enacts a parallel effort, he is especially helpful in assessing efforts to come to terms with (even redeem?) redemptive rhetoric.[27]

What is the problem with redemptive rhetoric? At the core of any critique is the question: *from what* do people seek redemption? Nietzsche's argument "against" redemption is that desire for it is motivated by resentment at what he calls the "fundamental pre-requisites of life." What do people resent from which they seek deliverance? In *The Case of Wagner*, he declares: "The need for *redemption* [is] the quintessence of all Christian needs.... The Christian wants to be *rid* of himself." Those who "suffer" from life see (their) suffering as an indictment of (their) life; they wish to be "rid" of themselves because they resent, and wish to escape, the past (the injuries and suffering) that constituted them as they are. For identities rooted in injury, "redemption" means reparation or vindication, as if it were possible to change what went wrong in the past.

"Fundamental pre-requisites" thus include suffering, injury, and the intractability of who we have become. But "Christians" also would be "rid of" the "problem" of the meaning of their suffering. They long for "the unconditional," a truth freed from contingency and motivation, which seem to threaten—to stain—the universality and certainty, and so the validity, of the meaning they would live by. Here, "fundamental pre-requisites" include plurality, perspective, and partiality, which are related to error, illusion, and change. "Timeless" truth, authored by God and not by humans, delivers "Christians" from such "all-too-human" aspects of meaning-making. "True worlds," he warns, devalue "the actual one."[28]

The critique of redemption as deliverance extends from the what to the how: stories of redemption (from captivity, affliction, or exile) project a clear and guaranteed path to redemption and promise an irrevocable and completed, fully "redeemed" condition, without remainder, regress, or further change. Such promises comprise a "true world"; if the way is certain and without moral risk, if the "end" stands in a direct and transparent relation to our intentions and hopes, then we are being delivered from actuality. If the way is certain and the end assured, if redemption means overcoming injustice, or pride, or idolatry *once and for all* and *completely*, then deliverance means closing the gap between aspiration and actuality, justice and life, words and the world.

Politics, I want to say, requires sustaining and not removing these tensions by facing the tragic or morally risky relationship between intentions and consequences, the morally ambiguous conditions of bearing partial perspectives, wielding power, and provoking conflict that make politics necessary and valuable. But Nietzsche's critique suggests that those who secularize redemption have remained "Christians" because, though they disavow divine agency, they invest in reason, moral deliberation, or communicative rationality, proletariat agency, technology, or nationhood, a redemption from the "fundamental pre-requisites" of life, and so from politics. If redemption as deliverance means resentfully devaluing crucial aspects of life, then, as Nietzsche says in reference to Wagner, "what is needed is redemption from the redeemer." To be redeemed—delivered—from the "redeemers" is to (re)turn to the actualities they malign or erase.

His critique of redemption thus compels his paradoxical demand for redemption from redemption:

> In a stronger age than this decaying, self-doubting present, he must yet come to us, the *redeeming* man of great love and contempt, the creative spirit . . . whose isolation is misunderstood . . . as a flight from reality while it is only his penetration into reality so that . . . he may bring home the *redemption* of this reality; its redemption from the curse that the hitherto reigning ideal has laid on it. This man of the future . . . will *redeem* us not only from the hitherto reigning ideal but also from what was bound to grow out of it, the great nausea, the will to nothingness, nihilism.[29]

To "redeem"—deliver—us from captivity to the ascetic ideal, and from the nihilism growing by its secularization, is to "redeem" (to make good, even restore to innocence) reality itself, long devalued by that ideal. So Nietzsche does not abjure but rather reworks the language of redemption, in its senses of deliverance, recovery or repossession, and making good.

Then is the "problem" in redemption *not* in the grammar of deliverance as such but *which* condition people specify? Is the problem (also?) whether they imagine that condition "resentfully," so as to be "rid" of it, rather than struggling *with* it? Is redemption problematic only if it means "cleansing" rather than struggling with obdurate realities (other people, pervasive historical practices, cultural differences, internalized dispositions) that we cannot erase—and whose value we may need to recognize? We thus might distinguish efforts to erase conditions depicted as a stain on life from efforts to wrestle with the conditions that constitute life. In that distinction lies the ambiguous meaning of Nietzsche's term "overcoming." We see how, in his vision of overcoming the ascetic ideal, he may be repeating the problem he identified.

Still, his poetry yields an effort to posit values differently than before. This learning is enabled by the ascetic ideal because its religious and secular forms drive people to cultivate capacities for self-reflection and self-overcoming. Nietzsche thus models how the "illness" of the bad conscience can be made a "pregnancy" by using these capacities to work through "hitherto reigning" ideals and "digest" the resentment he calls "the womb of all ideals." Zarathustra defines "my redemption" to evoke this struggle: "And it is all my art and aim to compose into one and bring together what is fragment and riddle and dreadful chance. And how could I endure to be a man if man were not also poet and reader of riddles and the redeemer of chance! To redeem the past and to transform every 'it was' into an 'I wanted it thus'—that alone do I call redemption."[30]

This account of redemption foregrounds not the idiom of deliverance but the idiom of making good, which Nietzsche applies to the past conceived as a problem. The problem appears in the ruling ideas people have incorporated and in their resentful relationship toward the injuries and contingencies that have shaped them. There is no redemption *from* the past, which they cannot change (or forget). Indeed, as long as people seek to be redeemed *from* the past, they remain imprisoned by it. But a past that is *unredeemed* is not "digested"; it haunts people, driving them to self-blame and vengefulness, to dreams of escape or reparations. So the past *must* be "redeemed"—made meaningful, justified, or made good. The *absence* of redemption is the most destructive (and most pressing) problem because, if we submit, resignedly or resentfully, to a future that seems dictated by a past taken passively as given, we relinquish our freedom.

Nietzsche describes this "redemption" in two related ways. Partly, it is a practice of what he calls *amor fati*, an effort "to transform every 'it was' into an 'I wanted it thus.'" The goal is to *alter, not his past but his relationship to it*. By accepting (or willing) the past that constituted him, he is enabled to consider, as if without rancor, what in himself he would and could change, who he might become now. He is no longer merely reactive to his past, for he takes what he merely resented and actively makes it a condition of possibility. But partly, this capacity to accept the past is entwined with a capacity to "compose into one and bring together"—to organize and endow with meaning—the fragments, riddles, and accidents, the contingencies and injuries that shaped identity. The "poet" is thus a "redeemer" of chance. By (re)telling the past to digest it, he both redeems himself from rancor and "redeems the past," that is, makes it a fruitful condition of further action.

By the art of narration and a practice of *amor fati* he recovers what Arendt calls natality. *Amor fati* is antithetical to the idiom of deliverance, since he accepts fate, whereas deliverance bespeaks a dream of freedom *from*, so that deliverance is then animated by the very resentment that *amor fati* would overcome. *Amor fati* then seems to "redeem" redemption, but its redemptive meaning includes deliverance from resentment and recovery of generative agency. This is no promised land to possess, but it is still a way forward and a whither, though it includes ways to go awry.

We thus can project Nietzsche's reworking of redemption in two directions. Surely he parallels Freud's hope, "where it was I shall be," since the "it" includes not only drives but also a past not yet claimed as one's own. For some, psychoanalysis thus embodies a this-worldly redemption practiced by coming to terms with the past. He also enters a tradition running from Blake through Whitman to Stevens, which locates redemption in poesis or art: if prophets are poets whose genius figured gods so powerfully as to become truths people lived by, and if faith in those truths has waned, then generative poesis must be reclaimed to take on the task of redeeming life consciously by making meaning (and bestowing value) through arts recognized as such. "Poetry" cast as a *public* vocation bears a collective (cultural if not avowedly political) purpose of making a meaning for the earth rather than a true world beyond it. As that meaning depends on confronting a collective past so "poetry" may bear on politics in ways that echo prophetic forbears.[31]

Redemption and Politics

It is a mistake to reduce redemption to a symptom of resentment or insist that the concept requires violence. It is a mistake to imagine erasing the idiom of deliverance, as if emphasizing the idiom of healing or repair could redeem redemption from its dangers. Nor should we reduce prophecy to redemption gone awry and attribute what is problematic in secular rhetorics of redemption to such "religious origins." It is more fruitful to see the rich ambiguities constituting redemption as a concept and the enduring tensions that shape how human beings use it. Rather than use Nietzsche to attack prophets, then, let us use their examples to return to Asad's account. Are there (more "political") ways of imagining and practicing redemption, by which to contest how redemptive rhetoric and democratic ideals are used now as an "authorizing discourse" for late modern forms of power?

Partly, Nietzsche reveals the key questions to ask regarding redemptive rhetoric and its political bearing. Surely, a first question is: from what do people seek redemption, and how do they conceive and practice it? A "more political" form of redemption, I want to say, accepts that any struggle for deliverance—from worldly domination, pride, or resentment—is incomplete and ongoing, open to revision and subject to regress. Whether people are enlarged and empowered or diminished by these struggles depends partly on whether they disown what stains life or wrestle with what constitutes it. A second crucial question is: what is the character of the truth by which people imagine deliverance or endow suffering with meaning? A "more political" form of redemption, I want to say, addresses suffering through a poesis that is conventional, local, subject to failure, open to revision. Meaning-making is more open to argument the more we recognize it as ongoing (because every moment becomes another "it was" that cannot be changed or escaped), incomplete (because the future always runs ahead of our capacity to "know" the "end"), and plural (because people make lives meaningful in multiple and contrasting ways).

Redemptive language is inescapable because it is entwined with aspirations for freedom, experience of temporality, and projections of meaning, but as a result of the grammar of the concept, redemption *can* go awry in identifiably recurring ways, which we might call false prophecy. The dangers are inherent, yet contingent, susceptible to chastening if we accept our incompletion and the limits and dangers in language. Such acknowledgments make redemptive language not a symptom of but an antidote to resentment; we can rework it to affirm rather than devalue political life.[32]

Nietzsche suggests that we should recognize the practice of redemption as contingent, open to a reworking. But Nietzsche's view of redemption is also profoundly unpolitical in ways that signal the value of earlier prophecy. After all, he speaks of "my redemption," implying that he can redeem his past, create his values, and produce his freedom *by himself,* as if to endorse the very sovereignty he criticizes. And despite his diagnosis of the disciplinary power authorized by democratic redemption or herd morality, his story of redemption (by a solitary hero) evades the political claim that redemption is a *collective* undertaking. Since deliverance for some ("our" redemption) has been premised on the domination of others, founding violence and ongoing conflict haunt every community, and coming to terms with the past is a paramount *political* problem. There is no centering "I" to redeem the "it" of a disclaimed past, but a "we" whose existence is itself a political artifact contingent on the speech and action of subjects differently positioned by and toward history. What political "art" can "compose and bring together" what is fragment (these subjects), riddle (the relatedness and meaning of their histories), and dreadful chance (the contingencies that produced their injuries and unequal powers)? What political arts can compose out of profound differences a "we" that is the agent and object of this redemption?

For Asad, the discourses of late modern power are authorized by this aspiration to forge a "we" and "redeem" it. The danger is only intensified by 9/11, which has enabled the ruling American elite to revitalize the myth of America as a "redeemer nation," to justify violence in the name of securing the freedom of some by freeing others (the unredeemed) from their captivity to nonliberal practices. This emancipatory promise *is* the redemptive meaning of American liberal nationalism, whose fruit always has been violence and repressive unity. The clash of redemptive dreams, twinned in their dogmatic animosity, squeezes out the space of politics to such a degree that democratic life thus seems to depend on disenchanting redemptive myths, layer upon layer, from human rights and liberal internationalism to Christian crusade and Islamic jihad. It is as if communities and political action must be drained of redemptive meaning to chasten dogmatism, unmask power, foster reverence for endangered human diversity. Then, the "office" of theorists is not to define better or worse forms of redemption but to criticize pervasive narratives and unsettle their promises of redemption, to expose the groundlessness—and humorlessness—of the meanings we relentlessly make for ourselves and impose on others.

Asad's critique of secularism, as a discursive practice that knots knowledge and power, takes this critical form, which is concerned less with "justifying" resistance than with revealing the practices by which every justification becomes a form of power. De-idealization of language, especially of redemptive and democratic rhetoric, is the only way to expose how ideals, taken up in the logics and ruses of power, are practiced at human expense. While exposing secularism as an ideology, then, Asad practices its distinguishing disillusionment as if this were the best or perhaps the only resource against disciplinary power.

Nonetheless, democratic projects, both within and against liberal modernity, may need to take seriously, not disavow, redemptive language. First, liberal nationalism can be challenged only by coming to terms with the historical amnesia that enables elites to repeat manifest destiny. To narrate a counterhistory of American empire is to take on a project of redeeming the past, to fashion an alternative legacy by which to act creatively toward the future. Political freedom in democratic forms may well depend on some such retelling; that is, a reworking of redemptive language may be indispensable to defending democratic practices from erasure. Second, Asad himself recognizes that power can be resisted only by power, but power requires solidarity, which depends on authorizing narratives that, in a present marked by domination and violence, project a better future and figure community to solicit desire and motivate action.

If assertions of state power in the name of liberalism endanger democratic possibility in this country and everywhere else, a *political* defense means taking on democracy's mythic meaning as an experiment bearing a redemptive significance. Since that redemption hinges on participation in rule, and thus on equalizing resources and power, it lives in tension with the liberal rhetoric and pluralist ideology that rules our grossly unequal society. To be sure, narrations of a democratizing future can be used to empower the state by replenishing its authority, and even democratically inflected solidarities cannot escape the paradoxes of power and exclusion. But the survival even of constitutional forms, let alone more democratized practices in politics and culture, may depend on those prophetic poets or mobilized constituencies who dramatize the redemptive meaning and elicit the redemptive energy of democratic possibility.

10

Subjects and Agents in the History of Imperialism and Resistance

Jon E. Wilson

I

One of the most powerful elements of Talal Asad's work over the last decade or so has been his genealogical critique of the "modern" use of the category of agency. Asad places the concept of agency at the center of the modern intellectual landscape he terms "secularism." Secularism is far more than a political doctrine about the separation of religious and secular institutions. It is a conceptual environment that presupposes certain ways of defining how religion, ethics, the nation, and politics relate to each other.[1] At the core of the discourse of secularism is the assumption that human subjects—whether individual people or collective groups—are agents who "make their own history." Asad shows that this simple suggestion is far more complex than it might otherwise seem. Through a series of genealogical studies of pain and ritual, law, religion, and imperialism, Asad's work points to the contested, ambivalent, and often contradictory styles of reasoning that secularism relies upon. Within these discourses, agency is never a clear-cut category. Its functioning relies on the operation of rules of inclusion and exclusion, tensions and contradictions that articulate and sustain the power differential between the West and the non-European world.[2]

Over the last twenty years the category of agency has become centrally important to the way in which historians and anthropologists write about the relationship between Europe and the non-European world. When it was initially invoked by historians and others, perhaps most notably by South Asian history's Subaltern Studies collective, the concept was used to challenge the elitist assumption that the poor and marginalized are merely passive victims of elite oppression. Progressive historians argued that subaltern peoples were self-determining historical agents who challenged, resisted, and attempted to liberate themselves from the oppressive social and political structures they inhabited. The assumption that subalterns were autonomous, self-activating agents whose history was "their own" required the historian to challenge teleological narratives that saw the peasant or worker as the passive subject of a process directed from elsewhere (by, for instance, abstract socio-economic forces, the colonial regime, or politically conscious elite politicians). This literature challenged the assumption that European history was both the model and the point of origin for the historical development (or otherwise) of the non-European world. Whether they emerged from colonial discourse or postcolonial liberalism and Marxism, global narratives of emancipation regarded Africa, Asia, the Middle East, and Latin America as laggard followers of a process of social change initiated by Europeans—whether that social change was industrialization, democratization, or social revolution. The subaltern critique of Eurocentric history required the historian to examine the forms of subaltern consciousness on its own terms, looking at the distinctive idioms of peasant protest—its religious and communitarian language and its ability to appropriate but also subvert elite political practice. The injunction of the subaltern historians of colonial South Asia, Latin America, and Southeast Asia is to look beyond Eurocentric universalizing grand narratives and examine the local and particular character of subaltern revolt.[3]

Yet, as a number of scholars have noted, the desire to discover agency is itself part of precisely such a Eurocentric narrative of historical change. The assertion of subaltern agency is one component of a modern style of reasoning that posits the autonomous, self-determining human subject (whether that subject is the individual person or collective group) as the beginning and end points in a process of global social transformation. It is the product of a form of secular political commitment that asserts that emancipation occurs only when human beings are freed from the social and political structures that prevent them from leading fulfilled, self-determining lives—whether liberation takes the form of a liberal democratic state or a socialist society. In order to resist "colonial and nationalist discursive hegemonies," a history that attempts to free subalterns from "the will of the colonial and national elite" needs to pose the autonomy of the subaltern's consciousness by invoking a category of agency produced by the kind of Eurocentric story about global emancipation that the subaltern critique was initially designed to overturn.

Many have noticed this tension and argued that politically engaged historians need to find ways to live and work comfortably in its interstices. For example, in a debate with Rosalind O'Hanlon and David Washbrook, Gyan Prakash argues that the historian needs to use both these contradictory forms of analysis at the same time—to, as he puts it, "ride two horses at once." Prakash quotes a passage from Gayatri Chakravorty Spivak about the necessity of saying an "impossible 'no' to a structure, which one critiques, but inhabits intimately."[4] The work of Gayatri Chakravorty Spivak, Gyan Prakash, and others has emerged into a powerful critique of the essentialistic assumptions that underpin the use of the category of agency. Historians and anthropologists have acknowledged the force of that critique but continue to see the category of agency as a necessary component for a politically engaged history that attempts to do justice to the life-worlds of the poor and marginalized. At the same time, scholars who were once practitioners of "history from below" have shifted focus to study the conditions of various elite forms of colonial and postcolonial knowledge. With a few excellent exceptions, sustained and theoretically sophisticated research into the forms of engagement and ways of life of the poor and marginalized have become fewer and farther between. In South Asian studies in particular, as a result of the theoretical difficulties that agency poses, forms of history-writing that depend upon its explicit use have been quietly abandoned.[5]

Even if the category of agency is no longer invoked quite as often as it once was, it remains an implicit component within many aspects of historical research. In the following pages, I suggest that the work of Talal Asad provides a set of tools that historians and others can use to prise apart the rather limiting terms of an old debate about agency—a debate whose aftereffects nonetheless continue to linger in the historiography of the non-European world.

Throughout the following pages, I will pick up on an important theme within Talal Asad's work: his discussion of the relationship between consciousness, subjectivity, and agency. In a number of places in his work, Asad challenges the tendency of historians and anthropologists to conflate subjectivity and agency. Asad notes that scholars tend to assume that an analysis of subjective consciousness is adequate to explain the agentive power human beings have in the world. But, as he puts it, "the *structures of possible actions* . . . are logically independent of the consciousness of actors." Asad asks us to separate conscious subjectivity from agentive power. He summarizes his argument as follows: "Contrary to the discourse of many radical historians and anthropologists, *agent* and *subject* (where the former is the principle of effectivity and the latter of consciousness) do not belong to the same theoretical universe and should not, therefore, be coupled."[6]

I agree with this suggestion; my aim is to show how historians have conflated agency and consciousness and how Asad's work helps us think about writing history that does not connect the two. But I think Asad's mode of analysis forces him to go further than this explicit attempt to delink consciousness and agency. Within his work, there is a less clearly articulated critique of the attempt to conflate agency and subjectivity in all its forms. This deeper challenge avoids imputing effective agentive power to *any* single subject, whether conscious or not. Certainly, one can talk of power relations that have particular trajectories and use specific strategies, but one cannot attribute them to singular subjects that are said to "possess" the power or agency to act. Taking such a view has radical consequences. It forces the historian or anthropologist to abandon an attempt to attribute causal efficacy (and thus responsibility) to collective social forces (the state, imperialism, class) or individual agents. Over the following pages, I will defend this argument. But its implications for the way in which we think about responsibility and political engagement are profound, and I will conclude by considering those implications.

II

So far I have sketched the outline of part of my argument in a schematic and abstract way. It is time to consider a concrete example of the theoretical points I am making.

Let me begin with a well-known story. In January 1783, the peasants of the district of Rangpur in Bengal—which had been directly governed by the English East India Company for a decade—rose up against their landlords and governors. Objecting to increased rates of rent and the coercive means used to extract it, they burned down government and landlord offices, killed revenue officials, and destroyed government records. The rebels appointed leaders and began to establish a government. The uprising was suppressed when a rebel encampment was attacked by a detachment of Company troops, with the loss of over sixty insurgent lives.[7]

How does the historian of colonial India make sense of this event? At first sight, it seems simple enough. Perceived from an anti-imperialist point of view, it appears to have been an early response to exploitation by the colonial regime and its Indian accomplices. The peasants aimed at "reversing [their] world." Their actions were guided by "the autonomous cultural traditions that informed the struggles of peasant, tribal and labouring communities."[8] Within such a narrative, the rebels appear as tragic heroes, using the conscious agentive power they possessed to replace with a social order all of their own the regime they saw as the cause their poverty.

In some ways, this mode of telling the story would not be very far removed from the way imperial officials and politicians described the same set of events. Some colonial officers perceived the rebellion as a dangerous threat to order and social stability that, for the good of both Britain and India, needed to be suppressed by overwhelming force. Others saw it as an inevitable—though unfortunate—response to the corruption and incompetence of an early phase of colonial rule, to be replaced by a more enlightened form of rule later on. The heroes in these colonial stories were the agents of the colonial regime who pacified the insurgency or the officials who abolished its causes.[9] Different historians may evaluate the merits of each side in the conflict in different ways, but imperial and anti-imperial historians agree about the nature of the encounter. The battle that occurred in the Rangpur countryside was a struggle for power between two opposing subjects, the peasants and the colonial regime. Like a cricket match between two national teams, it was an event played by two groups of people who each had a clear and coherent sense of their autonomous identity and already clearly knew who they were. It occurred over a limited period of time. It had a rather testing final denouement but resulted in clear victory for one side. The match was played out again and again in rebellions throughout India in subsequent years, with the same victor each time.

If one examines the rebellion of 1783 purely in terms of the thinking of its participants, it quickly becomes apparent that none of the parties involved acted from motives that existed within their own autonomous consciousness. Doing justice to the particularity of what the rebels thought makes it impossible to treat their consciousness solely "on its own terms." An approach that explains events such as the Rangpur uprising by seeing it as a clash between the autonomous consciousness of its participants does not help to provide an adequate explanation of how it happened because it does not explain how the consciousness of each participant (indeed their very sense of who they were) was shaped through his or her encounter with others.

If I can be forgiven for schematizing, one might be able to sketch three different social groups as participants within the rebellion of 1783—insurgent rebels, Indian landholders and British officials. Each of these groups had its own aims and objectives; each developed its own strategies to achieve them by relating to the strategies of others around them. Let me begin with the consciousness of the insurgents. Rangpur's rebellious peasants were not conscious of being the autonomous creators of a counterhegemonic social order. They regarded themselves as interlocutors and critics of an authority to which they were already subject, but which they had the ability to reform and amend for their own purposes. The rebellion consisted of an attempt to recreate a good social order that rebels believed had been broken by the actions of their rulers—not to create an entirely novel social order. Long after violence had broken out, the rebels presented themselves as supplicants and petitioners before the agents of the colonial regime, appealing for justice and ending each missive with the words "you are master, we are subjects." But as supplicants, the rebels did not believe they were powerless. They saw themselves as having the power to refuse to pay rent or to migrate elsewhere, able thus to undermine the landholder's livelihood. The possibility for these actions was structured by the demographics of eighteenth-century Bengal, in which the availability of land far outstripped the supply of labor to cultivate it. In this social environment, the landholders' demand for labor gave peasants a significant sense of their own power.[10]

From the insurgents' point of view, peasants and landlords inhabited a shared social world in which the peasants' labor was given voluntarily to the lord in exchange for "protection" and economic support in the face of an uncertain economic environment. Indeed, in the few surviving contemporary Indian descriptions of the rebellion, the peasants' gift of labor is seen as actively constituting the authority their lord possessed; it made the authority of the lord dependent on the maintenance of the economic and social conditions necessary for the peasants' survival. We can see this conception at work when, on a number of occasions, peasant action forced a landholder to dismiss particular local officials and replace them with others seen as more amenable to the peasants' interests. The poet Krsnahari Das describes these events, putting the following words into the mouth of the sacked *diwan*:

> Raiyats can do anything,
> they can raise someone to heaven,
> or throw them down to death,
> the Raiyat creates the kingly authority of the lord,
> all the gold bangles you see are their doing.[11]

My point here is that peasants did not perceive themselves as powerless. But neither did they believe that their power inhered permanently in their own subjectivity: it flowed from the peasant to the lord, and then back—in a conditional form—to the peasant again. It was the relationship between the two, and not the peasant's inherent, autonomous consciousness, that constituted the identity and motivated the actions of peasants in 1783.

This set of concepts was challenged by two rival discursive orders, those of Rangpur's landholding population and that of the colonial regime. Bengali landholders do not seem to have universally shared the peasants' conception of a normative moral order. In the language they use to communicate with the colonial regime (language that may have been adopted precisely because they were engaging with the colonial regime), many seem to have seen the protection of their tenants and subjects in purely instrumental terms, as nothing but a mechanism to maintain their local authority. The landholder's way of understanding the world, his or her sense of self, was defined by idioms of authority that did not always include the vast majority of his or her subjects or tenants. The landholding self was constituted in languages about kinship and lineage, about status and substance, which involved a dialogue with peers in civic bodies such as the *eka-jai* (community council) and in royal courts of one sort or another, not only with tenants and subjects of a significantly lower social status.[12] Nonetheless, these elitist idioms of self-constitution were undermined by the practical recognition that the landholder's authority could only be upheld in practice by maintaining a dialogic relationship with his or her subjects. The landholder would offer peasants concessions sufficient to prevent rebellion or mass migration, but would employ other means to retain that role when they were able to. Bengali landholders frequently complained to colonial officials about the Company's unwillingness to support means of coercion (imprisonment, dispossession, capture of peasants who "absconded" across district boundaries) that were seen as essential to the consolidation of local authority. But landholders also recognized that in order to keep their retinue of "subjects" in place, they needed to show a willingness to compromise and engage in dialogue with an armed body of the rural population. As we can see, an analysis that concentrates on the autonomous consciousness of either of these social groups is unable to explain the events or the unequal power relations that occurred. The consciousness and actions of Rangpur's landholding class were constituted by a process of engagement with a complex set of social forces.

How does one think about the collective consciousness of the colonial regime? Both peasants and landholders were aware that their ability to act was not created by the intrinsic potentialities they possessed but pragmatically constituted by the flow of power between different social groups. An examination of the thoughts and deeds of British officials shows that they took for granted their ability to act autonomously to a far greater degree than other groups we have looked at. Richard Goodlad, the district collector, saw himself as the agent of a sovereign authority that had the right and capability to impose order and security in the neighborhood. On an individual basis, he saw his authority as flowing unproblematically from his superiors in the Board of Revenue and from the Governor-General in Calcutta. Theoretically, the Company's collective authority came from two sources: the British Parliament and the East India Company's inheritance of the supposedly unitary sovereignty of the Mughal state in Bengal. The violence used against the Rangpur rebellion was legitimated as a suppression of elements within Bengal's population who were disturbing the static, propertied social order that the Company had been put in place to protect. Politicians and Company officials disputed the legitimacy of the actions of Raja Devi Singh, the Company's revenue agent whose repressive actions were seen by many to have instigated the revolt; some questioned Goodlad's readiness to bring in the forces of violence of the colonial regime so quickly to support him. Yet none doubted that the Company's sovereignty gave it both the right and the ability to act to suppress social revolt.[13]

We can make two points here. First of all, the very fact that the insurrection happened demonstrates that this conception of the Company's absolute authority was not adequate to explain how "its" power actually worked. The fact that a significant proportion of Rangpur's population acted violently against the agents of the colonial regime (even though they were not necessarily perceived as such by the rebels themselves) shows that the Company's authority could indeed be challenged—and challenged successfully for a limited period of time.

Secondly, the fact of this challenge (both in 1783 and on countless other occasions) broke open the univocality of the colonial voice. Alongside the language of absolute authority, a pragmatic language existed, which recognized the necessity for complex maneuvers and negotiations to occur if the authority of the colonial regime was to be secured. A tactical discourse of "expediency" was used to justify negotiations of one sort or another. In order to prevent "peaceful" peasants from joining the rebellion, Richard Goodlad made concessions to peasants who did not rise up in revolt. In the middle of the uprising, he publicly agreed to many demands of the insurgent peasants—even if he went back on his word and continued to collect rent at the same level as before. More importantly, the tactical vocabulary I am talking about created a process in which Company officials continually changed the administrative fabric of the colonial regime. In order to maintain their authority—to avoid the possibility of rebellion and secure a continuing revenue stream—the colonial regime reinvented itself on a regular basis. In doing so, it also transformed the language it used to legitimate its own authority.

Throughout the events of 1783, we can see that different players had different goals; they each employed a different set of strategies to try to achieve their objectives. The move each player made in each case was fundamentally dependent on the place of all the other pieces in the game. To attribute a set of events to the "autonomous" consciousness of one or more "agent" is to reduce a complex, dynamic process of interaction to a static set-piece encounter in which each player has no choice but to repeat the same move time and time again.

So far, I have agreed with Talal Asad's suggestion that "*agent* and *subject* (where the former is the principle of effectivity and the latter of consciousness) do not belong to the same theoretical universe and should not, therefore, be coupled." I have challenged the argument—which seems to have been held by the early generation of subaltern historians—that an analysis of consciousness can explain actions, at least the actions of peasant insurgents. But one needs to go beyond this and show how a historical process such as the one that occurred in late eighteenth-century Rangpur cannot be explained with reference to *any* coherent agentive subject, whether conscious or not. This is the case for two reasons. First of all, the historical process that produces particular events (e.g., "the rebellion") occurs as the consequence of a process of interaction between subjects (whether conscious or not) who are constituted in different ways, each with their own conscious and unconscious tendencies and trajectories. The agency that produced the rebellion and its repression did not exist inherently in one of those forces (such as "capitalism," the revenue-maximizing logic of the colonial regime, the consciousness of peasants, demographics, or whatever), but rather in a set of power-relations that flowed between them in their interaction. Secondly, the way the subjects that participated in these events were constituted was itself the *product* of the contingent historical relationship between the different forces I am speaking of. In Rangpur, the rebellion made the rebels; likewise, the rebellion and subsequent repression powerfully influenced the specific character of the colonial regime.

To demonstrate this argument, let me return to Rangpur and consider the supposedly objective reality of "the colonial state" as a potential subject-agent for a moment. We noted earlier that the East India Company's officials possessed a conception of the Company's absolute sovereignty, but this consciousness was continually undercut by a tactical vocabulary about the contingent means the Company needed to employ to consolidate its own authority. As I suggested, that pragmatic, tactical language emerged as a consequence of the Company's engagement with a variety of social forces in Bengal; it meant that the Company's officials continually reinvented the language they used to justify its authority, and continually transformed the mechanisms they used to assert it.

The idea of a subject-agent is rooted in the understanding that subjects are also agents that *possess* the capacity or *power* of acting with effect in the world—whether they are conscious of that capacity or not (I will return to the words I have italicized in a moment). To suggest that the Company's ability to act depended on the inherent capabilities it ("the colonial regime") *possessed* is a misnomer. This was certainly the case in Rangpur in 1783. The coercive apparatus the collector of Rangpur, Richard Goodlad, had at his disposal consisted of a detachment of Indian troops commanded by a European officer. This coercive force was the basis of the "power" Goodlad believed he possessed. But those troops were employed by the Company because of the dominant role the British had begun to play in the Indian military labor market, a role that in turn rested on the Company's ability to collect revenue from Indian landlords and peasants in order to pay a competitive wage. For this authority to be secure, officials such as Goodlad needed to use continually changing means to extract surplus from the process of agrarian production in Bengal. So to ask about the degree of power a Company official *possessed* is meaningless; his ability to act was based on a capacity to direct and dispose of the capabilities of others. The maintenance of the Company's authority (and a *conception* of its power) depended on a series of tactical interventions and relationships that the Company made with subjects that existed elsewhere.

These interventions transformed the character of the Company's rule. The Rangpur rebellion and similar instances of resistance and repression around the same time had an influence on the changing shape of British rule—so much so that it is impossible to talk about "the colonial regime" or "the Company regime" as a coherent subject over this period at all. The infamous "permanent settlement" of 1793—the attempt to fix the amount landholders paid to the British—emerged out of a critique of the mode of collecting revenue that had underpinned the Rangpur rebellion a decade before.[14] The language used during the 1790s emphasized the role of the Company as the guarantor of property and security, not its potential to intervene in order to transform the social fabric of Bengali society. Yet the mechanisms established in that decade failed to meet their initial objectives because they did not adequately account for the ways in which Bengal's landholders did in fact act. This failure occurred because colonial understandings were incapable of fully comprehending the ways in which Bengal's population engaged, responded, and resisted the institutions of the colonial regime. The result was that the mechanisms used by British officials to intervene in Indian power relations were reconstructed, as the Company's regime remodeled itself once again.

I don't have the space to explain this transformation in much detail, but let me briefly summarize two aspects of it. First of all, the East India Company's regime became much clearer about both its capacity and the limits on its capacity to "interfere" with social relations in Bengal. The way the Company acted upon the world around it changed fundamentally, as it began to see itself as an agency with an active capacity to intervene in the fabric of Bengali society, whether to reconfigure property relations, reorient the character of commercial transactions, or introduce English education as a way of realigning the conduct of its Bengali subjects. In Bengal itself, this transformation was fairly subtle, although it was marked by a new belief in the power of the colonial "state" to introduce innovative legislation in order to "improve" the social relations of Bengal. Outside Bengal, more transformatory schemes were put into place that overturned the basis of the "Bengal policy" of permanent settlement. Notionally at least, across Northern India, landholders (*zamindars* and *taluqdars*) were dispossessed and revenue collected directly from peasants. The Awadh settlement of 1856, which many see as a causative precursor of the insurrection of 1857–58, was an attempt to transform the fabric of Indian society in precisely this way.[15]

Secondly, this new conception of the colonial regime's role involved a transformation in the way officials perceived the colonial regime's relationship to temporality. Company policy in the 1770s and 1780s was based on an assumption authorized by past modes of practice, but it could be distanced from the state's activity in the present. British officials had talked of "custom" and the "ancient constitution" as ways to legitimate their rule. But later conceptions perceived the state as an agent that existed at the junction between two temporal structures, between the "tradition" of a homogeneous Indian past that needed to be sometimes reformed, sometimes protected, and a future Indian modernity authored and created by the British colonial regime.[16]

The forms of practice and thought that transformed the subjectivity of the colonial regime between 1780 and 1840 or so were not "imposed" from Britain. They were worked out in a series of colonial situations in which constantly changing concepts from Britain interacted with the activity of Indians and the cultural practices of the colonial regime. My argument is that this process transformed the character of the forces that engaged with each other to produce the continually changing character of colonial rule in the Indian subcontinent. It is impossible to attribute these changes to a coherent subject-agent such as "the colonial regime" because the colonial regime's very subjectivity—in other words, the way it existed as an entity with the capacity to act—was dramatically transformed in the process.

When historians attribute primacy within their research to the subjectivity of one agent (whether the colonial regime, the insurgent peasant, or the hidden hand of capitalist economic activity), that force is constructed as a coherent subject-agent with an abstract and almost metaphysical quality. The use of these transcendent categories within historical analysis prevents a satisfactory explanation of the process of historical change. Fundamentally, it prevents the historian or anthropologist from understanding how imperialism created a new political and moral landscape which itself created new limits upon and possibilities for human activity.

The construction of these transcendent categories of historical analysis bedevils any attempt to attribute autonomy to the consciousness and practice of non-European colonial subjects. I've discussed the history of the colonial regime at length in this paper because, almost invariably, constructions such as these presuppose the colonial—and often also nationalist—state as a monolithic entity with a single normalizing project that originates in European history. The existence of either Europe or the modern state as a coherent and static subject-agent is taken for granted. The critique only comes when historians argue that the state's ability to effectively impose its will is challenged by insurgent, if fragmented, modes of consciousness that assert rival indigenous forms of power and thought. In attempting to recover the autonomy of these indigenous forms, historians are driven to assume that they consist of a set of transcendent subjectivities, in precisely the same way as they assume the transcendent existence of the colonial regime.

More recently, Partha Chatterjee has argued that South Asian scholars should move beyond a delineation of the rigid autonomous spheres of "elite" and "subaltern" politics and begin to recognize "the mutually conditioned historicities" of each.[17] Yet these intentions are undermined by his analysis later in the text. Chatterjee's main concern is to isolate the "fragments" of a modern Indian mode of political thought in order to show how Indians asserted their difference by carving an autonomous space for themselves in counterpoint to the dominant role of colonial modernity in civil society and the state. Along with other scholars, he argues that Indian nationalists created a "different modernity," which consisted neither in a return to the past of precolonial Indian tradition nor the abandonment of the difference of being Indian for a universal or European form of social order.[18] In theory, his purpose is precisely to challenge the construction of transcendent categories of analysis. Yet the category he uses to discuss the characteristics of this modernity is a universal one: community. Community is presented as a transcendent category that is the antithesis of the individualism essential to modern, liberal political discourse and the antagonist of the logic of capital that European capitalism attempts to force upon the subcontinent.

Chatterjee's concern is to "claim for us, the once-colonized, our freedom of imagination." This concern for absolute autonomy and difference forces him to try to conjure up a space for truly "Indian" thought. The only way he can do so is by invoking community, a category that seems to be nothing but the transcendent antithesis of the transcendent logic he ascribes to capitalism and the colonial regime. Any concern with the particularity of Indian thought and practice, and its relationship to the changing moral and political landscape of nineteenth-century Bengal, is lost in the process.[19]

My point is that in asserting the difference of subaltern or Indian thought and practice, historians always have to presuppose the entity in opposition to which that difference is defined as a cohesive, monolithic category. The attempt to find subaltern autonomy ends up being reduced to a set of logical procedures in which the agency of an anticolonial subject is defined simply as the binary opposite of the different identities it ranged itself against (in Chatterjee's account of elite political discourse, these are the colonial state and Bengal's subaltern classes). Searching for agency consists simply in the identification of characteristics in the thought or conduct of the insurgent subject that differ from those perceived in other modes of practice or consciousness. These characteristics are then imputed to a transcendent subject that retains those characteristics throughout the historical process. The solution is not for historians to look for different kinds of subjects, but to question the link between subjectivity and agency in its entirety.

III

The word "agency" is a surrogate for the term "power"—the capacity to act, affect, or influence something else. Historians who search for agency, whether the agency of the colonial official or the subaltern peasant, believe that power is *possessed* by a particular individual or collective subject. Different subjects possess different levels of power. Few argue that the most oppressed peasant has the same amount of power as his or her master. But those who attempt to uncover the agency of the rural poor argue that peasants did have a limited capability to mold their lives according to their own will. The fact of rebellion—of a conscious, premeditated mode of defiance—is evidence of peasants' power over the world they inhabit, even though its suppression is proof that their power was opposed by a stronger force. At the center of this and many other debates about the relationship between imperialism and its colonial subjects is the question of who or what wields power and who or what does not, even if a conception of the subaltern's "power" is used to define the conditions in which she is able to make her own life under an extensive form of domination. The question posed in this debate is where a particular subject exists on a continuum from fully empowered to entirely powerless.

But as Michel Foucault suggests, to ask who has power in any given historical situation is to "pos[e] a labyrinthine and unanswerable question." To ask who has power requires the historian to presuppose the existence of abstract, transcendent subjects in a way that undermines the historian's attempt to explain the specific characteristics of the particular historical process they are describing. Power (agency) does not inhere in particular subjects. It flows between them, constituting, enabling, and constraining their actions as it does so. As Michel Foucault reminds us, "Power must be analysed as something which circulates, or rather as something which only functions in the form of a chain. It is never localized here or there, never in anybody's hands, never appropriated as a commodity or a piece of wealth. Power is employed and exercised in a netlike organization."[20] Foucault's argument here is often misinterpreted as an abstract and transcendent account of power that contrasts with a common-sense view in which power is the capacity agents have of doing things. Jürgen Habermas criticizes Foucault for merging his conception of power as a "pure, decentred, rule-guided operation with the ordered elements of a suprasubjectively constructed system"; power is said to have a "transcendent generality" in Habermas's interpretation of Foucault.[21] Yet if one uses Foucault's concept of power to analyze concrete historical situations, one soon sees that it is the presumption that power is something which subjects possess and wield that generates "transcendent generalities," and not Foucault's approach. The kind of empirical account of power relations that Foucault offers allows the historian to describe how particular subjects and courses of action are constituted and authorized whereas Habermas's conception of the universal character of human subjectivity does not.

    I do not want to suggest that historians should not attribute tendencies and strategies to impersonal social entities. It is impossible for historians to consider the infinite complexity of events; scholars need to find ways to reduce infinite difference and heterogeneity to a manageable form. One way to do so is to impute a coherent trajectory to an impersonal set of forces and use a single noun (the working class, peasants, the colonial regime) to describe them. The problem occurs when the operation of power is attributed to coherent entities of this sort, and terms like the peasantry, the working class, or the colonial regime are identified as the directing force behind a particular instance of historical change. Power possesses strategies and tactics, moves in particular directions, and even has certain intentions, but these are never firmly attached to particular subjects. "There is," as Foucault puts it, "no power that is exercised without a series of aims and objectives." But, "let us not look for the headquarters that presides over its rationality."[22]

A form of historical practice that took these arguments seriously would abandon all interest in the forms of agency responsible for particular phenomena and refuse to attribute them to particular subject-agents imbued with power. It would be a thoroughly Foucauldian history, in which a concern to trace everything back to origins is replaced with an interest in more contingent processes of emergence in which a complex range of untraceable forces intersect to produce different forms of subjectivity at particular points in time. Instead of imputing power to the consciousness or inherent tendencies of particular subject-agents, it would see subjectivity as something that emerges from the flow of power between different forms of subjectivity and agency.

Applied to the study of the colonized world, such a history would not abandon the category of imperialism or undermine attempts to uncover the processes of colonial power and domination. Neither would it be a story about the "indigenous" origins of colonial rule—a major concern for number of scholars in recent times. Along with Nicholas Dirks, Partha Chatterjee has vehemently challenged a style of historical reasoning they find in the work of C. A. Bayly and David Washbrook, which asserts the indigenous origins of colonial rule. Chatterjee suggests that Bayly and Washbrook write the colonial intrusion out of the history of imperialism; Dirks suggests that these scholars "blame the victim" for its own exploitation. These accusations are only possible because both critics assume that the meaning of "imperialism" and "victimhood" are stable. But insofar as Chatterjee and Dirks are correct in identifying this argument in Bayly and Washbrook's work (a debate I do not wish to enter into here), their scholarship is vulnerable to the same critique—that it takes for granted the existence of coherent subject-agents that are responsible for the course of colonial Indian history.[23]

In contrast to these rather limiting debates, an approach that refuses to conflate subjectivity and agency allows for the delineation of the specificities and peculiarities of the colonial in a far more nuanced fashion. Imperialism should not be understood as an encounter between an external power and an indigenous population, in which rival sets of forces struggle to assert their autonomy and dominance over each other. It makes more sense to see it as a process of interaction within a particular geographical space (in this case, India) that produced the subjects we perceive *as* indigenous and external and the relations of power and domination that ensued.

The "colonial" (British/imperial/modern/secular) and the "indigenous" are not agents responsible for the historical dynamics of imperialism, but consequences of these dynamics. Over the last two decades—in particular since the publication of Edward Said's *Orientalism*—historians and anthropologists have emphasized the role colonial discourse and practice played in defining the identity of the colonized. Hinduism, caste, and the Indian peasantry have all been seen as colonial constructions—and the implication is often that they were actively constructed by the agentive power of the colonial regime.[24] A more marginal strand of recent scholarly discussion suggests that the practice and subjectivity of the colonizers were constructed by imperialism to an equal extent. As we are frequently reminded, Europeans did things differently in the colony. In order to maintain a sense of their autonomy from and power over the subjects they ruled, they defined their subjectivity in different ways and engaged in forms of practice different from those in the metropolis. Many of these peculiarly colonial forms of European identity seeped back to inform life in Europe. Thus, for example, many British forms of dress and cuisine, styles of bureaucratic government, and notions of race and identity emerged in the colony to define a colonial concept of Britishness in India and elsewhere, and were then translated into a "metropolitan" British context.[25] I would not go so far as to suggest that empire was entirely constitutive of British identity—that would be to attribute agency to empire as a single coherent agentive subject and deny the role of the heterogeneous relations of power within Britain in the making of British or English identity. But a refusal to take the colonial subject-agent for granted opens up space for the historian to show that what it meant to be British in India, and occasionally elsewhere, was as much a product of the colonial process as what it meant to be Indian. As Franz Fanon, Albert Memmi, Ashis Nandy, and Ann Stoler all remind us, "The colonial system manufactures colonialists, just as it manufactures the colonised."[26] Yet the continued importance of imperialism in constituting European identities is effaced by those who emphasize the homogeneity of the European experience and assume that imperialism consisted in exporting, however ambiguously, the "modern" European state and "modern" forms of power.

As Talal Asad argues, imperialism should not be "thought of as the term for an actor contingently connected to its acts, for a player calculating what his next move should be in a game whose stakes are familiar to all participants, and whose rules are accepted by them." It is possible to discuss the autonomous agency of subjects who resist colonial power only if one excepts a view of imperialism as "an already constituted agent wh[ich] acts in a determinate way." Asad implies that the category of imperialism should be used instead to describe "the totality of forces that converge to create (largely contingently) a new moral landscape that defines different kinds of acts"—in other words, if it is considered as a process of interaction and convergence constitutive of subjectivity rather than a process constituted by subject-agents. Asad's argument here makes it impossible to speak coherently of agency or autonomy or resistance at all.

These comments occur in the midst of Asad's discussion of law reform in Egypt. He goes on to suggest that

> the basic question here . . . is not the determination of the "oppressors" and "oppressed," of whether the elites or the popular masses were the agents in the history of reform (both, of course, in various ways participated in the changes). It is the determination of that new landscape, and the degree to which the languages, behaviours, and institutions it makes possible come to resemble those that obtain in Western European nation-states.[27]

Here Asad refuses to attribute agency to any subject for the process of law reform and the new landscape it was part of. As a consequence, he avoids reifying the European and the Egyptian or locating the origin of the process of reform with one or the other. Law reform is instead seen as the consequence of a process of engagement between a range of European and non-European intellectual styles and traditions, in which the unequal power relations running through them played an important part.

The consequence of this process was the emergence of a peculiarly Egyptian variant of secularism. But Asad does not simply wish to argue that law reform had many sources. His point is that a new intellectual configuration occurred that transformed the identity of its constitutive elements. The moral landscape he terms secularism defined the spheres to be inhabited by the sources it used to create modern Egyptian legal practice. So, for example, the Islamic principles of sharia law were "transmuted" into a form of law that was relevant only to the domain of the family and personal status. In doing so, it was dramatically transformed into an instrument for regulating the modern domestic sphere. To argue that this transmutation continued to offer a space for autonomous Egyptian reasoning to occur would be to deny the fundamental nature of the transformation. Such an argument takes for granted the existence of the European and the indigenous as transcendent subjects, when the meaning of both these terms was transformed in the process of change. Instead, his concern is to argue that the process of sharia reform was both "the precondition and the consequence of secular processes of power."

Throughout *Formations of the Secular*, Asad argues that it is impossible to offer an a priori definition of "secularism" and "the secular." Nor is it possible to argue that it is a concept/set of practices/process with a unitary point of origin or "single line of filiation." The secular "is neither singular in origin nor stable in its identity."[28] So, for example, to say that secularism originates in the history of Western Europe is nonsensical, because our sense of what modern Europe is is constituted by a conception of Europe's secularism as much as the reverse. Although there are occasions when Asad refers to "the secular" as a "concept," he usually defines secularism as a set of concepts and practices that share family resemblances and operate through a common grammer.[29] Secularism is not a "subject" that itself has "agentive power" but the effect of an interaction between heterogeneous power relations. Like the process of imperialism, it does not consist of "an already constituted agent wh[ich] acts in a determinate way." Nor can it be wielded and imposed from outside on other social groups by agents (the colonial regime, the Egyptian middle class, etc.) who have agentive power. In Asad's analysis, it is described as a phenomenon that emerges without origins.

This approach allows Asad to brilliantly pick apart the contradictions and incoherences implicit in the use of the concept of secularism. At the core of this cluster of concepts is the assumption that "men make their own history." Secularism posits the individual and collective human subject as the creator of the world in which he or she lives. It does so by asserting the history-making human subject-agent as a universal category. But as Asad points out, this claim to universality is undercut by secularism's continual assertion of the particular *kind* of human being that the practice of secularism creates. The particular attributes of humanity envisaged by secular thought depend on the specific histories of particular institutions which have configured what it means to be human in different contexts. My reading of Asad's text leads to the argument that the definition of "secularism" is not and can never be universal because different societies have created their own conception of what it means to be human.

For example, Asad discusses the role of Muslims as a religious minority in Europe, noting the widespread perception that Muslims, "whose roots lie in Asia, do not belong in the Western family."[30] It is not a failure of Muslim values and practices to conform to the universalizing secular values Europeans profess to espouse that produces this perception. Rather Europeans, despite the supposed universality of secular humanism, subscribe to a conception of themselves as having an "unchangeable essence" that excludes (but can be allowed to tolerate) those—like Muslims—who are seen to lie outside it.[31] This essence is essentially historical. It is articulated in the belief that a single historical narrative can be told about a coherent entity called Europe, which Muslims are not part of. It asserts that there is a particular European variant of what it means to be human. This conception (or, more accurately, the belief that this conception exists) then structures attitudes toward those who are subsequently defined as lacking the essential attributes of humanity. But attempting to define the essence of Europeanness is an impossible task: Where is its center? What are its core values?[32] All there is is a range of narrative strategies that have been used to invoke the history of a single entity called Europe, and which are employed to define its difference from the rest of the world. The history of "the signs and symbols" institutions have used to define Europe is a history of heterogeneity. These narratives do not have a single stable referent. They never converge on a single, really existing subject called Europe that could provide an original point for such a discourse.

Asad's point here is that neither secularism nor Europe exist as subject-agents, whether or not one wishes to treat them as conscious entities. As much as the European Community might wish to deny it, there is no single "collective consciousness" that can provide a set of commonly shared values to define the essence of being European. Neither can one identify a common set of unconscious practices or tendencies that might serve to define the essence of the category "Europe." The histories of particular regions, nations, social groups, and institutions are heterogeneous and have produced their own distinct traditions and histories of what it is to be human. I am perhaps pushing Asad's argument further than he would wish, but the logic of his position is that that no single narrative of European capitalism, European state-formation, or European secularism is possible. Europe, as a cohesive subject with agentive power over the rest of the world, simply does not exist.

The heterogeneous multiple imaginings of Europe coexist with the idea that there *is* such a thing as Europe because, as Asad points out, the category "Europe" is forged to define its difference from the world outside. The only thing that is stable about the process by which Europe is constituted is that it is defined as different from its "others"—although the precise nature of its difference is itself heterogeneous, unstable, and impossible to define at a general level. The point here is not specific to Europe but could be applied to countless other abstract categories that are deployed within historical analysis and political life—nations, social classes, peasants, landholders, modes of production, and the colonial regime. Yet at the historical conjuncture we live in, the idea of Europe (or the idea that there is an idea of Europe) can be deployed with greater force than categories that our discursive order marginalizes. George Bush's recent assertion of the existence of common European values of freedom and democracy underpinning Euro-American relations—despite obvious differences about the way these supposedly common values were put into practice during the war in Iraq—is a good example; Vladimir Putin's attempt to assert the essentially European character of Russian civilization is another. In both cases, Europe is deployed as a coherent subject-agent having transformative power, even though it is conjured in very different ways.[33]

Throughout this paper, I have suggested that the power of categories such as "Europe" cannot be displaced if historians and anthropologists simply present counternarratives that conjure up antagonistic subject-agents to challenge its power (the non-European nation, the subaltern community, etc.). Narratives of this sort attempt to displace the category "Europe" by positing a rival subject that shares the same intellectual space and is vulnerable to the same critique. Stories about nationalist or subaltern autonomy present an insurgent version of what it means to be human, but they do so by taking for granted the coherence and univocality of the subjects they oppose—ultimately, they leave imperialism, modernity, or Europe standing on the same ground that inhabitants of those categories incoherently claim for themselves. A more fundamental critique is possible. By refusing to conflate subjectivity with agency, it is possible to challenge the transcendence of the modern, secular, or European. Doing so allows the historian or anthropologist to delineate the particular historical conjunctures—and the particular forms of inclusion and exclusion and specific relations of power—on which the heterogeneous operation of those terms relied.

IV

The position I have outlined in this chapter has political implications. A form of historical or anthropological writing that challenges the connection between subjectivity and agency undermines the secular claim that "man makes his own history." Historical change is regarded as the effect of a continual process of interaction between human subjects in one form or another, in such a way as to make it impossible to attribute autonomous power and consciousness to particular agents for specific events. Such a form of analysis would, to quote Foucault, provide a history of the "effects of power," without trying to answer the question of where—or with whom—power lies. Yet within the life-worlds we inhabit, political activity relies on the assumption that politics requires the activist to possess a conscious sense of her own agency to achieve particular radical ends. Many of the forms of engagement open to us are based on the assumption that subjects—collective or individual—are capable of making history. An approach that studies the effects of power without imputing its operation to particular subject-agents obviously undermines the secular foundations of political action.

But this style of reasoning is not nihilistic; it is just that a different kind of ethics and politics underpins the antifoundational approach I've outlined in this chapter. Using a rigid concept of agency to explain historical change involves the assumption that the sum total of activity that exists in the world can be attributed to the sum total of subjectivity and agency. Every human action or phenomenon—whether we see it as good or bad, whether it furthers the cause of human happiness or human suffering—is supposed to be attributable to a clearly identifiable autonomous agent, who can be regarded as responsible for it.[34] As Asad and others emphasize, this conception of responsible agency underpins our understanding of the way many modern institutions operate. It forms the basis for our legal systems (a criminal can be convicted because we believe he has singular responsibility for the crime he committed) and is crucially important for the operation of countless institutions, ranging from the global bodies that police human rights to the working of the machinery of electoral politics. In its attempt to map the quantum of human activity to exactly defined subject-agents who are singularly responsible for it, this perspective is uneasy with contingency, uncertainty, and contestability and results in a culture of blame and resentment.

As William E. Connolly suggests, a world in which everything happens for a reason and every occurrence has to be attributed to a subject that is its cause is also a world in which identities are unstable and contingent. Connolly discusses this question in the context of an argument about what he calls "the problem of evil"—how we, as late moderns, account for the existence of suffering in the world. Individuals try to bridge the gap between the contingency and contestability of their own identity by imputing responsibility for suffering and evil to the coherent, autonomous subjectivity of another. We—"the modern inheritors of the idea that the world was made good"—cannot believe that evil (suffering, pain, poverty, etc.) is fundamental to the world in which we live. As a result we blame a particular individual or social force for being the responsible agent that *causes* the evils of the world. Asylum-seekers are seen as responsible for crime; the downturn in the global economy is attributed to terrorism; the absence of peace and democracy in the Middle East is blamed on Islamic culture; Indian poverty is a legacy of colonial rule, and so on. In order to shore up identities for ourselves in a world riven by contingency and ambiguity, we attribute responsibility for the things we do not like to another. This move proceeds by discursively constructing blamable subject-agents that are other from ourselves.

Connolly's point is that if we could live more easily with contingency and inhabit a world in which all instances of human suffering did not need to be attributed to determinate, responsible agents, we could avoid the resentful attribution of evil to the other. But being at ease with contingency involves a radical epistemological shift and a vigorous critique of the secular foundations of political action. Fundamentally, it requires us to disconnect subjectivity and identity from agency. It involves a refusal to attribute all activity—good and bad—to coherent subjects, whether ourselves or another.

Connolly proposes a politics of "deep pluralism," in which subjects recognize the fractured character of their own identity and are "alert to elements of contingency in its relational constitution."[35] This form of politics would recognize deep-rooted forms of identity but see such identities as emerging from a contingent process of interaction with others and ourselves, not as the expression of an a priori position of autonomous agency. Connolly suggests that this would undermine the totalizing claims of particular forms of national identity, for example. It would do so by emphasizing the plural character of the heterogeneous identities possessed by the inhabitants of a nation. Both Connolly and Asad argue that this could coincide with a form of politics that recognizes the absence of a single majority form of national subjectivity; instead, they envision the nation as an agglomeration of minorities.[36]

The "deep pluralism" proposed by both Connolly and Asad requires that agency and responsibility be decoupled from subjectivity and identity, and involves a recognition of the contingent and interactive process by which subjects are constituted. As a consequence, it is critical of the foundations subjects create for themselves in order to engage politically in the world. The politically committed cannot, however, entirely reject the need to construct coherent forms of subjectivity that provide the basis for their willful, agentive attempt to change the world. Political activity requires the mobilization of particular groups who are perceived to share a common identity in order to provide the basis for political action. It depends on the fictive but effective assumption that there *are* coherent communities that can wield agentive power.

The political implications of Asad's genealogical critique of "what it takes to live particular ways of life continuously, co-operatively and unselfconsciously" exists in a discursive space fundamentally different from the assertion (however contingent and temporary) of homogenous forms of community required by political action. One can inform the other, but it is impossible to do both things at once. To see this as a problem is to conflate two separate roles and to assume that the purpose of the engaged, critical historian or anthropologist is to actively propel particular processes of historical change. It is to confuse critique with activism and to deny that one individual can occupy the role of critic and activist in different institutions at different points in time. A life as *both* a critic and activist is possible, but it cannot exist within a single institutional and intellectual site. The same genre of academic scholarship should not try to both critique the foundations of global inequality *and* offer alternative subject positions from which those injustices can be overturned. Familiar as we are with the existence of multiple worlds structured by heterogeneous, often incommensurate sets of cultural practices, there should be nothing strange about doing one thing according to one style of reasoning in one place, and another somewhere else.

Often, though, we end up being the victims of the totalizing claims that the academic institutions and discourses we inhabit apply to every aspect of our lives. It is too easy for academics to assume that every form of political engagement has to occur from within academia, but living in the world consists of involvement in many different institutions. Academics teach and conduct research in universities, but they are also consumers, fitness fanatics, lovers, community activists, and members of political organizations. In each case, they speak different languages and occupy different subject positions that cannot be assimilated into a single way of life. There is no reason why this shouldn't also be the case regarding the ways we choose to focus our political engagement. If we are to take seriously the assumption that the objects of our historical and anthropological inquiry have multiple identities and perform many different roles, we should apply this insight to our own lives.

For much of our lives we cannot but inhabit a secular world in which we assume that men, women, and the collective entities they form are subject-agents that are the authors of their own destiny. However, Talal Asad's work has opened up a space within the cultural practices of academia (and perhaps in some places beyond), in which to unearth and critique the complex and contradictory genealogies that produce these practices of secularism.

11

Responses

Talal Asad

I am grateful to the authors of these essays. All of them—and not least those who have taken strong issue with my arguments—have compelled me to think again about what I said. In *Formations of the Secular*, I tried to extend certain ideas that I touched on in *Genealogies of Religion*. In some ways, the former was harder to write than the latter. It is much more exploratory, and I am not satisfied with everything I said in it. This is why it has been valuable for me to elaborate some of the ideas that were incompletely or inadequately stated. Whether in doing so I have responded satisfactorily to each of the authors I don't know.

The only point I want to stress at the outset is that for me anthropology is a continuous exploration of received ideas about the way given modes of life hang together. More precisely: What is included or excluded in the concepts that help to organize our collective lives? How? Why? With what probable consequences for behavior and experience? Such an inquiry requires that one be ready to break out of the coercive constraints of Sociological Truth—the axiom that the social is the ground of being. The results, however provisional, can be uncomfortable, and they may sometimes point to politically incorrect conclusions. What we eventually do with them is another matter, because we are not abstract intellectuals. All of us live in particular forms of life that constantly demand decisions and that in general presuppose a variety of commitments. And we all have particular memories, fears, and hopes.

Critique, though indispensable, can occupy only a small part of a life that is lived sanely. It is nevertheless possible to be alert to the tension between the unconditional openness required by anthropological inquiry and the decisiveness demanded by ethical and political life. The two always go together but not easily. In my view, anthropological inquiry and political commitment should not be confused. It is not only that we do not know for certain what the long-term future will be. More importantly, we do not know which aspects of the past it will be reasonable (and vital) to restore or invoke when we get to the future. So we do not know what the past will be. In my view, anthropological inquiry is therefore an unending labor of revision and reconsideration, while political commitment requires decisive action (even calculated waiting is an action) regardless of how ignorant we are—and regardless of the fact that sometimes we may only be moving in time from one social distribution of pain and cruelty to another.

Response to Casanova

In the first few pages of chapter 6 in *Formations*, I tried to address Casanova's broad argument because it seemed to me—and still does—of considerable interest. In particular, I regard his disaggregation of the three main elements in the secularization thesis and his comments on them as an obvious advance in the debate. However, in the final analysis, his attempt to save the "core of the theory" did not seem to me successful. Casanova complains that I have misrepresented his attempt at reformulation, although he proposes that in our intellectual endeavors we are both in fundamental agreement. I plead that my concern in that chapter was not to write a review essay on *Public Religions in the Modern World*; it was to conduct a series of skeptical inquiries about secularism, beginning with a look at his reformulation of the thesis. I cannot pick up every disclaimer Casanova has made in his own defense, but I stand by my reading. Here I will confine myself to restating my objections to the basic argument of his book. Finally, although I admire his erudition and humanity, I am not persuaded that our projects *are* quite the same.

In Casanova's view, the core of the theory of secularization is the claim that modern society is characterized by "the differentiation of the secular spheres from each other *and* from religious institutions and norms." This claim he regards in his book as "still defensible." Now, as I see it, the first problem is that the characterization virtually equates secularization with modernity, as many sociologists have defined it, and I'm not sure how different this makes it from "the teleological theory of religious development" that Casanova rightly disparages. Secondly, it doesn't help us to identify the different kinds of secular life and the political reasoning on which they are based. For example, in the United States the population is largely religious and the federal government is constitutionally required to be neutral, and yet Christian movements have historically been able to mobilize effectively in support of important policies (antislavery, Prohibition, anti-abortion, pro-Israel, etc.). Conversely, the federal courts are frequently required to decide whether particular forms of public behavior deserve to be protected under the principle of freedom of religion; in this way, the legal apparatus of the state must continually define what is truly religion. In France, where the population is mostly nonreligious, the aggressively antireligious state owns all church property built before 1908, except in Alsace and Lorraine (which were at that time a part of Germany), where *all* church property is now state property and where priests, ministers, and rabbis are state employees. A state that maintains the basic conditions for the practice of religion in society is itself religious. Thus in these two societies the state responds very differently to religious institutions and norms, although in neither case are state and religion completely separate. Right through the nineteenth and twentieth centuries, American religiosity fed into federal policy-making in ways quite unparalleled in France; the French state, on the other hand, controls religious property in ways unthinkable in America. And yet both the United States and France are in theory and practice secular states. I'm sure Casanova is aware of these facts, but my point is that his core theory of secularization impedes their full investigation because it avoids examining the complicated prejudgments on which relations between religion and state appear to rest in constitutional law.

This brings me to my final difficulty with Casanova's thesis: if "the deprivatization of religion" is compatible with "modernity," doesn't this jeopardize the "core of the theory of secularization," according to which the structural differentiation of modern society requires that distinctive social activities belong to appropriate social spaces? I think Casanova senses the paradox here, which is why he says that "in the modern secular world, the boundaries between the religious and the secular are so fluid that one ought to be very cautious when drawing such analytical distinctions." I only wish he had explored the implications of this statement for his argument. The point I would stress here is not merely that religion and the secular interpenetrate, but that (a) both are historically constituted, (b) this happens through accidental processes bringing together a variety of concepts, practices, and sensibilities, and (c) in modern society the law is crucially involved in defining and defending the distinctiveness of social spaces—especially the legitimate space for religion. In *Formations of the Secular* I ended the chapter that began with Casanova's reformulated thesis by saying that in modern society the law finds itself continually having to redefine the space that religion may properly occupy because the reproduction of secular life ceaselessly disturbs the clarity of its boundaries. I observed that "the unceasing pursuit of the new in productive effort, aesthetic experience, and claims to knowledge, as well as the unending struggle to extend individual self-creation, undermines the stability of established boundaries." The point that interests me, therefore, is not that we need to be careful in drawing analytical distinctions—I take that for granted as a general requirement for clear thinking. My concern is with the *process* by which boundaries are established and by which they come to be defined as modern. Thus in the United States the courts have a tendency to define "religion" in terms of systems of belief in order to determine whether some local administrative constraint substantially burdens the "free exercise of religion." In France it appears that the state is primarily concerned with "the ostentatious display of religious symbols in public schools" regardless of belief. I simplify, of course, but what kinds of authorized memory and presentiment go into these contrasting definitions of religion in "secular" societies? My impression is that such questions do not interest Casanova.

I endorse Casanova's call to scholars "to abandon the eurocentric view that modern Western European developments, including the secularization of European Christianity, are general universal processes," but I am curious as to why the kind of global developments to which he refers approvingly in contemporary non-Christian religions seem largely to be linked (for good or for ill) to Western liberal conceptions of person and politics. Liberalism is of course a complex tradition: Locke is not Constant and Constant is not Mill and Mill is not Rawls, the history of liberalism in North America is not the same as that in Europe—or, for that matter, in parts of the Third World, where it can be said to have a substantial purchase. But as a value-space, liberalism today provides its advocates with a common political and moral language (whose ambiguities and aporias allow it to evolve) in which to identify problems and with which to dispute. Such ideas as individual sovereignty, freedom, limitation of state power, toleration, *and secularism* are central to that space, not least when they are debated. In referring to religion as liberal, I refer to its adjustment to these (often incompatible) ideas, but unfortunately this question is one that Casanova does not investigate.

More generally, I tried *not* to describe historical development here in terms of a linear sequence of ideas, as Casanova and other sociologists often do ("Protestant Reformation" as a cause and "secular modernity" as an effect), because a genealogical investigation presupposes a more complicated web of connections and recursivities than the notion of a causal chain does. When I referred to the Renaissance doctrine of humanism, the Enlightenment concept of nature, and Hegel's philosophy of history, I was talking not about causes but about doctrinal elements that are part of the genealogy of secularism. It's odd that Casanova should represent my reference to them as "triumphalist," because that implies I have an essentialist view of secularism. I wish that he had not confined himself to the one chapter of *Formations* in which I mention his book but instead had read it all, because then I think he would have been better able to understand what my genealogical efforts were aimed at.

Response to Caton

Caton is an excellent ethnographer and a fine linguist, so I find it a matter of regret that he hasn't grasped the basic point of *Genealogies of Religion*. The chapter in which I deal with Geertz is followed by a number of studies that are integral to its argument, yet Caton ignores them. Had he read the entire book, he might have realized that it was not a critique of Geertz (although I am critical of his influential approach to religion) but an attempt, through an engagement with an essentialist definition of religion, to create a conceptual space in which "the construction of religion as an anthropological category" (the title of my first chapter) can be avoided.

I do not have space here to deal with every one of Caton's countercriticisms in defence of Geertz, so I will confine myself to the larger argument.

To begin with, chapter 1 of *Genealogies* is not about how a religion acquires its authority in a particular society. It is about how religion is constructed as an anthropological category. My argument is that the very process of offering definitions of religion as a universal category has roots in a Christian history, a modern Christian history in which "belief" is given a unique place, and which is at the same time a history of comparative religion as an intellectual subject. It is in this context that I speak of "authorizing discourses" in the first chapter—the ways in which various elements are included or excluded historically to create the concept of religion. My concern is with the conditions of possibility of "religion" rather than with its substance. I refer primarily to a *constitutive* process (that which makes the concept "religion") and secondarily to a *regulative* one (that which enables practices to be properly "religious"). There is a complicated relationship between the two that certainly involves coercive force, but not always and never only.

Caton's Yemeni ethnography (his analysis of rain prayers) is intended to prove that my notion of religious authority is an impoverished one because it is "external": the question Caton asked his informants—"Whose words (or what text) authorized these prayers?"—could not be answered because no utterance or text did. Caton wants to say that the authority of the prayers he describes derived not from an external, textual source but from the semantic structure of the language of the rain prayer itself. The authority of that discourse, he tells us, depends on the recursive character of self-citation. Caton is right to seek an *intrinsic* structuration, but the lingualism he defends in Geertz is precisely what prevents him from seeing the embodied character of authoritative discourse, its articulation of the sensorium. In accounting for authority in terms of a determining linguistic structure, Caton reproduces Geertz's questionable assumption about the autonomy of signs. It will be recalled that according to the latter's definition of religion as *a cultural system*, it is precisely the *given* character of a system of symbols that determines observable "religious" behavior, a system that the anthropologist is asked to specify and interpret. The idea that he detects in Geertz—the self-authorization of religious symbols—is precisely a reflection of the latter's textualism.

In part, *Genealogies* is concerned to show that a hermeneutic approach to religion (what do religious symbols mean?) is not the only alternative to a functionalist one ("religion" as an ideological mask, or a justification for rule, or a compensatory device for psychological deficiency), and that, as definitions, *both functionalism and interpretivism are equally externalist.* I consider it mistaken to look for a universal answer to the question "What is religion?" So I consider it wrong to think that religious symbols need interpreting in a determinate way. Their authority depends neither on coercion nor on persuasion, although both kinds of discourse are part of people's religious life. The chapters in *Genealogies* that follow my analysis of Geertz's famous definition explore the internal character of authoritative discourse. But "authoritative discourse" is not, in that book, a purely linguistic phenomenon, and the internality I try to identify is not essentially linguistic. I use the term *authority* to refer to the internal structure of a relationship that brings into play a multiplicity of material components.

One aspect of that structure is willing obedience. People obey what they regard as commands because they are afraid, or because they wish to please someone, or from some other motive. What interests me, however, is *authority as an inner binding*, something that I maintain can't be explained through the science of linguistics—by analyzing self-citation or the language of command, for example. An encounter, not a communication, lies at the heart of authority. Hannah Arendt saw that authority depends neither on coercive force nor on persuasive argument. She recognized that an order (backed by force) is authoritarianism, not authority. I say that if we wish to analyze authority in Christian or Islamic traditions, it won't do to deal with it purely textually—as signs to be read and interpreted. Of course, one must attend to language here, but language as rooted in a somatic complex (hearing-feeling-seeing-remembering) and as involved in people's making/remaking themselves or others over time. My discussions of ritual as embodiment (chapter 2), of conviction and pain in medieval law and monastic discipline (chapter 3), of St. Bernard's teaching his novices how to restructure their secular desires (chapter 4), of cultural translation as a showing and a scandal (chapter 5), of Islamic advice-exhortation-confrontation as a passionate theologico-political phenomenon (chapter 6) are all directed at this question.

In *Genealogies* I regard "power" not merely as *struggle*—although that is important—but as *capability*, that is to say, not simply as the clash or imposition of (external) forces but also as the realization of (internal) potentiality—something that presupposes the interconnection of persons and things. The power of things—whether animate or inanimate—is their ability to act within a network of enabling conditions. Signs-in-action tell persons, animals, and machines something, but only when they are appropriately sited. This is why I devote so much space to Hugh of St. Victor's account of the sacraments as iconic *for subjects who have learned to feel and remember and hope as Christians.* Feeling, remembering, and hoping are as physical as they are mental. When I speak of the separation of symbol from power, I have in mind the difference between being informed and attending, between simple iteration and combinatorial recall. If Caton thinks that the authority of the Yemeni rain prayers lies in their internal semantic structure, he should ask himself why they were not authoritative for him.

If religious authority were just a matter of hearing/reading something (a message communicated by a sender and interpreted by a receiver), if it required the citation of "authoritative words" before it could take effect, it would be essentially a matter of the functioning of signs, of what signs meant. I would then agree with Caton that "discourse authorizes itself by commenting on itself," and regard this self-reference as an instance of an "internal" structure. But the conception of internality here is confined to the level of the message artificially isolated; it has nothing to say about the somatic processes that authoritatively bind persons to one another, of discourse as a physical process.

If we think of authoritative relationship as one person's ability to grasp and obey a compelling truth, then what matters is not that the subject interprets given signs by other signs, but that she connects to "the truth" of what is made apparent to her, and that she is thereby able to transform herself in that moment. It is *that moment*—extended through recollection and desire—that subjects her to its authority and alters her, that marks a beginning. She is struck by what she has not noticed before, by a "new presence" that works to become a spontaneous part of her self. Like someone love-struck, she lives in a compelling truth, she inhabits a relationship with someone who is at once internal and external. Of course, her body-heart-mind *and* the context in which she is placed all have to be right for her to be able to subjectify herself. Power in this sense spells a kind of fit between the individual's ability and all the practical conditions that have helped shape her desire and exercised it in a particular way. This is not a matter of communication as such, and therefore not a matter of the principles by which communication is analyzed in the science of linguistics. The doctrine that every authorizing event should be regarded as an exchange of signs between autonomous senders and receivers may be useful for some purposes, but it obliterates the crucial difference between communication and participation, between internalizing and appropriating. In exploring religious authority, I do not treat discourse as a separable linguistic realm, a domain of signification *to which metapragmatics can be added.* My concern is with the way the living body subjectifies itself through images, practices, institutions, programs, objects—and through other living bodies. And therefore with the way it develops and articulates its virtues and vices. I take the grammar of authority (authoritative discourse) to be rooted in continuously interacting materialities—the body's internal and external constitution, and the energies that sustain them—that make for its *compelling character.* It is not signs in themselves that explain people's recognition of authority; it is how people have learned to do, feel, and remember signs that helps explain it. Or (in another key) how they apprehend signs of the beloved when they "fall in love."

This brings me finally to Caton's claim that Geertz is a Wittgensteinian because, like the latter, he has an action-oriented notion of the symbol. The idea that the meaning of words lies in their use is certainly important to Wittgenstein, but it is not original to him, nor—when expressed by him—is it a simple idea that can be assimilated to pragmatics. For Wittgenstein, there is no distinction between the meaning of a sentence (symbol) and the way it is used/lived. Hence Geertz's conclusion (which I cite in disagreement in chapter 1) that "the anthropological study of religion is therefore a two-stage operation: first, an analysis of the system of meanings embodied in the symbols which make up the religion proper; and second, the relating of these systems to social-structural and psychological processes" stands in sharp opposition to Wittgenstein's treatment of language. In the latter, the power of authoritative discourses is always already a part of practical life and the capabilities that that life presupposes. There is no such thing as an independent sentence-meaning that is *complemented* by metapragmatics. (This, incidentally, is why I refer to Geertz's approach as cognitive.) In fact, Wittgenstein doesn't propound a *theory* of language (for example, that the meaning of symbols is always to be sought in action, or that linguistic signs form a system and should be analyzed as such). Wittgenstein's basic concern was to show, through what he called grammatical investigations, that various philosophical perplexities arise from ignoring the ways we actually employ words in ordinary life. How we use words in various circumstances is the most familiar thing about our knowledge of language—in that sense, signs-in-use are inseparable from the way we live. We tend to use them competently in ordinary life even if we don't know why the forms in which they appear are important to what we are doing. In order to grasp what is being done here, one relies not on *interpretation* but on observing the skill with which things are competently done. The meanings of words-in-use lie, as it were, on the surface of recognizable practices—they are not mysteriously hidden in those practices, waiting to be dug out by an interpretive science.

When Geertz says that religion "must, if it is not to consist of the mere collection of received practices and conventional sentiments we usually refer to as moralism, affirm something," he wants to be able to point to a meaning—an underlying worldview—over and beyond the practices and sentiments that bind individuals authoritatively to one another, and to do what Wittgenstein warns philosophers not to do. He wants to offer an interpretation of a theoretical object. Let's not forget: for all the talk about "thick description," Geertz isn't a mere storyteller or travel writer. Nor does he claim to be a mere translator of foreign languages. These valuable figures have existed for millennia, and all of them are familiar with "thick description." Geertz is claiming to initiate a new claim to knowledge: the Interpretation of Culture. And "the interpretation of culture" in his view presupposes an object ("culture as a system of symbols") that trained anthropologists can identify and interpret.

Theoretical statements about liturgical practices produced by a religious expert—interpretations of what they really mean within a wider scheme—are of course among the things that are said and done, and they often presuppose a distinction between authorizing discourse and discourse that is authorized. But taking a cue from Wittgenstein, I urge that anthropologists should not offer theoretical definitions of religion, whether taken from learned experts in the society studied or invented by ourselves, as the real site of its meaning or as the real (i.e., social-scientific) explanation of its manifestations. ("Theory," let us remember, has a cultic etymology: *theoros* was the impersonal onlooker who was sent as a representative of the Greek cities to the sacred ceremonies. *Theoria* then came to mean the contemplation that enabled the philosopher to distinguish the eternal truth of the cosmos from the uncertainty and fluidity of quotidian life.) I urge not that we give up theorizing—which is impossible—but that we observe its proper place. This includes examining how theoretical definitions are made by particular people in particular times and places and for particular purposes. If anything is hidden, it is the accidental pasts out of which practices have emerged, not the deep meanings of their present. Geertz offers a complex definition of religion through which he invites the reader to decipher the deep meanings of *religion*—not to investigate how this invocation or rite or discipline works, to what that memory or desire or pain is attached, but how to interpret "religion as a cultural system." It is precisely this claim to abstract universality that has made it so attractive to many religious studies scholars. Perhaps because it gives them the assurance that, even if they are atheists, in studying religion they are studying a transcendent object that constitutes an essence of universal humanness.

Response to Chatterjee

In his contribution, Chatterjee shows that attempts by the state of West Bengal to address educational (and security) problems pertaining to the Muslim minority are regarded with suspicion not only by members of that community but also by others for different reasons. Among Muslims there is, furthermore, a concern about who could legitimately represent them, focused this time on the problem of reform within the community. In particular, the growing Muslim middle class is concerned about the independent schools (*madrasahs*) that are used by the poorer segment of the Muslim minority, schools whose standards are very low and in which excessive emphasis is placed on religion.

Thus a crucial analytical question for Chatterjee is: "What are the ethical as well as the strategic considerations in carrying out a project of secularization that carries the imprint of popular legitimacy and democratic consent?" The answer that he proposes, in convincing detail, draws on the idea of "political society" that he has theorized so impressively in an important new book. He argues here that the way for minority communities to be properly reformed so that they can be fully integrated into a secular national polity is neither through coercive state action nor through the elitist intervention of Westernized citizens, but through the elected representatives of underprivileged subjects, who are thereby enabled to negotiate their own demands and norms.

But while I sympathize with the political intention behind this answer—and have great admiration for his work generally—my primary conceptual interest is a little different from his. I am concerned less with "the discovery of new paths toward secularism" and more with what secularism means historically—with how certain practices, concepts, and sensibilities have helped to organize, in different places and at different times, political arrangements called secularism. Chatterjee will agree, I'm sure, that the simple formulas most people produce if asked about secularism ("the separation of church and state," "the neutrality of the law toward different religions," "living together tolerantly in a modern plural society") are more problematic than they appear at first sight.

Let me illustrate this by reference to some of the problems I see in trying to understand secularism in France, a republic whose history constitutes an important part of the definition of "secularism-in-general," rather than talk about Bengal, a region with which I am much less familiar.

In the summer of 2003, I watched a young Muslim woman on French television, wearing a headscarf, respond to the interviewer's provocative questions about wearing it in school. She argued that as a French citizen she had the right to her religious beliefs—and since these included the belief that as a Muslim woman she was required to cover her head in public, she wished to exercise that right. The interviewer, however, insisted that the headscarf, being a religious symbol, violated the fundamental secular character of the republic. The eventual outcome of such debates in the media was the government's appointing of a commission of inquiry charged with reporting on the question of secularity in schools. The commission recommended a law prohibiting the display of any "ostentatious religious symbols," including headscarves, in schools. To me this seemed to be an argument not so much about social tolerance toward Muslim immigrants in a former colonial society, nor about the line between the public sphere (inhabited by equal citizens) and the private (where the inequalities of life and opinion are properly situated)—although both these aspects were present. It was first and foremost about *the structure of political liberties* on which this secular democratic state is thought to be built. The dominant position in this debate holds that in the event of a conflict between constitutional principles *the state's right to defend its personality*—which transcends the distinction between individual and state—*will trump all other rights*. The state's personality is expressed in and through particular signs, including those properly attached to the abstract individuals whom the state represents—and to which they owe unconditional obedience. Thus the headscarf worn by Muslim women is a "religious" *sign* that is held to conflict with the secular personality of the French state as expressed in its own symbols. The commission of inquiry recommended a law proscribing the display of "ostentatious religious signs" in public schools—citing headscarves, skull-caps, and crosses worn around the neck. It is worth noting that although the young women insist that their wearing of the headscarf in public is a religious *duty*, the secular state regards it as a *sign*: it is not intentions declared by the wearer that matter here but publicly produced symbols. The symbols have a "religious" meaning by virtue of their relation to a system of authorized representations (the cross means Christianity, the veil means Islam). It is the state through its agents, in other words, that determines the meanings of such symbols. In this way, a secular state that should have nothing to do with religion finds itself defining what religious duties are acceptable.

Thus in France "religious" symbols are seen to collide with the state's representation of itself as essentially secular, but it is the state that decides which are religious symbols. The motives of their carriers do not count, nor are *their* interpretations of these symbols legally decisive. At the same time, symbolic representations of the state, and what they mean, are themselves charged with powerful—and powerfully protected—emotions. Thus the headscarf is aggressively condemned by powerful voices, and it is defiantly defended.

Thus "secularism" appears here as a matter of social cohesion (or integration) within the body politic. The personality of the republic has a history and a repertoire of symbols anchored in deep emotions (the Revolution, empire, the creation of a unified nation independent of the Vatican). The move to ban the Islamic headscarf from schools is therefore not driven simply by the desire to emancipate all pupils from authority. The school is itself an authoritarian structure in which the republic seeks to secure its own symbolic dominance by representing *laïcité* as a space of emancipation—a space that, in contradictory fashion, at once enables the individual to affirm her self and imposes on her *an unconditional* loyalty to the nation-state. In this affair, at any rate, secularism isn't merely a rational solution to the political problem of living amicably together in a plural, modern society. It is a way of trying to secure the power of *a particular* kind of state, by pronouncing the *illegitimacy* of certain kinds of citizen-subject who are thought to be incompatible with it because they do not share fundamental national values. But given the contradiction within *laïcité* referred to above, it is not always clear when all individuals in the nation can be said to "share its fundamental values," the condition on which social cohesion is alleged to depend.

Defenders of *laïcité* (and this includes many assimilated Muslims) argue that the debate over the headscarf is to be understood as a reluctance on the part of the French state to recognize the *group* identity of a minority, especially a religious minority, within the republic that sees itself as a collection of citizens with individual rights. This argument is interesting, but it ignores the fact that in attempting to define the *acceptable* form of religion the state *does* find itself having to organize a new minority religion, Islam, with the idea of some kind of representation within the republic. This is why the government has asked Muslims to vote for their representatives in a "religious" council of their own, the French Council of the Muslim Religion. Clearly, *impeccably democratic means were used to achieve a "proper" representation of the "religious" minority*. What is worth noting is the fact that the move is presented as a "political" act, whereas wearing a headscarf is described as "religious," but it is the state that determines how each should be seen. Similarly, the mandatory "religious instruction"—Catholic, Protestant, and Judaic—in Alsatian public schools is determined by the constitutional modification made when the province was reintegrated into France after the First World War. It is emphasized that what is taught here are "facts" only, but the state, through its authorized educators, must decide how "religious facts" are to be distinguished from "religious interpretations." In brief, secularism turns out to be a particular pattern of political rule.

I stress that my purpose is not to criticize the French state for being unfair because it is inconsistent or inadequate in its secularity. My suggestion is that we need to explore the assumptions underlying judgments made by historically constituted states regarding the proper place of religion. No actually existing secular state should be denied its claim to secularity just because it doesn't correspond to some utopian model of secularism.

As I see it, for understanding secularism, more is at stake than the question of popular legitimacy in reaching it. It is quite evident that the madrasahs in Bengal, described by Chatterjee, would benefit greatly from reform through the working of "political society," as he argues. I am particularly taken by his argument that new and unforeseen democratic forms can emerge in what he calls political society, forms that may allow for a *decent* politics even if they do not guarantee it. This seems to me a very important point. But I am not persuaded that "political society" is the best place to identify the formation and reformation of secularism, whether in Europe or India.

Response to Connolly

I have long been attracted by Connolly's "deep, multidimensional pluralism" through which he seeks to articulate a theory of generous sensibility in ethical and political life. I have especially profited from his most recent book, *Neuropolitics*, in which that position is developed in rich detail. I was enlightened by the present essay's account of what he calls a minor European tradition, and particularly by his pointing to neglected aspects of Kant of which I was unaware. I find myself in agreement with virtually everything he has written here, but there are questions that still leave me uncertain as to how far I can follow him in his general argument. I will therefore take him seriously when he describes me as an agonistic partner—at once supporting his major vision and uneasy about some perplexities it seems to generate. My disagreements and questions (for what they are worth) are not due simply to my faith being "invested in something beyond pure immanence as well as in it."

The ruling idea that Connolly finds and values in the Spinozist-Deleuzian tradition is an ethic of cultivation that binds body, mind, and social life. I share this with him and endorse his call for anthropology to be brought into closer coordination with neuroscience so that the interconnections between "social traditions" and "embodiment" can be traced in their complexity.

From Deleuze, Connolly gets the notion of multiple temporalities: because different mental, corporeal, and cultural events occur at various speeds in completing themselves as identifiable events, existence consists in the emergence and disappearance of a plurality of things and their mutual interference. This seems to me a very fertile idea. However, I cannot quite see why Connolly regards it as a reason for optimism. "The Spinozist-Deleuzian wager," he observes, "is that effective movements of pluralization, and particularly of generous responses to such movements, are grounded in part on affirmative, generous energies—on *hilaritus*, and not on suffering alone." But isn't it *generous response* rather than pluralization in itself that is the critical issue? The experience of multiple, intersecting temporalities might dislocate the embodied subject, but will it make affirmative, generous energies more likely? Mightn't the continuous experience of unpredictable events make the cultivation of generous sensibilities more precarious? Connolly might, of course, respond that this is why the *cultivation* of such energies, as and when one finds them, is so important.

I was struck here by Connolly's reference to Deleuze's notion of "the suffering that subtends radical dislocation" and his concern to find ways "to mute the sense of existential suffering that accompanies the quickening of pace itself." I was struck by this because raising the problem of an appropriate cultivation of energies to deal with pain reminded me of some religious disciplines that I have dealt with whose concern is precisely with bodily and mental suffering. In the case of these religious disciplines, the aim is famously (or notoriously) to mute pain by transmuting it, partly by learning that nonaction can itself be agentive. So, how should one think about disciplines for dealing with suffering, one's own and that of others? Are all disciplines "coercive," even self-discipline? Is coercion always painful to bear, always unbearable? Can pain never be enjoyed? Other questions: What if one delivers oneself to the discipline of a teacher who can tell one that a demanding technique for dealing with suffering will "work for one" only at a particular stage in one's life and only after lengthy practice? Put another way: If personal experience has to be subordinated to disciplinary tradition (trust placed in its techniques, emotional investments, judgments), does this subject the learner to another's "transcendent" will? Is that transcendence (the attempt to overcome the limits of one's ego) what secularists identify as "religion"? Do they reject transcendence because it frustrates the individual's will? But what if it is one's "free" will to cultivate the virtue of obedience? (Is *the will* really ever "unfree" or only a means of implementing "unfreedom"?) Is transcendence rejected because it limits the impulse to generosity? But is generosity the "free" giving of something? Or is it (extending Mauss) the mutual obligation that binds giver and receiver, or teacher and pupil, in equal humility?

This brings me finally to my main uncertainty about Connolly's affirmation of "immanence" and his rejection of "transcendence." It is not that I object to a monistic metaphysic on principle, it's that I'm not sure how far this philosophical vocabulary of "substance" and "identity"—coming out of a long history of theological and post-theological definitions of "religion"—should be taken as universally valid for all of life and every mode of experience. In other words, I wonder whether descriptions of people's various experiences and practices relating to *their overcoming of limits* or to *their evasion of dominant demands* are always adequately made if we apply an a priori binary of "transcendence" versus "immanence." In my introduction to *Formations*, I argued that a modern state seeking to institute secularism was in effect trying to redefine particular, differentiated practices of the self (articulated in terms of class, gender, and religion) in terms of a transcendent political medium—that of citizenship. If the intrinsic constitution of the modern secular nation (or, for that matter, of the subject or of humanity) is to be regarded as an instance not of "transcendence" but of "immanence," can one escape the totalitarianism implicit in such a formulation?

I agree with Connolly that we always encounter a multiplicity of interacting events, but wouldn't he concede that these events are often hierarchically arranged so that some are hegemonic over (more powerful than) others. Could one not therefore say that some forces "transcend" individual events? As a follower of the Spinozist-Deleuzian tradition, Connolly might perhaps respond that they do but only temporarily and always in this world. But "this world," as he persuasively puts it, "refers in part to a time in which becoming has accelerated." If time is in this sense the ultimate determinant of being, it is not clear to me why another time, *the time of eternity*, in which everything exists always and forever, cannot also determine being. (Responding to a question about progress in philosophy, Deleuze somewhere says that it's pointless to do philosophy Plato's way "not because we've superseded Plato but because you can't supersede Plato, and it makes no sense to have another go at what he's done *for all time*." Does he mean that there's a sense in which Plato's philosophy inhabits eternity?) Eternity is the place of which many religious traditions speak, and in light of which their followers attempt to cultivate their bodies and souls. But the question, as I see it, is not whether such a time is "real" or "imaginary"—and not even whether it is best described as "transcendent"—but what difference it makes to the way people live and die when they invoke it as an object of experience or when they engage in disciplines that prepare them for that experience. Throughout *Formations* I stressed that people, even in modern societies, live in multiple temporalities, and that a central aspect of secularism as a commanding doctrine is precisely its attempt to transcend such pluralities through the homogeneous time of capital. When one unpredictably encounters something strange, demanding, and transforming, it does not seem to me important to ask whether it comes from inside or outside, whether it is immanent or transcendent. What matters is that through a familiar medium (a time, a place, an object) a totally unfamiliar sense opens up, a glimpse of "another world" that *grasps one's life.*

Connolly's vision of a multiplicity of minority traditions is clearly a precondition for developing the generous ethical and political sensibilities he endorses (and that I too support). However, it still remains for us to think through the weaknesses and contradictions that accompany the liberal conception of tolerance. Otherwise we may find ourselves simply restating the liberal doctrine that the government, in its role as umpire, must always ensure that the diverse religious beliefs and practices of its citizenry are protected. It is not that this doctrine is dishonorable but that we don't fully understand all its political implications for modern conceptions of liberty. (After all, the ability to tolerate another's religious behavior is not the same as the other's right to be religiously free.) What are we to make of the apparent conflict between the principle regarding the private inviolability of beliefs and the principle that all beliefs are publicly contestable? More concretely: Why is it that in America the wearing of headscarves in public schools is regarded as a matter of the right of the free individual to express her religious beliefs without harm to others, and in France it is considered to be an obstacle to the constitution of a free (because autonomous) subject-citizen?

Although the historical connection of secularism with the formation of the modern nation-state is well known (and we have some excellent accounts of the moral person that has been promoted by that formation), the way the nation-state's self-declared national personality affects the practical application of its religious neutrality, and its guardianship of freedom, needs to be examined more systematically. The specific practices, sensibilities, and attitudes that undergird secularism as a national arrangement—that give it solidity and support—remain largely unexplored, and yet it is these elements that shape the concepts of civil liberty and social tolerance. In *Formations of the Secular* I tried, in a very preliminary way, to explore this undergirding. Recognition of our ignorance in this matter is, in my view, equally central to anthropological inquiry, to democratic culture, and to modern ethical life. I get the sense that Connolly and I are in agreement on this basic point, although perhaps we differ in the reasons we give for that ignorance and for the ways people deal with its apparent consequences. Following Deleuze, Connolly may say that our ignorance is a function of the continuous and unpredictable emergence of the new; I think it is also a function of the infinite character of what is already there to be known. Finally, if I have understood him rightly, I think Connolly sees more scope for spontaneous generous energies than I do.

Response to Das

I must thank Das for her critical comments on *Formations*. She is quite right when she observes that I haven't paid any attention to how reproduction and birth are thought of in the secular state. My excuse for having omitted a matter of such importance is simply that I don't know enough about it. Her own speculations on this matter are provocative in the best sense of the word. They have helped me think further.

But first a few words about a small misunderstanding: Agamben's idea of "bare life" (which belongs to the argument that the physical body, *corpus*, has become the object of modern state power) is not, as I understand it, a feature of "the state of nature" that I mention in chapter 4. Bare life, or the life of *homo sacer*, was "the sacred man" in early Rome who could not be sacrificed but could be killed with impunity by anyone. It is true that Agamben translates Hobbes's account of "the state of nature" as the state in which every individual considers every other as *homo sacer*, but I think this is wrong, because *homo sacer* is constituted as such by divine and human law and is therefore not "in a state of nature." My concern in chapter 4 was, in any case, with the well-known idea of early natural rights theorists that certain rights—whether we classify them retrospectively as active or passive—are inherent in the human being as a creature of God and not derived from the individual's membership in a political society. In this conception, active rights (the individual's ability to do her own thing, as we might say today) are no closer to bare life, *zoē*, than passive rights (the individual to whom welfare is owed). In other words, bare life is not part of the natural rights story because not every living thing has rights attributed to it. My point was simply that various elements in the natural rights story, which I touched on very sketchily, help us to better understand the claim that human rights define the essence of the human. The connection between human rights and natural rights is well known, and it was to that theme that my attention was directed. As I pointed out, it is precisely the idea that "natural rights" are prior to any social and political arrangements in the world as we know it that allowed its use as a ground for criticizing those arrangements. My analytic distinction between the individual as citizen and the individual as human being refers not to my view of the entire arrangement of law, violence, and rights in modern secular states but to the binary that underpins the idea of human rights. I am concerned mainly with some of the paradoxes that seem to have been brought into being with the introduction of the secular idea of (moral and political) *sovereignty*. I make no claims about the fixed character of "nature" as such or about its simple opposition to "society." On the contrary: my brief discussion, at the end of that chapter, of the shifting human-animal line, of interventions by genetic engineering and neuroscience, is a recognition of the problematic character of "nature," which is now more clearly visible than ever before. Now, if even "human nature" can be seen as being itself a construct (or rather, as being literally constructed in crucial areas of life by some political-economic powers), the vantage point once afforded by the idea of *nature* to criticize existing legal arrangements seems to me to vanish.

I agree with Das that the Parsi child in the law case she cites is "a socially and legally constituted person already located in a system of relationships." But would a natural rights theorist dispute this? Wouldn't he say that the context here is the judicial authority of a sovereign state to define paternity as an unbreakable legal relationship? The justices, he would say, are not speaking of an original state of nature that is meant to explain the necessity of instituted government. At any rate, my concern in chapter 4 was to argue that the modern secular notion of human rights is unstable and incoherent partly because of its historical connections with natural rights theories. (This doesn't mean I propose that human rights must therefore be discarded. There may be good practical reasons for retaining it despite its incoherence.)

What Das's essay has made clearer to me, however, is that the idea of nature is of greater moment in the development of Western law than I had previously realized. It certainly doesn't have the same importance in Islamic law, although that law is equally patriarchal. So she has led me to think about the following question: in Islamic political theology, there is no *pater familias* in a state of nature, no heavenly father on whom paternity is modeled, and no conception of the earthly ruler as father of his people. What difference, if any, does this make to the concept and practice of patriarchy in Muslim societies? I don't know the answer yet, but I thank her for alerting me to the question.

Das rightly points out that the law is not a "unitary, sovereign presence." The passage she cites from *Formations* refers explicitly to "a scheme" that underlies the modern secular state. I would urge that it should not be read as amounting to a claim on my part that the law is indeed a unitary, sovereign presence. Nevertheless, I hope she will agree with me that legal judgments are made and followed through with appropriate sanctions, and on the whole with a substantial measure of predictability—except in the matter of the exception that is linked to sovereign power whose predictability resides precisely in the exercise of sovereignty. If there are debates about where the ultimate authority of the law resides, they are debates in and with reference to the language of law. Of course, that language is not completely determinate and not to be regarded as though it were a clearly bounded system—that is precisely what makes it possible for lawyers to argue against each other in court, and for jurists to propound or deny foundations. But the concept of "legality"—of what can be considered enforceable or allowable in the law—is still a central concern of those who use that language. And it is a concern even of the sovereign power that declares the state of exception (as in Guantanamo Bay) in which the law is affirmed by its suspension. So I share with her the view that the concept of "law" is not unvarying, not always fixed in the same context, and not always concerned with punishment—and that everyone is not in agreement about how legal rules should be understood in given contexts.

When Das chides me for having "a restricted notion of context," I am led to wonder how useful it is to talk about context in the abstract. Doesn't context depend on the thing to be contextualized? Surely, whether the context of a concept is too narrow, too wide, or just right depends on what we are trying to do with it. This is a central question in every trial, the thing that allows the dispute. My argument, however, is that even if the applicability of the concept is subject to varying interpretation and related to different contexts, there is a point at which a final judgment is reached for a case and a measure of "certainty" is secured (albeit in circular fashion), whether in the first instance or in a final court of appeal. Perhaps we do not agree on this, but in my view all legal judgments rest on relatively predictable forms of "legitimate" violence (or the threat of violence), which are always part of the judicial process and so of the state. The law may not be a "unitary, sovereign presence," but the state, of which the law is an expression, is a coercive body that has a (variable) measure of spatial and temporal continuity—and its legal violence is generally predictable.

None of this (especially the law's violence) is exclusive to the modern secular state, of course. As Das very properly notes, it is the way political and moral *sovereignty* is conceived in and through the law—the work it does socially—that distinguishes secularism. The sovereignty of the individual is enacted both in private spaces and in public, and legally speaking, "the family" is an instance of the former. Incidentally, the classification in Europe of laws relating to marriage, divorce, relations between parents and children, guardianship, and so on as "family law" is a relatively late one—in England it wasn't in use before the 1960s, when the welfare state was firmly constituted. As a subdivision of "private law," as a subject of legal scholarship, and as an object of administrative intervention, "the family" (excluding servants and distant relatives in the same household) owes its emergence to the fact that in the late nineteenth century the secularizing state acquired the power to regulate marriage, divorce, and so on from the ecclesiastical courts that had previously dealt with them. I therefore agree with the Foucauldian thesis that, as a modern legal category, "the family" is an element of governmentality—in England and France, as well as in

Egypt (a de facto British colony that acquired its judicial framework from French law). Even the reform of the sharia, redefined as "family law," is to be seen in this context, as I suggested with regard to the legal writings of the famous Egyptian reformer Muhammad Abduh and the subsequent arguments of the secularizing lawyer Ahmad Safwat.

If I have understood her rightly, Das's general concern is with the question of paternity and its ideological roots in conceptions of nature. She expresses her puzzlement over the importance of paternity even in the secular state. Why, she asks, does paternity remain an obsession even after the replacement of biblical time by secular time? This is an interesting question, and now that she has raised it, I too am puzzled. But then I also ask myself how important paternity is *now*. Given the extension of equal rights to women, hasn't paternity as a legal concept become less and less important in the modern secular state—even in such important matters as the acquisition of citizenship? Isn't this due in large measure to the extended application of the principle of equality, which is central both to the state of nature story and to modern secular liberalism?

I agree that the secular is not "a unitary system or a notionally complete totality of legal rules." The entire project of *Formations* is to argue against such an idea—not least through the distinction I try to make between the epistemological category of the secular (what are the practices, concepts, and sensibilities regarded as necessary for knowledge about reality?) and the political doctrine of secularism (how does the state try to ensure that it is neutral in relation to different religions?). The two are obviously connected, but I don't see them in a relationship of direct determination. It is precisely my concern to stress that the elements making up the secular and secularism are in each case contingent.

Nevertheless, I remain intrigued to know how Das would deal with the connection of the democratic principle of equality to the principle of individual autonomy, because the individual is important both to secular epistemology and to secular politics, to the family and the nation-state. I also wish she had dealt with bio-medical techniques of reproduction— from sperm banks to cloning—on which she is knowledgeable. She could then have discussed their implications for the legal status of *paternity* and their implications for notions of secular truth.

I found Das's reading of *Emile* especially suggestive. By citing the passage that ends with the rhetorical question, "Do you know what the price is of your being permitted to live and for whom you ought to die?" she urges me to think more carefully about the links between the family and the state in secular modernity, and about the power of that state to regulate reproduction and death. She makes an important point here that I think raises questions about natural rights not confined to those of the *pater familias*, questions that require further reflection. Thus it has been argued by abolitionists that the death penalty for murder violates the natural right of all human beings to life, and supporters of that punishment respond that legally convicted criminals have forfeited that right. Critics have pointed out that in effect this latter argument turns the right to life into a privilege for good behavior accorded by the state to those within its power. Most abolitionists who make this argument seem less concerned about other violations of natural rights that follow from legal penalties, for example, incarceration as a denial of the right to free movement. There are also other suspensions of rights that take place in "a state of emergency." Actually, there is no right that the state—including the liberal democratic state—cannot abrogate or suspend. This should lead one to the conclusion that *there is no such thing as a natural* (i.e., inalienable) *right in the modern sovereign state*. Does this also mean that ipso facto there is no such thing as a human right, only a legal rhetoric that is employed by nation-states, singly or in concert, to justify particular actions? What I find most helpful in Das's essay is the way it draws the reader's attention to the processes of state power and national sovereignty that underpin the rhetoric of "the natural right of the father/husband/citizen." It will be fruitful to think about this systematically.

Response to de Vries

This has not been an easy essay to read, but like everything I have read by de Vries, it has forced me to think. My difficulty is obviously a sign of my own inadequacy. I am not a philosopher, and worse, I have not read Levinas—except occasionally as he is cited or summarized by someone else. What I have read of him often leaves me very puzzled. So the first part of my response to de Vries is a struggle to understand Levinas as presented by him.

Thus when he says that "man is Europe and the Bible, and all the rest can be translated from there," I ask myself: doesn't "Europe *and* the Bible" appear to be a contingent coupling? And yet he also says that "the European" is the "convergence" of the tradition of Greek philosophical thought and the Bible, and then claims something less than a fusion: "Old or New Testament—but it is in the Old Testament that *everything*, in my opinion, is borne." This appears to mean the *original* possibility of a moral world and a world of science and technology. But "everything" from the Bible? Whereas Max Weber linked the Puritan ethic to the rise of modern capitalism (and thus to science, technology, and secularism), Levinas appears to insist on an earlier, more inclusive—and much more problematic—historical origin. Referring to Claude Lévi-Strauss's *The Savage Mind*, he exclaims triumphantly that "a European knew how to discover [the principles of primitive thinking], it was not the savage thinkers who discovered our thinking. There is a kind of envelopment of all thinking by the European subject." And from here he moves to undercut a possible *moralistic* objection: "Europe has many things to be reproached for, its history has been one of blood and war, but it is also the place where this blood and war have been regretted and constitute a bad conscience, a bad conscience of Europe which is the return of Europe, not toward Greece, but toward the Bible." But "a bad conscience" is no bar to further immoral action, it merely gives such action a distinctive style. Note the frequent hesitations and qualifications the European moral conscience has displayed when confronted with its own cruelties. (A well-known tactic for blunting moral criticism of one's own side, by the way, is to cast doubt on the moral behavior of one's enemies.) In any case, what does he want us to *do* with Europe's "conscience"? As I see it, the important question is not Europe's (regretted) bad behavior or its legitimate pride in the many good things it has achieved for itself and the world, but how various European empires—at different times and places—have opened up different kinds of mutually constitutive powers and knowledges.

Levinas seems to me to have abandoned too quickly the problem of how "the European subject" is constituted and of how *essential* its relation is to "a collective conscience." The result is that a complicated conceptual problem is apparently shifted by a stark moralistic claim. I am puzzled, first, by how "openness to the other" (to "the neighbor") is accomplished when all thinking is enveloped by "the European subject." But above all, I cannot make out what is at stake for Levinas in his insistence on "the European subject" and its capacity, through its bad conscience, to transcend itself. Why is it so important for him to insist on the *Europeanness* of "the subject"?

Commenting on the Russian novelist Grossman, Levinas observes that "the end of socialism, in the horror of Stalinism, is the greatest spiritual crisis in modern Europe." The totalitarian state (a European invention) collapses and the possibility of the totally free market (another European invention) can take its place—more successfully than ever, in every social space and throughout the globe. I did not see Levinas's critique of capitalism clearly enough, although this may well be my fault. But even so, while it is true that money facilitates *charity*, as Levinas stresses, doesn't the free circulation of money also do other things that are less than admirable? Is love inseparable from market exchange? Surely, it is *eros* that can be bought but not *caritas*. At any rate, my question now is this: is it the perception of "a spiritual crisis in modern Europe" that necessitates the construction of "the European subject" who can redeem himself? And is the succession of "European spiritual crises" partly what defines modern secularism? Is it that, by overcoming each successive European crisis, the European subject ensures "the progress of the human spirit"?

In a lengthy passage cited by de Vries, Levinas claims,

> The condemnation of technology has become a comfortable rhetoric. Yet technology is destructive of pagan gods. Through it, certain gods are now dead: those gods of astrology's conjunction of the planets, the gods of destiny, local gods, gods of place and countryside, all the gods inhabiting consciousness and reproducing in anguish and terror the gods of the skies. Technology teaches us that these gods are of the world, and therefore are things, and being things they are nothing much. In this sense, secularizing technology figures in the progress of the human spirit.

Victorian anthropologists held mistakenly that "primitive religion" was based on fear. But I want to ask Levinas whether he really believes that "things" are no cause for "anguish and terror"? Things are part of our world, they enable us to be, to do, and to be done to. Modern war and modern surveillance by the state, modern genocide and modern impoverishment, unlimited consumerism and depredation of the environment—it is not necessary to condemn modernity to see that these products of things are also gods in our world. Are modern cruelties better than those of the dark ages because we now have "moral standards"—or worse for just that reason? Is "a bad conscience" sufficient compensation for liberation from the old gods of the skies? Or should we look to the circulation of money to set all right again? Is the free market our salvation? Is this the style of secularization that Levinas offers humanity? I do not believe that this is what de Vries subscribes to.

What interests me more than Levinas, therefore, is de Vries' own idea of *global religion*, which he eventually connects with his reading of Levinas—a term by which he refers to "the qualities of a dislocation and deterritorialization that increasingly tend to characterize a terrain that has lost all fixed boundaries (such as, say, Europe, or the West) and that we . . . can begin to explore under the heading of 'religion.'" Here, I think, is something important, something worth thinking further about. Would de Vries agree that in this sense *global religion* is not the expansion of the "European subject" to encompass the world nor is it the reaction of the world Europe seeks to encompass, but another subject altogether? Europe itself tries hard to domesticate global religion, to fix it, subordinate it to nation-state proportions—as "French Islam" or "British Islam," for instance—as though it were part of the world still needing to be conquered.

The binaries of which de Vries speaks (the *trivialization* and *profanation* of religion itself together with a *purification* and *intensification* of its ultimate concern) may perhaps be a feature of global religion. But global religion is globalizing religion—a religionizing that accompanies but is not an element of global capitalism that Europe spawned. As such, it presupposes the beginning of traditions that stand beyond both those subjects. Am I right to think that for de Vries global religion isn't merely "universal religion"? Then categories like public versus private, or inclusive versus intolerant, or even technologically sophisticated versus technologically simple, do not apply to it. Would he agree that global religion stands apart from both "the European subject" and "the Third World" that Europe has sought to dominate? If he does, then perhaps we should approach global religion not through binaries but in terms that capture its tertiary character.

Response to Scott

Scott has recently published a complex book on tragedy as a political modality, in which he approaches that category through a famous study of a famous event in Caribbean history—C. L. R. James on the Haitian revolution—in order to understand the significance of modernity for the Third World today. My reason for discussing the tragedy of Oedipus in the latter half of chapter 2 was different: to explore some aspects of agency and pain in a secular context. It was not intended as a disquisition on tragedy as such. I was concerned neither with the thesis that human beings and their world are in fundamental disharmony (as Bernard Williams held in the book I cite) nor with the paradigmatic sequence of tragedy: confusion, violence, horror, and meaningless suffering resolved eventually into guilt, moral lucidity, the recognition of personal responsibility, and the calm recovery of meaning (*catharsis*, in the post-Christian understanding of that ancient Greek term). I simply wanted to say that if one read *Oedipus* purposefully, one might see more clearly that moral agency doesn't necessitate the ideas of intentionality (in contrast to consciousness), responsibility (answerability to authority), and "just punishment." So I am reluctant to use that piece—or anything else I have written—to claim a privilege for the tragic sensibility. He is right to say that I think that a malign fate rules us collectively, often by turning our best intentions against us. But I'm not sure that that amounts to a tragic vision.

However, I must admit that Scott has identified an apparent contradiction in my work: I am apparently attached at the same time to Foucault and to MacIntyre. He is right to insist that I have not explained anywhere how I can draw both on genealogy and on tradition. MacIntyre himself, as Scott notes, has written a book contrasting the two and arguing that the former is not viable. This book, like others MacIntyre has written, has been valuable for my thinking on the subject, even if (perhaps because?) I find myself in disagreement with its overall argument. I have long thought it necessary to rethink the connection/contrast between genealogy and tradition, and Scott's contribution has forced me farther in that direction, and for that alone I am grateful. But perhaps more important, Scott has caused me to wonder whether in this rethinking it may not be necessary to approach the concept of tragedy more directly than I have done so far.

Since this is the subject of my next project, what I say here will inevitably be very brief and inadequate. How do I see the *difference* between genealogy and tradition? First, by the way they *share* something: discipline. The latter sustains, elaborates, and sometimes argues over disciplinary practices; the former inquires into the contingent formation of their conditions of truthfulness. I do not use genealogy to uncover a succession of masks or to challenge the very idea of academic history. Nor do I regard tradition as mere continuity, mere imitation. Certainly MacIntyre is right to argue that a tradition-constituted position is necessary to any concept of moral action. But tradition is also the space in which one experiences a multiplicity of times and confronts a variety of memories. This is what gives disciplines both their authoritativeness and their openness.

So, as I use it, genealogy is a way of (re)telling history by tracing contingencies that have come together to form an apparently natural development. While it is not itself a moral narrative, it is relevant to moral narratives, for the notion of a tradition-constituted standpoint on which MacIntyre insists does not by itself explain *how* we come to argue for or against a particular position from within a tradition. Thus when some followers of a tradition argue over an established position, they try to show their opponents that what has been taken to be self-evident in the tradition is not necessarily so. This need not undermine the idea of tradition itself but only what has been taken to be its essence. Furthermore, while it is the case that we argue by narrating particular kinds of histories, our arguments do not depend only on representations that are narrative in form. Qualitative and quantitative analyses are also crucial to the way we argue within traditions to undermine *or to establish* disciplinary truths. That's where genealogy again becomes relevant.

But tradition, of course, is not just a matter of argument—indeed argument is mostly peripheral to it. Tradition is primarily about practice, about learning the point of a practice and performing it properly and making it a part of oneself, something that embraces Mauss's concept of *habitus*. Of course this doesn't mean that the traditional disciplines by which particular virtues are cultivated always produce what they are designed to do. Even the monks I wrote about in *Genealogies of Religion* knew that well when they employed the idea of original sin, and all confessors knew (or at any rate were supposed to know) about the fragility of human virtue. At all times, the implications of discipline are never fully grasped, even when resort is had to genealogy. Discipline always has to work through the tensions and contradictions that inhabit the individual and is therefore, as often as not, likely to undermine itself. So the self that is subjected to the disciplines of a tradition is, as MacIntyre rightly claims, accountable to the authorities of a community. But to the extent that the practices are part of her, she is also compelled from inside—passionately, precisely because not in a rationally calculative way. To that extent also, it is not *accountability* that matters but *necessity*—even if this leads to personal pain and public mourning. To act thus is to *live* (with body-and-mind) one's tradition in a total way, not to trade off some consequences for others according to a calculus that reconciles irreconcilable positions.

I don't mean to say that such attachment to tradition inevitably leads to human disaster. To belong to a tradition is not the same as playing in a drama. Most of the time there is no great moral conflict, no terrible choice to be made. It is not tradition in itself but the uncertainties of life that force moral conflicts on one. So what I mean is merely that there are different styles of confronting disaster—of explaining, justifying, living it. Thus the calculative mode of social relations, so characteristic of the modern state, has often been as indifferent to human loss as any other, but it has lived it in its own way. A genealogical mode of inquiry makes it clear that it is not only terrible conflicts of choices but also terrible indifference that leads to moral disaster.

Can all of this be articulated by the idea of tragedy? Perhaps. But there is also something else: as the human being becomes old, there is a tendency for him/her to lose many of the virtues necessary to moral habitus—attention, courage, passion. When the aging human body betrays the subject, what one gets is not tragedy but bathos.

Response to Shulman

Shulman writes impressively in defense of "redemption" against what he perceives as a flattening of its meaning in *Formations*. As always, I have benefited from what he has to say on this subject. However, I must remind him that I discuss redemption not only in chapter 1 in reference to Canovan but also in chapter 4, where it appears at length as part of an answer to the question, "Why does human rights language play such a marginal role in the reform history of the United States?" The redemptive language used by Martin Luther King Jr. (about which I first began to think after reading Shulman on prophetic narration) is, I note there, very different from the redemptive discourse I analyze in chapter 1. King's is not merely a Christian discourse (so too is the salvationist discourse of European missionaries in Asia and Africa) but a particular kind of Christian discourse—deployed by subjects to combat their own oppression, yet explicitly nonviolent in the face of state provocation and refusing the language of "the enemy." It articulates a distinctive grammar of redemption in which suffering isn't *inflicted* by the redeemer on the redeemed but *endured*. But although this distinguishes it from the redemptive project of the state, I suggest that its political and moral effectiveness depended on its punctuality—on its arrival at the right time and in the right context. King's discourse of redemption calls for the healing of past injuries and the regeneration of America itself, and in so doing it draws successfully on America's self-definition as Christian and more. In a prophesying mode, King typically declares,

One day the South will know that when these disinherited children of God sat down at lunch counters they were in reality standing up for the best in the American dream and the most sacred values in our Judeo-Christian heritage, and thus carrying the whole nation back to the great wells of democracy, which were dug deep by the founding fathers in the formulation of the Constitution and Declaration of Independence.

It is at such points that we find important overlaps with the language and thought of those who manage the nation-state. When I worry about this tension, it is not because I believe that the concept of redemption always affords (in banal fashion) a discourse that simply authorizes violence. It is because I find redemption as the master-trope of democratic politics a worrying thought. Its invocation by the Bush government is not an aberration, but belongs to an old American tradition that has helped define the relationship of the United States to the world.

Although I can't think of any form of government more acceptable than democracy, my enthusiasm for it is tempered, mainly because it is so closely tied to the nation-state—with all that is indispensable and frightening about the state in modern existence. And this is what makes the notion of redemption so ambiguous. I understand the value of redeeming one's promise, one's past, oneself. I understand the necessity of recognizing our dependence on other human beings, even of having a sense of responsibility toward a collective mode of life. But redeeming others? What kind of situation are we in when we can think this? Democracy is all very well, but I fear the power of the liberal democratic state, especially because it promises to deliver "the people's will." It is not that there are "good motives" and "bad motives" for redemptive acts, still less that there is a need for reworking the idea so that it no longer implies violence and resentment. I argue that the idea of political redemption is grotesquely out of place in the secular world, a danger to politics and a parody of spirituality. Of course redemptive language may be inescapable in modernity (as Shulman puts it), but then so much the worse for all of us.

The question of who is to be included or excluded from "humanity" remains as crucial as ever for the project of secular redemption. I wish Shulman had dealt with it. For, as Hannah Arendt once noted, "It is quite conceivable, and even within the realm of practical political possibilities, that one fine day a highly organized and mechanized humanity will conclude quite democratically—namely by majority decision—that for humanity as a whole it would be better to liquidate certain parts thereof." And she went on, more provocatively: "Here, in the problems of factual reality, we are confronted with one of the oldest perplexities of political philosophy, which could remain undetected only so long as a stable Christian theology provided the framework for all political and philosophical problems, but which long ago caused Plato to say: 'Not man, but a god, must be the measure of all things.'" In our modern world, where democratic politics is often presented as the highest public good, God is not dead but reincarnated in Man—that is, in a multiplicity of morally self-governing human beings brought together in transcendent polities. That's why liberal democratic states, representing and defending humanity as a whole, are entitled to decide on matters of life and death (natal policy and health care, war and judicial punishment, as well as various kinds of humanitarian intervention). That's why the claim that our democratic state is infiltrated (infected?) by aliens leads to a call for cleansing. And because the cleansing is carried out lawfully—by means of legislatures, courts of law, and a democratically elected administration—the imprisonment, expulsion, and punishment of alien captives, and the destruction of foreign civilians by war, are all regarded as acts in the service of a political order that is right in itself. How will democracy help us to distinguish "good" redemption from "bad"? In a democracy, as Arendt reminds us, "the people" *have a right* to make national decisions even if they are not *morally right.*

Even now there is a dispute about whether democratically formulated policies can be damaging to humanity as a whole. For example, although both the European Community and the United States publicly proclaim the virtues of a free-market economy for the well-being of humanity, they also provide substantial agricultural subsidies to their own farmers in response to the demands of their own electorate. Among the effects of such agricultural policies is damage done to a considerable part of humanity that inhabits Africa and Asia. Is this an unavoidable consequence of democratic politics (in which a national government must represent the interests of the voters)? Or is it yet another sign that our present concept of democracy (not redemption but democratic politics) needs to be rethought? And if the latter, how is that to be done in an interconnected world where the meaning of democratic politics has been learned in the context of the sovereign nation-state, one of whose functions is to demarcate "enemies of the people" from "patriots"? It seems to me that there are serious difficulties with the idea of redemption, which democratic politics (itself a vexed and often unclear notion) will not necessarily resolve.

Toward the end of my chapter on human rights, I argued that recent scientific developments in genetic engineering and neuroscience were beginning to undermine any fixed notion of the human. And since the task of the modern liberal state is the welfare and protection of its human population, the open destabilization of "the human" explodes the notion of political redemption. The possibilities of remaking as well as protecting the human are now endless. The processes by which individuals can be excluded or included within that category, and the different ways they can be defended against unending physical threats (epidemics, terrorism, economic crises) are legion. Perhaps that is why the task of political redemption becomes a permanent one, why, unlike the Old Testament idea of redemption (as well as the Christian idea), it is never achieved. The liberal democratic states devoted to increasing the security and happiness of their national populations deploy technological means that are never completely adequate to the multiplying dangers that seem to confront it. Everything must be surveyed so that anything that emerges as a threat to the redemptive project can be dealt with immediately. What kind of ground is this for redemptive projects of a political kind?

Response to Wilson

Wilson has presented a strong argument in favor of separating the concept of "agent" from that of "subject" in the writing of history, and I agree with him in most of what he has to say (clearly we are both indebted to Foucault).

Wilson is surely right to stress the interconnection of Bengali peasants with their landlords. I found this analysis very persuasive, in spite of its brevity. The fact of interdependence does not imply the *dissolution* of subject-agents, it indicates that they are mutually constitutive. The more radical perspective that he goes on to argue for, according to which persons and things are embedded spatial webs and temporal loops in relation to which acts and events emerge and dissolve, is important because it complicates the actions and passions of individuals and helps explain why they are never fully in control of their knowledge and action. The actions of an agent may be not fully his/her own but also (primarily) those of another— a client, a master (a human, a god, a spirit), an unconscious. To say that is to ask about the different ways the human subject is thought about and played out in different times and places. So although I would insist that the principle of effectivity (agency) be separated analytically from the principle of experience (subjectivity), I am reluctant to say that it is impossible to identify such a thing as a relatively coherent subject-agent (a human individual), if only because the very idea of "incompleteness" in relation to knowledge and action presupposes some notion of what "completeness" would be like in particular contexts.

What interests me is precisely how "the human" (differentiated, for example, from "animals" and "gods," as well as from "machines" and "natural environments") is realized in different societies and epochs—how the diverse elements of the idea of the human come together to form wholes. Thus it is that the human in modern secular society comes to be endowed with particular capacities for self-awareness, autonomy, and responsibility that make her capable of acting (an agent). These capacities do not necessarily depend on one another—they are contingent—but the human individual defined by them lies ideologically at the center of capitalist political economy—as worker, consumer, and citizen. And as the follower of various modern liberal religions. Because religion's ultimate justification is now widely believed to reside in the individual's experience of "the sacred" and his/her desire to connect with "transcendence," he/she now assumes an absolute right to choose in such matters. The agent is ultimately responsible for himself or herself because he or she is now presumed to have a self that can be inspected, evaluated, and guided autonomously. In previous epochs, the individual was often an integral part of family and institution, and his substance derived from particular places and kin.

Of course, internality is not a purely modern phenomenon. It is common knowledge that for thousands of years various ascetic traditions have cultivated reflexive subjectivities. I simply emphasize that the geography of what is "internal" to the person, and of the relationships of that "inside" to what is "external," is differently articulated in modernity—at least potentially if not always in reality. Religion thus becomes fully private in the sense of being able to do without *any* public organization or institutional discipline; the demands on the self of religious conversion tend increasingly to give place to the opportunities for religious choice now available to it (New Age, oriental cults, free-floating mysticisms, etc.). That this individual is an ideological construction does not *in itself* make it incoherent. The aspiration to coherence is a necessary condition of social life, in the sense that people's relations to one another (and to themselves) require some measure of consistency in the long term.

Finally, I completely share Wilson's skepticism regarding academia as the special space of insight from which rational political action can be designed. The fact that intellectuals have a professional interest in particular cultures and institutions doesn't make them more qualified than ordinary citizens to participate actively in politics. However, because they possess what many nonacademics regard as "authoritative knowledge," intellectuals may be sought by the media for its own purposes. It is not easy for them to negotiate the treacherous ground of public debate that is largely controlled by the media, with its own rules as well as its political and financial agenda. Because academics live in a tension between the open-mindedness required by intellectual research and the decisiveness required by political action, they may find themselves more easily manipulated by journalists and television hosts—as became evident during the buildup to the U.S. invasion of Iraq, when the mainstream media in this country had virtually become a propaganda organ of a state bent on war. (Such manipulation, incidentally, again presupposes some notion of a coherent subject.) But the political world itself can be recalcitrant and treacherous—even if this does not free us from having to act when we must.

Appendix: The Trouble of Thinking:
An Interview with Talal Asad

David Scott

> I should not like my writing to spare others the trouble of thinking.
> —LUDWIG WITTGENSTEIN, *Philosophical Investigations*

Beginnings

David Scott: Talal, let me start by asking what propelled you into anthropology in the first place, what idea of anthropology did you have at the time you started, what did you think anthropology would *enable*? Why not, for example, pursue philosophy?

Talal Asad: You know, actually, when I first came to England I studied architecture, because that was the choice my father made for me. But I had become interested in anthropology when I was still in Pakistan, just before I came to England. An American lady who was a teacher there, and whom I got to know briefly, gave me a copy of *Patterns of Culture*.[1] That was the first anthropology book I ever read, and I was really quite excited by it. So I had some conception then, obviously not very clearly formulated, of anthropology as a way of looking at different kinds of cultural experiences. I was very committed to the idea of total cultures—*patterns*, as the book put it.

DS: So there is a sense in which your first encounter with anthropology was through American cultural anthropology and not British social anthropology.

TA: Yes. And when I look back on it, I think it's rather interesting. But then I went to England in order to study architecture, and after a couple of years it became clear to me that this wasn't what I wanted to do. I then went to study anthropology at Edinburgh, where I did an Honors M.A. in Anthropology, which is a four-year undergraduate degree in Scottish universities as opposed to a three-year General M.A. And I did do a philosophy course, because in an honors degree you can choose to do various minor subjects together with your major. And I became more interested in this idea of different kinds of social experiences across different kinds of social terrain, as it were. And certainly the whole idea of the West-versus-the-Rest was something that came to me very early on. I was very conscious of it, having virtually grown up in the colonial world, in India and Pakistan. I was too young to understand the details of British rule, but we talked a lot about it in our household. So that was my experience when I was growing up, and it seems to me that thinking about different kinds of cultural experiences, and of European dominance in India, came almost naturally.

DS: Were there specific debates in British social anthropology around the time you were an undergraduate that you can remember particularly capturing your imagination?

TA: Well, of course, virtually all British anthropology regarded itself as being rather more intellectual than American anthropology. But Edinburgh was slightly different, in that we were also taught American anthropology, which must have had something to do with some of the teachers being familiar with the American scene. I think one of them had been in America for some years, although he was English. So we were taught some aspects of American anthropology. For example, we were taught psychological anthropology, Kardiner and Linton and Hallowell and so on. But it was taken for granted that anthropology in Britain was not only more rigorous than in America but that its proper concern was with social structure. So one of the debates going on at the time was about how to theorize social structure. Radcliffe-Brown was dead by then, of course. We are talking about the late 1950s.[2] And the idea that you could theorize culture was dismissed in a superior sort of way. Talk about culture was a sign of sloppy thinking; it meant confusing psychology with sociology, and as good Durkheimians we thought that that was a sin. That was one debate. There was also some argument over whether anthropology could be a real science. Nadel's textbook, *Foundations of Social Anthropology*, was much read at that time.³ There was also the burning question of history's relation to anthropology. And some concern about how to interpret symbols. We had a teacher who was very interested in symbolic anthropology. He talked to us about Suzanne Langer and Ernst Cassirer and their work on symbolism. I must confess this didn't attract me very much.

DS: Why did you choose Oxford University as the place to pursue your doctorate, rather than staying at Edinburgh?

TA: Well, I think in part I wanted to work with Evans-Pritchard. We had of course read and studied all of his work on the Sudan, and he had also written on other parts of the Middle East, you know, his study, *The Sanusi of Cyrenaica*.⁴ I wanted to do fieldwork in an area that was Arabic speaking, and I knew that he had worked in the Sudan and that he had also briefly taught for a year or so in Cairo. These were probably the main reasons—that is, both the intellectual status of Evans-Pritchard, who was regarded by many as the outstanding anthropologist, and as someone for whom anthropology was not a "science," and as somebody who had connections with the Middle East, however peripheral.

DS: What was your relationship with Evans-Pritchard like?

TA: Well, I'll come to that in a moment. I just want to quickly finish off about my undergraduate work in Edinburgh by saying that one of the things that I did was a master's thesis—remember that this was an undergraduate degree—which was a sustained critique of Radcliffe-Brown's theory of ritual. I had been reading all kinds of philosophical texts at the time (including Austin, Wittgenstein, Toulmin, Ryle), which then prompted me to do a critical reassessment of his work on ritual. One of my teachers in particular was very unhappy about that. He was extremely critical of my attempt because he thought I was being arrogant toward the great man. But I knew that the Oxford Institute was much more favorable to rethinking the Radcliffe-Brown legacy. When I got to Oxford, it seemed to me some people there were even a little too critical of Radcliffe-Brown. I wondered whether they weren't partly motivated by a desire to establish Oxford as a different place, with Evans-Pritchard now as their leader. Anyway, that was initially another reason why I went to Oxford—because I knew they would look more sympathetically on my criticism of Radcliffe-Brown— and indeed one of the things I submitted with my application was my thesis, a short little thing called rather grandly, "The Structural Analysis of Ritual." It was an attempt on my part to think about performativity. My argument there was that Radcliffe-Brown's whole thesis about the social function of ritual was psychologistic and that one could approach the whole question from a purely semantic, structural point of view. Structural in the sense of breaking down complex structures, not of Lévi-Straussian binarism. Structuralism in the Lévi-Strauss sense, by the way, was just beginning to come to our notice. I was never really very excited by Lévi-Strauss's structuralism, although I found some aspects of his thought suggestive. But that's another story. So these things pushed me to choose Oxford. I went and was interviewed and was admitted, and then later I was offered a small fellowship.

Now, what were my relations with Evans-Pritchard like? You know, I did a B.Litt. first, before I did a doctorate. And the B.Litt. was a historical study of changes in Muslim law and landholding in the Punjab under the British from the period of the conquest in the late 1850s to Independence. My supervisor then was someone called David Pocock, who had done work in India, and he was a very interesting and encouraging supervisor.[5] But, partly by chance, I then decided to go to the Sudan. The Department of Anthropology in Khartoum University was virtually set up by Oxford people so there was a very close connection between Oxford and Khartoum. And the head of the department, Ian Cunnison—who became a good friend later—used to come regularly to Oxford to recruit from among the graduate students, although he was a Cambridge man himself. Khartoum University had a very good arrangement, which was to offer you a five-year contract to teach, and in that time you would get research money and the equivalent of a year's time off to do field research locally. And that was very attractive because, you know, Britain wasn't a place with lots and lots of money for research. The kind of arrangement Khartoum offered was one of the ways in which research could be done. So then Evans-Pritchard became my supervisor. I admired him for many things, of course, but I must confess he wasn't the sort of person I felt very warm toward. He was in many ways a rather prejudiced man, and he reveled in his prejudice. He could say unkind things to make people uncomfortable. There were aspects of him that I thought were really not very likeable.

Nor did I get an awful lot out of him intellectually, even though he was a great anthropologist. I did go to his lectures on the history of anthropology, which were eventually published, and I found those very interesting.⁶ And I had him always as my supervisor, but I can't say I was very indebted to his ideas. Though I must add that in spite of everything, when I was in the field and I got terribly depressed after a few months there, he wrote me a number of brief but encouraging letters. They were psychologically very helpful. Anyway, when I wrote up my doctoral thesis, I was largely on my own. I don't know that I got much useful feedback from him. In any case, he was almost retired by then, and I talked much more with people like Rodney Needham and Godfrey Lienhardt and (later) Fredrik Barth and to them I'm much more intellectually indebted.⁷

DS: Was it unusual for an undergraduate thesis to be some sort of critique of a school or an author rather than itself an original piece of research?

TA: I think it was in a way a little unusual. The subjects that people wrote on for their thesis varied greatly. For example, a fellow student did a translation of Van Gennep's *Rites of Passage* from the French (it hadn't been translated into English by then) with a mini-introduction and conclusion.⁸ Other people did what was in effect an extended ethnographic essay of about forty to sixty pages. But somehow I stumbled into this argumentative mode and decided that Radcliffe-Brown, whom everybody in Edinburgh revered, was not entirely right, and so I critiqued him. And I was encouraged by one of my teachers in Edinburgh, an open-minded man called Michael Banton. He was the one person who was very, very encouraging.⁹ I must say I'm grateful to him. He suggested I should publish my M.A. thesis as an article, but I never did.

DS: Looking back, is there a sense in which you enter anthropology, or in which you inhabit anthropology from the beginning, in a very antagonistic or a very critical sort of way?

TA: A *combative* way?

DS: Yes, that's a good word. Do you have a *combative* relationship with anthropology from the beginning?

TA: Perhaps. I think I developed a habit of that kind very early on, partly even the *need* for it. In my missionary boarding school in India, where I was one of a handful of Muslim students, I found I had to argue with my Christian fellow students—even when I was about eleven. So I certainly had that sense of *combativeness*, of having to argue almost in self-defense as it were, from very early on.

Khartoum and the Kababish

DS: Tell me about your experience in Khartoum. What was it like teaching there?

TA: I loved it. I was really very happy during the five years (1961–1966) I was in the Sudan. And it was my first experience of teaching. There wasn't any such thing as graduate teachers at Oxford, so I had never had any experience teaching while I was there. So this was very exciting and I went through a whole lot of material, and really found myself doing what I've always done in different ways since then, and that is to use teaching occasions to read through and think about various texts and to teach myself. The students were very bright. Most of them were very keen just to get a degree—like everywhere. The university was a very cosmopolitan place. There were teachers from many countries, including India, Pakistan, Egypt, various countries in Europe, including [then] Eastern Europe, and from England of course. In that sense, it was cosmopolitan, and personal relations were very congenial between teachers as well as with students. I was also very concerned to be as much in touch with the Sudanese as possible and to improve my spoken Arabic. Because, after all, I had learned Arabic from my mother, and of course then I had studied Arabic as an undergraduate in Edinburgh but only to be able to read it. But the Sudan was a period that helped me to improve my command of Arabic. So I would meet with as many Sudanese as possible, perhaps more than some others might have done. I had many Sudanese friends, some of whom are still friends today because they live in the States.

DS: Did you ever go back to the Sudan?

TA: Yes, I did. I went back in 1970 and then for the last time in 1975. That was the time I spent a semester teaching at the University of Khartoum.

DS: The work that comes out of this period, of course, is your Ph.D. thesis, submitted in 1968, I believe, and then the book *The Kababish Arabs*, which was published in 1970.[10] I want to talk a little bit about this book, in particular about the questions it asks and its mode of questioning, because looking at it recently, I was struck by the continuities between your approach to inquiry then and your approach now. *The Kababish Arabs* is concerned with the political structure of the Kababish, and in particular the conditions that make political power only accessible to a small group of persons. There is of course a large amount of conventional anthropological description in it—kinship charts, photographs, and so on—but the central preoccupation of the book is a *conceptual* one. You are interested in the role of "consent" in British functional anthropology. Why is that? What brings you to that *mode* of inquiry? And what enabled you to direct your attention to the problematic of consent in British anthropology?

TA: May I go back just little bit in order to try and place another phase of what you've called my combativeness? That's to my first experience in England when I arrived. When I was young, from at least the age of fourteen, I developed an enormous admiration for the West—or rather, for a certain idea of the enlightened West. I was very much imbued with the idea that the West was where one would find Reason, where one would find Freedom, where one would find all the wonderful things which were lacking in Pakistan. And my experience in Britain and then here in the U.S.—and now I speak of a long *durée* in my life—was one of a slow *disabusement*. There were different phases, which are connected to my work and to which I will come later on, but put simply, I began to realize how *saturated* with prejudice people in England were. You might say I was terribly naïve to think otherwise. And I certainly was naïve, but I had to *learn* to see my naïveté. This seemed to me an incredible discovery, that I had failed for so long to see people in England as prejudiced, as *soaked* in prejudice. People are prejudiced everywhere, of course, but the English were supposed to be living in an enlightened Western country. So I began to be interested in the question of ideology. I read Marx, even as an undergraduate, and then later on in my early Oxford days as a graduate student. There I was both very attracted and puzzled by the way he talked about domination and ideology. Something that I gained from Marx very early on was the recognition that structures of domination need *not* be rooted directly in force or consent, but in what at that time I called "structural exclusion," something independent of what people might consciously think. Both force and consent were states of consciousness, but they were of minor significance, I thought, for explaining structures of domination—both political and intellectual.

It was also, I think, at that time that I happened to read Hobbes, for whom, interestingly enough, violence—the violence of the dominator—

also generates a kind of consent. Hobbes doesn't think that consent is inconsistent with coercion. He thinks that in the end, if the sword compels the person who's subordinated to give in to the will of the dominator, then that is almost the same as consent; it's a kind of consent in the sense that it's always possible to say no and choose death. Anyway, what I found so interesting about Marx, apart from the grand story of capitalism, and apart from his incisive critiques of modern liberal society, was the very idea that domination could be seen as a function of structural exclusion. After all, it's the very process of capitalist production that creates—without explicit consent or force—the subordination of the worker.

DS: So it is *through* Marx that you come at a conceptual analysis?

TA: Yes.

DS: In the preface to *The Kababish Arabs*, you say that you had actually meant to study the pastoral ecology and the kinship system of the Kababish, and it is while you are there that you shift your focus to the political structure of the society. Why would you have gone to study pastoral ecology? How would you have come to that? How do you recollect the shift that you undergo while you are there in the Sudan?

TA: I think I was tipping my hat at Evans-Pritchard, because, after all, even though his book on *The Nuer* deals with politics, it's really about modes of livelihood, about pastoral ecology. In fact, his monograph was at first the model for what I thought my study should be. So I thought, "Hah, I'll do an analysis of the pastoral system and the lineage system of the Kababish." In *The Nuer* he employs the notion of segmentary lineage systems to outline their political system in conjunction with their pastoral mode of livelihood. I expected to find something similar. I made an awful lot of lineage charts, and much to my delight I found that they *did* have segmentary lineages. But it slowly dawned on me that this was simply a function of the way in which genealogies are taken, and it doesn't necessarily have any significance for the way people organize or relate to one another. If you go and ask people, "Who was your father, and your father's father?" and then backward if you like: "How many children did each one have?" you'll find you've got a kind of inverted tree structure. And I thought, "Aha! segmentary lineage systems!" But of course that was nonsense. Except for the chiefly family, which had something approaching a lineage group, most of the others didn't have one at all. It was after some months of effort that I discovered I'd made all these charts for nothing, you know, and my segmentary lineage systems among the Kababish were just illusions.

I became interested then—since I'd started with the chiefly group, and it was quite clear that they had monopolized all sorts of offices, all sorts of functions within their family, and they dominated the local government structure—in how that had happened. Because the Kababish tribe was a relatively recent political entity. That's partly why my history of the Kababish is in the middle of my book rather than at the beginning, which was the conventional place for it in monographs at that time. You know, you had the history of the tribe and then the ethnographic account, whereas I come to it in the middle of the book because I wanted to try and understand how this particular structure of local domination came to be established. Much depended on the astuteness of the modern founder, Sheikh Ali al-Tom, who made use of the British to consolidate his power by bringing various small groups of pastoralists together.

DS: So from very early on, your attention is drawn to the problem of the way in which anthropological knowledge is fashioned, the idea that the kinds of knowledge that anthropology produces are, in part at least, a function of the kinds of questions it asks.

TA: Yes. I did in fact write something for a Festschrift for Evans-Pritchard on the concept of the tribe, in which I tried to argue that the concept of the tribe, at least among the Kababish, was a construct of several things: people within the tribe making certain historical claims, administrators who needed to have a category called the tribe, and the anthropologist who employed a social science concept of "tribe."[11]

DS: Besides Marx, what else were you reading at the time that was influencing the perspective that you took?

TA: I was very interested in the history of science. Michael Banton, whom I mentioned earlier on, was active in a small study group in Edinburgh consisting of scientists, historians, sociologists, and so on, interested in the history of science. I think it may even have been called the Darwin Group or something like that, because Darwin had studied at Edinburgh as an undergraduate. So I was interested in the history of science because it seemed to me part of what a modern rational postenlightenment man ought to concern himself with. Science was *the* legitimate approach to "reality." But at the same time, I was also very attracted to the later Wittgenstein. I can't recall now exactly who it was who introduced me to him—yes, I remember, a friend of mine in England. So perhaps that was slightly before I went to do anthropology at Edinburgh. At any rate, I was introduced to Wittgenstein. And I can remember that one of my most engrossing experiences as a student was reading *The Blue and Brown Books* (I don't think I ever mentioned this to you) on the train from Edinburgh right through to London, an eight-hour journey. I sat there and I read the whole thing in one go. I was so gripped by it! The *Books* was a preparatory study for the *Philosophical Investigations* that I had encountered earlier but never read right through. Wittgenstein certainly helped to complicate enormously my early, somewhat childish, attraction to logical positivism.

DS: That's interesting. You had not told me that before. So you're reading the Wittgenstein who is himself trying to get out of his earlier attraction to logical positivism.[12]

TA: Yes, I suppose. I hadn't thought of it quite that way. But certainly it helped me to see how incredibly naïve some of those assumptions that I had were. You know I'd read books like A. J. Ayers's *Language, Truth, and Logic* (I still have my copy of it for sentimental reasons), which had provided me with a marvelously simple way of sorting out sense from nonsense.[13] It is of course a brilliant young man's book, but terribly simpleminded in spite of its brilliance. And I realized that there were complexities that needed to be addressed, which I also thought anthropology would help me in some way to address. I began to see these as feeding into my sensitivity to the social and cultural experiences of people in different contexts. So Wittgenstein's work was certainly one of the things that influenced me, although I didn't draw explicitly on it for a number of years. It helped to reshape my whole conception of human relations, the complexities of language and language use, and so on.

DS: As you're reading Wittgenstein, reading Marx, formulating a perspective on anthropology, and so on, do you feel yourself to be intellectually alone? I mean, do you have other college-mates who you feel are questioning in a similar way?

TA: Not in those years. I mean I didn't feel I had intellectual mates as an undergraduate. I think as I began to talk with other graduates at Oxford (mostly nonanthropologists) I felt I wasn't quite so alone. Certainly there was much more interest in a Wittgensteinian approach, and indeed in people like your friend R. G. Collingwood, who was a very important figure there in the Oxford Institute in those years, though interestingly enough it was mainly *The Idea of History* that people read.

DS: But curiously enough, Talal, I have never seen you cite *The Idea of History*. What I see a lot of, though, is Collingwood's *The Principles of Art*.[14]

TA: That's right. That's what excited me. But it was precisely *The Idea of History* that tended to be taken up much more seriously in Oxford. And one of my complaints has been that I was never introduced by my Oxford teachers to *The Principles of Art*, or for that matter to *The Idea of Nature*, but only to *The Idea of History*.

DS: That is very interesting indeed, because Collingwood himself was a very *conceptual* thinker; that's what holds his attention.

TA: Right. And many things you have touched on in your own work are the kinds of things I started to think about much later, particularly after reading your work, in which you draw on him so fruitfully.[15] For example, the significance of the question-and-answer approach, so important to Collingwood, wasn't apparent to me at that time. Still, I found him to be a very stimulating writer. But he himself, as you know better than most, was very much an isolated intellectual figure in his lifetime. So, to answer that question: did I have a sense of being alone? Yes, on the whole I did. Anyway, I then went off to the Sudan. That was a very different context. And when we came back to England in 1966, I again had a sense of being somewhat alone, partly because I felt I had to try to think through some things for myself. Then came 1967 and the Six Days War. That was an enormous watershed in my life, intellectually as well as politically. The first thing was the reaction of the English, which astounded me. I couldn't get over the fantastic delight at the utter defeat of Egypt and the other Arab countries. Joy expressed in TV and newspaper reports and in photographs (I still have some of these) at the thousands of humiliated, exhausted, peasant soldiers, forced to walk barefoot over the hot desert. I could understand the joy that Israelis must have felt at their victory. But the English? What was the emotion that fueled the exultation of this enlightened nation toward the ignominious defeat of a wretched, oppressed oriental people? This question began as a rhetorical one for me, as a reproach, but slowly it pushed me to rethink the assumptions I had for so long carried with me about Rationality and Justice in politics.

DS: I want to come back to that in a moment, to the political context of the late 1960s, but I want to stay a wee bit longer with *The Kababish Arabs*. One of the striking features of that book, in addition to your attention to the political structure and the wider modern history in which the Kababish are embedded, is the distinctive way you shape the question about history. You are writing this inside of a British social anthropology that is itself—in Evans-Pritchard, in Edmund Leach—making a sort of historical turn. But still there is a distinctive way in which you pose the question about history. In one of the historical chapters, for example, you say, after talking a bit about the political life of the Kababish, that this indicates "from the earliest years of its modern history the political possibilities of the Kababish tribe were partly a consequence of calculated policy beyond the direct control of its rulers."[16] This seems to me to be a very Talal Asad kind of sentence; what holds your attention is the way in which possibilities for action, political in this case, are shaped by power. And this is something that has become a much more central part of your theoretical work in the years since then. But what is it that inclines you toward *that sense* of the question of history?

TA: This brings me back to the political context of 1967 and after. I was, after all, writing my book in 1968. I began at that time to be seriously interested in colonial history and the complex conditions that colonialism created—of which those who dominated and those who were dominated were joint authors—in the different countries with which I was more familiar. In a sense, everyone's fate was being partly decided somewhere else. Obviously I don't mean that everyone has the same power of decision, or that everyone is equally innocent in what he or she decides to do. On the contrary, the asymmetry of colonial and postcolonial power makes the lives of many people open to intervention by others in a nonreciprocal way. That seems to me a fairly straightforward proposition that was illustrated by the Middle East. Power is central in history both in the obvious sense of what some people can do to many, and also of what someone can do to himself or herself. That was what was so interesting about the student uprisings in the 1960s, in spite of their many absurdities and overall failure. It seems to me they were at once a confrontation with power and an exploration of the limits and possibilities of power. The Kababish "tribe" had, after all, created itself as a political unit within and through the colonial structure in ways I detail in my book. This doesn't mean I thought the Kababish were as powerful as the colonial rulers.

DS: Let's pause a little around this period, Talal. There is the Six Days War in 1967, and there are the student uprisings in 1968, both in France and in England. How do these tilt or reshape your politics, and are you drawn to some of the emerging theoretical trends, whether in the Marxism of the New Left or Cultural Studies, that are beginning to emerge in the late 1960s, early 1970s?

TA: I had been reading Marx very early on, and sort of naturally gravitated toward the Left even as a youth. And when I arrived at Oxford I subscribed to that short-lived journal called *Universities and Left Review*, of which Stuart Hall, Charles Taylor, Alasdair MacIntyre, and a number of others were the editors.[17] In that sense, I was very much drawn to that tendency already, but it became sharper for me immediately after 1967, because of both the war—a further expropriation of Palestinian land by Israelis—and the student uprisings, which articulated generosity and hope. I lectured much more systematically on Marx at that time to students. And I interacted intensively with academics who were Marxist activists, although I never joined any political group. Virtually everybody in our department was a member either of the SWP [Socialist Workers Party] or the IMG [International Marxist Group]—both of them Trotskyist groups—or the Communist Party, or the left wing of the Labour Party. I was very reluctant to join a group because of the unease I felt about making too tight a connection between intellectual work and political work. That is, I didn't see the two as being quite so straightforwardly connected. I felt myself to be unequivocally on the Left politically. But I didn't see that that fact should determine all the work I was doing and the kinds of questions I was asking.

I've always been somewhat pessimistic about the possibilities of political activism, and certainly skeptical about the idea of political revolution. I even became increasingly skeptical about the idea that a rational politics would lead to emancipation. As I say, 1967 was a traumatic moment for me, in which all sorts of questions were forming in my mind of which I was not fully aware at the time but which developed over time. So that is part of the context: politically committed to the Left, reading Marx, belonging to a *Capital*-reading group, construing the text as though it were a believer's Bible. I still have the old text, pencil marks and underlining and notes in the margin. And indeed from the late 1960s on, some of us began to be influenced by Althusserian Marxism. So, for example, we wouldn't start with chapter 1 [of *Capital*], but jump to later chapters. I certainly found Althusser enormously stimulating at the time, not only as a political thinker but as someone who made me more sharply aware of the finer questions of textual analysis, of temporalities inside texts, and the question of epistemological breaks and so on.

DS: What about the emergence of Cultural Studies? Are you aware of what's going on at the University of Birmingham with Richard Hoggart and Stuart Hall and does it interest you?

TA: I was aware of it, and I was interested in many of the things they were doing. I had read Hoggart and then, later on, Stuart Hall as well. I always found Hall was much more open to all kinds of theoretical developments and much less dogmatic than many other people around him. Because, you know, he drew on people like Althusser when the British Left was far more sympathetic to E. P. Thompson, a bitter anti-Althusserian. That was something that I appreciated. The empirical work by the Cultural Studies people was both interesting and somewhat dismaying to me. Interesting because of the studies of youthful fashions, of motorcycle gangs, of working-class schools, and so on.[18] Dismaying because they seemed to be reaching for a kind of Geertzianism, by which I mean a kind of textualization of cultural constructs. This was also a move in the direction of an anthropology (symbolic analysis and the interpretation of meaning) that I was trying to distance myself from.

Let me explain by quoting two short passages from Stuart Hall's *Culture, Media, and Language*. He writes: "*The Uses of Literacy* refused many of Leavis's embedded cultural judgements. But it did attempt to deploy literary criticism to 'read' the emblems, idioms, social arrangements, the lived cultures and 'languages' of working class life, as particular kinds of 'text,' as a privileged sort of cultural evidence." And then he says later on: "With the extension in the meaning of 'culture' from texts and representations to lived practices, belief systems and institutions, some part of the subject matter of sociology also fell within our scope."[19] So instead of extending the idea of "lived practices" to texts, as I would have urged, the Cultural Studies people choose to do the reverse.

DS: Would the question of culture have already seeped into British social anthropology? I mean, for Cultural Studies, it's really Raymond Williams who is drawn on.

TA: Was the concept of culture introduced into British social anthropology at this time? Well, there was Mary Douglas, and British Lévi-Straussians like Edmund Leach and Rodney Needham who wrote about culture. But this is a different lineage. Cultural Studies people remained independent pioneers, I think. They began to talk about culture in ways that most anthropologists in Britain had not wanted to. And they were able to do that partly by drawing on people like Roland Barthes, who had shown how *popular* culture could be subjected to a structural analysis. But they were not, strictly speaking, structuralists because while structuralists are primarily interested in the cultural processes by which meanings are produced, Cultural Studies people seemed more interested in interpreting social meanings. This is not an aspect of the modern history of ideas that I've seriously thought about, but it deserves to be studied. How anthropologists shifted their perspective on culture.

DS: You mean anthropologists in Britain?

TA: Yes, right. But all this was happening at a time when my own interest first in Althusser and then in Foucault pushed me *away* from being concerned with the interpretation of symbols in social life.

Anthropology and Colonialism

DS: There is an important endnote to the introduction to *The Kababish Arabs* (the content of which becomes much more important in your subsequent work), in which you are thinking much more explicitly about the relationship between anthropology and colonialism. I want to turn to this briefly. The note goes like this: "I believe it to be both mistaken and unjust to attribute invidious political motives to anthropologists studying primitive societies—as is sometimes done by opinion in ex-colonial countries and by left-wing writers in the West. Most social anthropologists held or still hold radical, or liberal, political views. Nevertheless, it remains true that classic functionalism prevented them from effecting a fruitful conjunction between their political commitments and their sociological analysis."[20] So by the time you write *The Kababish Arabs*, the discussion about anthropology and colonialism is in full swing. There are a number of articles in the early to mid-1960s that are beginning to problematize this. Again, for me what's really fascinating is the *angle* at which you come at the problem of anthropology and colonialism. Can you say what it is about the character of that emerging debate that presses you in this direction?

TA: It's interesting to be confronted with things that I wrote in 1968 or 1969, but I think the thing that concerned me at the time was both the importance of a colonial history and the tendency—on the part of many people, both friends and political comrades—to reduce understanding to moralistic judgment. I felt then, and I think this is perhaps reflected in that brief note, that there was a need for thinking again about how one could understand that kind of history and what such rethinking might both open and close in terms of actual political commitments. I wanted our political commitments to *generate* questions for investigation that might in turn constitute a challenge to them. I suppose I wanted to do without eternally fixed foundations. I wanted to understand the impact of Western societies, modern societies, on colonized or quasi-colonized modes of life. But I was increasingly reluctant to discuss it in terms of injustice, or in terms of the idea that collective suffering was often the price to be paid for historical progress. And I thought we needed to think about how colonial history threw up different kinds of possibilities and limits. I hadn't done that in *The Kababish Arabs*, I know. But I didn't see anyone who was doing it in anthropology. Even the people I was later much influenced by, people like Foucault and other poststructuralists, were uninterested in colonial history. And I felt that one had to somehow try and find a way of speaking about this without descending either into personal blame or describing the discipline as the "handmaiden" of colonialism. I thought that there were still many questions to ask about that history, and so about political commitments, and we didn't quite know how to do that yet.

DS: Well, one of the avenues that you foreground in your approach to the question of anthropology and colonialism, displacing the moralizing polemic against various anthropologists and the colonial enterprise, is to look at the ways in which a discipline like anthropology, because of the character of its theoretical analysis—not the attitude of its practitioners—reproduces a colonial ideology.

TA: Yes, I was concerned with that. Perhaps the text in which I tried to do this most self-consciously is my reanalysis of Abner Cohen.[21] I wanted to get at that whole question, again without any ad hominem arguments, because the question of anthropology seemed to me to be often grossly misconceived by its critics. I think I've said this on a number of occasions from then on: anthropology is a very small discipline, and when you widen your definition to include all sorts of people who are not formally anthropologists, you can make a case for saying, "Of course it was profoundly important for colonial rule." But I've always maintained that anthropology had a very peripheral role. But what interested me was not so much what individual anthropologists had done here or there, but what the historical situation of having to describe or analyze very different kinds of societies that are ruled from outside—what that did to some of the assumptions of the discipline. And here I was trying to think through what it meant to say that an ideological reproduction was the reproduction of a whole field of assumptions. And this is partly what I think I did in the Abner Cohen piece. There were lots of things, even about his personal role in the administration of Palestinian populations, to which I didn't refer at all. You know, this was a very poststructuralist phase, in which I wanted to uncover, as it were, what the unconscious structures of the text were. I think now I didn't quite succeed in this. I think I had interesting things to say in my article, but I took certain things too much for granted. But even so, it was an attempt. And you're right, it was an attempt to see texts as having a life of their own, and as carrying through certain kinds of assumptions that were part of that imbedded relationship between an intellectual academic discipline in the West and the places to which one went that had been ruled by the West.

DS: I want to come back to that essay on Abner Cohen in a moment. But I want to stay a bit with the question of anthropology and colonialism. Can you tell me a bit about the making of the seminar that led to the volume *Anthropology and the Colonial Encounter*?[22] How did that come about?

TA: Well, I was a member of the British Association of Social Anthropologists, which had annual meetings—much smaller than the American Anthropological Association circuses. And at the end of each session, which went on for two or three days, people were asked to suggest themes for further meetings. I think it was about 1969 or 1970, yes, 1970, when there was a meeting in Bristol. Various people suggested possible themes for the future, which were put up on the blackboard, and I suggested doing something on anthropology and colonialism. What I had in mind of course was not something that would simply be a mea culpa thing—you know, saying we've all been guilty and so on. I wanted to explore that relationship and what it meant for our concepts. I think somebody wrote it up on a blackboard, but then in a rather typical British way it just got lost in the ensuing discussion. It got marginalized. And so I talked to Ian Cunnison about this, and we discussed the possibility of having a small, low-budget conference on the subject at Hull.

DS: By this time, you are teaching at the University of Hull and Ian Cunnison is the head of the department.

TA: Yes. I came at the end of 1966, in September, just before the academic year started. So we decided in 1970 to do that conference. I was going away for a year to Egypt in 1971. I had just got a British Academy Fellowship to go to Egypt for a year because I wanted to do some thinking about the Middle East and to familiarize myself in particular with Egypt. So Cunnison agreed we'd hold it when I got back. And there were a number of people I thought of inviting, one or two in the Hull department, my historian friend Roger Owen at Oxford, and one or two Sudanese, and a few others.

DS: How did you select the participants?

TA: It was just a matter of serendipity. It wasn't done systematically. There were a number of people I knew about, who I thought would have something interesting to say. For example, there was someone called Richard Brown, who was working on the Rhodes-Livingstone Institute doing a serious piece of historiographical research. Cunnison got in touch with him because he had contacts with Manchester. There was Jim Faris, who was at the University of Connecticut, whom I had known from the Sudan—we overlapped a little bit when he arrived. There was Wendy James, an Oxford anthropologist who had also worked in the Sudan. And one or two others.

DS: But in some ways the disparate character of the pieces in the volume makes it a curious book on reflection, because your own particular take on the question of the unequal power between the West and the non-West and how this shapes anthropological knowledge is not really at the center of the other pieces. You are concerned with the ideological conditions of knowledge production, and the other pieces aren't really. What was the discussion like? How did other people respond to your shaping of the book? Because, of course, one of the things about *Anthropology and the Colonial Encounter* is that it is identified with Talal Asad and is in some sense *your* book.

TA: Well, that is curious, because it really was a collective effort. The discussion was interesting, and I am trying now to remember it after three decades. We had a whole day at least, maybe we had two days, discussing the papers. For most people the subject evoked a strong sense of its being a moral one, and that comes out in a number of the pieces. My own piece—and my introduction—was clearly struggling to get out of that. But I made absolutely no attempt to impose any kind of editorial control, because I wanted it understood—and I think I said this in my introduction—that the book was just the beginning of a discussion rather than anything definitive. And I wanted to push people to reflect on the matter, because there was nothing like it in Britain. And this was not out of any determination on the part of British academics to suppress something uncomfortable. It was simply the typical British way of pushing uninteresting things aside. The quasi-scientific approach to the discipline, which still obtained among many anthropologists, made the discipline's connection to colonialism quite uninteresting. I was hoping to press people to start a discussion. And I remember discussing the book at one of the Paris universities after it was published, as well as in Utrecht. But I don't think there was any discussion of it in Britain, absolutely nothing.

DS: So the reception of it in Britain was poor?

TA: By and large, many people felt they had been personally attacked. They had been morally impugned. The essay by the Sudanese anthropologist Abdel-Ghaffar Ahmed, a wild critique of Evans-Pritchard, seemed especially to have offended a number of people.[23] But by and large, apart from the feeling on the part of many people that I had done something really improper, there was virtually no *intellectual* reaction to it at all, at least openly. And it was in that context that three of us—Roger Owen, Sami Zubaida, and myself—started a Middle East group. We held regular discussions in Hull once a year. We did that for three years, publishing the articles presented at our seminar. Again, they were very uneven articles, but when you start a new venture like this, that often can't be helped. Anyway, it was in the first issue of the journal we established to publish our papers—*Review of Middle East Studies*—that my analysis of Abner Cohen's text came.[24] I considered it to be a continuation of what I had hoped people would do in *Anthropology and the Colonial Encounter*.

DS: How long did the *Review* go on for?

TA: Well, the *Review* went on for three years, to begin with. Then after a few years of silence, it was revived without my editorial involvement and with a new purpose. If you want me to talk a bit about the group for which the *Review* was established, I can do that. We were very dissatisfied with the level of theorization in Middle East Studies. And my concern was not simply with the political bias, but the enormous disparity between the sophisticated thinking that you would see in the historiography, sociology, political philosophy of Western societies compared to the stuff that was coming out about the Middle East. The theoretical level was abysmal. So having a reading group (that is, with Sami, Roger, and myself) in which we read and discussed things, sometimes our own stuff and sometimes texts by others, we decided to have a bigger annual do, which we held on three occasions, and whose presentations we published in the *Review*. Both the group and the journal have continued, though in a very different form, as I said. It now meets regularly in London. The journal has become "normalized," concerned more with political economy and political developments in the region from a progressive perspective, but I'm not sure how regularly it is now published.

For me, the whole project of anthropology and colonialism was carried into that group, which I felt ought to be doing two things. One was to do *counterpolemical* work against publications we considered politically biased or sloppy. There was other work of that kind coming out at that time. The one that became most famous, of course, is Edward Said's *Orientalism*, which appeared in 1978, after the last of our three issues of the *Review* had come out.[25] Its success gave us great encouragement. So I thought that on the one hand we should do that—show the kinds of political bias that existed in individual works about the Middle East and their historical context. But I *also* wanted us to do something else: to explore and rework existing material without being committed to any specific party line. We would then see where that led us, see how far we could generate new questions. This latter part of our project never really caught on, because most people felt that since a Marxist framework was already available, since a political economy framework was already there, we already knew what all the important questions were.

The first part of the project seemed less and less interesting to colleagues. But the other task wasn't even grasped by most of our group. So eventually I sort of disengaged myself from the group. I'm still an honorary member but not an active one. Now they're doing standard academic stuff from a somewhat leftwing perspective. When the *Review* was resuscitated, a new editorial noted the shift, arguing that things had now changed for the better because many of us who were originally junior lecturers or graduates now had jobs or were full professors, and this was a sign that our critical project had succeeded and was now being taken seriously by the larger academic community. This seemed to me an extraordinary argument. It almost implied that it was concern for our careers that had initially propelled our dissatisfaction. So I found myself working somewhat alone again, trying to think about things in a more exploratory way, prepared to find myself at the end of it in a different place from where I had begun, a place I didn't even know existed until I got there.

The Question of Ideology

DS: I want to come back now to the essay on Abner Cohen, which I read in *Economy and Society* and not in *Review of Middle East Studies.*

TA: Yes, it appeared simultaneously in both. I was then a member of the *Economy and Society* editorial board, having joined in 1974. The journal had a Marxist orientation at the time, having been founded in 1972 by a group of sociologists with strong Althusserian inclinations. I was invited to join at the same time as Ernesto Laclau, so the board got a political theorist and an anthropologist.

DS: In the 1970s you published a number of essays concerned with anthropology and ideology: concerned on the one hand with the ideological character of anthropological work, and on the other with the anthropological analysis of ideology. I am thinking of two texts: the essay on Cohen that you have just mentioned, published in 1975, and "Anthropology and the Analysis of Ideology," your Malinowksi Lecture, published in 1979.[26]

I want to pause a little over these two essays and ask you a couple of questions. The first question (which in some sense you may have answered) is about the intellectual and ideological fields in which you take these texts to be interventions—because their character is that of *interventions*. What is going on in anthropology or the human sciences more generally that prompts both the *character* and the *direction* of these interventions?

TA: Well, let me think about the Abner Cohen piece first, because that was the one that came out first. In it I used the Marxist idea of the articulation of modes of production. I was trying to marry my concern with political economy to the way in which the whole Israeli/Palestinian problem was being commonly presented, with its notable disdain for Palestinians and a great deal of sympathy and respect for the Zionist project. And then I was concerned with ideology and how it is that one comes to write about, speak about, things in a certain way given one's political convictions. I think I mentioned earlier that when I first came to Britain I was infatuated with the Enlightenment, its celebration of rationality, justice, tolerance, and so forth. And very reluctantly I came to the conclusion not only that there was much prejudice in Western societies, but that the problem of ideology, as Marxism saw it, was much more complicated than I had assumed. So that was what drew me to thinking about ideology. I am less satisfied with the results I arrived at. Not because I think my analysis was fundamentally wrong; there is quite a lot I would still stand by in the Abner Cohen piece. I am not so sure now about the way I used the "articulation of modes of production" as a framework. But even there, I think there are some points still worth pondering. But the idea that one could uncover certain mistaken assumptions by bringing them into daylight and that a reasonable mind would then be able to perceive them as such—this became increasingly problematic. That was both what attracted me to the concept of ideology and at the same time made me dissatisfied with the way in which classical Marxism had elaborated it.

Shortly after that, because of my mother's final illness, I left for Saudi Arabia. I spent just over a year there in 1978–79. I found myself again unhappy about the kind of society that I had to live in for the year. I had ambivalent feelings about it, actually. On the one hand, I spent time with my relatives and also got to know some very nice people. On the other hand, I felt an intense dislike for the religious bigotry that was being churned out on television and radio. And I was asked before I left Britain whether I would give the Malinowski Lecture, and I said I couldn't that year because of my having to go to Saudi Arabia, but that I would do so as soon as I came back. And when I came back, I began to try to rethink for myself from scratch the whole question of ideology, and the ways in which one thought of ideology as simply a kind of blind, which once removed would show all rational people what the answer was. I had become disturbed by my experience in Saudi Arabia, by media presentations of the Israeli/Palestinian conflict in Britain, by the media reactions to the student uprisings. All the rational demonstrations of what was wrong in each case—so it seemed to me—were clearly not having any significant effect. So I rediscovered the wheel: the assumption that rational argument will persuade people that they are wrong is an incredibly naïve idea. You ask any ordinary person in the street, and she knows this already without having read any philosophy, but for blinkered idiots like us, intellectuals, or rather for myself, rational criticism was thought to be the way to show somebody what the truth is. And so in a very primitive and blundering way I started to rethink this. That's what the Malinowski Lecture is about. I think it is not entirely coherent. In it several points are being made that are occasionally contradictory and certainly not as well made as they could be. But it was really my first attempt to shift myself out of what was a kind of intellectual morass and to start thinking for myself again.

DS: So in some sense the Malinowski Lecture is part of an exercise in self-criticism.

TA: Very much so.

DS: And partly therefore a criticism of the essay on Abner Cohen. But I want to ask you about a particular passage that speaks to this in the Cohen piece, which I have always found very helpful. You say, and I am quoting: "In order to evaluate the theoretical limitations of contemporary anthropological knowledge and its political implications, it is necessary to carry out detailed critical analysis of specific representative work. This is the only effective way of demonstrating the principle that the uncritical reproduction of an ideological work is itself ideological and therefore theoretically faulty."[27] You seem now to see in this formulation an excess of rationalism.

TA: I think so, yes. It's also, by the way, a very Marxist theorization.

It's not that critique isn't useful, indeed it is and doing *detailed* criticism is generally more useful—but for *tactical* purposes rather than in some absolute sense. Over time I have found myself becoming much more suspicious of theory. I was drawn again and again to currents that were suspicious of theory, of grand theory. The concern I once had with theoretical rigor, with logical demonstration of an overall theoretical argument, became less attractive to me. I became more concerned to explore things in ways that might have appeared theoretically unsatisfactory previously. I began to feel that one should be prepared to take risks in which one might say and write things that were sometimes wrong and be prepared to arrive at conclusions that might appear naïve. One has to take that risk. And I began to be more self-conscious about it. In the Middle East group I talked about earlier, I had had a sense of just that—of the necessity of taking risks. And that was partly what I was expressing in the Malinowski Lecture: a greater openness than one finds in the Abner Cohen article, where I know exactly what argument I am using and where I'm headed. It is through a Marxist political economy framework that I think I can demonstrate not only the working of certain political-economic processes and their clear outcomes, but also their ideological underpinnings, and so on. I'm now certainly no less critical of the Israeli state, but I am less interested in being able to convince myself that I have a rigorous framework and a rigorous methodology for getting at rational conclusions.

DS: Are you suggesting then that in the piece on Abner Cohen you could examine his anthropological text and draw out what you call here the political implications of that work, whereas from 1978/79 onward the idea of being able to identify clearly the political implications of theoretical work is something that you no longer believe to be possible or you no longer feel is a worthwhile strategy to adopt? I am interested in several things in the formulation I quoted. You say, "In order to evaluate the theoretical limitations of anthropological knowledge and its political implications...." Do you now, looking back, disagree with that formulation? Do you now think that we cannot in fact draw out the "political implications of theoretical work"?

TA: No. As I said, perhaps most of what I argued in that paper I would still stand by. What I am less persuaded by now is that this kind of argument can significantly convince others. The political implications of any theoretical work are not as tidy, as determinate as they might appear at first sight. "Implication" is a logical term, but the political activity that someone might engage in (or reject) doesn't depend on relations of logic. And I don't just mean that all of us are illogical much of the time. Perhaps there's a better way of putting it. What has interested me since the late 1970s is this: What is there about this process of drawing out implications that strikes me as evident, obvious, important, but doesn't so strike other people? This is not a plea for empathy but a recognition that I am leaving something *out* of this entire process, namely, how people engage with language and with their emotions too. This is where I began to be interested in reconceptualizing the question of ideology in terms of the experience of the body-mind-heart.

So I think I would say, yes, at one level I see that there are political implications, but what that means concretely is no longer always clear to me, and I want to do some more thinking on that. What does it mean to say there are political implications? Here's a text, I read it, I point to some of its assumptions and what I think are certain political implications. But what does this mean in the real world? I want to complicate for myself the whole question of how one interprets these texts and what it means to draw political implications from them for a particular situation. What does it mean to respond politically to "implications"? And how can they be grasped by someone other than myself? What is the difference between my seeing them and somebody else seeing them? How can a theoretical work be linked objectively to a particular situation?

DS: So in a sense you are saying it's not that you have given up the strategy of thinking about political implications of certain kinds of work, but that it's complicated by raising a question about what constitutes "political implications" and for whom?

TA: Yes, exactly.

DS: Why is the critical analysis of what you call "specific representative work" the way to gain a grasp of the yield and limit of anthropological knowledge?

TA: Well, you know, this was an indirect reference to Durkheim really, and his notion of the "average" being "representative." British social anthropology was very much indebted, as you know, to Durkheimian sociology. And in a way I was using a Durkheimian principle by saying the average is the representative. So when some people said to me, "But why don't you take a *famous* text and analyze that?" they were clearly taking it for granted that famous books are also socially significant books. Much to my delight later, this was precisely what Foucault questioned so well. He was more interested in popular historical texts by little-known people. That was the Durkheimian statistical principle: the more ordinary it is, the more run-of-the-mill it is, the more representative it is of what people are thinking and doing. There are a number of things in that article that perhaps you may not have noticed but I know people in Britain did. The Manchester School under Max Gluckman pioneered a kind of teaching seminar in which they took a particular text, an anthropological monograph, and analyzed it and tried to reconstruct its theoretical framework and the questions for field research that that framework generated. This kind of graduate seminar was widely known at that time in British anthropology departments as Anthropological Texts and Problems. So I gave it a twist in the title to my article by calling it "*ideological* texts and anthropological problems."

DS: This statement also suggests a relationship between the theoretical and the ideological. You say that the reproduction of ideological objects is not only itself ideological as well as theoretically faulty, but that it is theoretically faulty *because* it is ideological. Can you say a little bit more about what that relationship between the theoretical and the ideological is about?

TA: I was still grappling at the time with the Marxist idea of ideology as a kind of systematic distortion of reality that would be revealed by a truly scientific approach. To say that something was ideological was to say it was really not an adequate representation of reality. The ideology of the bourgeoisie—insofar as economics was that ideology—was a misrepresentation of the workings of modern capital. The writings of economists who took on board bourgeois ideas as part of their theory were not scientific accounts of economic reality; they failed to represent that reality properly. And to that extent, I think, now that you are reading the sentence out to me, I can recognize that it belongs to the phase before my Malinowski Lecture.

DS: Well, let's turn to that lecture, which I have always found to be a very complicated and fascinating essay, and which I have had to read and reread many times. I want to quote again from it and ask you about a passage. It's a passage that occurs very early in it, where you are setting up your argument, and you do so by referring again to the question of anthropology and colonialism: "The modesty of anthropologists regarding the ideological role of their discourses in the determination of colonial structures does not seem to be matched by a corresponding skepticism regarding the role of ideology generally in the determination of social structures which are objects of their discourse. Their science as discourse, so it said, is not determined by social reality and yet the social reality of which that science speaks is typically nothing but discourse."[28] You are setting up a kind of paradox here in which you are using the preoccupation with anthropology's relationship with ideology to launch into a discussion about how anthropology analyzes ideology and how it ought to do so. Why do you begin with that paradox, and what is it that you are trying to get at through stating the problem that way?

TA: I have to go back and look at the lecture in detail. I felt very strongly the need to rethink all sorts of things and at the same time I was conscious that I wasn't well enough prepared to do that. So I was grappling with older instruments and trying to make a newer kind of space for myself which I didn't know how to do well. I think I felt that there was something not quite right about the way anthropologists focused on symbolism, their uncontrolled (because unconscious) resort to interpretation, on interpretations being taken for things.

DS: A theorist who appears in this text and who clearly had some influence on your thinking is V. N. Voloshinov, and especially his book *Marxism and the Philosophy of Language*.[29] What did you take from Voloshinov? In what way did Voloshinov's considerations of language enable your rethinking of the problem of ideology?

TA: I was struck first of all by the fact that he is struggling with what appear to be two diametrically opposed positions in linguistics: Saussurean structuralism on the one hand and a kind of individualist expressivism on the other. And he is trying to criticize both by going from one to the other and admitting that each in a sense has some insights but that they are grossly misappropriated by the traditions they gave rise to. So that's one thing I liked, his concern to draw on the importance of insights from structuralism and expressivism. But more important, he tried to link language to what he called the materiality of the sign, to the fact that signs *are* things and not merely reflections of things. And if signs are *things*, they must have a physical presence apprehended by the senses—through hearing, feeling, and seeing. That stress on materiality seemed to me important, and I later saw that it was necessary to think about signs in relation to the body and its emotions. In other words, Voloshinov helped me to see the idealization of language itself in many theories.

The way forward, it seemed to me, was to further explore the materiality of the body. The phrase "authoritative discourse" that I used in my lecture was a way of reaching out in that direction. It wasn't intended to refer to language in the abstract. So in a way what I got most out of Voloshinov was something that wasn't fully and explicitly there in the book. Another thing he made clearer to me was why I had been dissatisfied with Lévi-Straussian structuralism. A lot of my anthropological colleagues were very drawn to Lévi-Strauss, and those who weren't were often too sociologistic, too inattentive to the question of language.

DS: At the heart of this essay, "Anthropology and the Analysis of Ideology," is a mode of argument that would later be called anti-essentialist. Those are not the terms you use, but your argument is that anthropology is preoccupied with identifying and representing authentic systems of meaning. And in your reimagining of an anthropological understanding of representation, you introduced the term "authoritative discourse." Anthropology should interest itself in the relationship between language and power, knowledge and power, not simply in representing essential meanings but in trying to grasp the conditions of power in which some kinds of knowledge displace others. What is carrying you toward that conception? Why do you characterize anthropology in that way, and how would you characterize the problem-space in which your recognition of that problem in anthropology emerges?

TA: This is a David Scott question! I am going to have to think very carefully both in general about what was happening at the time and specifically about how I was trying to reformulate these questions. Of course, I've always been concerned with the question of power. All my writings from the very beginning have been focused on it. But as I was trying to rethink questions of power Foucault became increasingly valuable.

DS: But Foucault doesn't appear in that essay.

TA: No, but I had already started to read him, although I didn't cite him. I think that, together with Wittgenstein, he was an important influence at the time. Definitely, because this is 1979 and I was already reading Foucault in the mid-1970s. I would not have absorbed all the implications of what he was saying, but it was just before this lecture that I read *The Archaeology of Knowledge*, though I hadn't absorbed it the first time I read it. In fact, I remember feeling very ambivalent about it when I first read it. I had to reread it afterward.

Anyway, I think I had a conception of anthropology as a discipline that was concerned with the description of other cultures in terms of what various things meant to people in those societies. And this tended to detach those societies conceptually from the wider nexus of relationships and processes. And because it assumed those societies to be closed, and because there was a focus on interpreting the meanings of what people did that I always found problematical, I think I was feeling my way toward an interesting positivistic strand in Foucault's thought, his concern to describe how things are actually done. This is also reflected in Wittgenstein's well-known advice: Don't look for meaning, look for use. Wittgenstein was an anti-essentialist who problematized simple assumptions about psychological causality. This was important for me in my concern with rethinking the category of power.

I also continued to be concerned about the way scholars wrote about Islam. There's a paper I wrote, which is better known to people in the Middle East than here, that engages with a Palestinian Marxist's account of the rise of Islam.[30] There I both analyze his book and offer a different take on the relationship between religion and society. I wanted to see religion (Islam in particular) as more processual and not as the fixed ideology of a particular class. So there was my concern to rethink ideas about religion as ideology, against the classic Marxist sense, not as a kind of distortion or external justification for power. I wanted to move away from an interpretativist approach. And that was partly helped, as I said, by thinking of power not simply as an external force but as an internal relationship, to think of power as potentiality, the ability to do something, to enact something, in connection with other persons, things, institutions, or whatever. And so my interest shifted toward the question of how one was able to do certain things (including persuading oneself or others) rather than with what meanings might be attributed to acts regarded as representative of given cultures. There were a number of people like Mauss who helped to crystallize my thoughts here. The *doing* was also partly a matter of language, so I am not suggesting that it has nothing to do with language, but this emphasis on *doing* helps one to avoid thinking of language as a window onto reality. All that language does is, after all, *a part* of reality. One aspect of that was to rethink authoritative discourse, and the problem of authority, not simply as a matter of somebody or something exercising the power of command over gullible subjects but as an *inner binding*. And that was, of course, what then eventually led me to many of the things I talk about in *Genealogies of Religion*. In *Genealogies* I begin to think of authoritative discourse in terms of *willing obedience*. I talk about monastic disciplines not as something that comes from outside but as an internal shaping of the self by the self. The term "authoritative discourse" was for me a means of getting away from a purely symbolic approach. I wanted to get away from having to make a choice between lingualism (everything is in the final analysis language, text) and sociologism (language is a product of social reality). And this was when I started to reread Wittgenstein, to whom I had been exposed much earlier.

DS: Let me ask you a question about symbolic anthropology, because a number of people who have invoked you take you to be a kind of symbolic anthropologist. A feature, I think, of the contemporary conditions of appraisal of symbolic anthropology or the anthropology of meaning very broadly speaking is that it often appears to many to be absurd *not* to be thinking inside of that aspect of the linguistic turn. Or, put differently, the linguistic turn has in many ways reshaped vast swathes of our intellectual landscape such that it appears very natural to understand yourself and others to be more or less symbolic anthropologists, or else it appears absurd that someone might *not* be interested specifically in the *meaning* of various kinds of practices or discourses.

TA: I think there is a confusion that we are often pushed into—all of us, at one point or another—which we must attend to carefully. It's not that one thinks one ought to study human beings as though they were rats, as though human language didn't matter. At a commonsense level, you are of course concerned with what people say. What is being contested is the idea that the primary goal of understanding human life is through uncovering the real meaning of what they do. That invests too much explanatory power in people's subjectivity or in the anthropologist's objectivity. It tends to separate the meaning of symbol from the power that creates and interprets symbol. One doesn't ask how capabilities produce modes of significant being and how capabilities are themselves shaped and created. In other words, because one sees power from this old external point of view—Foucault called it a juridical power, the command of No—one fails to see it as the development of a certain potentiality.

DS: For me, one of the fascinating things about that essay "Anthropology and the Analysis of Ideology" is its disciplinary preoccupation. Here and elsewhere in your work, the critique of anthropology is a trenchant one; it is not merely a critique of details, but a critique of fundamental aspects of the way in which the discipline understands itself conceptually, and how it goes about methodologically doing what it does in the "field." And one has a sense of you embattled inside of the discipline seeking to *reposition* but also to *conserve* it. My question is, why at that point do you continue to feel attached to something you would identify as anthropology?

TA: As far as the Malinowski Lecture is concerned, of course, one obvious thing is that it *is* the premier anthropology public lecture in Britain. Nevertheless my fundamental concern was with a certain tradition of anthropologizing, and I wanted to bring back again the question of anthropology and power but in a way that I felt should not be misunderstood. I had to keep repeating that what interested me was not merely the question of what anthropologists did in the colonies but the question of power and the discourses through which it operated and the concepts that anthropologists dealt with. That was a particular occasion—if you like, an *anthropological* occasion. But there's more to it than that, and you are quite right to keep pushing that question at me. I am going to try and give you an answer, but I must admit I'm not one hundred percent sure it's satisfactory. I think that there is something to be conserved in anthropology because there are many studies about other modes of life that have helped us to understand something about ours in sophisticated ways, especially compared to Orientalism. As a project of understanding different modes of life—especially nonmodern, non-European ways—it has been immensely fruitful. This is because it's concerned with different ways of reasoning about practical matters (how to make a good tent for winter and summer, how to rear healthy animals well, how and when to fulfill a social obligation aptly) and not with Reason—that universal psychological faculty whose operation is known in advance.

But I agree that I've been constantly trying to pull away from established anthropological positions and move in interdisciplinary directions. One reason is simply that even if you think of British anthropology, its most fruitful moments have involved engagements with something outside: theology in the nineteenth century, classics at the beginning of the twentieth century, sociology through Durkheim, linguistics through Saussure, political economy and history through Marxism, and so forth. Whatever one might say about each of these, about the results of each of these encounters, they have certainly been fertile moments generating interesting questions. So I see myself as somebody who was educated in this very loose discipline called anthropology, familiar therefore with most of the major texts in its history, valuing it as a tradition.

I've been talking so far mainly about some practical reasons for my investment in anthropology. But there's something else too, and it may be wishful thinking but I think not. What first attracted me to anthropology was that it encouraged one to think of human beings as having different kinds of possibility. One of the things modernity has done, as you know, is to extinguish various possibilities. I think anthropology is important when it comes to questioning the hegemony of our modern capitalist assumptions. I think that that aspect of anthropology needs to be kept alive in thinking about human existence. My point is not simply the familiar one about anthropology as the mirror of humankind. I believe that the serious study of different modes of being and thinking helps us conceptually. It provokes us to think about the assumptions that underlie some of our most cherished and taken-for-granted notions, which mobilize our ways of life, and it disturbs us by other, very different kinds of assumption. Out of this, perhaps, there can emerge other things that are equally human, so to speak, but entirely new.

DS: And anthropology in your view is the best suited to this endeavor?

TA: I don't know if it is the *best* suited. I don't think of a kind of ready-made ship there, which is off to sail to a particular destination and is best fitted to do it. I just think that understanding as I do a particular intellectual tradition that has its roots in Western academic sites, it can be made, it *should* be made, to yield questions about itself. And I think that is an aspect of anthropology I would like to see developed much more and not simply left to abstract philosophical critique or critique from an established tradition of political economy. Is anthropology *best* suited to that endeavor? I don't know. And when I see something that is better suited, I'll try to jump ship even if there is a danger of my falling into the water. But at present here we are in this intellectual tradition that has partly formed us. And it offers interesting possibilities.

DS: Anthropology encourages us to think of human beings as having different kinds of possibility. This is also the sense in which for you Foucault's a kind of anthropologist of Europe.[31]

TA: That's right, that's what struck me when first I read him. I don't know if you felt that too when you read him—he suddenly had made strange all those things that are so familiar to us, forced us to think about the assumptions on which they are built, and that's exactly what we have got to do, I think. And that's one of my principal disagreements with anthropologists like Geertz. You know, Geertz argues somewhere that all one has to do in translating across cultures is to make strange concepts familiar.[32] I argue that that's too *comforting*. In translation we ought to be bringing things into our language even though they cause a *scandal*. Now, one can respond to scandal in two ways: one can throw out the offending idea or one can think about what it is that produces the horror. I would like to think that that kind of translation forces one to rethink some of our own traditional categories and concepts. If you just say, "Well, I am going to find an equivalent word that is nice and familiar in our own language," you are simply domesticating the original. I think that is a very unanthropological way of doing things, at least that's how *I* see anthropology. Do you see what I mean? I think we should shake ourselves up. I'm not suggesting a permanent revolution in which everything must be continually questioned. I'm saying that every time one encounters something really strange, really outrageous, one should stop and think about what we normally do. We shouldn't take the standards by which we understand the rest of the world as always fixed.

DS: Well, let me ask you a connected question, not specifically about anthropology but about *disciplines* as such. Are you committed to the idea of disciplines? Are disciplines important for your conception of knowledge formation? In other words, you wouldn't see yourself as in principle *anti*-disciplinary. You take disciplines as a crucial way of examining the world.

TA: Yes, I think they are important, because I see the whole question of widening inquiry, of examining assumptions, *in and through* particular disciplines. Even if one wants to question some of the most fundamental aspects of a discipline—let's say, anthropology—then it seems to me one begins with a concrete situation. I see the discipline of anthropology as being a particular tradition, however loosely that is thought of, and so the possibility of questioning and arguing from *within* a tradition, because it provides the problems that need confronting and a vocabulary that needs modifying, and it does this initially through an accumulating body of literature and an oral knowledge about how anthropologists teach, write, and generally *do* anthropology. So in that sense, the discipline of anthropology gives one the materiality, if you like, or the *matter* from which one begins to reason, and against which one reasons. If one were to insist on being totally against disciplines per se, one would, I think, not know quite where one was, and so not know quite how to begin. And this is partly why, as you know, from very early on I tried to question and reanalyze various representative texts, starting with Fredrik Barth.[33] In other words, I feel I am bound to what already exists, to what one has inherited from the past.

DS: Is the question of discipline connected in any way to the idea of *location*, to the idea of, say, *metropolitan* locations, or to locations in which the disciplines are an entrenched form of knowledge-production in which you have been interpellated professionally and intellectually. In other words, suppose one were intellectually and politically elsewhere, in a location where, say, the discipline of anthropology doesn't have the authoritative place that it has in the West in the construction of certain kinds of objects-as-problems, would disciplines still have the same kind of significance for you?

TA: Aren't there other disciplines, even in the West, for which the anthropological objects of investigation and analysis are by no means central? One thinks here of political theory, which particularly interests you, or philosophy, or economics. So whether it is in the West or not, I think the question still remains the same, the question that you pose. And I'd say the idea of discipline for me remains the same. The value of what I find worth contemplating and analyzing is, of course, not universally binding. On the contrary, it is precisely *because* I know that there are other disciplines in other (geographical or historical) places, which are concerned with other objects of understanding and inquiry, *because* I know that they are also connected with other political predicaments, I think that they can be sources of *enlargement* for myself.

I find—and I think you find that too—that many of the things that are being dealt with in political theory and philosophy and literature are provocative for us in anthropology. But I think this is in part *because* they themselves come out of certain disciplines and they have a different valence for us, they have different suggestions for us. Our discipline is not one that imposes absolute boundaries, beyond which one can never go or which one can never question. On the contrary, it's the fact that there are these other disciplines that makes it possible for one to ask in a helpful way how one can regenerate some of the dead ends we find ourselves in.

DS: Yes, but I want to press you a little bit on this. I once heard Richard Rorty remark that the only difference between literary critics and philosophers is that they have read different books. And in a sense part of what he seems to me to mean is that literary critics and philosophers have been *brought up* in different traditions of reading. And therefore one of the requirements of something like interdisciplinarity is that one has to have a grasp of the traditions of reading out of which other disciplines come, or on the basis of which they have constructed the objects they construct. It's no use anthropology saying it has a grasp on democracy or political systems, a better grasp on these things than does political theory because it goes to the field, if it hasn't acquainted itself with the tradition of reading of political theory through which those objects (democracy or whatever) come to acquire their conceptual uses.

TA: I think I would agree in principle, except that I would be a little hesitant about saying that it's just a matter of different books that people have read. Of course there are different books that they have read. There are different kinds of conversations they've had. There are also different *disciplinary lives* that they've led, because there are organizations as well, which function to discipline people in certain ways. I don't think that one can jump in and out of different disciplines so easily. I don't think that all I have to do now is to read all those books that philosophers read and, "hey, presto," I am now a philosopher, because being in a discipline is also *living* in a certain way, intellectually, socially, practically.

Thinking about Religion

DS: Right, and I think that Rorty was being slightly glib, but I think that what he wanted to get at was that you can't adequately make claims about other disciplinary objects or knowledges unless you have a sense of the *tradition* through which that discipline has founded its objects and argues about them. I want to come back to the question of traditions in a moment, but I want to turn to the question of religion. At what point and in what intellectual and ideological circumstances do you begin to formulate your ideas about religion? When and how does it occur to you that a fundamental revision of anthropological and other considerations of religion is necessary?

TA: I suppose that was a longish process, and it came out of a variety of dissatisfactions, including a dissatisfaction with Marxist and Freudian approaches to religion, taking religion to be ideology in the classic Marxist sense of a masking, or the Freudian sense of a pathology, a surrogate for the unbearable character of reality. I was dissatisfied with that for some time and I think I came at it in that way rather than directly out of a concern about anthropological theories of religion. I think it was around 1980 when I wrote my review article of an Arabic book about the origin of the Islamic state, in which I tried to grapple with Marxist and Orientalist writings rather than anthropological texts.[34] I think there I was able to bring in some anthropological questions that seemed to me to destabilize many of the assumptions that the author of the book was making. And that, together with a concern about the way in which people had been writing about religion in the Middle East, was what worried me. It seemed intellectually unsatisfactory and it somehow didn't correspond to my own experiences, having been brought up in a religious household. So I began to think more systematically about that, and I thought that I would examine anthropological views of religion with which I had been vaguely familiar. The first text that I took was one that was already beginning to be very influential as a definition, a complicated sophisticated redefinition of religion—Clifford Geertz's.[35] And I had a thought that I might look at a number of them, including Dumont and others, but I would also then try to look at aspects of Western religion and religiosity historically. And then at Islam as well.

DS: Before you elaborate on that (and I want to come back to the specific question of why it is that medieval Christianity enters as the historical instance through which you think religion systematically), I want to press you on the ideological as well as the intellectual context in which your thinking about religion emerges. Are there other factors besides your dissatisfaction with Marxist and Orientalist conceptions of religion? Are there perhaps political-ideological factors in the late 1970s or early 1980s that lead you to believe that rethinking religion is a crucial enterprise to be engaged in?

TA: Yes, I had had arguments with close friends in Egypt and the Sudan who were Marxists or secular nationalists. The trouble with quite a lot of Middle Eastern secularist approaches to the question of Islam and religion was a certain kind of theory that prevented politically active people from making real intellectual contact with the traditions and experiences of ordinary people. Many of my friends at the time agreed with that and admitted that one of the reasons why most communist parties in the Middle East had not made a significant impact was that they had never been able to recruit the masses. This was also a time when Islamist movements were beginning to mobilize people. But part of the problem, it seemed to me, was that this concession of failure could be seen too easily as a tactical or strategic matter. In other words, an attitude was beginning to emerge among secularists that if they were to make contact with the masses they would have to be careful not to be quite so dismissive of their traditional religious beliefs. This still seemed to me to foreclose the question of what one might learn about possible political futures from traditions other than the ones modernists and secularists recognized and revered as their own.

I go back here to my intellectual concern in the mid-seventies, when I was trying to organize the Middle East study group, when I was hoping we could carry out the two functions of an intellectual project, one of which was to be counterpolemics and the other an exploratory exercise. This was a similar concern. I felt that both intellectually and politically one needed greater humility toward other traditions in order to learn about and from them—even though one remained within one's own.

DS: Why does this emerging set of questions lead you to the study of medieval Christianity specifically?

TA: Well, you know, the first thing I did was to engage in a critical dialogue with Geertz on religion. And the more I went into it, the more I read around the whole question, the more it became apparent to me that his was a particular, historical conception of religion being used anachronistically. So I felt it was necessary for me to inquire into the genesis of that conception—a conception from the sixteenth and seventeenth centuries, from early modernity, the beginnings of modern Western Europe. And my first thought was to investigate the conditions in which this conception had emerged, to follow its development. The more I read around some aspects of that early modern history, the more I came to feel that I needed to take a step back in order to have a sharper contrast with what was actually emerging. In other words, instead of tracing the emergence of a familiar outline (at least now beginning to be familiar to me) of the modern Western conception of religion, I wanted to look at what had been the case in some respects in the earlier period, before the Reformation and the Renaissance, so that I could look more sharply at that contrast. And as far as I can recall, this was one of the decisions I made at the time. So instead of doing other anthropological studies, studies of theorists like Dumont, I thought I would deal with some historical material.

The first study was on body/pain. As I've said to a number of friends over the years, including historians, I found myself a bit like an ethnographer getting more and more interested in the European Middle Ages. I began to find aspects of medieval thinking and practice very impressive. The first essay is, if I might use that expression, perhaps a little hard-nosed; in it I highlighted some (to modern liberal sensibilities) alarming aspects of medieval Christianity, which were already well known and well studied, such as the Inquisition. The second essay is, I think, more reflective. I was then discovering things that I hadn't thought about. For example, many medieval theological writings, such as Hugh of St. Victor on the sacraments, turned out to be enormously sophisticated, much more so than anthropological theory on the nature of ritual ceremony. And the same goes for St. Bernard of Clairvaux's sermons in which he offers his monks the possibility of reinterpreting their past lives in preparation for a future life of obedience.

DS: This is where your idea of "willing obedience" comes in.

TA: Yes. And then there were other things written by St. Bernard (and others) on the idea of obedience. These served to problematize for me some modern conceptions of power, such as the one contained in Weber's famous definition of power as the probability that someone will be able to impose his will on another.

DS: This might be a somewhat vulgar way of putting it, but is there a sense that initially the question of Christianity emerges for you partly polemically, as a way of producing a contrast-effect with standard conventional conceptions of religion, but that having entered the field, so to speak, it opens up and becomes itself an object of fascinating inquiry?

TA: I think that's a fair way of putting it. And it became an educative process; it opened up new questions for me. I mean I found that I was being educated and I wasn't any longer able to simply deploy a thesis for which I needed empirical information.

DS: But still, Christianity enabled a kind of leverage, a kind of *epistemic* leverage that was larger than colonialism, larger than the modern West, through which you could talk in a different way about the characteristic features of such modern disciplines as anthropology.

TA: Yes, and about Islam too. Because that history's educative quality consisted in my noticing aspects of the Islamic tradition that had escaped me before. I certainly don't mean by this that there is a historical parallel between Christian religion in the Middle Ages and Islam. I was forced to notice that Islam and Christianity are very different even in the Middle Ages.

DS: So would you say that it's a critique that shows the ways in which a presumptively secularist-universalist conception (namely anthropology's) of, say, religion turns out to have its roots in a very specific Christian tradition?

TA: Well, it is and I think that toward the end of the Middle Ages, this becomes clearer. I think it was clearer in the sense that in the sixteenth and seventeenth centuries some scholars were beginning to categorize certain experiences and behaviors encountered in different parts of world in universalizing ways. This is happening at the same time, of course, as the expansion of Europe overseas, and that aspect of universality is also reflected in a variety of different concerns to assimilate other ways of thinking and being into European or Western experience.

DS: Is the investigation of Christianity for you also a way of coming to grips with the question of Europe?

TA: In a sense. As a general principle, I've found myself constantly having to think about *both* Europe and the Middle East. It's not just a matter of the center and the periphery that interests me; it's not just the whole question of imperialism (which continues to be important for me). It's also the possibility of being able to push the experience and the formation of certain kinds of tradition in the Middle East against those in the modern West, and vice versa. Some of my most interesting results and encounters have come precisely in this way. As I said, it was through an understanding of aspects of medieval Christianity that I began to notice something about traditions in the Middle East, Islamic traditions. Conversely, too. For example, it was one of the things that, you know, having been brought up as a strict Muslim, that first made me skeptical about some generalizations in Geertz's conception of religion. The proposition that you have to believe and once you believe, other things will follow didn't make sense to me given the way I was brought up.

That personal knowledge of Islamic tradition enabled me to begin questioning the way in which religion was being conceived of in this universalizing framework. I had eventually, as you know, to go back to a book of Wilfred Cantwell Smith's that I'd read before, and I did a rereading of that because it seemed to me that that too (although it was really a very interesting book from the point of view of the definition of religion) was marred by a certain essentialism.[36] So, to go back to your question about whether Christianity was a way of getting at certain aspects of the West, yes it was. But I am skeptical of any notion that the West is the flowering or playing out of a kind of Christian destiny. It's rather that Christianity is regarded as a central tradition in "the West," even for atheists, and the constant reinterpretation of its history is part of what "the modern West" is about.

DS: Partly, my question goes like this: in the 1970s or around the period of *The Kababish Arabs* and *Anthropology and the Colonial Encoun-*

ter, there is a problematization of the ways in which Europe's knowledges of the non-West are conditioned by the enterprise of colonialism. In the 1970s you are exploring the ideological character of various kinds of representative anthropological texts. In the 1980s one begins to see the emergence of a strategy, in some ways similar to the earlier one, in which you are still trying to characterize the conditions of Europe's knowledges of non-European practices, but here it is not "the colonial" that is the problematized site, but Christianity. So my question is whether Christianity for you is the name of an encompassing *epistemic space* that gives you a critical vantage that colonialism doesn't?

TA: That's not an easy question to answer. I hadn't thought of it in quite that way. I'll certainly think more systematically about it. I mean I tried to describe the way in which I gradually drifted into various kinds of projects that never seem to get completed. I hadn't thought about this as a specific *strategy* for understanding that relationship, which is still for me very central. As you know, I'm not impressed by the attempts (and there have been so many) to try and dissolve the conceptual opposition of the West to the non-West. Reflecting on Christian history has certainly opened up for me a range of questions about the nature of physical discipline, or discipline in more than an intellectual sense, which can be deployed outside the West. I am trying now to think about the question you asked me, which is one I haven't thought about before, and I'm finding it difficult at the moment. I am trying now to think of how my last book was conceived—*Formations of the Secular*—in great measure as a continuation of my dissatisfaction with this universal category of religion and of the kind of binaries that are constantly deployed. They've been fairly dominant, these binaries, in the deployment of certain kinds of power. I tried to trace that in the first chapter. I bring this up because I'm trying to think about what you've just asked me in relation to what I tried to do in that chapter. You may remember that I go through a series of instances of the use of "myth," whose consideration seems to me to be important for subverting the neat categories that cluster around "religion" and "secularism." Christian traditions in the eighteenth and nineteenth centuries play a pivotal part in that sequence of cases. My last case is, of course, that of the political theorist Margaret Canovan, who endorses what she calls the myth underlying modern liberalism.[37] But myth by now has acquired a double valence, negative and positive, and the positive thrust of myth was largely the product of a secularized reading of the Christian scriptures in the eighteenth and nineteenth centuries. One might say it was the Christian use of the quasi-religious notion of myth that helped to usher in a modern consciousness of reality as finally *social.*

DS: Let me ask the question in one more way and perhaps in a much more blatantly mischievous way. Is Christianity a useful theoretical/historical site from which to *unmask* the pretensions of Western conceptions of non-Western practices? Clearly none of your work is simply polemical, but does Christianity enable a vantage from which to demonstrate that, however secular the West's conceptions may be in its own self-image, it can be demonstrated that they have roots that are in fact *not* secular?

TA: The brief answer to that would be "no," because the question assumes that the categories of the secular and of the religious are clear-cut, and *that* is precisely what I criticize. Indeed, it is part of my dissatisfaction with those anthropologists and other social theorists who have talked about certain state forms being secular only in appearance but not in reality. The claim that the apparently secular is masking the truly religious is something that I don't find very helpful. In the first place, it's not *unmasking* that I want to pursue; it's simply reminding my readers of connections that will, I hope, make it evident that sharp distinctions are not as sharp as they might seem to be, that continuities are not as continuous as they might seem to be. Both these contradictory things are what I'm concerned to say rather than to unmask. Which is partly why I end the opening essay of *Formations of the Secular* with Walter Benjamin as the one I recommend as a guide, so to speak, rather than Paul de Man. For Paul de Man, the truth is something one can see, and it is our duty to see reality as it really is, to face up to it stoically and not to romanticize it. Whereas it seems to me that Benjamin is pointing us in a different direction. He is constantly sliding what are conventionally thought of as religious categories into what are thought of as secular ones, and vice versa. And for him signs are a part of reality and not a way of pointing to it.

So if I were to think of my investigation of Christianity as a way of subverting the West's view of itself, I would be doing something that I'm not consciously trying to do. I'm trying in fact to take a distance from that endeavor. I'm trying to complicate descriptive categories. I'm trying to complicate the Western tradition of secularism. I'm aware, incidentally, that there are vigorous and contradictory tendencies in Christianity from the rise of modernity onward, whose outcomes are never quite clear, never decisive and final, but which have to negotiate massive breaks that have occurred in history. I certainly don't see Christianity as being at the root either of capitalism or of the modern drive for world domination. Nor at the root of modern intolerance, something now being attributed not merely to Christianity but to all monotheism.

One of the things in Carl Schmitt's political theology that I find myself dissatisfied with is his attempt to show that many secular political ideas are essentially Christian.[38] I find this overlooks really fundamental breaks in the way many of these political terms are deployed in the modern state. One needs to pay attention to that—to what Wittgenstein called "the grammar of concepts"—in order to see that Christian discourse is not being played out as it was earlier.

DS: I am going to come back to your conception of history, historical change, and in particular modernity, in which you think of historical breaks. But I want to ask one more question around this matter. Given what you've just said, I can see why the preoccupation in *Genealogies* is less with the *deconstruction* of an anthropological category (although it does that) and more with the *reconstruction* of a particular understanding of medieval Christianity. What is your suspicion of subversion as a critical strategy?

TA: I'll begin by saying that strategies of translation and those of subversion are not necessarily compatible. Translation, in my view, requires a kind of faithfulness to an original, even if that often proves impossible. However one conceives of it, subversion is an *act of war*, and while there is a place for subversion, I think it's often misplaced in talk about translation. Subversion might in fact require not translation at all but simply the introduction of particular knowledges to a new site, so that their sheer weight then begins to subvert a particular configuration of things. I am not against subversion per se, because I try for example in *Formations of the Secular* to subvert a certain rigid polarity. But I'm concerned that subversion shouldn't be used as a strategy in inappropriate situations so that everything becomes an act of subversion.

DS: I want to press this question of subversion a little bit. I want to ask about subversion in the context of tradition, partly to get at some of the ways in which I suspect you depart from Michel Foucault, or at least the stance with which Michel Foucault is often connected, namely as the great *subverter*. It has always seemed to me that you make a rapid move from destabilizing particular conventions, assumptions, and so on, which might be called *unmasking* or *subverting*, to the attempt to *reconstruct* a different understanding than the one that has been in place. So the anti-essentialist preoccupation with subverting conventions appears to me in your work a very *limited* strategy. In that move are you conscious of being critical of Michel Foucault?

TA: No, but I think I'm aware that my interest in the idea of tradition has been a matter of disapproval for some people who are particularly interested in subversion as a strategy. This seems to me to indicate that there is more work to be done in thinking about where one can construct a relation to reconceived pasts and where one can't. The disjunctions one makes between past and present should not be thought of in a simple way. I haven't been directly critical, but I am conscious of the fact that I stand apart from aspects of Foucault's thinking. I think that there are often moments when you get the feeling that he needs to think about temporality more deeply than he does. Especially in his later work on Greek discipline, where he seems to me to work with a very conventional periodization and leave aside questions of temporality. The result is that you get a very one-dimensional view of the past as something that is finished. Once something has been subverted, it can't be put together again. Subversion brings down a structure, disables an enemy. If one begins from a notion of discursive tradition, then you might be able to think of the fact that what's been subverted might be reconstructed again within the tradition. What I'm trying to say is that the question of subversion versus translation is built around a too-simple notion of time. I need to think more about that.

I think this is also true of MacIntyre, whom I find enormously stimulating, as I know you do too. I think that he too has only a singular notion of temporality. This connects up with an aspect of secularity that I still need to explore further, and that is the very notion of history, which gives us our modern notion of truth about the past. In many ways, that is a rather *literal* notion, built on a notion of a linear succession employing empty time. The whole idea of homogeneous, empty time is, as so many since have reminded us, absolutely crucial for the idea of modern history. I want to think more carefully about that and the question, therefore, of whether when Foucault is effectively engaged in subversion, his strategy takes homogeneous, empty time for granted. Thus his historical breaks, of modernity, of the classical period, and so forth, are breaks within a linear modern narrative. And that is why historians have often argued with him and said, "No, no, your periodization of X or Y or whatever is inaccurate."

DS: In your exploration of medieval Christianity, the body emerges as a crucial site of inquiry; why is that? What is the contrast-effect with modern conceptions or modern *Christian* conceptions that's at stake there?

TA: Perhaps I can slightly rephrase that, if I may, because you might notice that what has constantly fascinated me is *pain* rather than simply the body in all its aspects.

DS: I want to come to pain, but part of the contrast I am after is your critique of Geertz's assumptions regarding the centrality of "belief" to religion, a view that gives priority to a kind of *cognitivist* orientation.

TA: Yes, indeed. In modern liberal thinking, *belief* is the core of religion and therefore the core of that which is private, truly one's own. This goes back to a sharp body-mind distinction that was established in early modernity. But, you know, Christians right from early modern times have disputed this distinction. Some Christian traditions have disputed it, but by and large liberal thinking has maintained it. And I include various Christian tendencies as part of that liberal thinking. The body, of course, is enmeshed in *traditions of cultivation*. Not just the physical body, but the body in its capacity to sense things, to be persuaded and convinced. So I'm less interested in the body simply as the object of a certain kind of domination, something about which a lot has been written. This interests me less. I've often said that taking the idea of "the docile subject" to mean the worker who is exploited by capital, the woman who is oppressed by patriarchy, is all very well, but it's not that sense that interests me in the first place. I point to the etymology of "docile," that is, "teachable." So I'm interested in "the docile subject" as someone who is *teachable* and therefore as someone who has the capacity to be taught. A taught body is one to which "belief" (as a conscious supposition of what is the case in the world, or as a proposition to which one assents) is at best secondary.

This seems to me the trouble with a lot of postcolonial theorizing on this topic, where we move from the notion of, you know, a totally constructed mannequin to something that has absolutely no center and therefore no effectivity. One needs to think about causality in different ways. I think that Connolly's last book, *Neuropolitics*, is an intriguing attempt to deal with some of these issues, and I'm sympathetic with his move.[39] Still, I think that one has somehow to think about all these things when one is thinking about the body. One has to think about temporality and causality, and one has to steer clear of the notion of a totally passive, malleable subject, of a totally decentered subject, as well as of a totally self-directing subject.

DS: I've heard you say somewhere that part of the problem with MacIntyre's conception of a tradition is that he doesn't pay sufficient attention to the body and to the literally *embodied* character of tradition; that bodies, so to speak, *bear* traditions. And this is connected, isn't it, with your uses of the concept of *habitus*. So that *habitus* and tradition are for you interconnected concepts.

TA: Yes. But I must say that he was for me the first philosopher who made me aware that one could think productively about tradition.[40] What I liked about MacIntyre's conception of a tradition is that he points to the possibility of its being a space of different interpretations, a space of argument. The old idea that tradition means nonargument and modernity means argument really just won't do any longer. But what I find disappointing in MacIntyre is, as you said, his leaving out the body. This is not a matter of simply leaving out a dimension that is very real in people's lives and that enables them to be carriers of a tradition. It raises questions about the autonomy of a space for argument. Because argument is itself interwoven with the body in its entirety, it always invokes historical bodies, bodies placed within particular traditions, with their potentialities of feeling, of receptivity, and of suspicion. So much of this is part of everybody's experience of what argument is about. We know it's not a matter simply of "the mind." Argument is always rooted in temporal processes, it's always embodied. That's why persuasion and agreement can be so difficult. Thinking about the notion of tradition meant for me a different opening, a more promising one.

DS: And *habitus* is the concept that allows you to bring together body-heart-mind.

TA: Yes, that's right. And that's without needing to pursue the question of how structures of domination are reproduced—something Bourdieu is concerned with when he employs the notion of *habitus*. I employ *habitus* to refer to the predisposition of the body, to its traditional sensibilities. There's a crucial difference between *habit* as the disposition the body acquires through repetition and inertia, through the generally unconscious and uncontrollable circuits of energy, emotion, feeling, and *habitus*, that aspect of a tradition in which specific virtues are defined and the attempt is made to cultivate and enact them. MacIntyre doesn't seem to me to appreciate adequately how closely this latter aspect of tradition depends on corporeality.

DS: What is the relationship between tradition and the anthropological conception of culture? Are these rival categories? Is one, in your mind, to displace the other? What does the work of tradition do for you that the concept of culture can't do?

TA: Well, I'm often asked that. My first response is to ask: *which* concept of culture? Since tradition is an older concept, one might even want to reflect on a further question: what does the concept of culture enable one to do that the idea of tradition couldn't? I think one thing culture eventually enabled was the textualization of social life, regarding it as a set of legible meanings. The idea of tradition, on the other hand, has always been concerned with the conditions that produce meanings (compelling meanings or taken-for-granted ones)—and so with time and embodiment, with the disciplines that cultivate thought, desire, and behavior, and aim at particular virtues. I certainly haven't found in culture, in the way that people who follow Geertz, say, talk about it, the kind of questions that thinking in terms of tradition raises. Especially questions about the body in its various modalities, receiving traces and exercising capabilities. In my view, tradition is a more mobile, time-sensitive, more open-ended concept than most formulations of culture. And it looks not just to the past but to the future. A tradition is in part concerned with the way limits are constructed in response to problems encountered and conceptualized. There's always a tension between this construction of limits and the forces that push the tradition onto new terrain, where part or all of the tradition ceases to make sense and so needs a new beginning. And looked at another way: with each new beginning, there is the possibility of a new (or "revived") tradition, a new story about the past and the future, new virtues to be developed, new projects to be addressed.

DS: Meaning that there is something there that is worked on, something there that is cultivated?

TA: A tradition certainly provides some of the means to cultivate oneself or to help others cultivate themselves—without which there's no continuity in social life. It also allows one to address the question of causality in other than mechanical terms. As something akin to what Althusser used to call structural causality, where time is not a linear sequence of before and after. It seems to me that most Marxists, being still very much caught up in the classical notion of ideology, missed the opportunity of thinking about different kinds of causality.

DS: It is precisely around this question of ideology that Foucault departs from Althusser. Let's come to the question of pain, because this is connected. Why does pain fascinate you so? What is it that focusing on pain, agency, and the body illuminates for you?

TA: I think it helps me to think about a number of things. First, the experience of pain seems to bear out the most empiricist of claims about knowledge, the claim that truth is essentially "bodily." I think this claim is questionable. The assumption is that pain can't itself be constituted in different ways through different traditions of embodiment. So there is this epistemological assumption about the *priority* of the body, something called the body, as opposed to something else called the mind or spirit. I want to problematize this by exploring how pain is actually experienced.

There's also something else about pain. Liberal theory is ideologically committed to the overcoming of conditions in which people undergo pain and suffering. There's the pain that people feel when tortured, the pain they feel when they're hungry, when they are slighted. Liberalism is committed to the idea of a society in which pain and suffering have been done away with. Torture is an interesting case of pain, and that is why I talk a bit about it. Torture is often subject to a kind of regulation. There's also the case of pain that is valorized: in sports, for example. That is acceptable, just as pain is acceptable in curative surgery. So everybody is aware that there are different conditions in which pain is acceptable. Also, in a utilitarian scheme, it's acceptable if it's adequate to its purpose. So I've been interested in pain for two interconnected reasons: one epistemological (how does pain mediate the interpretation of experience?) and the other political and moral (what kinds of pain are thought to be good to prevent or to endure?).

Powers of Modernity

DS: Modernity is a category you make use of, modern *power* specifically. In the 1980s in a number of essays the question of the distinctiveness of the modern arises, and part of the critique of Geertz and your mobilization of medieval Christianity is to enable a contrast-effect that demonstrates the distinctiveness of *modern* conceptions. I am thinking in particular about that very powerful little essay in the Festschrift for Stanley Diamond, "Conscripts of Western Civilization," and also the review essay on Eric Wolf, "Are There Histories of Peoples without Europe?"[41] Why does the conception of modernity become so crucial for you, and *what* concept of modernity is important to you?

TA: I think the point at which I start is colonial power and the power over citizens in a modern state—state power generally. In fact, I see the state, the modern state, as a total structure that has its origins in the West and that has been established in different parts of the Third World. Those aspects of power are still for me the central ones from which I start to think about modernity. I'm not persuaded by all those people in the Middle East who say that there's only one way to move out of the present mess, and that is to become truly modern, and they know exactly what being modern is. It's being like the West. More precisely, this now means acquiring "liberal democracy," a free market and free elections to a representative parliament. Reformation of the state is a central objective of modernity and its central obstacle. The world's most powerful state (the United States) says the truly modern state must be at once liberated and confined. Both secularists and Islamists recognize this, that's why both of them want to control the state and through it all its citizens. But this ambition is not rooted in the Islamic tradition at all, or in other premodern traditions. You know, one of the things that is totally ignored by people like Bernard Lewis when talking about Islam, about "what's wrong with Islam," is of course the fact that the powers and ambitions of the modern state do not emerge out of an Islamic tradition; there is nothing Islamic about them.[42] The modern state opens up and closes markets of goods and money. It controls the movement of populations. It tries to manage a national economy. It employs specific modalities of violence, both internally and externally to defend its interests.

So that is one aspect of how I see modernity—in terms of the modern state. And I find it deeply troubling. Of course, in many respects I think one must still work through the modern state, but working through it also means trying to rethink whether all the forms in which it appears—whether in the West or in the Middle East—are *fated* forms. I have this sense that claiming something as modern is a kind of closure. That closure evokes certain fundamental transformations in our economy, in our conception of legitimate knowledge, in the way we think about and practice politics and religion, in our celebration of the autonomous individual. There are a number of things that relate to what we call the modern. But what strikes me as extraordinary is the fact that in the West, in modern Western societies, a number of things are actually contested (even if not always effectively), a number of things are questioned and argued over without dragging in the categories of modern and nonmodern. The arguments are about whether something is just or unjust, workable or unworkable, whether a proposal for change is adequate to the problem in hand or not. When you come to people arguing in the Third World, the conception of modernity always haunts the discussion. This means that modernity there presents a singular face, whereas *inside* the West it has a multiplicity of faces and voices.

DS: But suppose someone were to say, well not exactly, but the kind of conception of modernity that *you* seem to be preoccupied with precludes a discussion of the *variousness* of the effects of modern power in different parts of the Third World. You seem to be much less concerned with different trends, indeed to preclude a focus on different trends and to be much more concerned with the *sameness* of that face that modernity presents to the Third World.

TA: Yes, one can't deny the differences evident in the Third World, but I'm talking about the projects being urged on us by modernists. What I'm worried about, I think, are two things. First, that in spite of what people tell us about global "differences," there is a very strong thrust toward basic homogeneities throughout the world as a consequence of the way imperialism works. It destroys and at the same time points to a certain *kind* of rebuilding. I know that people do things differently in different parts of the world in spite of this, that they have different experiences and so on. But you know, there *is* a fundamental push in a *recognizable* direction—whether this is the way we furnish our houses or the way we dress, whether it is the kinds of music we profess to enjoy, or entertainments we spend much of our time and money on. You might think these are minor matters, but they do serve to create similar sensibilities. I've got nothing against that in principle, but all these things are part of that homogenizing thrust. As such, I have the Middle East in mind, where many people (often responding to explicit prodding from the West) argue: "Look, there is no other option. We are now in the modern world. We must move with it. We must respond to its demands." Okay, but what exactly does that mean? What does saying "there is no other option" mean here? You know, does it mean you know exactly what options we have, that you dismiss the possibilities that others try to argue for? Is modernity an inescapable fate to which one must bend or a paradise that invites us to enter?

DS: But again I might respond that it appears that it is really you who is suggesting that the modern imposes a singularity, not us, who talk about multiple modernities. I might ask why it is you think it is more important to focus on the thrust of modern power that is transforming conditions and not on the various kinds of resistances that are reimagining themselves in ways different from what the European modern might have led them to expect?

TA: Well, I find myself constantly thinking about that, and I must confess I'm torn in two different directions. On one hand I am persuaded that modern power creates conditions in which new kinds of desire, new kinds of possibility, are opened up. But what those possibilities are, how far they are written in stone, still need to be thought about carefully. On the other hand I find myself sympathizing with some of the attempts to rethink various kinds of Islamic future in the Middle East. The idea that you can simply catalogue Islamic movements as reactionary, as a revolt against modernity, is, I think, quite unhelpful. My point here is not that these movements are really headed in a progressive direction. It's that we ought to ask whether some of them might not be trying to think about things that have not been thought about before, ways of existing. That is why I'm sympathetic to some of these movements some of the time but also rather pessimistic about the possibility of their being able to construct something really new and interesting. I think that the powers of modern universalism, the powers of modern capitalist hegemony, are such that it's very difficult for certain new things to arise. Ironically, anti-essentialism can become a ruse of hegemonic forces, as I argued in my chapter on Muslims in Europe. So, I think it's much more likely that there's going to be a replay of the way in which the Catholic church has gradually adjusted itself over the years to secular democratic politics. You might find, if this is allowed in places like Turkey, that Islamic movements become liberal democratic parties. These movements aren't going to pose a threat to liberalism. So I think you point to a contradiction in my thinking, born out of, on the one hand, the conviction that modernity has created powerful conditions for change in limited directions and, on the other hand, a sympathy for people aiming at far-reaching alternatives but also a pessimism about the realizability or sanity of these alternatives.

DS: In your discussions of the distinctive character of the modern world, law is often a very significant site for you. Why is that? What does law illuminate about the modern world?

TA: The modern state describes itself as the law state. Law is central to how it sees its structures and processes. And the modern world is inconceivable without the modern nation-state. There is a conception in the modern world of something transcendent that civilizes subjects, that legitimizes the conditions in which they can develop, in which they can be administered. Law is a mode of universalization that civilizes, legitimizes, and administers.

Looking at it historically, law is the domain in which the secular plays itself out through the modern notion of the social and the modern notion of the self. It's pitted, in its effectivity and in its truth, against canon law. This also applies to Islamic law, the law said to be derived from divine injunctions. I see law as a very interesting expression of modern power, a power to shape the modern subject-citizen. I'm intrigued by the idea that while premodern law is said to invoke the transcendent, modern law depends only on human sovereignty. But this works because human sovereignty then becomes a kind of transcendent principle, although it does so in a very different way, imposing a different kind of universality.

DS: So in your view law is central to what Foucault might call governmentality?

TA: It is central to governmentality but not only that. I think that, yes, law is central to governments that predated what Foucault described as governmentality. You sometimes find anthropologists talking mistakenly about governmentality as though it meant government, but of course that's wrong. In pregovernmentality the law is also important, but it has different implications, different functions, makes different claims. Its premise is a different kind of subject-citizen and a different kind of politics. So, yes, law is clearly central to governmentality but not *only* to governmentality.

DS: I want to go back to the question of history and historical change and to your essay on Eric Wolf's *Europe and the People without History*, and to a particular image that you deploy in your discussion. The image is of historical change as *glacial*. And part of what you seem to be aiming at is displacing the centrality of consciousness and, in particular, conscious resistance to understanding historical change. Can you spell that out a little bit for me?

TA: I think that there are a couple of reasons why that image seemed to me to be appropriate. It is, of course, aimed against a Marxist view of history, which has its laws of motion. I wanted an image to convey something more contingent and less law-governed. The notion of glacial shift seemed to me apt for that reason. Also I wanted something that would accommodate the notion of changes occurring slowly through, as it were, a vast number of accumulated pressures and movements. This is not to deny that there are cataclysmic events, big earthquakes or storms that change things more dramatically and sharply. But a glacial shift is also one in which slow accumulated changes occur at different rates in the different levels of a terrain. I wanted an image of contingency having a multiplicity of little causes, but which nevertheless produce an overall shape. And, of course, that pattern would not depend on a conscious project.

DS: Why do you abandon the image, though? Take, for example, the introduction to *Genealogies*, in which you are once again disagreeing with the focus of some kinds of historical anthropology that are preoccupied with the sovereign agent making history. That would have seemed to me to be one place where that image of glacial change might have been useful. I was struck by the fact that it doesn't reappear.

TA: Well, the introduction was written in the space of a few days when I was under pressure to finish my manuscript. As you know, I write very slowly; I think through my writing, revising it several times, trying to connect what I'm writing about with what I've thought about in the past. In the introduction I simply stated some of my major concerns; I didn't try to develop my earlier ideas. If I had had the opportunity to write it at leisure, the introduction would have been different. You are right, that image should have been brought in and developed further.

DS: I mean, one of the reasons why I've always found that image a very powerful one is that you have the picture of shifts and changes in which the individual subject gradually finds her- or himself standing, so to speak, on a different terrain, and finds that her or his consciousness does not adequately fit with the terrain that he or she now stands on. And it seems to me to be a very fitting image for our present, insofar as there is a sort of misfit between the radical or revolutionary consciousness and a terrain that seems not to be enabling for revolutionary activity.

TA: I agree with you. I think you've developed that idea very elegantly in your latest book on C. L. R. James on the Haitian Revolution.[43] I was trying to get at some of this when I used the image of paths that cease to be viable as a result of glacial shifts. Old paths go nowhere, as it were, and new paths now become possible. So if you left an old path, it wouldn't be because you had rationally concluded that another path would be better but because, as you said, the terrain had so changed that you simply couldn't follow the old path any longer. It no longer led to a meaningful destination. I think, you know, these were aspects of my trying to rethink our connections with the past and our possibilities for the future. I thought of that image as an *intimation* of the way our collective lives move, and I was rather pessimistic about that.

DS: Another reason why that image resonates with me is that it comports very nicely with the idea I take from R. G. Collingwood—questions and answers—and the idea that old paths now seem to go nowhere suggests that those old paths were connected to one particular kind of question/answer complex and that the answers are perhaps still recognizable, but the questions that underlay the compunction toward those answers are no longer there, are no longer useful. And that suggests, then, the need to abandon the questions that propelled one along those old paths toward answers that were already to hand—and what's important to understand now are the new questions that are suggested by the shifted terrain of problems. In other words, the idea of old paths seems to suggest that, for whatever set of reasons, an old question/answer complex has faded in terms of its efficacy and a new complex of question-and-answer has emerged, and what the present demands is deciphering of what the new questions are.

TA: Right. This is, of course, work you've elaborated and developed illuminatingly. But, as I say, for me it's been an *image* rather than a systematic theoretical proposition. The image of a glacial shift reflects my pessimism about possibilities. However, I don't think my sense of pessimism deserves serious consideration because it's the result of accidental experiences and I don't think that anybody who's beginning to think productively and creatively should be pessimistic. I sometimes find myself using such expressions as "the malignancy of the present"—and I don't mean simply Bush, by the way.

DS: You are referring to the present's seemingly *intractable* character.

TA: No. I use malignancy literally in the sense of there being something malign, antihuman, which seems to be gathering in (or dissipating) the present. But perhaps on reflection "intractable" is a better word because it implies an indifferent state of affairs, something one can't quite get a grip on but that might be dealt with successfully at a future stage. Whereas if there is a sense of an opposing *force* that is malign—which is what I sometimes think—then one is simply unable to see the present clearly. I am attracted very much by the way you develop this idea of the problem-space and how you use Collingwood's notion of question-and-answer and its connection to a changed present.

DS: How would you describe the connection between *Genealogies of Religion* and *Formations of the Secular*? Do you think of one as taking up where the other left off? Are the strategies you deploy similar in both instances? Is *Formations* in part a working out of dissatisfactions with *Genealogies*?

TA: Well, in the first place, I think it is . . . it is a continuation in the sense that I mention secularism very briefly in *Genealogies* but I really don't discuss it adequately; I don't discuss its conditions of existence. In that sense, *Formations* takes up where I left off; it's an elaboration of some things I said earlier. So there is this continuity. But I think it also expresses some dissatisfaction with the too-quick suggestion that in modern life religion has been secularized to the extent that it has now become entirely privatized. I think I took the dichotomy between the public and private too much for granted. Perhaps I implied that law and morality were too clearly separated. After *Genealogies* I wanted to try something seemingly paradoxical—to problematize "the religious" and "the secular" as clear-cut categories but also to search for the conditions in which *they were* clear-cut and were sustained as such. In other words, you know, I wanted to ask not only "how can people make these distinctions when they aren't sustainable?" but also "what are the conditions in which these dichotomies, these binaries, *do* seem to make some sense?" I really want to question this impression that *Genealogies* is a kind of debunking of religion and that *Formations* is an attempt at defending it. In my view that whole battle between "religion" and "secularism" is itself an ongoing modern battle and it needs to be analyzed as such.

DS: There are at least two things that are striking to me in the introduction to *Formations of the Secular*. One is that there seems to be a much more self-consciously *tentative* sense of exploration in the idea (as you just mentioned) that you are going to proceed *indirectly*. You say that the secular is so much a part of modern life that it is necessary to approach it *indirectly*.[44] And I immediately asked myself, why wasn't that necessary in *Genealogies*? The second thing is the *positional* character of *Formations*. The introduction explicitly calls attention to various aspects of the very present in which you are writing. It is clear to the reader that you are writing in the wake of September 11, 2001, and so the book is *located* in a much more deliberate way than *Genealogies*. It's that too that prompts me to ask about the difference in critical strategy between these books.

TA: I suppose in *Genealogies* I was primarily concerned with a different level of the whole question of ideology—that is, how can one understand religion in a different way from the way classic Marxism does? What happens to the classic notion of ideology when one recognizes the importance of the body? Freud, of course, takes the body seriously but in a way that I didn't find persuasive as far as "religious experience" was concerned. What happens if we take the body seriously in a non-Freudian way? And then, beyond that, in *Genealogies* I was very interested in how we come to have this category called religion, with the concern to find universal characteristics. I have much less problem in talking about Christianity, in talking about Islam, than I have in talking about religion. So my concern there was to examine some Christian traditions to do with things like the Inquisition and the law. But it's a concern with aspects of the Christian tradition that slowly becomes transformed. Historians of the Middle Ages tend to describe these changes as progressive ones, as being propelled in a rational direction. I was concerned to problematize that, to argue for the earlier stage being equally rational. As an anthropologist, this came naturally to me in the sense that I had learned to see every way of life as having its own reasons. But I was also concerned not to give an alternative definition of religion but to ask how embodiment enabled certain kinds of willing subjects, so to speak, and what part discipline played in that, regardless of whether it was to be called secular or religious. I was concerned to question the simple progressivist story.

In *Formations* I took up the theme of secularism directly, a theme I had touched on in the first book. But I wanted to do more than simply say you shouldn't give an essentialist definition of secularism. I wanted to look at, or to suggest that we look at, combinations of ideas, practices, institutions, and so on that shifted over time and helped to give us our ideas of "the secular." The secular, legitimized as the secular, itself shifted over time. So that something that was seen as illegitimate at one time might be seen as a legitimate form of living-in-this-world at another time. I was looking deliberately for these kinds of connection at a much more conceptual level. I felt I had to be more tentative because I was less sure about how to proceed in such an inquiry. I was also much less interested in the straightforward institutional narratives that I had to some extent offered in *Genealogies*.

DS: Now to the *positioned* character of *Formations of the Secular*.

TA: Virtually everything except the introduction was written before 9/11, including the Egypt chapter. I was totally knocked out by 9/11 and also by the way "informed" public opinion represented it. Not since 1967 had I been so disoriented. The attack itself was shattering. But then even more so was the torrent of stuff that started coming out in the electronic and print media about Islam and Arabs. For me it was a very personal experience, as well as an intellectual one. The confidence and sense of security one had had in everyday life was seriously dented, of course. And I'm not referring here to a fear of further terrorist attacks. I began to see how one could be thoroughly unnerved even though living in a modern secular society. And when I say unnerved, I don't mean myself, I mean the population in general and the Muslim immigrants in particular. Muslims and Arabs have been beaten, and a few killed. Mosques have been burned and vandalized, individuals have been arrested on mere suspicion and not allowed access to lawyers, and so on. All of this is familiar now. But I must say I felt stunned when I opened "serious" newspapers like the *New York Times* and whenever I watched television news. The rapidity with which an entire population felt its nationalistic sentiments aroused, the cleverness with which the Bush administration exploited them, the slyness of so many public intellectuals and politicians, who had at last found something they could together denounce, all of this was not merely disturbing but eye-opening. I was watching open intimidation being practiced by a secular nation-state. Many people here and in Europe described this as "fully understandable," by which they seemed to mean fully justifiable.

In my introduction, I couldn't help but locate myself and try to analyze the political situation as I found it. One could see public discourse producing a whole series of equations—religion, religious violence, Islam, intolerance, terrorism, and so on. And it was also feeding into old prejudices about religion in general and about Islam in particular. Of course, there were many people who talked about "true" religion and "real Islam," and even about "the clash of fundamentalisms" (meaning Bush and Bin Laden).[45] But these are simply ways to reinforce established prejudices. I began to be further interested in the whole question of responsibility—of the state (whether secular or religious) having to find someone responsible for a national disaster, of needing to blame and punish "badies" and absolve "goodies." I try to deal with that in the book. It then occurred to me that it was all very well to go on denying that religious traditions (whether Islam, Judaism, Christianity, Hinduism, or whatever) must as such be connected with violence and intolerance—which, of course, is what secularism has always insisted, which is part of its claim to legitimacy. I asked myself, what is it that is being done when one attributes responsibility for acts of violence, for intolerant behavior, to a certain tradition. Responsibility is literally the duty to "answer." You are answerable for something. There is a judge and there is a power in and through the law, the ability to punish physically. It's a matter of trying to find somebody who is responsible for an act, somebody on whom blame can be pinned, or who can be exonerated from blame. The whole business is a kind of blaming machine, and the machine's purpose is to reduce the complexity of different ways people and things are involved in the emergence of particular events. We carve out something called an "act" and "an actor" and we identify "a responsible person." The motive for that, it seems to me, is paradigmatically the law. This is the law in its punishing mode, the law in its demanding mode. It is also the law in its enabling mode, because in our capitalist culture all hurt and loss calls for pecuniary recompense, and that means someone must be found to pay.

DS: I suppose my question has to do with the contrast between *Genealogies*, in which there is much more of an intellectual location for your intervention (speaking loosely), and *Formations*, in which there is both an intellectual location and also a very deliberate *moral-political* framing of the intervention. *Formations* is much more *aware* of an historical-political shift in relation to which the book and its preoccupations need to be read, whereas that is not as sharply so in the case of *Genealogies*.

TA: You are right. I hadn't quite thought of it that way. Despite the fact that there were also certain concerns at that time, such as the polemical bit on the Rushdie affair, in which I am very concerned also to intervene in a certain way, because both of those essays were published separately in journals prior to being brought together in the book. But I think certainly you are right, apart from the Rushdie piece, which is polemical and which I call a polemic.

But I believe that as anthropologists we should be suspicious of our intuitions and preferences when confronted with social/cultural phenomena. Yes, of course, anthropology cannot be isolated from politics. But the connection between the two is rarely direct and simple. There is always a tension between the need for decisiveness in political commitment and the need for openness in anthropological inquiry. I think in *Formations* I am more aware that that tension must be worked through again and again.

DS: *Formations of the Secular* opens with the question, What is the relation between the secular as an epistemic category and secularism as a political doctrine? And yet *Formations* is divided into three parts, and not two: secular, secularism, and secularization—secularization being understood as a historical process. What is the relationship between the secular as an epistemic category, secularism as a political doctrine, and secularization as a historical process?

TA: I suppose I simply wanted to shift my investigation into another register. In the final chapter, I am closer to telling a story—that is, from the beginning of the twentieth century a series of changes occur, and I am focusing in particular on the changes that have to do with the modern way of thinking about the law: the confining (as it's been described) of the religious law to the family, to what's called civil status. I do try to bring some aspects of both the idea of the secular as an epistemic space and of secularism as a self-conscious political doctrine, which carried weight in the period I deal with. I think I was hoping that many of the concerns of the first part—which had to do with "the secular," with sensibilities, with the different ways in which human beings are supposed to feel and think, to sense through their bodies as well as through their social relations—would somehow be reflected in the narrative of "legal reform." I am conscious of not having done this satisfactorily. And by the way, "legal reform" is not my term here. It is the term used in histories of modern law for European-initiated changes in the law in the Third World in the late nineteenth and early twentieth centuries. So, in a way this section represents first a move from a section that consists largely of tentative explorations to a more questioning section—"secularism." I then conclude with a more skeptical but also more narrativized section, "secularization." Thinking back over it now, there's increasing weight on skepticism as the book proceeds. It's in the final chapter that I express explicitly my skepticism about the way in which secularism and the secular are set within a progressivist story.

I think I should have stressed something that I didn't in the final chapter: how different ("modern") feelings, experiences, helped to define altered conceptions of "the real"—of reality that was knowable by *legitimate* methods—and how that contributed to the need for particular kinds of "reform," because feelings always come charged with emotion, and *that* makes one desire to maintain or to eliminate their cause. But the notion of *legitimate* methods of knowing tends to render some desires valid and some invalid—as distortion, illusion, sickness. And so there is increasingly the sense that "secularism" as a political doctrine gives that need for reform a legitimate direction. This is implicit in what I say, but it isn't made explicit in the final chapter.

DS: Where do you go from here? And will we see a book on rethinking the concept of a tradition?

TA: Well, I don't know if we will see a book. Everything becomes more and more difficult as one gets older. As you know, David, I find writing painful; I'm very dissatisfied with almost everything I've written. I really dislike rereading what I have written except—except perhaps in a few cases and then only after many, many years. And sometimes I find with surprise that it's not quite as bad as my memory had it. But in the longer term, I do want to write something on tradition. As you know, I've been thinking about tradition for many years, ever since I touched on it in a preliminary way in *The Idea of an Anthropology of Islam*, but I really haven't addressed it adequately.[46] I want to think about it in a sustained way. I want to draw on some notes that I've made, I want to do lot more reading. Whether eventually it will amount to a book or an article I don't know. But it's something I'd like to do. And again I'd like to move conceptually between the Middle East, between Islamic concepts and practices of tradition, and Western understandings of modernity.

Notes

INTRODUCTION

1. One source for this view, of course, is Ludwig Wittgenstein, *On Certainty*, ed. G. E. M. Anscombe and G. H. von Wright (Oxford: Blackwell, 1969). Asad has always been a keen reader of Wittgenstein.
2. Bronislaw Malinowski, *A Diary in the Strict Sense of the Term* (New York: Harcourt Brace, 1967).
3. Talal Asad, *The Kababish Arabs: Power, Authority and Consent in a Nomadic Tribe* (London: Christopher Hurst, 1970). This book was based on Asad's doctoral research among the Kababish, a nomadic Arab people in northern Sudan, carried on while holding a teaching post at the University of Khartoum between 1961 and 1966. See David Scott, "The Trouble of Thinking: An Interview with Talal Asad," in this volume.
4. Asad, *The Kababish Arabs*, 2.
5. Ibid., 10n.1.
6. Talal Asad (ed.), *Anthropology and the Colonial Encounter* (London: Ithaca Press, 1973).
7. Asad, "Introduction," in *Anthropology and the Colonial Encounter*, 12.
8. Ibid., 17.
9. Asad, "Two European Images of Non-European Rule," in *Anthropology and the Colonial Encounter*.
10. One thinks especially of Talal Asad, "Anthropological Texts and Ideological Problems: An Analysis of Cohen on Arab Villages in Israel," *Economy and Society* 4, no. 3 (1975): 251–82; and "Anthropology and the Analysis of Ideology" *Man* (n.s.) 14, no. 4 (1979): 607–27.
11. James Clifford and George E. Marcus (eds.), *Writing Culture: The Poetics and Politics of Ethnography* (Berkeley: University of California Press, 1986).
12. See Talal Asad, "Ethnographic Representation, Statistics and Modern Power," *Social Research* 61, no. 1 (1994): 55–88; and "Introduction," in *Formations of the Secular: Christianity, Islam, Modernity* (Stanford, CA: Stanford University Press, 2003).

13. Talal Asad, "The Concept of Cultural Translation," in Clifford and Marcus (eds.), *Writing Culture*, 163.

14. Clifford Geertz, "Religion as a Cultural System," in *The Interpretation of Cultures* (New York: Basic Books, 1973).

15. Asad, "Religion as an Anthropological Category," in *Genealogies of Religion: Discipline and Reasons of Power in Christianity and Islam* (Baltimore, MD: Johns Hopkins University Press, 1993), 42–43. This is a revised version of "Anthropological Conceptions of Religion: Reflections on Geertz," *Man* (n.s.) 18, no. 2 (1983): 237–59.

16. Asad, "Religion as an Anthropological Category," 53.

17. Asad, "Pain and Truth in Medieval Christian Ritual" and "Discipline and Humility in Christian Monasticism," both in *Genealogies of Religion*.

18. Hans Gumbrecht, "A Farewell to Interpretation," in Hans Gumbrecht and K. Ludwig Pfeiffer (eds.), *Materialities of Communication* (Stanford, CA: Stanford University Press, 1994), 94.

19. Alasdair MacIntyre, *After Virtue: A Study in Moral Theory* (Notre Dame, IN: University of Notre Dame Press, 1984).

20. Talal Asad, "The Idea of an Anthropology of Islam," *Occasional Paper Series* (Washington, D.C.: Center for Contemporary Studies, Georgetown University, 1986).

21. See Marcel Mauss, "Techniques of the Body," *Economy and Society* 2, no. 1 (February 1973): 70–88. Asad's use of the notion of human (as in "human objectives") has a certain similarity to Wittgenstein's idea of human ways of doing things, as well as "instinctual action," a similarity that becomes all the more evident in Asad's most recent writings on pain. See Ludwig Wittgenstein, *Philosophical Investigations*, trans. G. E. M. Anscombe (Oxford: Oxford University Press, 1968).

22. See Michel Foucault, *Discipline and Punish: The Birth of the Prison* (New York: Vintage Books, 1979); *Technologies of the Self: A Seminar with Michel Foucault* (Amherst: University of Massachusetts Press, 1988).

23. Asad, *Formations of the Secular*.

24. Asad, "Thinking about Agency and Pain," in *Formations of the Secular*, 84 (italics in original).

25. Asad, "Reconfigurations of Law and Ethics in Colonial Egypt," in *Formations of the Secular*.

CHAPTER 2

1. Talal Asad, *Formations of the Secular*, 182–83.

2. In the following presentation I will follow closely, often literally, my *Public Religions in the Modern World* (Chicago: University of Chicago, 1994), particular-

ly those passages that appear in the index under "secularization." In order not to overburden the text, however, I will only use quotations to signal those passages that indicate Asad has misinterpreted my position.

3. *Public Religions*, 7.
4. *Formations of the Secular*, 182.
5. *Public Religions*, 219.
6. *Formations of the Secular*, 182.
7. *Public Religions*, 6.
8. *Formations of the Secular*, 183.
9. *Public Religions*, 233–34.
10. See my more recent statement, "Beyond European and American Exceptionalisms: Towards a Global Perspective," in *Predicting Religion*, ed. G. Davie, P. Helas, and L. Woodhead (Aldershot: Ashgate, 2003).
11. Cf. Jon Butler, *Awash in a Sea of Faith: Christianizing the American People* (Cambridge, MA: Harvard University Press, 1990); Roger Finke and Rodney Stark, *The Churching of America, 1776–1990: Winners and Losers in Our Religious Economy* (New Brunswick, NJ: Rutgers University Press, 1992); Andrew Greeley, *Religious Change in America* (Cambridge, MA: Harvard University Press, 1989).
12. Rodney Stark, "Secularization RIP," *Sociology of Religion* 62, no. 2 (1999); Rodney Stark and William S. Bainbridge, *The Future of Religion* (Berkeley: University of California Press, 1985).
13. Kirk Hadaway, Penny Long Marler, and Mark Chaves, "What the Polls Don't Show: A Closer Look at U.S. Church Attendance," *American Sociological Review* 58 (1993).
14. David Martin, *A General Theory of Secularization* (Oxford: Blackwell, 1978); Grace Davie, *Religion in Modern Europe* (Oxford: Oxford University Press, 2000).
15. R. Stephen Warner, "Work in Progress toward a New Paradigm for the Sociological Study of Religion in the United States," *American Journal of Sociology* 98, no. 5 (1993).
16. Alexis de Tocqueville, *Democracy in America*, 2 vols. (New York: Vintage, 1990); Karl Marx, "On the Jewish Question," in *Early Writings* (New York: Vintage, 1975).
17. Rodney Stark and Laurence Iannaccone, "A Supply-Side Interpretation of the 'Secularization' of Europe," *Journal for the Scientific Study of Religion* 33 (1994).
18. I still consider valid the schematic analytical reconstruction of the historical process of differentiation presented in *Public Religions*, 20–25.
19. *Public Religions*, 18.
20. *Formations of the Secular*, 191.
21. Ibid., 192.

22. Cf. Karl Löwith, *Meaning in History* (Chicago: University of Chicago Press, 1949); and Hans Blumenberg, *The Legitimacy of the Modern Age* (Cambridge, Mass.: MIT Press, 1983).

23. Talcott Parsons, "Christianity and Modern Industrial Society," in Edward Tiryakian, ed., *Sociological Theory, Values and Sociocultural Change* (New York: Free Press, 1963).

24. This has been the customary practice of European analysts, namely to discount the evidence of American religiosity by claiming that it is somehow "inauthentic" and therefore does not serve as invalidating evidence against the thesis.

25. *Formations of the Secular*, 193.

26. Knut Walf, "Gospel, Church Law and Human Rights: Foundations and Deficiencies," in Hans Küng and Jurgen Moltmann, eds., *The Ethics of World Religions and Human Rights* (*Concilium* 1990/2) (Philadelphia: Trinity Press International, 1990), 36.

27. As papal nuncio in Paris, Monsignor Roncalli, later Pope John XXIII, played some role in the formulation of the Universal Declaration of Human Rights by the United Nations in 1948 through the support and assistance it gave to the French delegation. See Leonard Swidler, "Human Rights: A Historical Overview," in Küng and Moltmann, *Ethics of World Religions*, 19–20.

28. Cf. Peter Hebblethwaite, *Pope John XXIII: Shepherd of the Modern World* (New York: Doubleday, 1985); David Hollenbach, *Claims in Conflict: Retrieving and Renewing the Catholic Human Rights Tradition* (New York: Paulist Press, 1979); David Hollenbach, ed., *Human Rights in the Americas: The Struggle for Consensus* (Washington, D.C.: Woodstock Theological Center, 1981).

29. See John Courtney Murray, "The Problem of Religious Freedom," *Theological Studies* 25 (1964): 503–75; George Weigel, *The Final Revolution* (New York: Oxford University Press, 1992).

30. For a more elaborate analysis of the transformation of the modern papacy, see José Casanova, "Globalizing Catholicism and the Return to a 'Universal' Church," in Susanne Rudolph and James Piscatori, eds., *Transnational Religion and Fading States* (Boulder, CO: Westview Press, 1997).

31. See José Casanova, "Global Catholicism and the Politics of Civil Society," *Sociological Inquiry* 66, no. 3 (Fall 1996).

32. One could claim that this was truly the first ecumenical, i.e., global, council in the history of Christianity. Vatican I (1875) was still a mainly European event, even though the forty-nine prelates from the United States comprised already one-tenth of the gathered bishops. The 2,500 Fathers who participated at Vatican II, by contrast, came from practically all parts of the world. Europeans no longer formed a majority. The U.S. delegation, with over two hundred bishops, was the second largest, though it was already smaller than the combined group of 228 indigenous Asian and African bishops at the end of the Council. The number

is significant, considering that only under the papacy of Benedict XV (1914–22) did the Vatican begin to promote the recruitment of indigenous clergy and the formation of native hierarchies, thus abandoning the European colonial legacy of considering missions as religious colonies.

33. *Formations of the Secular*, 195.

34. John Paul II, *The Acting Person* (Boston: Reidel, 1979); *Toward a Philosophy of Praxis* (New York: Crossroad, 1981); *Return to Poland: The Collected Speeches of John Paul II* (London: Collins, 1979).

35. The 1937 collective Pastoral Letter of the Spanish episcopate officially supporting and legitimating the 1936 military uprising against the constitutional republican government in the midst of the Spanish Civil War is one of those rare instances.

36. José Casanova, "Civil Society and Religion: Retrospective Reflections on Catholicism and Prospective Reflections on Islam," *Social Research* 68, no. 4 (Winter 2001).

37. The literature is vast. As an illustrative sample of relevant texts, c.f. Saïd A. Arjomand, "Civil Society and the Rule of Law in the Constitutional Politics of Iran under Khatami," *Social Research* 67, no. 2 (Summer 2000); Dale F. Eickelman, "Islam and the Languages of Modernity," *Daedalus* 129, no. 1 (Winter 2000); Dale F. Eickelman and Jon W. Anderson, eds., *New Media and the Muslim World: The Emerging Public Sphere* (Bloomington: Indiana University Press, 1999); John L. Esposito and John O. Voll, *Islam and Democracy* (Oxford: Oxford University Press, 1996); Robert W. Heffner, *Civil Islam: Muslims and Democratization in Indonesia* (Princeton, NJ: Princeton University Press, 2000); Charles Kurzman, ed., *Liberal Islam: A Sourcebook* (New York: Oxford University Press, 1998); Ann Elizabeth Mayer, *Islam and Human Rights: Tradition and Politics* (Boulder, CO: Westview Press, 1999); Armando Salvatore, *Islam and the Political Discourse of Modernity* (Reading: Ithaca Press, 1997); Armando Salvatore and Dale F. Eickelman, eds., *Public Islam and the Common Good* (Princeton, NJ: Princeton University Press, 2004); Jenny B. White, *Islamist Modernization in Turkey: A Study in Vernacular Politics* (Seattle: University of Washington Press, 2002); Muhammad Qasim Zaman, *The Ulama in Contemporary Islam: Custodians of Change* (Princeton, NJ: Princeton University Press, 2002).

CHAPTER 3

1. Clifford Geertz, *The Interpretation of Cultures* (New York: Basic Books, 1973).

2. Asad, *Genealogies of Religion*, 29.

3. Geertz, *Interpretation*, 90 (my emphasis).

4. Steven C. Caton, "The Importance of Reflexive Language in George H. Mead's Theory of Self and Communication," in *Reflexive Language: Reported Speech and Metapragmatics* (Cambridge: Cambridge University Press, 1993), 315–37.

5. Geertz, *Interpretation*, 91.
6. Asad, *Genealogies of Religion*, 30.
7. Ibid.
8. Ibid., 31.
9. Ibid. (my emphasis).
10. Geertz, *Interpretation*, 11–12.
11. Ibid., 17 (my emphasis).
12. See also David Schneider, "Notes Toward a Theory of Culture," in Keith H. Basso and Henry A. Selby, eds., *Meaning in Anthropology* (Albuquerque: University of New Mexico Press, 1976), 197–220.

13. Kenneth Burke, *Language as Symbolic Action* (Berkeley: University of California Press, 1966).

14. Kenneth Burke, *Philosophy of Literary Form* (Berkeley: University of California Press, 1949).

15. Ibid.
16. Eric Wolf, *Europe and the People without History* (Berkeley: University of California Press, 1982); William Roseberry, "Balinese Cockfights and the Seduction of Anthropology," in *Anthropologies and Histories* (Rutgers, NJ: Rutgers University Press, 1989), 17–29.

17. Clifford Geertz, *Negara: The Theater-State in Nineteenth Century Bali* (Princeton, NJ: Princeton University Press, 1980).

18. Asad, *Genealogies of Religion*, 32.
19. Ibid., 36–37.
20. Talal Asad, *The Idea of an Anthropology of Islam*, Occasional Paper Series (Washington, D.C.: Georgetown University Center for Contemporary Arab Studies, 1986), 14.

21. Ibid., 15 (emphasis in the original).
22. Ibid.
23. Ibid., 14–15 (emphasis in the original).
24. Asad, *Genealogies of Religion*, 36 (my emphasis).
25. See Roman Jakobson, "Linguistics and Poetics," in Thomas A. Sebeok, ed., *Style in Language* (Cambridge, Mass.: MIT Press, 1960), 350–70.

26. Jakobson, "Linguistics and Poetics"; Michael Silverstein, "Shifters, Linguistic Categories, and Cultural Description," in Keith H. Basso and Henry A. Selby, eds., *Meaning in Anthropology* (Albuquerque: University of New Mexico, 1976), 11–55; Michael Silverstein, "Metapragmatic Discourse and Metapragmatic Function," in John A. Lucy, ed., *Reflexive Language: Reported Speech and Metapragmatics* (Cambridge: Cambridge University Press, 1993), 33–58.

27. M. M. Bakhtin, "Discourse of the Novel," in Michael Holquist, ed., *The Dialogic Imagination*, trans. Caryl Emerson and Michael Holquist (Austin: University of Texas Press, 1981), 279.

28. Ibid., 338.

29. Ibid., 339.

30. Steven C. Caton, "Salam TaHiya: Greetings from the Highlands of Yemen," *American Ethnologist* 13, no. 2 (1986): 290–308.

31. L. Gardet, "Duʿa," in *The Encyclopedia of Islam*, new edition, vol. 3, ed. C. G. Lewis, C. Pellat, and J. Schacht (Leiden: E.J. Brill, 1983), 617–18.

CHAPTER 4

1. "Secularism and Toleration," in *A Possible India: Essays in Political Criticism* (Delhi: Oxford University Press, 1997), 228–62.

2. Selections from this debate have been collected in Rajeev Bhargava, ed., *Secularism and Its Critics* (Delhi: Oxford University Press, 1998).

3. Asad, *Formations of the Secular*.

4. Bryan Wilson, *Religion in a Secular Society* (London: Watts, 1966).

5. Asad, *Formations of the Secular*, 181–83.

6. Ibid., 184–87.

7. Ibid., 205–56.

8. Asad, *Genealogies of Religion*.

9. *Telegraph* (Calcutta), 29 January 2002.

10. *Times of India* (Calcutta), 31 January 2002.

11. Ibid., 30 January 2002.

12. Ibid., 1 February 2002.

13. Ibid., 2 February 2002.

14. Ibid., 3 February 2002.

15. Ibid., 5 February 2002.

16. *Ganasakti* (Calcutta), 5 February 2002.

17. *Times of India*, 7 February 2002.

18. *Ganasakti*, 7 February 2002.

19. *Telegraph*, 8 February 2002; *Anandabajar Patrika*, 8 February 2002; *Ganasakti*, 8 February 2002; *Times of India*, 8 February 2002.

20. *Times of India*, 12 February 2002.

21. Milan Datta, "Madrasar biruddhe prachar: Age satyata jene nin," *Anandabajar Patrika*, 29 January 2002; *Telegraph*, 30 January 2002.

22. *Anandabajar Patrika*, 29 January 2002.

23. Anisur Rahaman, "Ladener roja," *Ganasakti*, 29 January 2002.

24. *Times of India*, 1 February 2002.

25. *Telegraph*, 1 February 2002.

26. *Anandabajar Patrika*, 1 February 2002.

27. Mainul Hasan, "Madrasah shiksha: Bartaman samay o Muslim samaj,"

Ganasakti, 6 February 2002.

28. *Telegraph*, 12 February 2002.

29. Ibid.

30. Letter by Fatema Begum, Bagnan, Howrah, in *Anandabajar Patrika*, 28 February 2002.

31. Partha Chatterjee, *The Politics of the Governed: Reflections on Popular Politics in Most of the World* (New York: Columbia University Press, 2004).

CHAPTER 5

1. Talal Asad, "Re-reading a Modern Classic: W. C. Smith's 'The Meaning and End of Religion,'" in Hent de Vries and Samuel Weber, eds., *Religion and the Media* (Stanford, CA: Stanford University Press, 2001), 216. I would like to thank Jane Bennett, John Docker, Gyan Pandey, and Lars Tonder for the thoughtful comments they made on the first draft of this essay.

2. Ibid., 220.

3. Asad, *Formations of the Secular*, 38.

4. Ibid., 38–39.

5. Ibid., 55.

6. Ibid., 90.

7. Ibid., 169.

8. Ibid., 205.

9. I pursue a related agenda in *Why I Am Not a Secularist* (Minneapolis: University of Minnesota Press, 1999). There I explore the relation between technique and being, drawing upon that exploration to project a pluralist "ethos of engagement" appropriate to the late-modern time. In his study of secularism, Asad assesses an earlier essay of mine pointing in the same direction.

10. Kant, *Critique of Practical Reason*, trans. Lewis Beck (New York: Macmillan, 1993), 78. For a thoughtful close discussion of the pivotal role that humiliation plays in Kant's philosophy of morality and politics, see Paul Saurette, "Challenging the Kantian Imperative: Common Sense Recognition and the Ethics of Cultivation," Ph.D. diss., Johns Hopkins University, 2001. Saurette says, "I want to suggest that on one hand, Kant portrays our common sense recognition of the moral law as an apodictic fact (which functions . . . to secure . . . the imperative image of morality) and on the other, devises a set of strategies to make it become apodictically recognized in fact" (72).

11. Immanuel Kant, *The Metaphysics of Morals*, trans. Mary Gregor (New York: Cambridge University Press, 1991), 274.

12. Ian Hunter, *Rival Enlightenments: Civil and Metaphysical Philosophy in Early Modern Germany* (Cambridge: Cambridge University Press, 2001). Hunter does

not identify Spinoza as a founder of one of the rival enlightenments, perhaps because he is focusing on Germany and those in Germany who contested the Kantian version.

13. Folio 408 of *Livro dos Acordos da Nacam*, cited in Yirmiyahu Yovel, *Spinoza and Other Heretics: The Marrano of Reason* (Princeton, NJ: Princeton University Press, 1989), 3.

14. An absorbing book that delineates this history and explores what Europe could look like if the golden age of Spain provided a normative model from which to build today is John Docker, *1492: The Poetics of Diaspora* (London: Continuum, 2001).

15. Benedict Spinoza, *Ethics*, trans. Samuel Shirley (Cambridge: Hackett Publishing, 1992), 103.

16. For a rich history of the "Radical Enlightenment" in Europe, the pivotal role Spinoza played in it, the harsh punishments meted out for a hundred years to the numerous priests, theologians, and philosophers in Holland, France, Germany, and England who either avowed Spinozism or were accused of it, and the ways in which the political advent of Spinozism helped create space for the better-known "Moderate Enlightenment," see Jonathan Israel, *Radical Enlightenment: Philosophy and the Making of Modernity, 1650–1750* (Cambridge: Cambridge University Press, 2001). I was not aware of this book when the present essay was completed. Had I been, I would have emphasized, in line with Israel's account, how pervasive and influential the Spinozist strain of the Enlightenment was, although it subsisted beneath the glare of the moderate Enlightenment and the latter's struggle with ecclesiastical faith. Spinozists were active in almost every European country, and they were met with far more violent repression than that faced by advocates of the moderate Enlightenment. The historical tendency to forget this side of the Enlightenment provides contemporary neo-Kantians with an excuse to define the authors discussed in this essay as opposed to "the Legacy of the Enlightenment" when in fact they express the contemporary evolution of one of its major wings. For a closer engagement with Israel and Antonio Damasio (discussed briefly below), and an examination of the importance to contemporary political thought of coming to terms with this minor tradition, see Connolly, "The Radical Enlightenment: Theory, Power, Faith," *Theory & Event* (Spring 2004), available at http://muse.jhu.edu/journals/tae/.

17. Stuart Hampshire, *Spinoza* (London: Faber and Faber, 1960).

18. Stuart Hampshire, *Freedom of Mind* (Princeton, NJ: Princeton University Press, 1971), 213 and 218, respectively.

19. Hampshire joins most Anglo-American interpreters of Spinoza in focusing on the role of the propositions in the *Ethics*. But these propositions are placed into dissonant communication with the *Scholia*, those vibrant and sometimes explosive paragraphs situated around them, which do so much to enliven the reader

and pull one along. For those who think the key to the text resides in the relays between the *Scholia* and the propositional demonstrations, then Hampshire's translation of Spinoza's demonstrations into contestable formulations marks a shift in orientation, but it does not, perhaps, constitute as radical a break as he suggests.

20. Hampshire, *Freedom of the Mind*, 203–4.

21. Antonio Damasio, *Looking for Spinoza: Joy, Sorrow, and the Feeling Brain* (New York: Harcourt, 2003), 192.

22. I outline the idea of a body/brain/culture network in chapter 1 of *Neuropolitics: Thinking, Culture, Speed* (Minneapolis: University of Minnesota Press, 2002).

23. One place where this is now occurring is in the exchanges taking place between Buddhist monks and neuroscientists about the effects of meditation on brain/body processes and the introduction of new instruments developed by neuroscientists to aid meditation. See, for instance, Francisco Varela, ed., *Sleeping, Dreaming, Dying: An Exploration of Consciousness with the Dalai Lama* (Boston: Wisdom Publications, 1997). Varela, who died recently, was a neuroscientist and a Buddhist.

24. Gilles Deleuze and Felix Guattari, *A Thousand Plateaus*, trans. Brian Massumi (Minneapolis: University of Minnesota Press, 1987), 407.

25. Gilles Deleuze, *Cinema II: The Time Image*, trans. Hugh Tomlinson and Robert Galeta (Minneapolis: University of Minnesota Press, 1989). These formulations appear between pages 170 and 173.

CHAPTER 6

1. Asad, *Formations of the Secular.* Further references to this book are incorporated in the text. I am grateful to Ali Khan for many discussions on the issues discussed here, and to Ranendra Das for his help in getting past some sticky problems. Talal's friendship and his capacity to sustain conversation are truly precious gifts for me.

2. Thomas Hobbes, *De Cive* (1651), in *Man and Citizen: 'De Homine' and 'De Cive,'* ed. Bernhard Gert (Indianapolis, IN: Hackett Publishing Company, 1991), 205.

3. Carole Pateman, *The Sexual Contract* (Stanford, CA: Stanford University Press, 1988).

4. Seyla Benhabib, *Situating the Self: Gender, Community and Postmodernism in Contemporary Ethics* (Cambridge: Polity Press, 1992).

5. Giorgio Agamben, *Homo Sacer: Sovereign Power and Bare Life*, trans. Daniel Heller-Roazen (Stanford, CA: Stanford University Press, 1998).

6. The cases reported here can be found in Sir Eskine Perry, *Cases Illustrative of Oriental Life and the Application of English Law to India decided in H.M. Supreme Court of Bombay* (London: S. Sweet Publishers, 1853).

7. Agamben, *Homo Sacer*.

8. Charles Taylor asserts that the modern democratic state needs a healthy degree of patriotism—"a strong sense of identification with the polity and a willingness to give of oneself for its sake." See Charles Taylor, "Modes of Secularism," in Rajeev Bhargava, ed., *Secularism and Its Critics* (New Delhi: Oxford University Press, 1998). Asad provides a stringent critique of the simplistic notion of belonging in this text. I simply want to add to Asad's points that the entire question of what it is to give oneself—to be ready to die for your country—requires a complete description of who is called to die, whose death counts, and who determines what constitutes the state of exception in which one can be asked to die for a country. One aspect of this call to patriotism is that a myth of voluntary sacrifice has to be carefully maintained and stories of suffering of soldiers—and especially their dissent—are carefully suppressed in the creation of myths of patriotism. In any case, with the new doctrines and technologies of high-tech wars, the risks of death are disproportionately distributed and major casualties are now inflicted on civilians as collateral damage. See Michael Humphrey, *The Politics of Atrocity and Reconciliation: From Terror to Trauma* (London: Routledge, 2002).

9. Asad, *Formations of the Secular*, 192.

10. The precise nature and direction of the influence of religious thought on political philosophy is a subject of much debate, but see the classic contributions of John Dunn, *The Political Thought of John Locke* (Cambridge: Cambridge University Press, 1969); John Marshall, *John Locke: Resistance, Religion, and Responsibility* (Cambridge: Cambridge University Press, 1994); J. G. A. Pocock, *Politics, Language, and Time* (New York: Atheneum, 1971); Joshua Mitchell, "Hobbes and the Equality of All under the One," *Political Theory* 12, no. 1 (1993).

11. Sir Robert Filmer, *Patriarcha and Other Writings*, ed. Johann P. Sommerville (Cambridge: Cambridge University Press, 1991).

12. Mary Laura Severance, "Sex and the Social Contract," *ELH* (2000): 453–513.

13. While for Filmer it is the natural affection of the father that preserves the child, Hegel introduces the idea that children have a right to be brought up and supported at the expense of the family. G. W. F. Hegel, *Elements of the Philosophy of the Right*, ed. Allen W. Wood (Cambridge: Cambridge University Press, 1991), esp. paragraph 174.

14. Johann Jakob Bachofen, *Myth, Religion and Mother Right: Selected Writings of J. J. Bachofen*, trans. Ralph Manheim (Princeton, NJ: Princeton University Press, 1967); John Ferguson McLennan, *Primitive Marriage: An Enquiry into the Origin of the Form of Capture in Marriage*, ed. Peter Rivière (Chicago: Chicago University Press, 1970); Lewis Henry Morgan, *Ancient Society: Or, Researches in the Lines of Human Progress from Savagery through Barbarism to Civilization* (London: Macmillan, 1877).

15. Friedrich Engels, *The Origin of the Family, Private Property and the State: In the Light of the Researches of Lewis H. Morgan* (London: International Publishers, 1942), 125.

16. Jean-Jacques Rousseau, *Emile* (New York: Everyman's Library, 1974).

17. Ronald Grimsley, "Rousseau and His Reader: The Technique of Persuasion in *Emile*," in R. A. Leigh, ed., *Rousseau after Two Hundred Years: Proceedings of the Cambridge Bicentennial Colloquium* (Cambridge: Cambridge University Press, 1982), 225–38.

18. The theme of incorrect children being born of sexual violence and jeopardizing the honor of the nation is pursued in Veena Das, "National Honour and Practical Kinship," in *Critical Event: An Anthropological Perspective on Contemporary India* (New Delhi: Oxford University Press, 1995).

19. Mario Feit has examined the implications of Rousseau's theory of the relation between sexuality and mortality for same-sex marriage in an innovative and interesting way. While I see that there are important implications of Rousseau's thesis of citizenship for non-normative forms of sexuality, I am much more interested here in the way in which the figure of the father places Rousseau in the debate on fatherhood in Filmer, Hobbes, and Locke. I have learned much from Mario Feit's discussion on population. Mario Feit, "Mortality, Sexuality, and Citizenship: Reading Rousseau, Arendt, and Nietzsche," Ph.D. diss., Johns Hopkins University, 2003.

20. One can see the slippage between reproduction as an act of biological begetting, and reproduction as an act of socially creating the child in such statements of the tutor as "It is I who am the true father of Emile, it is I who made him into a man." The dispersal of the "I" in the text often allows a slippage between the tutor and the author; here the functioning of the father as a Name is evident.

21. In assembling the authors in the manner that I have done, my intention is not to give a comprehensive account or even to consider the chronological developments of ideas discussed here but to see how specifically the mutual determination of theological and political informs the way that the father is positioned.

22. Severance gives this marvelous quote from Locke: "The Husband and Wife, though they have one common Concern, yet having different understandings, will unavoidably sometimes have different wills too; it therefore being necessary that the last Determination, i.e., the Rule be placed somewhere, it naturally falls to the Man's share as the abler and stronger" (quoted in Severance, "Sex and the Social Contract," 18).

23. Perry, *Cases Illustrative of Oriental Life*, 525. Gauri Viswanathan has rightly regarded conversion as an extremely important issue for understanding the relation between belief, self, and community, and has argued that in tightly controlling conversion the British were maintaining the status quo. The question of whether converts were to retain the rights that accrued to them from membership

in their previous community was indeed a complex one. I find it curious, though, that the kinds of anxieties that Justice Perry repeatedly expresses when he imagines situations in which a Christian wife's husband has converted to Islam and the case comes before a Muslim judge do not find any place in Viswanathan's thesis about conversion. In general her observations on the rights of the converted spouse do not take up the kind of issues I have treated here, since she takes categories like family and patriarchy to be self-evident in her analysis. See Gauri Viswanathan, *Outside the Fold* (New Delhi: Oxford University Press, 1998).

24. U.S. Department of Labor, Office of Policy Planning and Research, *The Negro Family: The Case for National Action* (Washington D.C.: U.S. Government Printing Office, 1965).

CHAPTER 7

1. Jacques Derrida, *Acts of Religion*, ed. Gil Anidjar (New York: Routledge, 2002), 44.
2. Asad, *Formations of the Secular*, 13–14.
3. Ibid., 14.
4. Ibid., 21.
5. Ibid., 22.
6. Ibid., 14–15.
7. Ibid., 16.
8. Ibid.
9. Ibid., 16–17.
10. Ibid., 17.
11. Jacques Derrida, *L'écriture et la différence* (Paris: Seuil, 1967), 120; translated by Alan Bass under the title *Writing and Difference* (Chicago: University of Chicago Press, 1978), 81, trans. modified. Subsequent references give page numbers for the English translation followed by the French edition.
12. Derrida, *Writing and Difference*, 81 and 311n.4 / 120 and 120n.2.
13. Ibid., 311n.4/120n.2 (translation modified).
14. Ibid., 311–12n.4/120n.2.
15. Ibid., 81/120 (translation modified).
16. Ibid., 81/121 (translation modified).
17. Ibid. (translation modified).
18. Ibid., 82/122.
19. Levinas, *Is it Righteous to Be? Interviews with Emmanuel Levinas,* ed. Jill Robbins (Stanford, CA: Stanford University Press, 2001), 164.
20. *Is It Righteous to Be?* 64; François Poirié, *Emmanuel Levinas: Essais et entretiens* (Arles: Actes Sud, 1996), 136. The reference is to Claude Lévi-Strauss, *La pensée sauvage* (Paris: Plon, 1962).

21. *Is It Righteous to Be?* 64–65; Poirié, *Emmanuel Levinas*, 136.

22. Ibid., 78–79/161–62.

23. Emmanuel Levinas, *Dieu, la mort et le temps* (Paris: Grasset & Fasquelle, 1993), 190; translated by Bettina Bergo under the title *God, Death, and Time* (Stanford, CA: Stanford University Press, 2000), 166. Levinas's reference is to the classical fable of the belly and the attempted rebellion of the other parts of the body against it (a fable repeated in this chapter of *Pantagruel*).

24. Ibid.

25. *God, Death, and Time*, 166; *Dieu, la mort et le temps*, 190–91.

26. Emmanuel Levinas, *Autrement qu'être ou au-delà de l'essence* (The Hague: Martinus Nijhoff, 1974), 186n.13; translated by Alphonso Lingis under the title *Otherwise than Being, or Beyond Essence* (The Hague: Martinus Nijhoff, 1981), 199n.13.

27. Roger Burggraeve, *Emmanuel Levinas et la socialité de l'argent* (Leuven: Peeters, 1997), 46. Levinas refers to the French translation of Grossman's novel, entitled in Russian *Zhizn' i sud'ba* and translated as *Vie et destin* by Alexis Berelowitch (Paris: Editions l'Age d'Homme, 1980), which he himself read in the Russian language. See also *Life and Fate: A Novel*, trans. Robert Chandler (New York: Harper & Row, 1986); and John Garrard and Carol Garrard, *The Bones of Berdichev: The Life and Fate of Vasily Grossman* (New York: Free Press, 1996).

28. Burggraeve, *Emmanuel Levinas et la socialité de l'argent*, 46.

29. Ibid., 47.

30. *Is It Righteous to Be?* 80–81 (trans. modified); Poirié, *Emmanuel Levinas*, 165.

31. Ibid.

32. Burggraeve, *Emmanuel Levinas et la socialité de l'argent*, 47.

33. *Is It Righteous to Be?* 81; Poirié, *Emmanuel Levinas*, 165.

34. Ibid.

35. Ibid., 81/166.

36. Ibid., 89–90.

37. Ibid., 90.

38. Ibid., 207.

39. Cited in Levinas, *Is It Righteous to Be?* 79.

40. Ibid., 72 and 73.

41. Ibid., 73.

42. Ibid., 38, 74; and Emmanuel Levinas, *Entre nous: Essais sur le penser-à-l'autre* (Paris: Grasset & Fasquelle, 1991), 41; translated by Michael B. Smith and Bararah Harshav under the title *Entre nous: Thinking-of-the-Other* (New York: Columbia University Press, 1998), 41.

43. Burggraeve, *Emmanuel Levinas et la socialité de l'argent*, 74.

44. Ibid. (emphasis added).

45. Ibid.
46. Ibid.
47. Ibid.
48. Ibid., 74–75.
49. Ibid., 37.
50. Ibid., 75.
51. Ibid. (I have corrected the ungrammatical structure of the first phrase: "il ne doit pas considérer que la règle universelle qu'il découvre sont [sic] des règles universelles.")
52. Ibid.
53. Ibid., 39.
54. Ibid., 40.
55. Ibid.
56. Ibid.
57. Ibid.
58. Emmanuel Levinas, *Humanisme de l'autre homme* (Montpellier: Fata Morgana, 1972), 110n.9; translated by Nidra Poller under the title *Humanism of the Other* (Champaign: University of Illinois Press, 2003), 76n.9.
59. Burggraeve, *Emmanuel Levinas et la socialité de l'argent*, 75.
60. Ibid.
61. Ibid., 76.
62. See also Levinas, *Entre nous*, 52.
63. Cited in Burggraeve, *Emmanuel Levinas et la socialité de l'argent*, 76.
64. Ibid., 37.
65. Ibid.
66. Levinas, *Is it Righteous to Be?* 164; Christian Delacampagne, ed., *Entretiens avec 'Le Monde,'* vol. 1: *Philosophies* (Paris: Editions de la découverte/Le Monde, 1984), 147.
67. Raymond Aron, "L'Idolâtrie de l'histoire," in *L'Opium des intellectuels* (Paris: Hachette, 2002).

CHAPTER 8

1. The remark comes from Talal Asad, "Thinking about Agency and Pain," in his *Formations of the Secular*, 96.
2. See Talal Asad, "Anthropology and the Analysis of Ideology," *Man*, n.s. 14 (1979): 607–27.
3. Worthy of consideration in this regard are the following: Thomas Kuhn, *The Structure of Scientific Revolutions* (Chicago: University of Chicago Press, 1962); Ian Hacking, *Historical Ontology* (Cambridge: Harvard University Press, 2002); Stephen Toulmin, *The Uses of Argument* (Cambridge: Cambridge University Press,

1958), and *Return to Reason* (Cambridge: Harvard University Press, 2003); and Albert R. Jonsen and Stephen Toulmin, *The Abuse of Casuistry: A History of Moral Reasoning* (Berkeley: University of California Press, 1988).

4. The metaphor, of course, comes from Wittgenstein's preface to his *Philosophical Investigations*, trans. G. E. M. Anscombe (Oxford: Blackwell, 1968), v. Asad's debt to Wittgenstein is, I believe, a large one. My sense is that *Philosophical Investigations* in particular exercised considerable influence on his thinking, indeed, on his preoccupation with the very idea of "thinking."

5. "Genealogy is not intended here as a substitute for social history ('real history,' as many would put it) but a way of working back from our present to the contingencies that have come together to give us our certainties." Asad, introduction to *Formations of the Secular*, 16.

6. Michel Foucault, "Nietzsche, Genealogy, History," in Paul Rabinow, ed., *The Foucault Reader* (New York: Pantheon, 1984), 86.

7. Ibid., 81, 83.

8. Ibid., 97.

9. Asad, *Genealogies of Religion*.

10. Clifford Geertz, "Religion as a Cultural System," in his *Interpretation of Cultures*. Asad's "Anthropological Conceptions of Religion: Reflections on Geertz" first appeared in *Man* (N.S.) 18(2)(1983): 237–59, and in revised form as "The Construction of Religion as an Anthropological Category," in *Genealogies of Religion*, chapter 1.

11. "My argument is that there cannot be a universal definition of religion, not only because its constituent elements and relationships are historically specific, but because that definition is itself the historical product of discursive processes." Asad, "The Construction of Religion as an Anthropological Category," 29.

12. Readers of Asad's earlier—pre-Foucault—book, *The Kababish Arabs: Power, Authority, and Consent in a Nomadic Tribe* (London: Christopher Hurst, 1970), will remember that he is already attuned by Marx to the problem of how dominant anthropological categories—in this instance functional ones about power and kinship—shape the ways understandings of the non-West are constructed. See also his "Two European Images of Non-European Rule," in Asad (ed.), *Anthropology and the Colonial Encounter* (London: Ithaca Press, 1973).

13. Alasdair MacIntyre, *Three Rival Versions of Moral Enquiry: Encyclopaedia, Genealogy, and Tradition* (Notre Dame, IN: University of Notre Dame Press, 1990). This book is often thought of as completing his trilogy of moral philosophical revision. The first two, of course, are *After Virtue: A Study in Moral Theory* (Notre Dame, IN: University of Notre Dame Press, 1984), and *Whose Justice? Which Rationality?* (Notre Dame, IN: University of Notre Dame Press, 1988). For a useful discussion of MacIntyre's project, see John Horton and Susan Mendus, *After MacIntyre: Critical Perspectives on the Work of Alasdair MacIntyre* (Cam-

bridge: Polity Press, 1994); and Michael Fuller, *Making Sense of MacIntyre* (Aldershot: Ashgate, 1998).

14. MacIntyre, *Three Rival Versions of Moral Enquiry*, 14.

15. Ibid., 36.

16. This aspect of Nietzsche's thought is developed with acute insight by R. J. Hollingdale, *Nietzsche: The Man and His Philosophy* (New York: Cambridge University Press, 2001).

17. MacIntyre, *Three Rival Versions of Moral Enquiry*, 41.

18. Ibid., 44. As he goes on to say cogently: "It is one sign of the inescapable character of this metaphysics of reading that those who proscribe it so often fail nonetheless in the eyes of their post-Nietzschean colleagues to eliminate all traces of it from their own work. Thus Heidegger has accused Nietzsche of retaining in his thought an unacknowledged metaphysical remnant and so Derrida has in turn similarly accused Heidegger" (46).

19. Ibid., 49.

20. Ibid., 53.

21. Ibid.

22. Ibid., 203.

23. See, in this regard, Charles Segal's wonderful book on Sophocles' tragedies, *Tragedy and Civilization: An Interpretation of Sophocles* (Norman: University of Oklahoma Press, 1981), as well as his book on the *Oedipus* specifically, *Oedipus Tyrannus: Tragic Heroism and the Limits of Knowledge* (New York: Oxford University Press, 2001).

24. See J. Peter Euben, *The Tragedy of Political Theory: The Road Not Taken* (Princeton, NJ: Princeton University Press, 1990); and his edited volume, *Tragedy and Political Theory* (Berkeley: University of California Press, 1986). This section makes use of parts of my book, *Conscripts of Modernity: The Tragedy of Colonial Enlightenment* (Durham, NC: Duke University Press, 2004), chapter 5.

25. Michel Foucault, *Discipline and Punish: The Birth of the Prison*, trans. Alan Sheridan (New York: Pantheon, 1979), 217.

26. Euben, *Tragedy of Political Theory*, 25.

27. Ibid., 30.

28. Ibid.

29. Ibid., 5.

30. Talal Asad, "Thinking about Agency and Pain," in his *Formations of the Secular*, chapter 2.

31. See Asad's remarks on *Genealogies* and *Formations* in David Scott, "The Trouble of Thinking: An Interview with Talal Asad," in this volume.

32. Asad, "Thinking about Agency and Pain," 92.

33. Ibid.

34. Ibid.

35. Asad has in mind the reading of the *Oedipus* by Michael Dillon, "Otherwise than Self-Determination: The Mortal Freedom of Oedipus Asphaleos," in Hent de Vries and Samuel Weber (eds.), *Violence, Identity, and Self-Determination* (Stanford, CA: Stanford University Press, 1997).

36. Asad, "Thinking about Agency and Pain," 93.

37. Sophocles, "Oedipus at Colonus," in *The Three Theban Plays*, trans. Robert Fagles (New York: Peguin, 1984), 299.

38. Ibid.

39. Ibid., 95. The concept of *habitus* is in fact fundamental to the conception of *Formations of the Secular* as a whole. Known to most contemporary readers from Pierre Bourdieu's work (for instance, *Outline of a Theory of Practice*, trans. Richard Nice [Cambridge: Cambridge University Press, 1977], or *In Other Words: Essays Toward a Reflexive Sociology*, trans. Matthew Adamson [Cambridge: Polity Press, 1990]), Asad has always been inspired by Mauss's little essay, "Techniques of the Body," *Economy and Society* 2, no. 1 (February 1973): 70–88. There is perhaps work to be done in distinguishing Bourdieu's idea of *habitus* from Mauss's and Asad's.

40. Asad, "Thinking about Agency and Pain," 95.

41. Ibid., 96.

42. One of the more incisive discussions of this Kantian conception and its implications for secular ethics and liberal-rationalist politics (specifically in John Rawls's *A Theory of Justice* [Cambridge: Harvard University Press, 1971]) is to be found in Michael Sandel, *Liberalism and the Limits of Justice* (Cambridge: Cambridge University Press, 1982).

43. Asad, "Thinking about Agency and Pain," 98.

44. Reinhart Koselleck, *Futures Past: On the Semantics of Historical Time* (Cambridge: MIT Press, 1985). I discuss aspects of Koselleck's conception of "futures past" in my *Conscripts of Modernity*, chapter 1.

CHAPTER 9

Acknowledgments: I am indebted to Peter Euben, Victoria Hattam, Melissa Orlie, Hanna Pitkin, Mark Reinhardt, and Linda Zerilli for their help in clarifying my view of redemption. After writing this essay, I found many of my intuitions eloquently expressed in "Redemption and Violence," a special issue of *Public Culture* (15, no. 1, Winter 2003) edited by Patchen Markel and Candace Volger. Their introductory essay and the essay by Michael Warner, "What Like a Bullet Can Undeceive?" are illuminating.

1. Talal Asad, *Formations of the Secular* (Stanford, CA: Stanford University Press, 2003), 44.

2. William Blake, "The Marriage of Heaven & Hell"; Percey Bysshe Shelley, "In Defense of Poetry"; Walt Whitman, "Song of Myself."

3. Asad, *Formations of the Secular*, 52.
4. Asad, *Formations of the Secular*, 53.
5. Simon Critchley, *Very Little . . . Almost Nothing* (New York: Routledge, 1997), 86–103.
6. Asad, *Formations of the Secular*, 56.
7. Canovan quoted in Asad, *Formations of the Secular*, 59 (Asad's emphasis).
8. Asad, *Formations of the Secular*, 59-60.
9. Asad, *Formations of the Secular*, 61.
10. Asad, *Formations of the Secular*, 61.
11. These paragraphs describe the core problematic in my forthcoming book, *Prophecy and Redemption in American Political Culture* (Minneapolis: University of Minnesota Press, 2006).
12. Phillip Roth, *The Human Stain* (New York: Houghton Mifflin, 2000). In my argument about redemption, first, human beings always imagine and enact their salvation or redemption, so that second, our task is to judge forms of redemption. Prophets thus distinguish between forms of redemption (call them idolatry) that produce self-enslavement and barrenness, and ways of conceiving and practicing redemption that are fruitful and freeing. This is a political rather than metaphysical distinction, though claims to truth matter. But third, we judge the Hebrew prophets, whose view of redemption warrants criticism by the same logic they used against idolatry. In turn, the redemptions fashioned by critics like Marx and Nietzsche generate further criticism. But we thereby may extend the meaning of "redemption" so broadly that no one can escape holding onto it.
13. Classic accounts of biblical prophecy, in addition to Weber, include: Joseph Bleinkensopp, *A History of Prophecy in Israel* (Philadelphia: Westminster Press, 1983); John Bright, *Covenant and Promise* (Philadelphia: Westminster Press, 1976); Walter Brueggerman, "Trajectories in Old Testament Literature and the Sociology of Ancient Israel," *Journal of Biblical Literature* 98, no. 2 (1979); Martin Buber, *The Prophetic Faith* (New York: Harper, 1949); Frank Moore Cross, *Hebrew Epic and Canaanite Myth* (Cambridge, MA: Harvard University Press, 1973); Delbert Hillers, *Covenant: The History of a Biblical Idea* (Baltimore, MD: Johns Hopkins University Press, 1969); Douglas Knight, "Revelation through Tradition," in Douglas Knight, ed., *Tradition and Theology in the Old Testament* (New York: Sheffield Academic Press, 1991); George Mendenhall, *Tenth Generation* (Baltimore, MD: Johns Hopkins University Press, 1973); Walter Zimmerli, "Prophetic Reclamation and Reinterpretation," in Knight, ed., *Tradition and Theology in the Old Testament*.
14. Max Weber, *Ancient Judaism* (New York: Free Press, 1952), 126.
15. Nevertheless, does reimagining the past as a resource mean idealization? Yes, if we look at the example of the prophets, and of many American critics, including Arendt in *On Revolution*. Most jeremiads about a decline from origins posit only what Machiavelli calls "original goodness" and not also the violence

or domination entailed in establishing (and violating) origins. Hebrew prophets complain that people were *never* "truly" monotheist, but their story does not (also) link monotheism to exclusionary violence. In the American case, though, slavery and white supremacy has compelled some critics to create a more complex jeremiad, founding the nation in declarations of independence and in slavery. Redemption then means (re)turning, not to an unalloyed resource but to a tainted and morally ambiguous legacy.

16. Abraham Heschel, *The Prophets* (New York: Harper, 1962).

17. It is no coincidence that Toni Morrison chooses this promise (though quoted from Paul rather than Hosea) as the epigraph to *Beloved*.

18. Roth, *Human Stain*, 2. Blake says "honest indignation is the voice of God" in "The Marriage of Heaven and Hell."

19. At first, Hebrew prophets emphasize redemption in the form of human atonement and divine pardon, which together deliver—redeem—people from guilt by ending the conduct that incites it, putting trespass into the past. In the face of invasion, prophets denounce a guilty people whose assertions of innocence signal false prophecy. In this moment, prophecy endorses violence on the chosen people rather than their adversaries. But after exile, prophets imagine not a guilty people but "god's suffering servant," whose suffering proves his innocence and whose redemption means *vindication* (not pardon). Prophecy here shifts toward a more internalized and individualized religiosity after national autonomy is lost and Israel is a province in an empire, but also we see an endorsement of violence against Israel's enemies, whose destruction parallels redemption from exile. Whether defined in terms of guilt or of innocence, though, redemption links identity, injury, and moral categories in a story that invests people in their suffering in the name of ending it. A contemporary version of this problematic can be found in Wendy Brown, *States of Injury* (Princeton, NJ: Princeton University Press, 1995).

20. By their theodicy about a judging, punishing, and forgiving god, prophets articulate two premises of the grammar of redemption: people always can act differently and always bear the consequences of prior actions. They are "responsible" in both senses; God's forgiveness is a way to recognize—and yet suspend—these facts. Partly, by forgiving the past conduct of others, the injured subject lets the past be past: forgiveness releases us from rancor about what cannot be changed to effect what can be changed, the future. Forgiveness enables people to begin anew. Partly, by forgiving we can (re)constitute community because, as Lawrence Weschler notes, "true forgiveness is achieved in community; it is something people do for each other and with each other and at a certain point for free. It is history working itself out as grace but it can only be accomplished in truth." *A Miracle, a Universe* (Chicago: University of Chicago Press, 1990), 281–82.

I am indebted to Melissa Orlie, *Acting Ethically, Thinking Politically* (Ithaca,

NY: Cornell University Press, 1997) for my understanding of forgiveness in Arendt.

21. In *Exodus and Revolution* (Basic Books, 1985), Michael Walzer defends a "this-worldly" redemption against the millennialism he attributes to the experience of exile and associates with Christianity. The problem is not redemptive language as such, but the wish for deliverance from historical time and human limitation, which are accepted, he argues, by a social democratic politics. For Walzer, Marxism is "Christian" rather than "Jewish" for this reason.

22. Paul and Milton are cited in Orlando Patterson, *Freedom* (New York: Basic Books, 1991), 329. A longer version of this argument should address the relationship between Jesus and earlier prophecy in the representation of redemption and the difference between Jesus and Paul.

23. Cf. Sacvan Bercovitch, *American Jeremiad* (Madison: University of Wisconsin, 1978).

24. Karl Marx, "Contribution to the Critique: Introduction," in Robert C. Tucker, ed., *Marx-Engels Reader* (New York: Norton, 1978), 64.

25. Karl Marx, "For a Ruthless Criticism of Everything Existing," in ibid., 15.

26. Like Weber, Marx locates a flight from politics in the inner-worldly and other-worldly dimensions of religiosity, which are developed by the cultural shifts that produce Christianity. In "On the Jewish Question," Marx thus recovers and affirms a "Jewish" focus on "terrestrial" and "earthly" benefits and freedom, in response to a Christianity that abstracts from earthly needs to project a "celestial" other world. Beginning with the reality of "practical need" rather than trying to transcend it, he calls his own materialism "judaical" in its return to the earth from an invented world beyond it. Yet he invokes Christian universalism to overcome the "narrowness" or exclusivity of redemption conceived in national (and so narrowly political) terms. At the same time, he seeks redemption from the authority of the "internal priest" or bad conscience that he (like Nietzsche) associates with a "priestly nature." To "have their sins forgiven," he argues, "mankind needs only to declare them to be what they really are." As Nietzsche argues too, these sins "really" are aggression and inventiveness, or pride and poesis. Identifying with Prometheus, Marx "declares" their necessity for world-building in a universe without God.

27. Phillip Roth, *The Human Stain* (Boston: Houghton Mifflin, 2000).

28. Friedrich Nietzsche, "Epilogue," in *The Case of Wagner* (New York: Vintage, 1967), 191–92, and *The Anti-Christ* (Harmondsworth: Penguin, 1968).

29. Friedrich Nietzsche, *The Genealogy of Morals* (New York: Vintage, 1969), 96.

30. Friedrich Nietzsche, *Thus Spake Zarathustra*, trans. Walter Kaufman (New York: Viking, 1966), 141.

31. By suggesting these two paths from Nietzsche, I mean to complicate Fou-

cauldian readings of Nietzsche and his legacy, which are deconstructive (or "genealogical") and resolutely antipsychoanalytic.

32. For Stanley Cavell, philosophers are driven to metaphysics by the effort to defeat skepticism. Both skepticism and its "answer" drive people out of the ordinary world of language and its criteria, but skepticism can be addressed by showing how it makes a problem of knowledge out of a failure to acknowledge human finitude. Perhaps something parallel is true with respect to redemption: an effort to defeat it repeats the problem of deliverance, rather than acknowledging how an all-too-human aspiration for freedom can entail an all-too-human denial of finitude. Among his many texts, cf. Stanley Cavell, *The Claims of Reason* (New York: Oxford University Press, 1979).

CHAPTER 10

Acknowledgments: I would like to thank Talal Asad, Carrie Gibson, Ben Page, and Timothy Wilson for their critical engagement with earlier drafts of this text.

1. Asad, *Formations of the Secular*, 6.
2. Talal Asad, *Genealogies of Religion*; *Formations of the Secular*.
3. In particular, Ranajit Guha, ed., *Subaltern Studies: Writings on South Asian History and Society*, vols. 1–6 (Delhi: Oxford University Press, 1982–89); Florencia E. Mallon, "The Promise and Dilemma of Subaltern Studies: Perspectives from Latin American History," *American Historical Review* (1994): 1491–1515. James Scott's argument in *Weapons of the Weak: Everyday Forms of Peasant Resistance* (New Haven, CT: Yale University Press, 1985) has certain similarities, although it also shows significant differences from the position expounded by subaltern historians.
4. Gyan Prakash, "Can the Subaltern Ride? A Response to O'Hanlon and Washbrook," *Comparative Studies in Society and History*, 43, no. 1 (1992): 173; Gayatri Chakravarty Spivak, "Can the Subaltern Speak?" in Cary Nelson and Lawrence Grossberg (eds.), *Marxism and the Interpretation of Culture* (Urbana: University of Illinois Press, 1988), 271–313. A similar argument is made in the concluding chapter of Dipesh Chakrabarty's *Provincialising Europe: Postcolonial Thought and Historical Difference* (Princeton, NJ: Princeton University Press, 2000); and in his *Habitations of Modernity: Essays in the Wake of Subaltern Studies* (Delhi: Permanent Black, 2002).
5. My point is not to lament the "decline of the subaltern," as Sumit Sarkar does in "The Decline of the Subaltern in *Subaltern* Studies" in his *Writing Social History* (Delhi: Oxford University Press, 1997), 82–108, but simply to note the reasons for its decline. An exception seems to be in the history of India's indigenous or tribal populations. See Ajay Skaria, *Hybrid Histories: Forests, Frontiers and Wildness in Western India* (Delhi: Oxford University Press, 1999), for example.

6. Asad, *Genealogies of Religion*, 16.

7. For a more detailed discussion of the rebellion, see Jon E. Wilson, "'A Thousand Countries to Go To': Peasants in Rulers in Late Eighteenth-Century Bengal," *Past and Present*, no. 189 (2005).

8. Rosalind O'Hanlon, "Cultures of Rule, Communities of Resistance: Gender, Discourse and Tradition in Recent South Asian Historiographies," *Social Analysis* 25 (1989): 107–8.

9. The narrative in E. G. Glazier, "The District of Rangpur," in Walter K. Firminger, ed., *Bengal District Records, Rangpur*, Vol. 1: *1770–1779* (Calcutta, 1914), sees the rebels as having a legitimate cause but also asserts the necessity of the colonial state's imposition of law and order once it got "out of hand."

10. For the process by which landholders engaged in a series of marketlike transactions to attract cultivators to their land, see David L. Curley, "Kings and Commerce on an Agrarian Frontier: Kalketu's Story in Mukundu's *Candimangal*," *Indian Economic and Social History Review* 38, no. 3 (2001): 299–324; and Richard M. Eaton, *The Rise of Islam and the Bengal Frontier, 1204–1760* (Berkeley: University of California Press, 1993).

11. Quoted in Sukumar Sen, *History of Bengali Literature* (Delhi: Academic, 1979), 269. Sen's translation has been slightly modified.

12. See, for example, Ronald B. Inden's now very dated *Marriage and Rank in Bengali Culture: A History of Caste and Clan in Middle-Period Bengal* (Berkeley: University of California Press, 1978).

13. For expressions of the Company's absolute power, see Charles Boughton-Rouse, *Dissertation Concerning the Landed Property of Bengal* (Calcutta: Upjohn, 1791), 170; and letter from G. H. Barlow to Lord Cornwallis, 14 February 1794, Oriental and India Office Collection, British Library, IOR Pos 4211 [n.p.].

14. Existing accounts of the permanent settlement—and the debate that ensued—assume its origins *can* be attributed to a single causal agent. Ranajit Guha's *A Rule of Property for Bengal: An Essay on the Idea of Permanent Settlement* (Delhi: Orient Longman, 1963) argues that the reform was framed from a radical ideology imported from Britain and France. Ratnalekha Ray suggests it was a pragmatic response to preexisting Indian social relations in *Change in Bengal Agrarian Society, c. 1760–1820* (Delhi: Manohar, 1979).

15. Rudrangshu Mukherjee, *Awadh in Revolt, 1857–8: A Study in Popular Resistance* (New Delhi: Oxford, 1984). Mukherjee argues that the revolt in Awadh was instigated by the British destruction of a moral economy in which there was a symbiotic relationship between landholder and peasant.

16. I am relying here on Talal Asad's reading of Reinhard Koselleck's account of the temporality of modernity in *Futures Past: On the Semantics of Historical Time* (Cambridge, MA, MIT Press, 1984). Asad, *Formations of the Secular*, 192–93.

17. Partha Chatterjee, *The Nation and Its Fragments* (Princeton, NJ: Princeton University Press, 1993), 12.

18. In his *Another Reason: Science and the Imagination of Modern India* (Princeton, NJ: Princeton University Press, 1999), Gyan Prakash makes this point about Indian's "different modernity" while criticizing aspects of Chatterjee's argument.

19. Chatterjee, *The Nation and Its Fragments*, 13, 234–39.

20. Michel Foucault, "Two Lectures," in Michael Kelly, ed., *Critique and Power: Recasting the Foucault/Habermas Debate* (Cambridge, Mass: MIT Press, 1994), 34–35, 36.

21. Jürgen Habermas, "Critique of Reason," in ibid., 64. The mistake Habermas makes in his interpretation of Foucault (and Heidegger) is to presuppose that just because Foucault rejects the sovereign individual as the locus of truth and power, he must have replaced it with a transcendent subject somewhere else.

22. Michel Foucault, *The History of Sexuality*, vol. 1: *An Introduction* (London: Pelican Books, 1981), 95.

23. See Chatterjee, *The Nation and Its Fragments*, 27–34; Nicholas B. Dirks, *Castes of Mind: Colonialism and the Making of Modern India* (Princeton, NJ: Princeton University Press, 2001), 303–16; C. A. Bayly, *Indian Society and the Making of the British Empire* (Cambridge: Cambridge University Press, 1988); and D. A. Washbrook, "Progress and Problems: South Asian Economic and Social History, c. 1720–1860," *Modern Asian Studies* 22, no. 1 (1988).

24. See, for example, Dirks, *Castes of Mind.*

25. E. M. Collinham, *Imperial Bodies* (London: Polity, 2001); Jon E. Wilson, "Taking Europe for Granted" (review article), *History Workshop Journal* 50 (2001); Catherine Hall, *Civilizing Subjects: Metropole and Colony in the English Imagination, 1830–1867* (London: Polity, 2002).

26. Gary Wilder and Albert Memmi, "Irreconcilable Differences," *Transition* 71 (1996): 160. See also Frantz Fanon, *The Wretched of the Earth* (New York: Grove, 1963); Albert Memmi, *The Colonizer and the Colonized* (London: Beacon, 1965); Ashis Nandy, *The Intimate Enemy: Loss and Recovery of Self under Colonialism* (Delhi: Oxford University Press, 1983); Ann Laura Stoler, "Rethinking Colonial Categories: European Communities and the Boundaries of Rule," *Comparative Studies in Society and History* 31, no. 1 (1989): 134–61.

27. Asad, *Formations of the Secular*, 216–17.

28. Ibid., 25.

29. For example, ibid., 24–25.

30. Ibid., 161.

31. Ibid., 165.

32. One could contrast Hugh Trevor-Roper's *The Rise of Christian Europe* (London: Thames and Hudson, 1965), which Asad discusses in *Formations of the Secular* (166), with Norman Davies, *Europe: A History* (London: Pimlico, 1997). Trevor-Roper narrates the emergence of a Christian European identity by focusing on Britain, France, and Germany. Davies asserts the centrality of Eastern Europe, especially Poland.

33. Elisabeth Bumiller, "Praising Alliance, Bush asks Europe to Work with US," *New York Times*, 1 June 2003; "President Putin: Together, Russia and the EU Will Make Europe Secure," *Pravda*, English edition, 31 June 2003.

34. My argument here is indebted to William E. Connolly, *Identity | Difference: Democratic Negotiations of Political Paradox* (Minneapolis: University of Minnesota Press, 1991).

35. William E. Connolly, *Identity | Difference*, 173.

36. Asad, *Formations of the Secular*, 178. Intriguingly, an argument similar to this was espoused by British Labour politicians from Scotland soon after the 1997 general election. See Gordon Brown and Douglas Alexander, *New Britain, New Scotland* (London: John Smith Institute, 1998).

APPENDIX

Acknowledgments: This interview took place in New York, May 29–30, 2003. I am very grateful to Talal Asad for patience throughout. I would also like to thank Suren Pillay for transcribing the audiotapes.

1. Ruth Benedict, *Patterns of Culture* (New York: Houghton Mifflin, 1934).

2. Alfred Reginald Radcliffe-Brown (1881–1955), a powerful shaping influence on British social anthropology, was the author of many important books, including *A Natural Science of Society* (Glencoe: Free Press, 1957).

3. S. F. Nadel (1903–1956) was a scholar of the Nupe and the author of such books as *A Black Byzantium: The Kingdom of Nupe in Nigeria* (London: Oxford University Press, 1942), in addition to *The Foundations of Social Anthropology* (Glencoe: New Press, 1951).

4. Edward Evan Evans-Pritchard (1902–1973) was famously the editor with Meyer Fortes of *African Political Systems* (London: Oxford University Press, 1940), and the author of many books, including *The Nuer* (Oxford: Clarendon Press, 1940) and *The Sanusi of Cyrenaica* (Oxford: Clarendon Press, 1954).

5. See David F. Pocock, *Kanbi and Patidar: A Study of the Patidar Community of Gujarat* (Oxford: Clarendon, 1972).

6. See E. E. Evans-Pritchard, *A History of Anthropological Thought*, ed. André Singer (New York: Basic Books, 1981).

7. Rodney Needham is the author of a large number of books, including *Structure and Sentiment: A Test Case in Social Anthropology* (Chicago: University of Chicago Press, 1962); Fredrik Barth is the author of such studies as *Political Leadership among Swat Pathans* (New York: Athlone Press, 1965).

8. Arnold van Gennep (1873–1957), *The Rites of Passage*, trans. Monika B. Vizedom and Gabrielle L. Caffee (Chicago: University of Chicago Press, 1960).

9. Michael Banton is perhaps best known for his studies of race relations in Britain. One of his early books was *The Coloured Quarter: Negro Immigrants in an English City* (London: Cape, 1955).

10. Talal Asad, *The Kababish Arabs: Power, Authority and Consent in a Nomadic Tribe* (London: Christopher Hurst, 1970).

11. See Talal Asad, "Political Inequality in the Kababish Tribe," in Ian Cunnison and Wendy James (eds.), *Essays in Sudan Ethnography Presented to Sir Edward Evans-Pritchard* (London: Christopher Hurst, 1972).

12. On Wittgenstein's *Blue and Brown Books* and their relation to his *Philosophical Investigations* and philosophical development generally, see Ray Monk's splendid work, *Ludwig Wittgenstein: The Duty of Genius* (London: J. Cape, 1990).

13. A. J. Ayer, *Language, Truth, and Logic* (London: Gollancz, 1936). Ayer was a philosopher at Oxford whose famous paper on Wittgenstein's *Tractatus* is often credited with stimulating the positivist revolt against the metaphysical philosophers. For a fascinating reflection on Austin, Ayer, and Oxford Philosophy, see Isaiah Berlin, "Austin and the Early Beginnings of Oxford Philosophy," in G. J. Warnock (ed.), *Essays on J. L. Austin* (Oxford: Clarendon Press, 1973).

14. R. G. Collingwood (1889–1943), *The Principles of Art* (London: Oxford University Press, 1958).

15. The reference is to David Scott, *Refashioning Futures: Criticism after Postcoloniality* (Princeton, NJ: Princeton University Press, 1999), and *Conscripts of Modernity: The Tragedy of Colonial Enlightenment* (Durham, NC: Duke University Press, 2004).

16. Asad, *The Kababish Arabs*, 207.

17. On the *Universities and Left Review*, see Stuart Hall, "The 'First' New Left: Life and Times," in Oxford University Socialist Group (ed.), *Out of Apathy: Voices of the New Left Thirty Years On* (London: Verso, 1989).

18. See, for example, Stuart Hall and Tony Jefferson (eds.), *Resistance through Rituals: Youth Subcultures in Post-War Britain* (London: Hutchinson, 1976).

19. Stuart Hall et al. (eds.), *Culture, Media, and Language: Working Papers in Cultural Studies, 1972–79* (London: Hutchinson, 1980), 18, 23.

20. Asad, *The Kababish Arabs*, 10n.1.

21. Talal Asad, "Anthropological Texts and Ideological Problems: An Analysis of Cohen on Arab Villages in Israel," *Review of Middle East Studies* 1 (1975): 1–40, and *Economy and Society* 4, no. 3 (1975): 251–82.

22. Talal Asad (ed.), *Anthropology and the Colonial Encounter* (London: Ithaca Press, 1973).

23. See Abdel-Ghaffar M. Ahmed, "Some Remarks from the Third World on Anthropology and Colonialism: The Sudan," in Asad (ed.), *Anthropology and the Colonial Encounter*, 259–70.

24. Asad, *Anthropology and the Colonial Encounter*.

25. Edward Said, *Orientalism* (New York: Random House, 1978). See Asad's "short notice" of it in *English Historical Review* 45 (1980): 648–49.

26. Talal Asad, "Anthropology and the Analysis of Ideology," *Man* (n.s.) 14 (1979): 607–27.

27. Asad, "Anthropological Texts and Ideological Problems," *Economy and Society* 4, no. 3 (1975): 251.

28. Asad, "Anthropology and the Analysis of Ideology," 607.

29. V. N. Voloshinov, *Marxism and the Philosophy of Language* (New York: Seminar Press, 1973).

30. Sulayman Bashir, *The Balance of Contradictions: Lectures in Pre-Islamic and Early Islamic History* [in Arabic] (Jerusalem, 1978).

31. See Asad, *Genealogies of Religion*, 89.

32. See Clifford Geertz, "The Strange Estrangement: Taylor and the Natural Sciences," in James Tully (ed.), *Philosophy in an Age of Pluralism: The Philosophy of Charles Taylor in Question* (Cambridge: Cambridge University Press, 1994). He writes: "Those who, like myself, find the argument that the human sciences are most usefully conceived as efforts to render various matters on their face strange and puzzling (religious beliefs, political practices, self-definitions) 'no longer so, accounted for,' to be altogether persuasive" (83–84).

33. See Asad, "Market, Model, Class Structure and Consent: A Consideration of Swat Political Organization," *Man* 7, no. 1 (1972): 74–94; reprinted in Joan Vincent (ed.), *Readings in Political Anthropology* (Oxford: Blackwell, 2002).

34. See Asad, "Ideology, Class, and the Origin of the Islamic State," *Economy and Society* 9, no. 4 (1980): 450–73.

35. Clifford Geertz, "Religion as a Cultural System," in *The Interpretation of Cultures* (New York: Basic Books, 1973); and Asad, "Anthropological Conceptions of Religion: Reflections on Geertz," *Man* (n.s.) 18, no. 2 (1983): 237–59.

36. Wilfred Cantwell Smith, *The Meaning and End of Religion: A New Approach to the Religious Traditions of Mankind* (New York: Macmillan, 1963); Asad, "Re-reading a Modern Classic: W. C. Smith's *The Meaning and End of Religion*," *History of Religions* 40, no. 3 (2001): 205–22.

37. See Margaret Canovan, "On Being Economical with the Truth: Some Liberal Reflections," *Political Studies* 38 (1990).

38. See Carl Schmitt, *Political Theology: Four Chapters on the Concept of Sovereignty*, trans. George Schwab (Cambridge, MA: MIT Press, 1985).

39. William E. Connolly, *Neuropolitics: Thinking, Culture, Speed* (Minneapolis: University of Minnesota Press, 2002).

40. See especially Alasdair MacIntyre, *After Virtue: A Study in Moral Theory* (Notre Dame, IN: University of Notre Dame Press, 1984).

41. Talal Asad, "Conscripts of Western Civilization," in Christine Gailey (ed.), *Dialectical Anthropology: Essays in Honor of Stanley Diamond*, Vol. 1: *Civilization in Crisis: Anthropological Perspectives* (Tallahasse: University Press of Florida, 1992),

333–51; and "Are There Histories of Peoples without Europe?" *Comparative Studies in Society and History* 29, no. 3 (1987): 594–607.

42. Bernard Lewis, *What Went Wrong? Western Impact and Middle Eastern Response* (New York: Oxford University Press, 2002).

43. See David Scott, *Conscripts of Modernity*.

44. Asad writes in *Formations of the Secular*: "But precisely for this reason, because the secular is so much a part of our modern life, it is not easy to grasp it directly. I think it is best pursued through its shadows, as it were" (16).

45. See Tariq Ali, *The Clash of Fundamentalisms: Crusades, Jihad, and Modernity* (London: Verso, 2002).

46. Asad, *The Idea of an Anthropology of Islam*, Occasional Paper Series (Washington, D.C.: Center for Contemporary Studies, Georgetown University, 1986).

Talal Asad: A Bibliography

Compiled by Zainab Saleh

BOOKS

The Kababish Arabs: Power, Authority and Consent in a Nomadic Tribe (London: Hurst, 1970).
Genealogies of Religion: Discipline and Reasons of Power in Christianity and Islam (Baltimore, MD: Johns Hopkins University Press, 1993).
Formations of the Secular: Christianity, Islam, Modernity (Stanford, CA: Stanford University Press, 2003).

BOOKS EDITED

Anthropology and the Colonial Encounter (London: Ithaca Press; New York: Humanities Press, 1973).
Sociology of "Developing Societies": The Middle East (New York: Monthly Review Press, 1983), co-editor and contributor (with Roger Owen).

PRINCIPAL ARTICLES

"Seasonal Movements of the Kababish Arabs of Northern Kordofan," *Sudan Notes and Records: Incorporating Proceedings of the Philosophical Society of the Sudan*, vol. 45 (Khartoum, Philosophical Society of the Sudan, 1964), 49–58.
"Settlement of Nomads in the Sudan: A Critique of Present Plans," with I. Cunnison and L. Hill, *Proceedings of the Thirteenth Annual Conference, December 3–6, 1965: Agricultural Development in the Sudan*, ed. D. J. Shaw, vol. 1 (Khartoum: Philosophical Society of the Sudan, 1966), 102–25.
"A Note on the History of the Kababish Tribe," *Sudan Notes and Records: Incorporating Proceedings of the Philosophical Society of the Sudan*, vol. XLVII (Khartoum: Philosophical Society of the Sudan, 1966), 79–87.
"Market Model, Class Structure and Consent: A Reconsideration of Swat Political Organization," *Man* (n.s.) 7, no. 1 (1972): 74–94; *The Anthropology of Politics: A Reader in Ethnography, Theory, and Critique*, ed. Joan Vincent (Oxford: Oxford University Press, Blackwell Publishers, 2002), 65–82.

"Political Inequality in the Kababish Tribe," in *Essays in Sudan Ethnography Presented to Sir Edward Evans-Prichard*, ed. Ian Cunnison and Wendy James (London: Christopher Hurst & Company, 1972), 126–48.

"Introduction," in *Anthropology and the Colonial Encounter*, ed. Talal Asad (London: Ithaca Press; New York: Humanities Press, 1973), 9–19.

"The Bedouin as Military Force: Notes on Some Aspects of Power Relations between Nomads and Sedentaries in Historical Perspective," in *The Desert and the Sown: Nomads in Wider Society*, Research Series 21, ed. Cynthia Nelson (Berkeley: University of California, Institute of International Studies, 1973), 61–73.

"Two European Images of Non-European Rule," in *Anthropology and the Colonial Encounter*, ed. Talal Asad (London: Ithaca Press; New York: Humanities Press, 1973), 103–18; *Economy and Society* 2, no. 3 (1973): 263–77.

"The Concept of Rationality in Economic Anthropology," *Economy and Society* 3, no. 2 (1974): 211–18.

"Anthropological Texts and Ideological Problems: An Analysis of Cohen on Arab Villages in Israel," *Economy and Society* 4, no. 3 (1975): 251–82; *Review of Middle East Studies*, no. 1 (1975): 1–40; as "Class Transformation under the Mandate," *Middle East Research and Information Project Reports*, no. 53 (1976), 2–8, 23.

"The Rise of Arab Nationalism: A Comment," in *Israel and the Palestinians*, ed. Uri Davis, Andrew Mack, and Nira Yuval-Davis (London: Ithaca Press, 1975), 93–96.

"Concepts of Modes of Production," with Harold Wolpe, *Economy and Society* 5, no. 4 (1976): 471–506.

"Politics and Religion in Islamic Reform: a Critique of Kedourie's Afghani and Abduh," *Review of Middle East Studies*, no. 2 (1976): 13–22.

"Equality in Nomadic Social Systems? Notes towards the Dissolution of an Anthropological Category," *Critique of Anthropology* 3, no. 11 (1978): 57–65; in *Pastoral Production and Society*, ed. L'Equipe écologie et anthropologie des sociétés pastorales (Cambridge: Cambridge University Press, 1979), 419–28.

"Anthropology and the Analysis of Ideology," *Man* (n.s.) 14, no. 4 (1979): 607–27 (translated into Italian and reprinted in *Materiali Filosofici*, no. 3, 1980).

"The Critique of Orientalism: A Reply to Professor Dodd," with Roger Owen, *Bulletin (British Society for Middle Eastern Studies)* 7, no. 1 (1980): 33–38.

"Ideology, Class and the Origin of the Islamic State," *Economy and Society* 9, no. 4 (1980): 450–73 (translated into Arabic and republished in *Al-Mustaqbal Al-Arabi*, no. 22, 1980).

"Indigenous Anthropology in Non-Western Countries: A Further Elaboration," *Current Anthropology* 21, no. 5 (1980): 661–63; as "A Comment on the Idea of a Non-Western Anthropology," in *Indigenous Anthropology in Non-Western Countries: Proceedings of a Burg Wartenstein Symposium*, ed. Hussein Fahim (Durham, NC: Carolina Academic Press, 1982), 284–88.

"Short Notices," on Edward Said's *Orientalism*, *English Historical Review*, vol. 45 (1980): 648–49.

"The Middle East: An Anthropological Approach," *International Journal of Middle Eastern Studies* 14, no. 1 (1982): 102–3.

"Anthropological Conceptions of Religion: Reflections on Geertz," *Man* (n.s.) 18, no. 2 (1983): 237–59 (translated into Arabic and republished in *Kitabat Mu'asira* 7, no. 28, 1996).

"General Introduction," with Roger Owen, in *Sociology of "Developing Societies": The Middle East*, ed. Talal Asad and Roger Owen (New York: Monthly Review Press, 1983), 1–5.

Introductions to Part I, II, and III, with Roger Owen, in *Sociology of "Developing Societies": The Middle East*, ed. Talal Asad and Roger Owen (New York, Monthly Review Press, 1983), 7–15, 69–76, 159–63.

"Notes on Body Pain and Truth in Medieval Christian Ritual," *Economy and Society* 12, no. 3 (1983): 287–327 (translated into Italian and republished in *Potere Senza Stato*, ed. C. Pasquinelli, Rome, 1986).

"Primitive States and the Reproduction of Production Relations: Some Problems in Marxist Anthropology," in *On Social Evolution: Contributions to Anthropological Concepts: Proceedings of the Symposium Held on the Occasion of the Fiftieth Anniversary of the Wiener Institute fur Volkerkunde in Vienna, 12th-16th December 1979*, ed. Walter Dostal (Horn-Wien: F. Berger & Sohne, 1984), 93–109; *Critique of Anthropology* 5, no. 2 (1985): 21–33.

"Translating Europe's Others," with John Dixon, in *Europe and Its Others*, vol. 1: Proceedings of the Essex Conference on the Sociology of Literature, ed. F. Barker (Colchester: Essex University Press, 1985), 170–77.

"The Concept of Cultural Translation in British Social Anthropology," *Writing Culture: The Poetics and Politics of Ethnography*, ed. James Clifford and George E. Marcus (Berkeley: University of California Press, 1986), 141–64 (translated into German and republished in *Kultur, Soziale Praxis, Text*, ed. by E. Berg and M. Fuchs, Suhrkamp, 1993).

"The Idea of an Anthropology of Islam," Occasional Papers Series (Washington D.C.: Georgetown University for Contemporary Arab Studies, 1986).

"Medieval Heresy: An Anthropological View," *Social History* 11, no. 3 (1986): 354–62.

"Religion, Power, and Protest in Local Communities: The Northern Shore of the Mediterranean," *American Ethnologist* 13, no. 1 (1986): 164–66.

"Are There Histories of Peoples without Europe?" *Comparative Studies in Society and History* 29, no. 3 (1987): 594–607.

"On Ritual and Discipline in Medieval Christian Monasticism," *Economy and Society* 16, no. 2 (1987): 159–203.

"Towards a Genealogy of the Concept of Ritual," in *Vernacular Christianity: Essays in the Social Anthropology of Religion Presented to Godfrey Lienhardt*, Occasional Papers 7, ed. W. James and D. M. Johnson (Oxford: JASO, 1988), 73–87.

"Ethnography, Literature, and Politics: Some Readings and Uses of Salman Rushdie's *The Satanic Verses*," *Cultural Anthropology* 5, no. 3 (1990): 239–69.

"Multiculturalism and British Identity in the Wake of the Rushdie Affair," *Politics and Society* 18, no. 4 (1990): 455–80.

"From the History of Colonial Anthropology to the Anthropology of Western Hegemony," in *Colonial Situations: Essays in the Contextualization of Ethnographic Knowledge*, ed. George Stocking (Madison: University of Wisconsin Press, 1991), 314–24.

"Conscripts of Western Civilization," in *Dialectical Anthropology: Essays in Honor of Stanley Diamond*, Vol. 1: *Civilization in Crisis: Anthropological Perspectives*, ed. Christine Ward Gailey (Tallahassee: University Press of Florida, 1992), 333–51.

"Religion and Politics: An Introduction," *Social Research* 59, no. 1 (1992): 3–16.

"A Comment on Aijaz Ahmad's *In Theory*," *Public Culture* 6, no. 1 (1993): 31–39.

"Ethnographic Representation, Statistics and Modern Power," *Social Research* 61, no. 1 (1994): 55–88.

"Europe Against Islam: Islam in Europe" (in Dutch), *Nexus* 10 (1994); *The Muslim World* 87, no. 2 (1997): 183–96.

"A Comment on Translation, Critique, and Subversion," in *Between Languages and Cultures: Translation and Cross-Cultural Texts*, ed. Anuradh Dingwaney and Carol Maier (Pittsburgh: University of Pittsburgh Press, 1995), 325–32.

"Comments on Conversion," in *Conversion to Modernities: The Globalization of Christianity*, ed. Peter van der Veer (New York: Routledge, 1995), 263–74.

"Ideology and Cultural Identity: Modernity and the Third World Presence," *American Ethnologist* 22, no. 4 (1995): 1013–14.

"Honor," *Journal of the American Oriental Society* 116, no. 2 (1996): 308–9.

"On Torture, or Cruel, Inhumane, and Degrading Treatment," *Social Research* 63, no. 4 (1996), 1081–109; in *Social Suffering*, ed. Arthur Kleinman, Veena Das, and Margaret Lock (Berkeley: University of California Press, 1997), 285–305; in *Human Rights, Culture and Context*, ed. Richard Wilson (London; Chicago: Pluto Press, 1997), 111–33.

"Provocations of European Ethnology," *American Anthropologist* 99, no. 4 (1997): 713–30.

"Remarks on the Anthropology of the Body," in *Religion and the Body: Comparative Perspectives on Devotional Practices*, ed. Sarah Coakley (Cambridge: University of Cambridge Press, 1997), 42–52.

"Religion, Nation State, Secularism," in *Nation and Religion: Perspectives on Europe and Asia*, ed. Peter van der Veer and Hartmut Lehmann (Princeton, NJ: Princeton University Press, 1999), 178–96.

"Agency and Pain: An Exploration," *Culture and Religion* 1, no. 1 (2000): 29–60.

"Muslims and European Identity: Can Europe Represent Islam?" in *Cultural Encounters: Representing 'Otherness,'* ed. Elizabeth Hallam and Brian V. Street (New York: Routledge, 2000), 11–27; in *The Idea of Europe: From Antiquity to the European Union*, ed. Anthony Pagden (Cambridge: Cambridge University Press, 2002), 209–27.

"What Do Human Rights Do? An Anthropological Enquiry," *Theory and Event* (online journal) 4, no. 4 (2000).

"Reading a Modern Classic: W. C. Smith's *The Meaning and End of Religion*," *History of Religion* 40, no. 3 (2001): 205–22; in *Religion and Media*, ed. Hent de Vries and Samuel Weber (Stanford, CA: Stanford University Press, 2001), 131–47.

"Thinking about Secularism and Law in Egypt," Occasional Papers Series (Leiden: Isim, 2001).

"Boundaries and Rights in Islamic Law: Introduction," *Social Research* 70, no. 3 (2003): 683–86.

"Kinship," entry for *Encyclopedia of the Qur'an*, ed. Jane MacAuliffe, vol. 3 (Leiden: Brill, 2003), 95–100.

"Where Are the Margins of the State?" in *The State and Its Margins*, ed. Veena Das and Deborah Poole (Santa Fe, NM: School of American Research Press, forthcoming).

PERIODICALS EDITED

Full-time joint editor (1974–92), *Economy and Society*, published by Routledge, London.

Founded and edited, together with Roger Owen, the first three volumes (1975–78) of the *Review of Middle East Studies*, published by Ithaca Press, London.

Guest editor of special issue of *Social Research*, "Politics and Religion" (59, no. 1), published by New School for Social Research, New York.

INTERVIEWS

An interview in *Conference: A Journal of Philosophy and Theory* 5, no. 1 (1994).

"Modern Power and the Reconfiguration of Religious Traditions," an interview by Saba Mahmood, *Stanford Humanities Review* 5, no. 1 (Stanford, CA: Stanford University Press, 1995): 1–16.

An interview in *Al-'almaniyya wa-l-mumana'a al-islamiyya: Muhawarat fi al-nahda wa-l-hadatha* [Secularism and the Islamic Opposition to It: Conversations on the Arab Revival and Modernity], ed. Ali al-Imayr (London: Saqi Books, 1999).

"*Majallat al-'ulum al-ijtima'iyyah*" (in Arabic), *Journal of the Social Sciences* 29, no. 1 (2000).

AsiaSource [online publication of Asia Society], available at *www.asiasource.org/news/specialreports/asad.cfm,* December 16, 2002.

Contributors

Talal Asad is Distinguished Professor of Anthropology at the Graduate Center, City University of New York. He is the author of *The Kababish Arabs* (1970), *Genealogies of Religion* (1993), and *Formations of the Secular* (2003), and the editor of *Anthropology and the Colonial Encounter* (1973).

José Casanova is Professor of Sociology at the New School University. He is the author of *Public Religions in the Modern World* (1994) and *The Opus Dei and the Modernization of Spain* (forthcoming).

Steven C. Caton is Professor of Anthropology and Contemporary Arab Studies and Director of the Center for Middle Eastern Studies at Harvard University. His most recent book is *Lawrence of Arabia: A Film's Anthropology* (1999).

Partha Chatterjee is Director of the Centre for Studies in Social Sciences, Calcutta, and Professor of Anthropology at Columbia University, New York. He is the author of many books, including *Nationalist Thought and the Colonial World* (1986), *The Nation and Its Fragments* (1993), and most recently, *The Politics of the Governed* (2004).

William E. Connolly is Krieger-Eisenhower Professor of Political Science at the Johns Hopkins University. He is the author of several books, including *The Ethos of Pluralization* (1995), *Why I Am Not a Secularist* (1999), and *Neuropolitics: Thinking, Culture, Speed* (2002).

Veena Das is Krieger-Eisenhower Professor of Anthropology at the Johns Hopkins University. She has written extensively on the themes of violence, social suffering, and the linkages between urban poverty and health. She is a Foreign Fellow of the American Academy of Arts and Sciences. Currently she also serves on the Governing Board of the International Center of Ethic Studies, Colombo, and the Institute for Socio-Economic Research on Development and Democracy, Delhi.

Hent de Vries is Professor in the Humanities Center and in the Department of Philosophy at Johns Hopkins University. He is the author of *Philosophy and the Turn to Religion* (1999, 2000), *Religion and Violence: Philosophical Perspectives from Kant to Derrida* (2001), and of *Minimal Theologies: Critiques of Secular Reason in Theodor W. Adorno and Emmanuel Levinas* (2005). He is the editor (with Samuel Weber) of *Religion and Media* (2001).

Charles Hirschkind is Assistant Professor of Anthropology at the University of California, Berkeley. He is the author of *The Ethics of Listening: Media, Affect, and the Islamic Revival* (2006).

Zainab Saleh is a Ph.D. student in the Anthropology Department at Columbia University. Her research focuses on issues of nationalism, identity, and governance in relation to the interaction and networks among Shiites in Iran and Iraq.

David Scott teaches at Columbia University, where he is Professor of Anthropology. He is the author most recently of *Conscripts of Modernity: The Tragedy of Colonial Enlightenment* (2004) and is the editor of the journal *Small Axe*.

George Shulman is an Associate Professor in the Gallatin School of Individualized Study at New York University. He works in the areas of political thought and American studies, and his second book, *Prophecy and Redemption in American Political Culture*, is forthcoming from the University of Minnesota Press.

Jon E. Wilson teaches history at King's College, London. He has written on peasant politics in early colonial Bengal, on law in South Asia, and more broadly on the historiography of the British Empire. He is writing a book on law and government in early colonial Bengal entitled *The Making of a Colonial Order: Government and Its Objects in Bengal, 1780–1835.*

Index

Abduh, Muhammad, 228
Adorno, Theodor, 115, 124
Advani, L. K., 63, 64
Africa, 61, 62, 114, 181, 236, 238, 308n32
Agamben, Giorgio: on bare life, 95, 98, 224
agency: Asad on, 9–10, 135, 137, 148–51, 180, 182–83, 189, 197–203, 204, 204–5, 233, 239–40, 287–88, 295–96, 300–301; of colonial officials, 185, 186, 187–92, 194, 196–97; of Indian landholders, 185, 186–87, 191, 239; individual vs. collective, 181, 183, 194; Kant on, 80–81, 150, 151, 322n42; in Rangpur peasant revolt of 1783, 184–92, 239; and redemption, 166, 177–78; relationship to contingency, 189, 197–98, 203–4; relationship to politics, 183, 202–5; relationship to power, 187, 189, 190, 194–98, 202, 204; relationship to responsibility, 149–51, 202–4, 233, 240; of the state, 191–93, 197; and structure, 7–8, 146; of subalterns, 181–82, 184–86, 187, 189, 192–94, 196–97, 201, 239; vs. subjectivity, 183, 186, 189, 192–94, 195–96, 197–98, 199–202, 203–5, 239–41; subjects as making own history, 152, 180, 181–82, 190, 202; and tragic drama, 145–46
Ahmed, Abdel-Ghaffar, 261
Althusser, Louis, 256, 263, 290
anthropology: Asad on, 2–3, 4, 5–7, 10, 32–33, 116, 117, 132, 139–40, 145, 183, 206–7, 210–11, 215–16, 220, 224, 231, 243–47, 251, 256–79, 281, 282, 283, 289–90, 295, 299, 301, 320n12; concept of culture in, 4–5, 7, 8, 9, 10, 38, 39–41, 75, 76, 215, 243, 244, 256–57, 275, 289; ethnographic writing, 4–5; ethnoscience/cognitive anthropology, 38; and Marxism, 7–8, 40, 41, 255–56; relationship to colonialism, 2–3, 257–60, 269, 283; relationship to history, 245; in United Kingdom, 2–3, 243–47, 249, 254, 256–60, 267–68, 274, 329n2; in United States, 4–5, 243, 244, 259
Arendt, Hannah: on authority, 212; on democracy, 237, 238; on forgiveness, 325n20; on natality, 175; *On Revolution,* 323n15; on redemption, 161, 163, 167, 169
Aron, Raymond, 132
Asad, Talal: on agency, 9–10, 135, 137, 148–51, 180, 182–83, 189, 197–203, 204, 204–5, 233, 239–40, 287–88, 295–96, 300–301; and Althusser, 256, 257, 263, 290; on anthropology, 2–3, 4, 5–7, 10, 32–33, 116, 117, 132, 139–40, 145, 183, 206–7, 210–11, 215–16, 220, 224, 231, 243–47, 251, 256–79, 281, 282, 283, 289–90, 295, 299, 301, 320n12; on authorizing discourse, 32, 33–34, 35, 42–45, 50, 54, 56, 176, 179, 211–14, 270, 272; and Bakhtin/Voloshinov, 51–54, 269–70; and Begriffsgeschichte School, 101; on St.

Bernard, 212, 280–81; on Canovan, 156–57, 235–36, 283; on capitalism, 231, 232, 238, 240, 250, 274, 285, 294, 301; on Casanova, 12–15, 20, 207–10; on Caton, 210–16; on Chatterjee, 216–20; on Christianity, 6–7, 8, 32, 35, 77, 79, 140, 157, 211, 212, 213, 234–35, 236, 238, 272, 279, 280–82, 283–85, 287, 291, 299; on citizenship, 93–94, 102, 112, 219, 222, 223, 225, 228, 278, 291, 295; on cognitivism, 35–38, 214, 287; and Collingwood, 253, 296, 297; on colonialism and imperialism, 2–4, 140, 180, 197–98, 199, 228, 244, 254–55, 257–61, 269, 282, 283, 291, 292–93; on complex space and time, 132, 133–34; on Connolly, 220–24, 288, 312n9; on contingency, 228, 234, 240, 295; on Das, 224–29; on de Vries/Levinas, 229–32; on discipline, 8, 9–10, 35, 77, 154, 157, 159, 178, 221–22, 234–35, 277–78, 286, 299; in Edinburgh, 244, 245–46, 247, 248, 251–52; on Egypt, 60, 102, 198–99, 228, 299; on embodiment, 7–10, 34, 35, 77, 92, 132, 135, 150–51, 212, 214, 220, 270, 287–89, 299; on the Enlightenment, 1, 21, 101, 136, 210, 264; on Europe, 10, 76, 78–79, 139, 200–202, 217–20, 230–31, 232, 282, 294, 328n32; on faith and belief, 77–79, 211; and Foucault, 8, 15, 32, 35, 82, 137, 138–40, 145, 227–28, 233–34, 239, 257, 258, 270–71, 273, 275, 286, 295; on France, 208, 209, 217–20, 223, 227–28, 255; on functionalism, 2–3, 4, 212; on Geertz, 6–7, 32, 33–42, 44, 139–40, 210–13, 214–15, 275, 279, 280, 282, 287, 289, 291; on Gellner, 5; as genealogist, 15, 20–21, 28–29, 79, 80, 101, 131, 135, 137, 138–40, 145, 146, 148–49, 180, 204, 210–12, 233–35, 320n5; and *habitus*, 136, 137, 150–51, 234, 235, 288–89, 322n39; on Hegel's philosophy of history, 21, 101, 210; on historical change, 295–97; on Hugh of St. Victor, 213, 280; on human rights, 9, 24, 28–29, 94, 95, 156, 224–26, 229, 236; on ideology, 1, 2–3, 135–36, 154, 178, 212, 249, 258–59, 263–75, 290, 298; on Islam, 8, 10, 23, 32, 42–44, 76, 77–79, 140, 212, 226, 232, 271–72, 278, 279, 282, 291–92, 293–94, 299, 300, 303; on Kant, 80, 220; at Khartoum University, 246, 248–49, 305n3; on knowledge formation and disciplines, 276–78, 281, 289; on law, 94, 102, 180, 198–99, 209, 217, 225–28, 294–95, 299, 301, 302; on liberalism, 10, 27, 28–29, 154, 156–59, 209–10, 223, 228, 236–37, 283, 290, 291, 294; and MacIntyre, 8, 137, 140–41, 145, 233, 234–35, 255, 286, 288–89; and Marxism, 7–8, 135–36, 249, 250, 255–56, 257, 264, 265–66, 268, 274, 278, 279, 290, 298, 320n12; and Mauss, 8, 117, 133, 222, 272; on Middle East, 245, 253, 254, 255, 260, 261–63, 264, 265, 266, 271, 278, 279, 282, 291, 292, 293, 303; and Milbank, 132; on modernity, 116, 135, 154, 155–57, 239–40, 274, 288, 291–95, 302, 303, 332n44; on Muslim minorities in Europe, 10, 78–79, 200–201, 217–20, 232, 294; on myth, 154, 155–57, 283–85; on nature, 21, 101, 112, 156–57, 224–26; on obedience, 212, 221–22, 272, 280–81; on Orientalism, 4, 273, 278, 279; at Oxford University, 245, 246–47, 248, 249, 252–53, 255; on pain, 8–9, 137, 180, 212, 221–22, 233, 280, 287, 290–91; and Peirce, 37; on pluralism, 79, 80, 92, 220; on poetry, 155–56, 157; on politics, 2–3, 10, 14, 59–60, 78–79, 93–94, 102, 104, 112, 136, 154, 158–59, 176, 178, 179, 180, 207, 210, 217–20, 222, 223–28, 229, 235, 236–39, 240–41, 248–49, 250–51, 253–56, 258, 264, 266–67, 277, 278, 279, 285, 291–92, 294–95, 299–300,

301; and poststructuralism, 4, 7, 136, 258, 259; on power, 5, 6, 7, 8–9, 10, 35, 41–42, 52, 139, 154, 158–59, 176, 178, 179, 198, 212–14, 254–55, 270–73, 281, 291, 293; on practice, 7–8, 9, 38, 41, 42–45, 52, 56, 59–60, 76, 77–79, 84–85, 86, 88, 92, 93, 132, 140, 154, 157, 178, 215, 221, 228, 234–35, 256; on prophets, 155; on rationality, 136–37, 249, 253, 265–66, 274; on redemption, 155, 156–59, 176, 178, 235–39; relationship with Evans-Pritchard, 245, 246–47, 250–51; on religion, 5–7, 12–15, 23–24, 32–36, 41–42, 56, 59, 75–76, 78–79, 116, 132, 135, 139–40, 154, 180, 210–16, 221, 223, 231–32, 240, 271–72, 278–87, 297–300, 320n11; on Renaissance humanism, 21, 101, 210; on responsibility, 137, 148–51, 183, 202–3, 233, 240, 300–301; in Saudi Arabia, 264–65; on Scott, 233–35, 296, 297; on the secular, 7, 10, 15, 20–21, 28–29, 60, 74, 79, 80, 101, 102, 112, 115, 116–17, 131, 132, 135, 154–57, 199, 207–10, 228–29, 239–40, 283–85, 298, 299, 301–2, 332n44; on secularism, 9, 15, 20–21, 27, 59–60, 75–76, 93–94, 101, 115, 116, 117, 135–36, 154, 178, 180, 198–202, 205, 207, 210, 216–20, 222, 223–24, 227, 228, 231, 279, 283, 297–98, 299, 300–302, 312n9; on secularization, 12–15, 20–21, 23, 59–60, 62, 101, 115, 116, 117, 154, 207–10, 222, 223–24, 227–28, 232, 301–2; on Shulman, 235–39; on William Cantwell Smith, 76–77, 116, 255, 282; on social action, 35–36, 37, 38–40, 44–45; on subjectivity, 7–8, 183, 189, 197–98, 199–202, 204, 239–40; on subversion as critical strategy, 285–87; on suffering, 93–94; on symbols and meaning, 7, 33–34, 36–40, 41, 211–15, 217–20, 245, 257, 269–71, 272–73; on technology, 231–32, 238–39; on time, 220–23, 286–87, 289; on torture, 9, 290; on tradition, 8, 27, 42–44, 50, 135, 137, 138, 140, 145, 146, 148–49, 233–35, 276–78, 286, 287–90, 303; and the tragic, 134–35, 137, 138, 145, 146, 149–51, 233, 235; on translation between cultures, 5, 275, 322n35; on truth, 228, 234; on United States, 116, 208, 209, 223, 236, 241, 249, 297, 299–300; at University of Hull, 2, 260–62; on violence, 9, 93, 94, 154, 157, 158, 225, 227, 236, 249–50, 292, 299–300; on virtue, 136, 140, 214, 221–22, 234, 235, 289; and Vygotsky, 35–36; on Jon E. Wilson, 239–41; and Wittgenstein, 1, 116, 133, 137, 214–16, 243, 245, 252–53, 271, 272, 285, 305n1, 306n21, 320n4

Asad, Talal, works of: Abner Cohen essay, 259, 262, 263–66, 305n10; "Anthropology and the Analysis of Ideology" (Malinowski Lecture), 263–66, 268–71, 273, 305n10; *Anthropology and the Colonial Encounter*, 3–4, 259–61, 282–83; "Are There Histories of Peoples without Europe?," 291, 295–97; "The Concept of Cultural Translation," 5–6; "Conscripts of Western Civilization," 291; "The Construction of Religion as an Anthropological Category," 320n11; *Formations of the Secular*, 8–10, 12–15, 30, 58–60, 60, 77–79, 116, 148–51, 199, 206, 207–10, 209, 222, 223–24, 226, 228, 235–36, 283, 284–85, 297–98, 299–302, 320n5, 322n39, 328n32, 332n44; *Genealogies of Religion*, 32–41, 44–45, 60, 116, 139–40, 148–49, 206, 210–11, 234–35, 272, 285, 295, 297–99, 301, 306n17; "The Idea of an Anthropology of Islam," 8, 10, 42–44, 303; *The Kababish Arabs*, 2–3, 248–51, 254–55, 257–58, 282–83, 305n3, 320n12; "The Structural Analysis of Ritual," 245–46; "Two European

Images of Non-European Rule," 3–4
Asia, 61, 62, 236, 238, 308n32; South Asia, 181, 182, 193
atheism, 77, 123, 282
Austin, J. L., 245, 330n13
Ayer, A. J.: *Language, Truth, and Logic*, 252, 330n13

Bachofen, Johann, 105
Bakhtin, Mikhail, 51–54, 55, 269–70
Baldwin, James: on redemption, 160, 162, 167
Bangladesh, 67
Banton, Michael, 247, 251, 329n9
Baptists, 24
Barth, Fredrik, 247, 276, 329n7
Barthes, Roland, 257
Basu, Jyoti, 65
Bayly, C. A., 196
Begriffsgeschichte School, 101
Benedict, Ruth: *Patterns of Culture*, 243
Benedict XV, 309n32
Benhabib, Seyla, 91, 95
Benjamin, Walter, 284
Bergson, Henri, 82, 120; on intellectualism, 79
Berlin, Isaiah, 330n13
Bernard of Clairvaux, St., 212, 280–81
Bhattacharya, Budhadeb, 62–67, 71
Bible, the: exodus from Egypt, 159, 161–62, 170, 325n21; Hebrew prophets in, 130, 160, 161–70, 238; Levinas on, 121, 122
Bin Laden, Osama, 68, 300
Biswas, Kanti, 66–67
Blake, William: on redemption, 155, 165, 170, 176
Blanchot, Maurice, 125
Blumenberg, Hans, 21
body, the: Agamben on, 95, 98, 224; Asad on, 7–10, 34, 35, 77, 132, 135, 150–51, 212, 214, 220, 270, 287–89, 299; Mauss on, 8, 322n39. *See also* pain
Bose, Biman, 65

Bourdieu, Pierre, 289, 322n39
Brown, Richard, 260
Buber, Martin, 163
Buddhism, 114, 122, 314n23
Burke, Kenneth: on symbolic action, 40–41
Bush, George W., 201, 236, 297, 300

Canada, Quebec, 18
Canovan, Margaret: Asad on, 156–57, 235–36, 283; on liberalism, 156–57, 283
capitalism: Asad on, 231, 232, 238, 240, 250, 274, 285, 294, 301; circulation and concentration of capital, 118; globalization, 113, 120, 231, 232, 238; in India, 193; money in, 127–28, 129, 130, 133, 231, 232; and Protestantism, 22; relationship to secularization, 12–13, 22, 24; Weber on, 22, 230
Casanova, José, Asad on, 12–15, 20, 207–10
Cassirer, Ernst, 245
Castells, Manuel, 118
Catholic Church: Benedict XV, 309n32; and common good, 27, 28; Gregory XVI, 25; and human rights, 24–29; Inquisition, 82, 280, 299; John Paul II, 25, 26, 27–28; John XXIII, 25, 308n27; and modernity, 22, 25–29, 294; and morality, 27–28; *Pacem in Terris*, 25; Pius IX, 25; Pius VI, 24–25; and political authority, 28–29, 309n35; Vatican Council, Second, 25, 26–27, 308n32
Caton, Steven C., Asad on, 210–16
Cavell, Stanley, 326n32
Chacha, Rahman, 69
Chatterjee, Partha, 193–94, 196; Asad on, 216–20; on political society, 73, 216–17, 220
China, 60
Christianity, 114, 178; Asad on, 6–7, 8, 32, 35, 77, 79, 140, 157, 211, 212, 213, 234–35, 236, 238, 272, 279, 280–82,

283–85, 287, 291, 299; conversion to, 96–101; and human rights, 24–25; Jesus Christ, 27, 125, 126, 170, 325n22; Kant on, 80, 81; love of God and neighbor in, 170; in Middle Ages, 7, 8, 23, 24, 77, 140, 212, 213, 272, 280–82, 285, 291; and natural religion, 6; and politics, 28–29, 61, 309n35; postmillennial eschatology in, 21, 325n21; redemption in, 157, 159, 170–71, 238, 324n17, 325nn21,22; Reformation, 21, 29; relationship to Europe, 78, 82–83. *See also* Catholic Church; Protestantism

Clifford, James: *Writing Culture,* 4–5

Cohen, Abner: Asad on, 259, 262, 263–66, 305n10

Coleridge, Samuel Taylor, 155

Collingwood, R. G., 296, 297; *The Idea of History,* 253; *The Principles of Art,* 253

colonialism, 24, 181, 309n32; Asad on, 2–4, 140, 180, 197–98, 199, 228, 244, 254–55, 257–61, 269, 282, 283, 291, 292–93; identity of colonized and colonists, 197; in India, 96–101, 184–92, 196–97, 244, 246, 316n23; and law, 96–101, 111; and natural rights, 96–102, 111–12; relationship to anthropology, 2–3, 257–60, 269, 283

communitarianism, 15

Confucianism, 19–20

Connolly, William E.: Asad on, 220–24, 312n9; on identity, 203–4; *Neuropolitics,* 220, 288

Constant, Benjamin, 209

constructivism, 145–46, 152, 153

contingency: Asad on, 228, 234, 240, 295; in Greek tragedy, 134–35, 148, 149, 152–53; of identity, 203–5; relationship to agency, 189, 197–98, 203–4

Critchley, Simon, 156

Cultural Studies, 256–57

Cunnison, Ian, 246, 260

Damasio, Antonio, 82, 86, 313n16

Darwin, Charles, 251–52

Das, Krsnahari, 186

Das, Veena: Asad on, 224–29

Davies, Norman: *Europe: A History,* 328n32

Deleuze, Gilles: Asad on, 220–23, 224; on belief in the world, 88–89; *Cinema II,* 88–90; and existential suffering, 88, 221; and Spinoza, 82, 86–88, 90; on time and becoming, 87–89, 220–22

democracy, 28, 182, 224, 228, 277, 291, 294; Arendt on, 237, 238; and minority communities, 58, 61–62, 73–74, 216–17, 220; relationship to redemption, 155, 157, 158–59, 160, 168, 170–71, 176, 178–79, 236–38

Derrida, Jacques: "Faith and Knowledge," 115; on God, 119; on Heidegger, 321n18; on Levinas, 119, 120–21, 131; on the other, 119; on religion, 115; *Writing and Difference,* 119, 120–21

Descartes, René, 155

de Vries, Hent, Asad on, 229–32

Dillon, Michael, 322n35

Dirks, Nicholas, 196

discipline. *See* Asad, Talal, on discipline

discourse: as authorizing, 32, 33–34, 35, 42–45, 50, 54–56, 176, 179, 211–14, 270, 272; Bakhtin/Voloshinov on, 51–54, 55; Foucault on, 32; metapragmatic function of, 34, 42, 45, 50–56, 210–14

Dostoyevsky, Fyodor: *The Idiot,* 126

Douglas, Mary, 257

Douglass, Frederick, 163

Dumont, Louis, 279, 280

Durkheim, Emile, 14, 132, 244, 267–68, 274

Dutta, Narayan, 67

education, 19; Islamic education, 29, 62–74, 216–17

Egypt: Asad on, 60, 102, 198–99, 228, 299; secularization in, 10, 60, 77–78, 102, 198–99, 228
Elliot, T. S., 155–56
Engels, Friedrich: on the family, 105
England: marriage in, 99; patriarchal authority in, 103; secularization in, 60
Enlightenment, the, 120; Asad on, 1, 21, 101, 136, 210, 264; critique of religion during, 13, 14–15, 17–18, 19, 22, 78; Foucault on, 147; and Kant, 80, 81, 91, 312n12; and nature, 21, 101; and Spinoza, 81–82, 84, 90–92, 312n12, 313n16
Epicurus, 81
equality, 79, 156, 163, 228
Euben, J. Peter: on Greek tragedy, 146–48; on Nietzsche, 148
Europe: Asad on, 10, 76, 78–79, 139, 200–202, 217–20, 230–31, 232, 282, 294, 328n32; Eurocentric history, 181–82; Levinas on, 121–22, 123–24, 230–31; Muslims in, 10, 61, 76, 78–79, 217–20, 223, 232, 294; relationship to Christianity, 78, 82–83; secularization in, 6, 15–20, 21–22, 75–76, 78–79, 80, 82, 83, 84, 101, 102, 199; vs. United States, 15–19, 21–23. *See also* France; United Kingdom
Evans-Pritchard, Edward Evan, 254, 261; *African Political Systems*, 329n4; *The Nuer*, 250; relationship with Asad, 245, 246–47, 250–51; *The Sanusi of Cynrenaica*, 245
evolution, biological, 87, 105, 106

family, the: relationship to the state, 94, 98–99, 100–101, 102–6, 107–8, 110–12, 225–26, 227–28, 229, 316n19
Fanon, Frantz, 197
Faris, Jim, 260
fascism, 88, 123, 125
Faulkner, William, 160
Feit, Mario, 316n19

Feyerabend, Paul, 151
film, 88–89
Filmer, Sir Robert: *Patriarcha*, 103–4, 105, 108, 110, 315n13, 316n19
forgiveness, 46–47, 49, 55, 165–66, 167, 168, 324n20
Fortes, Meyer, 329n4
Foucault, Michel: vs. Althusser, 290; *The Archaeology of Knowledge*, 271; and Asad, 8, 15, 32, 35, 82, 137, 138–40, 145, 227–28, 233–34, 239, 257, 258, 270–71, 273, 275, 286, 295; *Discipline and Punish*, 147; on discourse, 32; on the Enlightenment, 147; as genealogist, 15, 137, 138–40, 141, 143, 145, 146, 147, 233–34; on governmentality, 295; on Greek tragedy, 147; *History of Sexuality*, 145; on Hyppolite, 138; on modernity, 147; on Nietzsche, 138, 143, 325n31; on power, 8, 147, 194–96, 202, 270–71, 273, 328n21; on progress, 147; and Spinoza, 86; as subverter, 286–87; on time, 286–87
France: Alsace and Lorraine, 208, 219; Asad on, 208, 209, 217–20, 223, 227–28, 255; Declaration of the Rights of Man, 24–25; Jacobins, 60; May 1968 in, 130, 253; Muslims in, 61, 217–20, 223; secularism in, 60, 208, 209, 217–20, 223; vs. United States, 208, 209, 223
Frazer, Sir James George, 32
freedom, 28, 210, 249; of conscience, 14, 25–26, 27; relationship to redemption, 161–62, 163, 169, 170–71; of religion, 14, 22, 25–26
Freud, Sigmund, 176, 278, 298
functionalism, 2–3, 4, 212, 257–58, 320n12
fundamentalism, religious, 19, 30, 66, 68, 72

Geertz, Clifford: Asad on, 6–7, 32, 33–42, 44, 139–40, 210–13, 214–15,

275, 279, 280, 282, 287, 289, 291; on models, 37, 52; on religion, 6–7, 32, 33–36, 41–42, 139–40, 210–16, 279, 280, 282, 287, 289; "Religion as a Cultural System," 33–41, 44; on Schneider, 38–40; on science, 331n32; on social action, 35–36, 37, 38–40, 44–45; on symbolic action, 38, 40–41; on symbols and meaning, 7, 33–34, 36–41, 211–12, 214–16; on thick description, 38–39, 53–54, 117, 215; and Wittgenstein, 39, 40, 214–16

Gellner, Ernest: "Concepts and Society," 5

genealogy: Asad on, 15, 20–21, 28–29, 79, 80, 101, 131, 135, 137, 138–40, 145, 146, 148–49, 180, 204, 210–12, 233–35, 320n5; Foucault on, 15, 137, 138–40, 141, 143, 145, 146, 147, 233–34; MacIntyre on, 141–44, 148; Nietzsche on, 141–44, 145, 148; relationship to tragic drama, 137, 146–48; vs. tradition, 137, 138, 140–41, 143–45, 146, 148, 233–35

Gennep, Arnold van: *Rites of Passage*, 247

Ghosh, Dipen, 67

Glazier, E. G., 327n9

globalization, 113, 120, 231, 232, 238

Gluckman, Max, 268

God: death of, 156, 157; theodicy, 165–67

Goodenough, Ward, 38

Goodlad, Richard, 187–88, 190

Gould, Stephen, 87

Greek philosophy, 120–21, 130–31, 146, 222–23, 230, 237

Greek tragedy, 145–53; Asad on, 149–51, 233; contingency in, 134–35, 148, 149, 152–53; Euben on, 146–47; and *habitus*, 137, 150–51, 152; necessity in, 134–35, 138, 146, 150–51, 152–53; rationality in, 134–35, 149; relationship to genealogy, 137, 146–48; relationship to philosophy, 146; relationship to tradition, 137, 146–48;

Sophocles, 134, 137, 146, 147–48, 149–50, 233, 321n23, 322n35

Gregory XVI, 25

Grimsley, Ronald, 106

Grossman, Vasili: *Life and Fate*, 125–26, 231

Guattari, Felix, 87

Guha, Ranajit, 327n14

Gumbrecht, Hans, 7

Gutmann, Amy, 91

Habermas, Jürgen, 91; on Foucault, 195, 328n21; on modernity, 118–19; on public sphere, 14; on rationality, 121; on subjectivity, 195

habitus: and Asad, 136, 137, 150–51, 234, 235, 288–89, 322n39; vs. belief, 78; and Greek tragedy, 137, 150–51, 152; Mauss on, 150–51, 234, 322n39

Hacking, Ian, 136

Hall, Stuart, 255, 256

Hallowell, A. Irving, 244

Hampshire, Stuart, 82, 313n19; on thought and body, 84–86

Harris, Marvin, 40

Hasan, Mainul, 70–71, 73–74

Hastings, Warren, 65

Hegel, G. W. F.: *Early Theological Writings*, 21; on the family, 315n13; philosophy of history, 21, 101, 210

Heidegger, Martin, 115, 120, 124, 321n18, 328n21

Heschel, Abraham, 164

Hinduism, 63–64, 67, 72, 114, 197

history, 286–87, 295–97; agency in writing on, 181–82, 183, 192–94, 202, 204–5; Eurocentrism in writing on, 181–82; subaltern historians, 181–82, 326nn3,5

Hobbes, Thomas: mushroom analogy of, 94–95, 106, 110; on the state, 94–95, 103–4, 108, 110, 316n19; on state of nature, 94–95, 103–4, 110, 224–25; on violence and consent, 249–50

Hoggart, Richard, 256

Holland, 82, 83
Horkheimer, Max, 124
Hugh of St. Victor, 213, 280
humanism, 21, 101, 152, 210
human rights, 178; active vs. passive, 94, 95, 109; Asad on, 9, 24, 28–29, 94, 95, 156, 224–26, 229, 236; and Christianity, 24–29; freedom of conscience, 14, 25–26, 27; freedom of religion, 14, 22, 25–26, 217–20, 223; as natural rights, 24, 94, 95, 224–26, 229; right to life, 229; Universal Declaration of Human Rights, 308n27
Hunter, Ian, 81, 312n12
Husserl, Edmund, 87, 120
Hyppolite, Jean, 138

identity: of colonized and colonists, 197; identity politics, 123, 159; local identity, 113–14; personal identity as contingent, 203–5
ideology: Asad on, 1, 2–3, 135–36, 154, 178, 212, 249, 258–59, 263–75, 290, 298; Bakhtin/Voloshinov on, 51–53; Levinas on, 125–26; official vs. behavioral, 51–53; secularism as, 17
immigration, 60–62, 78, 111
imperialism, 180–81, 192, 194, 196, 197–98, 199, 282, 291, 292–93. *See also* colonialism
India: American Center in Calcutta attacked, 62–63, 68; Awadh settlement of 1856, 191; Babari Masjid demolition, 67; Bharatiya Janata Party (BJP), 63–64; colonialism in, 96–101, 184–92, 196–97, 244, 246, 316n23; Communist Party of India (Marxist), 64, 65, 67, 68–69, 70; East India Company, 184–85, 186, 187–92; Gujarat, 74; Hindu right wing in, 63–64, 67, 72; insurrection of 1857–58, 191, 327n15; Jamiat-e-Ulema-Hind, 64; Lashkar-e-Taiba, 66; madrasahs in, 62–74, 216–17; nationalism in, 193; Parsis in, 96–101, 225–26; paternity and conversion to Christianity in, 96–101, 111–12, 225–26, 316n23; permanent settlement of 1793, 190–91, 327n14; Rangpur peasant revolt of 1783, 184–92, 239, 327n9; religious minorities in, 57–58, 60, 62–74; secularism in, 57–58, 60, 216–17; the state in, 57, 60, 72–73; West Bengal, 62–74, 216–17
individualism, 19, 27, 155, 193, 210, 228
Iraq, 201, 241
Ireland, 16
Islam, 114, 178; Asad on, 8, 10, 23, 32, 42–44, 76, 77–79, 140, 212, 226, 232, 271–72, 278, 279, 282, 291–92, 293–94, 299, 300, 303; charitable donations in, 48, 69, 70; faithfulness toward God (*imam*) in, 77–78, 81; fundamentalism, 66, 68, 72; hadith, 42, 43, 55; madrasahs in India, 62–74, 216–17; and modernity, 29–30; Muslims in Europe, 10, 61, 76, 78–79, 200–201, 217–20, 223, 232, 294; Muslims in India, 62–74, 216–17; Muslims in middle-class, 71–72, 73, 216; and political authority, 4; Prophet Muhammad, 48; Qur'an, 42, 43, 54–56; religious education, 29, 62–74, 216–17; Rushdie Affair, 32, 301; sharia law, 198, 226, 228, 246, 294; Shias, 55–56; sin in, 48–49; Sufism, 55; Yemeni rain prayers, 31–32, 45–50, 54–56, 211, 213; Zadis, 55–56
Israel, Jonathan, 313n16
Israel, modern, 264, 265, 266; Six Days War, 253, 255

James, C. L. R., 233, 296
James, Wendy, 260
James, William, 82; on intellectualism, 79
Jefferson, Thomas, 24
John Paul II, 25, 26, 27–28

John XXIII, 25, 308n27
Judaism, 81, 114
Juergensmeyer, Mark: *Global Religions*, 114
justice, 111–12, 128–30, 164–65, 166–67, 171–72, 173, 253

Kafka, Franz, 82
Kant, Immanuel: Asad on, 80, 220; on Christianity, 80, 81; and the Enlightenment, 80, 81, 91, 312n12; on faith, 80; on humiliation, 80–81, 312n10; on the moral/autonomous agent, 80–81, 150, 151, 322n42; on the moral law, 80–81, 150, 312n10; vs. Nietzsche, 142–43; on reason, 80, 85, 151; on religion, 119; vs. Spinoza, 85–86
Kardiner, Abram, 244
Kidwai, A. R., 66, 68
King, Martin Luther, Jr., 160, 169, 236
Koselleck, Reinhart, 152
Kuhn, Thomas, 136

Laclau, Ernesto, 263
Langer, Suzanne, 245
Latin America, 181
law: Asad on, 94, 102, 180, 198–99, 209, 217, 225–28, 294–95, 299, 301, 302; and colonialism, 96–102, 111; as embodied by father/monarch, 104; regarding marriage, 99–100, 102; regarding paternity, 96–99, 225–26; relationship to nature, 95, 96–101; sharia law, 198–99, 226, 228, 246, 294; writ of habeas corpus, 95, 98, 111–12
Leach, Edmund, 254, 257
Levinas, Emmanuel, 119–26, 229–32, 318n23; on antisemitism, 125; vs. Asad, 132–33; on being Jewish, 131; on the Bible, 121, 122, 230; on ethics, 120–21, 123, 124, 126, 128–30; on Europe, 121–22, 123–24, 230–31; *God, Death, and Time*, 123; on Grossman, 125–26, 231; on ideology, 125–26; on Jesus Christ, 125, 126; on justice, 128–30; vs. Marx, 124; on Marxism, 125, 130; on money, 127–28, 129, 130, 133, 231, 232; on organization, 125–26; on the other, 122–23, 125, 127–28, 166–67, 230–31; on religion, 123, 124, 131–32, 231–32; on social space, 132, 133; on Stalinism, 123, 125, 129; on the state, 129–30; on structuralism, 122; on subjectivity, 124–25; on technology, 122, 123–24, 231–32; and tradition, 120–21
Lévi-Strauss, Claude, 38, 246, 257, 270; *La Pensée sauvage*, 121–22, 230
Lévy-Bruhl, Lucien, 132
Lewis, Bernard, 291
liberalism, 95, 103, 117, 123, 129, 171, 182, 193, 322n42; Asad on, 27, 28–29, 154, 156–59, 209–10, 223, 228, 236–37, 283, 290, 291, 294; Canovan on, 156–57, 283; and nationalism, 170, 178–79. *See also* democracy; individualism; secularism; toleration, religious
Lienhardt, Godfrey, 247
Lincoln, Abraham: *Gettysburg Address*, 168–69
linguistic pragmatics, 33–34, 42, 45, 50–56, 210–14
Linton, Ralph, 244
Locke, John, 91, 209; on paternity, 105–6, 110, 316n19, 316n22
logical positivism, 252, 330n13
Lounsbury, Floyd, 38
Löwith, Karl, 21
Lucretius, 81

Machiavelli, Niccolò, 162, 163, 164, 323n15
MacIntyre, Alasdair: and Asad, 8, 137, 140–41, 145, 233, 234–35, 255, 286, 288–89; on encyclopedia, 141, 142, 143, 144; on Foucault, 143, 144; on genealogy, 141–44, 148; on Kantian ethics, 151; on Nietzsche, 141–44; on

the self, 144–45, 235; on time, 286; on tradition, 8, 137, 141, 143–45, 234–35, 288–89; on truth, 144, 145

Madison, James, 24; *Remonstrance,* 22

Malinowski, Bronislaw, 2

Man, Paul de, 284

Marcus, George: *Writing Culture,* 4–5

Martin, David, 21–22

Marx, Groucho, 172

Marx, Karl: *Capital,* 255–56; *Communist Manifesto,* 130; on domination, 136, 149, 250, 320n12; on history, 295; on ideology, 249, 264, 268, 290, 298; vs. Levinas, 124; on modes of production, 264; on money, 127; "On the Jewish Question," 325n26; on religion, 18, 325n26

Marxism, 40, 41, 58, 125, 130, 181; and Asad, 7–8, 135–36, 249, 250, 255–56, 257, 264, 265–66, 268, 274, 278, 279, 290, 298, 320n12; redemption in, 159, 160, 170, 171–72, 323n12, 325nn21,26

Marxism and the Philosophy of Language, 51–54, 55, 269–70

materialism, 115

Mauss, Marcel, 117, 133, 222, 272; on body techniques, 8; on *habitus,* 150–51, 234, 322n39; "Techniques of the Body," 322n39

Mclennan, John, 105

Memmi, Albert, 197

Merleau-Ponty, Maurice, 121

Middle East, 181, 203; Asad on, 245, 253, 254, 255, 260, 261–63, 264, 265, 266, 271, 278, 279, 282, 291, 292, 293, 303; Six Days War, 253, 255. *See also* Egypt; Yemen

Milbank, John, 132

Mill, John Stuart, 209

Milton, John, 170

modernity: Asad on, 116, 135, 154, 155–57, 239–40, 274, 288, 291–95, 302, 303, 332n44; and Catholic Church, 25–29, 294; Foucault on, 147; Habermas on, 118–19; and Islam, 29–30; and pain, 8–9; relationship to secularization, 6, 12–15, 17–20, 23–24, 28–30, 58–59, 101, 113–14, 116, 117–19, 207–10, 222, 332n44

morality: common good, 27, 28; justice, 111–12, 128–30, 164–65, 166–67, 171–72, 173, 253; Kant on, 80–81, 150, 151, 312n10, 322n42; moral agency, 80–81, 135, 148–51, 233; moral responsibility, 149–51, 233; moral suasion, 59–60; relationship to religion, 119, 131

Morgan, Lewis H., 105

Morrison, Toni, 160; *Beloved,* 324n17

Moynihan, Daniel Patrick, 112

Mukherjee, Rudrangshu, 327n15

Murray, John Courtney, 25

myth: Asad on, 154, 155–57, 283–85

Nadel, S. F.: *Foundations of Social Anthropology,* 244–45, 329n3

Nandy, Ashis, 197

nationalism, 76, 78, 154, 156, 158, 170–71, 178–79, 193, 201, 300

naturalism, 115, 118

natural law, 24, 27, 28, 104

natural rights: and colonialism, 96–102, 111–12; human rights as, 24, 94, 95, 224–26, 229; of paternity, 96–101, 225–26

Needham, Rodney, 247, 257, 329n7

New Zealand, 18

Nietzsche, Friedrich, 82, 140, 167, 321n18; on *amor fati,* 161, 175–76; aphorisms used by, 142; *Beyond Good and Evil,* 142; *The Case of Wagner,* 172–73; on Christianity, 172–73; Foucault on, 138, 143, 325n31; as genealogist, 141–44, 145, 148; *The Genealogy of Morals,* 142–43; *Human, All Too Human,* 142; vs. Kant, 142–43; perspectivalism of, 141–43; on redemption, 159, 160, 161, 162, 166, 169, 172–78, 323n12; on resentment, 172–73, 174, 175–76; on truth, 141–42, 173; on will-to-power, 141–42, 144

Nussbaum, Martha, 91

obedience, 78, 81, 84, 103, 218; Asad on, 212, 221–22, 272, 280–81
O'Hanlon, Rosalind, 182
Orientalism, 4, 273, 278, 279
Orlie, Melissa, 324n20
other, the, 116, 119, 139, 147, 201; Levinas on, 122–23, 125, 127–28, 166–67, 230–31
Owen, Roger, 260, 261–62

pain. *See* Asad, Talal, on pain
Paine, Tom, 170
Pakistan, 243, 244, 249; intelligence services of, 62, 63
Parsons, Talcot, 21, 35, 39
Pateman, Carol: on Hobbes, 94–95
paternity and patriarchal authority: in colonial India, 96–101, 111–12, 225–26, 316n23; Filmer on, 103–4, 105, 108, 110, 315n13, 316n19; law regarding paternity, 96–99, 225–26; Locke on, 105–6, 110, 316n19, 316n22; natural rights of paternity, 96–101, 225–26; relationship to the state, 98–99, 100–101, 102–6, 107–8, 109, 110–12, 225–26, 227, 228, 229, 316n19
Patterson, Orlando, 170
Paul, St.: on redemption, 170, 324n17, 325n21
Peirce, Charles S., on signs, 37
Perry, J., 96, 97–98, 99–100, 111–12, 316n23
Persian Gulf states, 69
phenomenology, 10
Pius IX, 25
Pius VI, 24–25
Plato, 222–23, 237
pluralism, 84, 90, 91–92, 204, 217; Asad on, 79, 80, 92, 220
Pocock, David, 246
poetry: Asad on, 155–56, 157; as redemptive, 156, 176
Poland, 16, 328n32

political society, 73, 216–17, 220
politics: and academia, 204–5, 240–41, 301; Asad on, 2–3, 10, 14, 59–60, 78–79, 93–94, 102, 104, 112, 136, 154, 158–59, 176, 178, 179, 180, 207, 210, 217–20, 222, 223–28, 229, 235, 236–39, 240–41, 248–49, 250–51, 253–56, 258, 264, 266–67, 277, 278, 279, 285, 291–92, 294–95, 299–300, 301; identity politics, 123, 159; and redemption, 155, 156–61, 167, 168–69, 170–71, 173, 176–79, 236–39; relationship to agency, 183, 202–5; role of consent in, 2, 7–8, 58, 61, 62, 103, 104, 110, 112, 123, 249–50. *See also* democracy; fascism; Stalinism; state, the
Portugal, 82–83
postcolonialism, 136, 181, 288
poststructuralism, 4, 7, 136, 258, 259
power, 14, 56; Asad on, 5, 6, 7, 8–9, 10, 35, 41–42, 52, 139, 154, 158–59, 176, 178, 179, 198, 212–14, 254–55, 270–73, 281, 291, 293; as discursive practice, 52; Foucault on, 8, 147, 194–96, 202, 270–71, 273, 328n21; relationship to agency, 187, 189, 190, 194–98, 202, 204; relationship to disciplinary knowledge, 4, 6–7; Weber on, 281
practice. *See* Asad, Talal, on practice
Prakash, Gyan, 182
pride, 164–65, 166, 168, 177
Prigogine, Ilya, 82
profanization, 114–15, 119, 232
prophets, Hebrew: Amos, 130, 165–66; Asad on, 155; Hosea, 164, 165, 324n17; Isaiah, 161, 164, 166; Jeremiah, 160, 163, 168; Micah, 161; on pride, 164–65, 166, 168; redemptive language of, 157–58, 160, 161–70, 171, 176, 177, 323nn12,15, 324nn19,20; theodicy of, 165–67, 324n20
Protestantism, 23, 170; Reformation, 21, 29; Weber on, 22, 159, 230
psychology, 35–36
Putin, Vladimir, 201

Rabelais, François: *Pantagruel*, 123, 318n23
Radcliffe-Brown, Alfred Reginald, 244, 245–46, 247, 329n2
Rahaman, Anisur, 68–69
rationality, 19, 59–60, 122, 125, 136, 148; Asad on, 136–37, 249, 253, 265–66, 274; instrumental reason, 124, 155, 159; Kant on, 80, 85, 151; unity of reason, 80, 85, 141; Weber on, 121, 165
Rawls, John, 91, 209, 322n42
Ray, Ratnalekha, 327n14
redemption: and agency, 166, 177–78; Arendt on, 161, 163, 167, 169; Asad on, 155, 156–59, 176, 178, 235–39; Baldwin on, 160, 162, 167; Blake on, 155, 165, 170, 176; in Christianity, 157, 159, 170–71, 238, 324n17, 325nn21,22; definitions of, 161, 174; and Hebrew prophets, 157–58, 160, 161–70, 171, 176, 177, 323nn12,15, 324nn19,20; in Marxism, 159, 160, 170, 171–72, 323n12, 325nn21,26; Nietzsche on, 159, 160, 161, 162, 166, 169, 172–78, 323n12; Paul on, 170, 324n17, 325n21; and poetry, 156, 176; redemption from vs. redemption of, 161, 164, 168–69, 171; relationship to democracy, 155, 157, 158–59, 160, 168, 170–71, 176, 178–79, 236–38; relationship to freedom, 161–62, 163, 169, 170–71; relationship to politics, 155, 156–61, 167, 168–69, 170–71, 173, 176–79, 236–39; relationship to resentment, 159–60, 168, 172–73, 174, 175–76, 177; relationship to responsibility, 162; relationship to violence, 159, 160, 162, 163, 165, 166, 169, 176, 177, 178, 236, 324nn15,19; Roth on, 161, 165, 172, 323n12; secularization of, 159, 170, 171–74, 236–37; and United States, 158, 160, 161, 163, 169, 170–71, 178–79, 236, 324n15
religion: Asad on, 5–7, 12–15, 23–24, 32–36, 41–42, 56, 59, 75–76, 78–79, 116, 132, 135, 139–40, 154, 180, 210–16, 221, 223, 231–32, 240, 271–72, 278–87, 297–300, 320n11; church attendance, 15, 16–17; as cognitive/metaphysical system, 32; definitions of, 6–7, 32, 33–36, 41–42, 76–77, 114, 116, 131–32, 139–40, 209, 210–13, 215–16, 222, 279, 282, 320n11; Derrida on, 115; as discursive practice, 32–33; fundamentalism, 19, 30, 66, 68, 72; Geertz on, 6–7, 32, 33–36, 41–42, 139–40, 210–16, 279, 280, 282, 287, 289; genitive theologies, 114; as global, 113–14, 115, 117–19, 131–32, 232; Levinas on, 123, 124, 131–32, 231–32; in liberal democracies, 13–14; liberation theology, 114; natural religion, 6; prayer, 15, 31–32, 44, 45–50, 54–56, 211, 213; privatization of, 12–13, 27, 58, 59, 61, 75, 78–79, 240, 298; profanation of, 114–15, 119, 232; relationship to morality, 119, 131; role of faith/belief in, 15, 77–79, 80, 209, 211, 287; William Cantwell Smith on, 76–77, 116, 282; in United States, 15–19, 21, 22–23, 208, 223, 236, 308nn24,32. *See also* Catholic Church; Christianity; Islam; Protestantism; secularism; secularization
Renaissance, humanism in, 21, 101, 210
resentment: Nietzsche on, 172–73, 174, 175–76; relationship to redemption, 159–60, 168, 172–73, 174, 175–76, 177
responsibility: Asad on, 137, 148–51, 183, 202–3, 233, 240, 300–301; relationship to agency, 148–51, 202–4, 233, 240; relationship to redemption, 162
Review of Middle East Studies, 262–63
romanticism, 155–56
Rorty, Richard, 277–78
Roseberry, William, 41
Roth, Philip: on redemption, 161, 165, 172, 323n12
Rousseau, Jean-Jacques: *Emile*, 106–9,

111, 228–29, 316nn19,20; Feit on, 316n19
Rushdie, Salman: *The Satanic Verses*, 32, 301
Ryle, Gilbert, 117, 245

Safwat, Ahmad, 228
Said, Edward: *Orientalism*, 4, 197, 262
Salim, Mohammed, 64, 66, 69
Sandel, Michael, 322n42
Sarkar, Sumit, 326n5
Saudi Arabia, 69, 264–65
Saurette, Paul, 312n10
Saussure, Ferdinand de, 36, 40, 269, 274
Schmitt, Carl, 285
Schneider, David, 38–40
science, 122–24, 125, 331n32; history of, 251–52; relationship to secularization, 13, 19, 22
Scott, David, Asad on, 233–35, 296, 297
secular, the: Asad on, 7, 10, 15, 20–21, 28–29, 60, 74, 79, 80, 101, 102, 112, 115, 116–17, 131, 132, 135, 154–57, 199, 207–10, 228–29, 239–40, 283–85, 298, 299, 301–2, 332n44; relationship to reproduction, 94, 96–101, 102, 103, 107–8, 109, 111, 224, 228, 229, 316n20; relationship to suffering and death, 93–94, 96, 103, 107–9, 111; secular intellectualism, 79, 91
secularism: Asad on, 9, 15, 20–21, 27, 59–60, 75–76, 93–94, 101, 115, 116, 117, 135–36, 154, 178, 180, 198–202, 205, 207, 210, 216–20, 222, 223, 223–24, 227, 228, 231, 279, 283, 297–98, 299, 300–302, 312n9; in Egypt, 77–78; in France, 60, 208, 209, 217–20, 223; in India, 57–58, 60, 216–17; relationship to secularization, 17–18, 22, 60–62
secularization: Asad on, 12–15, 20–21, 23, 59–60, 62, 101, 115, 116, 117, 154, 207–10, 222, 223–24, 227–28, 232, 301–2; coercion during, 60, 62; as decline in social significance of religious institutions, 16–17, 18–19, 58–59; as decline of religious beliefs and practices, 12, 16–17, 18–19, 58–59; as differentiation of the secular from the religious, 12–15, 19, 20–30, 58–59; in Egypt, 10, 60, 77–78, 102, 198–99, 228; in Europe, 6, 15–20, 21–22, 75–76, 78–79, 80, 82, 83, 101, 102, 109; as privatization of religion, 12–13, 27, 58, 59, 61, 75, 78–79, 240, 298; of redemption, 159, 170, 171–74; relationship to capitalism, 12–13, 22, 24; relationship to modernity, 6, 12–15, 17–20, 23–24, 28–30, 58–59, 101, 113–14, 116, 117–19, 207–10, 222, 332n44; relationship to science, 13, 19, 22; relationship to secularism, 17–18, 22, 60–62; relationship to technology, 124; relationship to the state, 12–13, 22, 24, 59–60, 61, 62, 70, 78–79, 93–94, 102, 208, 222, 223–24, 227–28; secularization thesis, 12–30, 58–59, 207–10, 308n24; in United States, 15–19, 22–23; Weber on, 58
Segal, Charles: *Oedipus Tyrranus*, 321n23; *Tragedy and Civilization*, 321n23
self, the: constructivism regarding, 145–46, 152, 153; MacIntyre on, 144–45; relationship to the past, 152–53
Severance, Mary Laura: on Hobbes, 104; on Locke, 105–6, 110, 316n22
Sheikh, Waris, 64
Shelley, Percy Bysshe, 155
Shulman, George: Asad on, 235–39
Singh, Raja Devi, 188
Six Days War, 253, 255
Skaria, Ajay, 326n5
slavery, 170
Smith, William Cantwell: on religion, 76–77, 116, 282
social action, 56; Asad on, 35–36, 37, 38–40, 44–45; Geertz on, 35–36, 37, 38–40, 44–45
Sophocles: *Antigone*, 146, 147; *Oedipus at Colonus*, 150; *Oedipus Tyrannus*, 134, 137, 146, 147, 149–50, 233, 321n23,

322n35; Segal on, 321n23
Soviet Union, 51, 60, 123
Spain, 82–83; Civil War, 309n35
Spinoza, Benedict, 81–88, 313n19; on the *conatus essendi*, 128; on cultivation of *hilaritus*, 84, 85, 86, 88, 90, 220–21; and Damasio, 86; and Deleuze, 82, 86–88, 90; and the Enlightenment, 81–82, 84, 90–92, 312n12, 313n16; excommunication of, 82; and Foucault, 86; and Hampshire, 84–86; on ideas and affect, 83, 86; on immanance of God/Nature, 83, 85, 87, 222; vs. Kant, 85–86; on monism, 83, 87, 222; on parallelism of mind and body, 83–84, 86
Spivak, Gayatri Chakravorty, 182
Stalinism, 51, 123, 125, 129, 231
state, the: as agent, 191–93, 197; Asad on, 78–79, 93–94, 102, 104, 112, 154, 158–59, 179, 208, 210, 217–20, 222, 223–28, 229, 235, 236–39, 278, 291–92, 294–95, 300; citizenship in, 93–94, 96, 98–99, 100–101, 102, 104, 107–9, 219, 222, 223, 225, 316n19; Hobbes on, 94–95, 103–4, 108, 110, 316n19; in India, 57, 72–73; Levinas on, 129–30; and patriotism, 94, 315n8; relationship to paternity/patriarchal authority, 98–99, 100–101, 102–6, 107–8, 109, 110–12, 225–26, 227, 228, 229, 316n19; relationship to secularization, 12–13, 22, 24, 59–60, 61, 62, 70, 78–79, 93–94, 102, 208, 222, 223–24, 227–28; relationship to the family, 94, 98–99, 100–101, 102–6, 107–8, 110–12, 225–26, 227–28, 229, 316n19; role of women in, 94–95, 106–9, 111; sovereignty of, 96, 100–101, 102, 103–6, 109, 110–11, 112, 225–26, 229. See also democracy; nationalism; politics
Stevens, Wallace, 156, 176
Stoler, Ann, 197
structuralism, 38, 122, 246, 257, 269–70

Subaltern Studies collective, 181
subjectivity: vs. agency, 183, 186, 189, 192–94, 195–96, 197–98, 199–202, 203–5, 239–41; Asad on, 7–8, 183, 189, 197–98, 199–202, 204, 239–40; Descartes on, 155; Habermas on, 195; Levinas on, 124–25; subjects as making own history, 152, 180, 181–82, 190, 202
Sudan, 245; Kababish, 2, 248–51, 254–55, 257–58, 305n3; Khartoum University, 246, 248–49, 305n3
suffering, 8, 9, 88, 93–94, 168–70, 171, 172–73, 177, 222, 236

Taoism, 19–20
Taylor, Charles, 255, 315n8
technology, 113, 125; Asad on, 231–32, 238–39; Levinas on, 122, 123–24, 231–32
Thackeray, Bal, 63
Thompson, E. P., 256
Thoreau, Henry, 163
Tocqueville, Alexis de, 18–19, 157
toleration, religious, 6, 10, 13–14, 59–60, 76, 78–79, 210, 217, 223
torture, 9, 290
Toulmin, Stephen, 136, 245
Tracterianism, 60
tradition: Asad on, 8, 27, 42–44, 50, 135, 137, 138, 140, 145, 146, 148–49, 233–35, 276–78, 286, 287–90, 303; vs. genealogy, 137, 138, 140–41, 143–45, 146, 148, 233–35; MacIntyre on, 8, 137, 141, 143–45, 234–35, 288–89; relationship to tragedy, 137, 146–48
tragedy. *See* Greek tragedy
Trevor-Roper, Hugh: *The Rise of Christian Europe*, 328n32
Troeltsch, Ernst, 21
truth, 177; Asad on, 228, 234; MacIntyre on, 144; Nietzsche on, 141–42, 173
Turkey, 60, 294

Ultramontanism, 60

United Kingdom: anthropology in, 2–3, 243–47, 249, 254, 256–60, 267–68, 274, 329n2; Association of Social Anthropologists, 259–60. *See also* colonialism

United States: African Americans in, 112; American Anthropological Association, 259; American Dream, 159; anthropology in, 4–5, 243, 244, 259; Asad on, 116, 208, 209, 223, 236, 241, 249, 297, 299–300; vs. Europe, 15–19, 21–23; First Amendment to Constitution, 18–19, 22; foreign policy, 116, 201, 236, 241; vs. France, 208, 209, 223; Iraq invaded by, 201, 241; the media in, 89, 241, 299–300; Muslims in, 300; and redemption, 158, 160, 161, 163, 169, 170–71, 178–79, 236, 324n15; religion in, 15–19, 21, 22–23, 61, 208, 223, 236, 308nn24,32; secularization in, 15–19, 22–23; September 11th attacks, 155, 158, 169, 178, 298, 299–300

Uruguay, 18

Varela, Francisco, 314n23
Vatican Council, Second, 26–27, 308n32; *Dignitatis Humanae*, 25; vs. First Vatican Council, 308n32; *Gaudium et Spes*, 26
Vigotsky, Lev, 35–36
violence: Asad on, 9, 93, 94, 154, 157, 158, 225, 227, 236, 249–50, 292, 299–300; relationship to redemption, 159, 160, 162, 163, 165, 166, 169, 176, 177, 178, 236, 324nn15,19
Virginia Statute on Religious Liberty, 22, 24
Viswanathan, Gauri, 316n23
Voloshinov, V. N.: *Marxism and the Philosophy of Language*, 51–54, 55, 269–70

Wagner, Richard, 173
Walzer, Michael: *Exodus and Revolution*, 325n21
Washbrook, David, 182, 196
Weber, Max, 21, 35, 325n26; on asceticism, 159, 171; on capitalism, 22, 230; on the exodus, 161–62; on Hebrew prophets, 161–62, 165; on power, 281; on Protestantism, 22, 159, 230; on rationality, 121, 165; on secularization, 58
Weschler, Lawrence, 324n20
Whitman, Walt, 155, 176
Williams, Bernard, 233
Williams, Raymond, 257
Wilson, Jon E.: Asad on, 239–41
Wittgenstein, Ludwig: and Asad, 1, 116, 133, 137, 214–16, 243, 245, 252–53, 271, 272, 285, 305n1, 306n21, 320n4; *Blue and Brown Books*, 252, 330n12; and Geertz, 39, 40, 214–16; on grammar, 116, 133, 285; on language games, 1; on meaning as use, 39, 40, 214–16, 271; *On Certainty*, 305n1; *Philosophical Investigations*, 40, 243, 252, 306n21, 320n4, 330n12; on sketching landscapes, 137; *Tractatus Logico-Philosophicus*, 330n13
Wolf, Eric, 41; *Europe and the People without History*, 291, 295
Woytyła, Cardinal Karol. *See* John Paul II

Yemen: Ibb, 48–49; al-Muqaddishah, 48; rain prayers in, 31–32, 45–50, 54–56, 211, 213

Zionism, 264
Zubaida, Sami, 261–62

Cultural Memory | in the Present

David Scott and Charles Hirschkind, *Powers of the Secular Modern: Talal Asad and his Interlocutors*

Gyanendra Pandey, *Routine Violence: Nations, Fragments, Histories*

James Siegel, *Naming the Witch*

J. M. Bernstein, *Against Voluptuous Bodies: Late Modernism and the Meaning of Painting*

Theodore W. Jennings, Jr., *Reading Derrida / Thinking Paul: On Justice*

Richard Rorty, *Take Care of Freedom and Truth Will Take Care of Itself: Interviews with Richard Rorty*, edited and with an Introduction by Eduardo Mendieta

Jacques Derrida, *Paper Machine*

Renaud Barbaras, *Desire and Distance: Introduction to a Phenomenology of Perception*

Jill Bennett, *Empathic Vision: Affect, Trauma, and Contemporary Art*

Ban Wang, *Illuminations from the Past: Trauma, Memory, and History in Modern China*

James Phillips, *Heidegger's* Volk: *Between National Socialism and Poetry*

Frank Ankersmit, *Sublime Historical Experience*

István Rév, *Retroactive Justice: Prehistory of Post-Communism*

Paola Marrati, *Genesis and Trace: Derrida Reading Husserl and Heidegger*

Krzysztof Ziarek, *The Force of Art*

Marie-José Mondzain, *Image, Icon, Economy: The Byzantine Origins of the Contemporary Imaginary*

Cecilia Sjöholm, *The Antigone Complex: Ethics and the Invention of Feminine Desire*

Jacques Derrida and Elisabeth Roudinesco, *For What Tomorrow . . . : A Dialogue*

Elisabeth Weber, *Questioning Judaism: Interviews by Elisabeth Weber*

Jacques Derrida and Catherine Malabou, *Counterpath: Traveling with Jacques Derrida*

Martin Seel, *Aesthetics of Appearing*

Nanette Salomon, *Shifting Priorities: Gender and Genre in Seventeenth-Century Dutch Painting*

Jacob Taubes, *The Political Theology of Paul*

Jean-Luc Marion, *The Crossing of the Visible*

Eric Michaud, *The Cult of Art in Nazi Germany*

Anne Freadman, *The Machinery of Talk: Charles Peirce and the Sign Hypothesis*

Stanley Cavell, *Emerson's Transcendental Etudes*

Stuart McLean, *The Event and its Terrors: Ireland, Famine, Modernity*

Beate Rössler, ed., *Privacies: Philosophical Evaluations*

Bernard Faure, *Double Exposure: Cutting Across Buddhist and Western Discourses*

Alessia Ricciardi, *The Ends Of Mourning: Psychoanalysis, Literature, Film*

Alain Badiou, *Saint Paul: The Foundation of Universalism*

Gil Anidjar, *The Jew, the Arab: A History of the Enemy*

Jonathan Culler and Kevin Lamb, eds., *Just Being Difficult? Academic Writing in the Public Arena*

Jean-Luc Nancy, *A Finite Thinking*, edited by Simon Sparks

Theodor W. Adorno, *Can One Live after Auschwitz? A Philosophical Reader*, edited by Rolf Tiedemann

Patricia Pisters, *The Matrix of Visual Culture: Working with Deleuze in Film Theory*

Andreas Huyssen, *Present Pasts: Urban Palimpsests and the Politics of Memory*

Talal Asad, *Formations of the Secular: Christianity, Islam, Modernity*

Dorothea von Mücke, *The Rise of the Fantastic Tale*

Marc Redfield, *The Politics of Aesthetics: Nationalism, Gender, Romanticism*

Emmanuel Levinas, *On Escape*

Dan Zahavi, *Husserl's Phenomenology*

Rodolphe Gasché, *The Idea of Form: Rethinking Kant's Aesthetics*

Michael Naas, *Taking on the Tradition: Jacques Derrida and the Legacies of Deconstruction*

Herlinde Pauer-Studer, ed., *Constructions of Practical Reason: Interviews on Moral and Political Philosophy*

Jean-Luc Marion, *Being Given That: Toward a Phenomenology of Givenness*

Theodor W. Adorno and Max Horkheimer, *Dialectic of Enlightenment*

Ian Balfour, *The Rhetoric of Romantic Prophecy*

Martin Stokhof, *World and Life as One: Ethics and Ontology in Wittgenstein's Early Thought*

Gianni Vattimo, *Nietzsche: An Introduction*

Jacques Derrida, *Negotiations: Interventions and Interviews, 1971-1998*, edited by Elizabeth Rottenberg

Brett Levinson, *The Ends of Literature: The Latin American "Boom" in the Neoliberal Marketplace*

Timothy J. Reiss, *Against Autonomy: Cultural Instruments, Mutualities, and the Fictive Imagination*

Hent de Vries and Samuel Weber, editors, *Religion and Media*

Niklas Luhmann, *Theories of Distinction: Re-Describing the Descriptions of Modernity*, edited and Introduction by William Rasch

Johannes Fabian, *Anthropology with an Attitude: Critical Essays*

Michel Henry, *I am the Truth: Toward a Philosophy of Christianity*

Gil Anidjar, *"Our Place in Al-Andalus": Kabbalah, Philosophy, Literature in Arab-Jewish Letters*

Hélène Cixous and Jacques Derrida, *Veils*

F. R. Ankersmit, *Historical Representation*

F. R. Ankersmit, *Political Representation*

Elissa Marder, *Dead Time: Temporal Disorders in the Wake of Modernity (Baudelaire and Flaubert)*

Reinhart Koselleck, *The Practice of Conceptual History: Timing History, Spacing Concepts*

Niklas Luhmann, *The Reality of the Mass Media*

Hubert Damisch, *A Childhood Memory by Piero della Francesca*

Hubert Damisch, *A Theory of /Cloud/: Toward a History of Painting*

Jean-Luc Nancy, *The Speculative Remark: (One of Hegel's bon mots)*

Jean-François Lyotard, *Soundproof Room: Malraux's Anti-Aesthetics*

Jan Patočka, *Plato and Europe*

Hubert Damisch, *Skyline: The Narcissistic City*

Isabel Hoving, *In Praise of New Travelers: Reading Caribbean Migrant Women Writers*

Richard Rand, ed., *Futures: Of Jacques Derrida*

William Rasch, *Niklas Luhmann's Modernity: The Paradoxes of Differentiation*

Jacques Derrida and Anne Dufourmantelle, *Of Hospitality*

Jean-François Lyotard, *The Confession of Augustine*

Kaja Silverman, *World Spectators*

Samuel Weber, *Institution and Interpretation: Expanded Edition*

Jeffrey S. Librett, *The Rhetoric of Cultural Dialogue: Jews and Germans in the Epoch of Emancipation*

Ulrich Baer, *Remnants of Song: Trauma and the Experience of Modernity in Charles Baudelaire and Paul Celan*

Samuel C. Wheeler III, *Deconstruction as Analytic Philosophy*

David S. Ferris, *Silent Urns: Romanticism, Hellenism, Modernity*

Rodolphe Gasché, *Of Minimal Things: Studies on the Notion of Relation*

Sarah Winter, *Freud and the Institution of Psychoanalytic Knowledge*

Samuel Weber, *The Legend of Freud: Expanded Edition*

Aris Fioretos, ed., *The Solid Letter: Readings of Friedrich Hölderlin*

J. Hillis Miller / Manuel Asensi, *Black Holes / J. Hillis Miller; or, Boustrophedonic Reading*

Miryam Sas, *Fault Lines: Cultural Memory and Japanese Surrealism*

Peter Schwenger, *Fantasm and Fiction: On Textual Envisioning*

Didier Maleuvre, *Museum Memories: History, Technology, Art*

Jacques Derrida, *Monolingualism of the Other; or, The Prosthesis of Origin*

Andrew Baruch Wachtel, *Making a Nation, Breaking a Nation: Literature and Cultural Politics in Yugoslavia*

Niklas Luhmann, *Love as Passion: The Codification of Intimacy*

Mieke Bal, editor, *The Practice of Cultural Analysis: Exposing Interdisciplinary Interpretation*

Jacques Derrida and Gianni Vattimo, editors, *Religion*

Jennifer A. Jordan, *Structures of Memory: Understanding Urban Change in Berlin and Beyond*